Witchcraft

IN THE MIDDLE AGES

Other Books by Jeffrey Burton Russell

Dissent and Reform in the Early Middle Ages (1965)
Medieval Civilization (1968)
A History of Medieval Christianity: Prophecy and Order (1968)
Religious Dissent in the Middle Ages (1971)
The Devil: Perceptions of Evil from Antiquity to Primitive Christianity (1977)
A History of Witchcraft: Sorcerers, Heretics, Pagans (1980)
Medieval Heresies: A Bibliography (with C. T. Berkhout) (1981)
Satan: The Early Christian Tradition (1981)
Lucifer: The Devil in the Middle Ages (1984)
Mephistopheles: The Devil in the Modern World (1986)
The Prince of Darkness: Radical Evil and the Power of Good in History (1988)

WITCH-CRAFT IN THE MIDDLE AGES

JEFFREY BURTON RUSSELL

Cornell University Press

Ithaca and London

First published 1972 by Cornell University Press
First printing, Cornell Paperbacks, 1984

Library of Congress Cataloging in Publication Data

Russell, Jeffrey Burton.
    Witchcraft in the Middle Ages.

    Bibliography : p.
    1. Witchcraft—History. I. Title
BF1569.R88   1972   914'.03'1   72–37755
International Standard Book Number (cloth: alk. paper) 0-8014-0697-8
International Standard Book Number (paper: alk. paper) 0-8014-9289-0
Library of Congress Catalog Card Number 72–37755
PRINTED IN THE UNITED STATES OF AMERICA

Cornell University Press strives to use environmentally responsible suppliers and materials to the fullest extent possible in the publishing of its books. Such materials include vegetable-based, low-VOC inks and acid-free papers that are recycled, totally chlorine-free, or partly composed of nonwood fibers. Books that bear the logo of the FSC (Forest Stewardship Council) use paper taken from forests that have been inspected and certified as meeting the highest standards for environmental and social responsibility. For further information, visit our website at www.cornellpress.cornell.edu.

Cloth printing   10 9 8 7 6

Paperback printing   10 9 8

For William

Acknowledgments

M Y work in the history of medieval heresy and witchcraft has been in progress for the past fifteen years, and it is impossible for me to acknowledge all the help and support that I have received during that time. Let me simply say thank you to all who in conversation, by letter, by offprint, or in whatever way, have contributed to my understanding of the phenomenon of witchcraft. In particular I want to thank those who have been especially helpful during the past few years, while this book has been under way. For their financial support of this study I am deeply indebted to the John Simon Guggenheim Memorial Foundation, the Social Science Research Council, the American Council of Learned Societies, and the Research Committee of the Academic Senate of the University of California, Riverside. For the facilities provided me at various stages of my research, I want to thank the interlibrary loan staff of the University of California, Riverside, especially Hazel Schupbach; the Cornell University Libraries; the University of Pennsylvania Library; the Wellcome Medical Institute Library; the Bodleian Library; the British Museum; the Harry Price Collection of the Library of the University of London; and the Warburg Institute. I am especially grateful to the Warburg Institute for providing me with a quiet place to work in London.

Among the many kind people who have given me support,

ideas, and criticism I wish to thank particularly Alphons A. Barb, Sona Rosa Burstein, Christina Hole, Malcolm Lambert, Will-Erich Peuckert, Rossell Hope Robbins, Hugh Trevor-Roper, and Walter Wakefield. I remember with pleasure the students in the joint undergraduate seminar in the history of witchcraft that Professor Robbins and I gave at UCR in 1969, one of the first courses in the subject offered in an academic institution. The students in my graduate seminar, especially Leon McCrillis and Mark Wyndham, contributed to my understanding of the subject. A superlative research assistant as well, Leon McCrillis deserves double mention. Dennis Simpson, Gary Woods, and Joseph Leroy were also very helpful.

I want to thank Wayland Hand, the Director of the Center for the Study of Comparative Folklore and Mythology at UCLA, for his kindness in allowing me to use his vast card index of folklore motifs relating to witchcraft. Thanks also to Claudine Black and the late Oras Black for the photograph from which the picture on the dust jacket is taken. Cornell University Press is an agreeable publisher and I am indebted to its staff.

To my wife and children, who are not quite numerous enough to form a coven, thanks for enabling me to witness the activity of demons firsthand.

JEFFREY BURTON RUSSELL

Riverside, California

Contents

1   The Meaning of Witchcraft   1

2   Witchcraft in History   27

3   The Transformation of Paganism, 300–700   45

4   Popular Witchcraft and Heresy, 700–1140   63

5   Demonology, Catharism, and Witchcraft, 1140–1230   101

6   Antinomianism, Scholasticism, and the Inquisition,
    1230–1300   133

7   Witchcraft and Rebellion in Medieval Society, 1300–
    1360   167

8   The Beginning of the Witch Craze, 1360–1427   199

9   The Classical Formulation of the Witch Phenomenon,
    1427–1486   227

10 Witchcraft and the Medieval Mind   265

    Appendix: The *Canon Episcopi* and Its Variations   291

    Notes   295

        Abbreviations   295

    Bibliography   345

        Theorists of Witchcraft, 1430–1486   346
        Books and Articles   350

    Index   379

Witchcraft in the Middle Ages

1

The Meaning
of Witchcraft

O understand witchcraft we must descend into the
darkness of the deepest oceans of the mind. In our
efforts to avoid facing the realities of human evil, we
have tamed the witch and made her comic, dressing
her in a peaked cap and setting her on a broom for
the amusement of children at Hallowe'en. Thus made silly
she can easily be exorcised from our minds, and we can con-
vince our children—and ourselves—that "there is no such
thing as a witch." But there is, or at least there was. A
phenomenon that for centuries gripped the minds of men
from the most illiterate peasant to the most skilled philosopher or scientist, leading to torture and death for hundreds
of thousands, is neither joke nor illusion.

Yet if suffering is at the heart of the world, there is a profound comedy in the heart of suffering. Christ is the God
of those who laugh, and as Peter Berger has pointed out, the
sense of the comic is a Christian virtue enabling us to see
through the façades and pretenses of the world. Having
learned that any vision of things is "precarious" and perceiving our own follies as well as those of others, we take
ourselves less seriously. In the terrible, burning comedy of
Flannery O'Connor, the comfortable illusions of this world
are devastated by the detonation of prophetic laughter.
Witchcraft is a human comedy in which the prophetic

spirit can discern the essential and immutable folly of our race.

The study of witchcraft is therefore of fundamental significance for the understanding of man. It illuminates theology. It adds to the understanding of individual and social psychology. It is of particular significance in the history and sociology of ideas, in the study of folk religion, in the history of social protest, in the history of the Church, and in that of religious suppression. This book, which is in some respects an effort in the sociology of knowledge, inquires why in one time and place eternal human folly and viciousness took the particular form of witchcraft. The central questions asked are how such a phenomenon came about, how it developed during the Middle Ages, and to what degree and by whom it was accepted.

The history of folklore and folk religion helps us grasp European witchcraft in the context of the sociology of knowledge. We must judge to what extent European witchcraft was normal, in the sense of being similar to the beliefs and practices of sorcery in other societies such as the Chinese or the Navaho, and to what extent it was aberrant and peculiar to western Christian society.

Witchcraft also has an important part in the history of social protest. Toward the end of the Middle Ages, the simultaneous appearance of numerous movements—flagellants, dancers, millenarians, mystics, and others—indicates that powerful currents of social unrest existed in a period of plague, famine, war, and rapid social change. As always in a society where religious values are ultimately important, these movements were expressed in religious terms. Later, when in the Western mind money replaced Christ at the right hand of God, popular discontent more frequently expressed itself in economic terms.

During the Middle Ages, these social-religious protests were directed against the Church. In the history of Christianity, witchcraft is an episode in the long struggle between authority and order on the one side and prophecy and rebellion on the other.

The development of medieval witchcraft is closely bound to that of heresy, the struggle for the expression of religious feeling beyond the limits tolerated by the Church. Sometimes that struggle was directed by fanatics whose conviction of self-righteousness enabled them to justify any excess so long as it hurt established society.

Because any challenge to the authority of the Church was, in medieval terms, a challenge to the order of society and to the majesty of God himself, society naturally responded to heresy and witchcraft with repressive measures. The judges of the bishops' courts, the secular courts, and the Inquisition believed themselves God's defenders. These men were, by and large, neither venal nor extraordinarily depraved; rather, they were carried away, with man's infinite capacity for self-delusion, by ecclesiastical self-righteousness. The truest judgment against them is that they showed "bad faith—the willingness to replace choice with fictitious necessities."[1] It should not be difficult to understand how men could torture and kill in the name of the Prince of Peace when at Dresden and My Lai men could torture and kill in the name of democracy and freedom. Viciousness is excusable in neither rebel nor Inquisitor. To understand is not to forgive. If tolerance is taken to the point of tolerating the destruction of those processes by which toleration is itself guaranteed, then it becomes intolerable. But ours is not to judge the fanatic or the Inquisitor: ours is to experience the shock of recognition of the fanatic and the Inquisitor in ourselves.

The witch was a rebel against Church and society at a time when the two were wholly identified. The modern popular conception of the witch as a bent, toothless old hag with a pointed hat, a broomstick, and a black cat has roots in the past, to be sure, but is a caricature of little historical value. Yet the search for a better definition is not easy. We need not ask of a definition that it be true—by their very nature, definitions are human inventions not necessarily equivalent to objective reality—but we are entitled to demand that it be useful. The most useful approach to the definition of witchcraft is to recognize it as a phenomenon: a human perception. The definition will then be dynamic rather than static, for perceptions of what the term witchcraft meant have varied widely and have often been vastly imprecise. The best definition will take into account the development of the concept of witchcraft in the Middle Ages and, in addition, the development of the conception of that developing concept by historians in the more recent past, a question that will be treated in the next chapter.

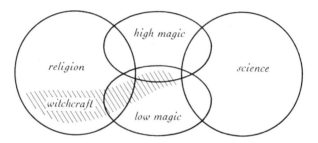

Magic, religion, science, and witchcraft

To obtain a relatively precise idea of witchcraft, we must place it in the context of an ambient magical world view, but we must also distinguish it from high magic, black magic, low magic, white magic, and religion. As semanticists have long pointed out, the most useful way of working toward a definition of a term is to show its relationship to other terms by means of word-clusters that can be illustrated in the form of Venn diagrams. The accompanying Venn diagram illustrates the place of witchcraft in a cluster of related terms.

Witchcraft appears as a phenomenon located in the areas of two other phenomena: religion and the magical world view. Magic, which has been common in all places and times, including the contemporary, took many forms during the Middle Ages. It is best understood, not as an inferior variety of science or religion, but as an independent world view. Ancient cultures knew no distinction between magic, science, or religion, or indeed between these and philosophy, poetry, and art; all were aimed at understanding and controlling the universe. Only in some sophisticated societies did these functions slowly become differentiated.[2] Anthropologists and historians have often perceived magic as a kind of superstition, but it is difficult to see how this helps.[3] "Superstition" is a pejorative term connoting ignorance or even stupidity, and far too many people simply apply it to anything in which they themselves do not happen to believe. It is more accurately defined as a belief not consistent with a coherent view of the universe. High magic, at least, was not superstitious. It formed a coherent world view that was related to both science and religion, particularly the latter, but independent of both.

The essence of the magical world view is belief in a homocentric universe. Man is literally the microcosm reflecting the macrocosm, so that the macrocosm in turn is a projection of man. Hence all things—stars, herbs, stones, metals, planets, the elements and elementals—mesh with man, his longings, his lusts, his desires, his fears, and even his physical appearance and health. Each natural object and natural phenomenon has a direct influence upon some aspect of man's body or psyche, and man's actions can in turn affect the elements. All things are made for man and on the model of man. Magic is a doctrine that, far more than religion or science, exalts man to the loftiest regions of glory: hence its perennial attraction, and hence its particular appeal for the Renaissance, when man's ambitions and his ability to achieve them seemed unlimited. Thus do all portents predict the death of Shakespeare's Caesar; thus do the elements crack and break with the destruction of Lear's mind; and thus can Marlowe's Faustus meditate:

> Shall I make spirits fetch me what I please,
> Resolve me of all ambiguities,
> Perform what desperate enterprise I will?
> I'll have them fly to India for gold,
> Ransack the ocean for orient pearl,
> And search all corners of the new-found world
> For pleasant fruits and princely delicates;
> I'll have them read me strange philosophy,
> And tell the secrets of all foreign kings . . .

For there is nothing so deep or so far away or so great that the magician cannot reach out for it, and no force that he cannot hope to compel.

Such beliefs reveal something about the individuals who hold them; they are likely to be held by people who are frustrated and who act out their hopes in ritual with the aim of realizing them.[4] On the other hand, magic is more a phenomenon of social than of individual psychology, since it is a world view usually handed down by tradition, deriving its strength from the values of society as a whole, and fulfilling definite social functions.[5]

The variations of magic described by Frazer and his successors —sympathetic magic, contagious magic, and so on—are only peripherally important to the study of witchcraft. One distinction firmly impressed in the popular mind, that between "white" and "black" magic, is the creation of modern writers, mainly occultist, and seldom appears in the history of world magic. The attitude of medieval Christianity was that all magic, benevolent or not, is evil, because it relies upon evil spirits and sets itself against God by trying to compel the powers of the Universe.

A much more useful distinction is that between low and high magic. The connection of witchcraft with low magic is close; its connection with high magic is much more tenuous. Low and high magic, although they sometimes meet, have always been different. In the Middle Ages, for example, theologians like Alexander of

Hales distinguished clearly between *divinatio*, the central aspect of high magic, and *maleficium*, evil-doing, the central aspect of low magic. Low magic is practical and aimed at obtaining immediate effects, for example, urinating into a ditch to cause rain or sticking a wax doll with a pin to cause pain; high magic is akin to religious, scientific, and philosophical speculation and reaches out through occult knowledge to understand, grasp, and ultimately control the Universe.

The two have discrete histories. No references to astrology or alchemy appear in medieval witch trials and few hints of the other varieties of high magic. Nor were high magicians often accused of employing the crudities of low magic. The two are distinct in origin. Even the fifteenth-century treatise *Malleus Maleficarum*, notorious for its efforts to extend the boundaries of the definition of witchcraft, clearly distinguishes it from astrology. Hugh Trevor-Roper argues that in the Middle Ages and Renaissance the two were encouraged by separate and distinct philosophical traditions, high magic drawing its sustinence from Platonism and Neoplatonism, and low magic its strength from Aristotelianism. Thus he is obliged to argue that the chronological conjunction in the Renaissance of the rapid rise of the influence of high magic and the phenomenal surge of the witch craze is coincidental. A connection is suggested by the fact that many Renaissance theologians, like Del Rio, were interested in both high magic and witchcraft. Moreover, the influence of high magic upon medieval theologians, which Thorndike has shown was very great, eventually filtered down to the Inquisitors and to the people in general, reinforcing the magical world view and encouraging the belief in witchcraft.

High magic was immensely sophisticated. The Comtian view that human thought has progressed from magic to religion to science is now thoroughly discredited, for the three have often been indistinguishable, and in any event varying degrees of sophistication in each have been found at all levels of societies from the primitive to the modern. The idea of primitive society's being necessarily inferior or unsophisticated has been discredited, and high magic of great coherence and complexity has existed throughout history. High magic in Western Europe has its ultimate sources in the science, particularly numerological and astrological, of Babylonia, in the philosophical speculations of Pythagoras and the Greeks, and in the religious traditions of Persia, whence the Magi (*magoi:* wise men, seers, magicians) came. It entered the Judaeo-Christian tradition and was an important element of gnosticism and of Neoplatonism. The *Corpus Hermeticum,* a collection of magical writings allegedly of immense antiquity but actually composed in the second and third centuries A.D., was formed in the Gnostic context. This *Corpus* became the basis of the magical cabala of the medieval Jews and in turn of medieval Christian and modern magic. The tradition of high magic was dealt a severe blow when in the seventeenth century Casaubon discovered the relative modernity of the hermetic writings, but it has been artificially revived in the nineteenth and twentieth centuries in an apparently endless panoply of spurious and puerile occultism. At its best, high magic sought union with the divine: the Neoplatonist Pseudo-Iamblichus wrote that communion with the gods was obtained through magic, and in the Renaissance Pico della Mirandola claimed that "No science gives greater proof of the divinity of Christ than magic and the Cabbala."[6] At its moral worst, yet with equally lofty aspirations, high magic sought to master the Universe for selfish purposes: this is the tradition of Faustus, and of Simon the Clerk in Charles Williams' great novel, *All Hallows' Eve.*

All varieties of high magic have shared the view that the world is controlled by Fate. Nothing is accidental; everything in the macrocosm has been designed for man the microcosm. One characteristic function of high magic was therefore divination of the

8

future through the examination of entrails, dreams, books, mirrors, bones, numbers, water, wine, wax, and other substances.* A second, the investigation of the natural universe in an effort to understand its workings upon man, promoted the study of herbs and plants, rocks, animals, the heavens (astrology), and metals (alchemy). In alchemy, where magic, science, and religion were perhaps most closely bound, the assumption was that man can change his spiritual nature by changing the chemical composition of things. As the alchemist caused base metals to be refined into gold in a seven-step process, his soul advanced concomitantly to purification. The third function of high magic was to try to summon up and concentrate the force of cosmic powers by containing them in a pentacle or other magically defined space, or by constraining them by using their names in incantations. *Incantatio,* originally a "chanting," came to mean a "spell" and has yielded the word "enchantment." Word magic has always been a powerful element in both high and low magic; the belief that power over a thing's name is power over the thing itself is worldwide, and in magic, as the modern occultist Eliphas Levi correctly observed, to have said is to have done. The most powerful and terrible magical spells in the Judaeo-Christian tradition used the Tetragrammaton (YHWH, the four transliterated Hebrew letters of the Name of God), preferably reversed.

---

* Divination in Greek is *manteia;* hence the suffix *-mancy* is used in technical descriptions of divination, e.g., oneiromancy (dreams), hydromancy (water), and so on. Necromancy, the art of exhuming dead bodies and causing them to prophesy, was understandably regarded by nonmagicians as the most sinister aspect of divination. In medieval Latin, the original Greek root (*nekros:* a corpse) was corrupted to the Latin *niger* ("black"), whence *nigromancy,* the "black art." It is largely from this etymological confusion that the term "black magic" derives. Divination by opening books, often the Bible, at random, was called in Latin *sortilegium,* literally meaning "the reading of the lots," but often applied to magic in general or even witchcraft.

Rel. +
Magic

The connection of high magic and religion has sometimes been denied and clear distinctions have been drawn between them. Sir James Frazer's distinction has become classical: magic attempts to compel the powers of the Universe; religion supplicates them.[7] The Swedish theologian Nathan Söderblom argues, "The essence of religion is submission and trust. The essence of magic is an audacious self-glorification. Magic knows no bounds to its power; religion, in the proper sense, begins when man feels his impotence in the face of a power which fills him with awe and dread. . . . Magic is thus in direct opposition to the spirit of religion."[8] Tillich identifies religion with ultimate concern and with *response* to the revelation of God, as opposed to magic, which reaches out and seizes in order to possess or control. The anthropologist William J. Goode places at the magical, as opposed to the religious, pole, the following characteristics: (1) concrete specificity of goal; (2) manipulative attitude; (3) emphasis on professional-client relationship rather than prophet-follower; (4) emphasis upon individual rather than social ends; (5) practice mainly by individuals rather than communal worship; (6) ready change of technique in the event of failure; (7) lesser degree of emotion; (8–10) emphasis on evading or bending the nature of the Universe as opposed to accepting and implementing it; (11) instrumental use for specific goals.[9]

In practice, as when prayers contain elements of constraint (do this for me, God, or I won't do that for you), the distinctions blur. Most modern historians of religion reject the idea of a dichotomy of religion and magic. No religions lack magical elements, and both magic and religion view the Universe as essentially alive, responding to man, in one way or another, in an I-Thou relationship. Modern anthropologists also reject clear distinctions between the two. The Waxes, for example, argue that the idea that magic is practical and religion theoretical is clearly untenable in view of the evidence to the contrary among many peoples; the distinction between magic as individualistic and religion as communal breaks down in the same way. Another fundamental source of muddle is that new religions often consider the practices of older religions as magic: the Christian attitude that paganism, whether Greco-Roman, Germanic, or Celtic, was magical and diabolical failed to recognize the distinction between magic and religion among those peoples themselves. There were magicians among the Romans, but adherents of the Roman religion were not necessarily magicians. Christianity itself was scarcely free from magical conceptions, high or low. Prayers were used as incantations, God and the saints were compelled by threats, the sacraments were used for magical purposes, and wonders were sought often without distinguishing between magic and miracle.[10] Magical elements are not lacking in the scholastic definition of transubstantiation itself, where the bread and wine become in essence the Body and Blood of Christ while retaining all the attributes of bread and wine. Similar shapeshifting is a common element in witchcraft: the black cat "really" remains the witch though having adopted totally feline attributes.

Yet when all the similarities between magic and religion have been observed, the essential differences remain. The Church of the Middle Ages and the Renaissance certainly believed that they did. It was the Church that made every effort to restrain magic, high and low, whereas natural scientists eagerly pursued magical practices.

The existence of an essential link between science and magic much stronger than that between religion and magic should not, since the appearance of Thorndike's work, surprise anyone, but the closeness of that connection is still not generally grasped. The astonishing and incontrovertible argument of Frances Yates' *Giordano Bruno and the Hermetic Tradition* is that not only were the greatest scientists of the Renaissance—Ficino and Giordano Bruno, for example—magicians, but the very nature of their scientific work and their attitudes toward science were magical. The opposition of the Church to some of the developments of natural science in the Renaissance was consequently part and parcel of its resistance to magic. In these sorcerer-scientists Christianity was opposing the magical world view that it had opposed since the days of Simon Magus; science had not yet developed its own world view and to a great extent accepted that of magic.

This explains why most of the attempts to define the differences between the science of the time and magic fail. Some valid distinctions exist. Magic is traditional and science, experimental; magic seeks to control and science, to learn: explanations in science are material as opposed to spiritual, for magic often calls in supernatural forces. But even today these distinctions do not always hold, and in the Middle Ages and Renaissance they scarcely did so at all: we must avoid the trap of comparing modern science with medieval magic. The distinction that holds most often is that explanations of how things occur in magic tend to be diffuse, general, undefined, and occult ("hidden"), whereas in science they are based as much as possible upon relationships between perceptible facts.[11] But even great anthropologists and historians of science like Malinowski or Thorndike insisted that magic is merely pseudo-science, because they failed to grasp to what extent magic offered a coherent view of the world that scientists of the time often shared. The distinction between science and high magic, and even that between science and low magic or witchcraft, is often very difficult to define.

The relationship between witchcraft and high magic is tenuous. The concentration and control of cosmic forces often entailed the invocation of spiritual beings defined as demons either by those who invoked them or at least by orthodox Christians condemning the practice. The cabala, for example, contains a detailed demonology, and cabalistic studies were considered heretical by both Jews and Christians. Witchcraft has echoes of the incantations,

12

sacrifices, ritual secrecy, recitation of prayers backwards, and other traits of cabalistic high magic.

Witchcraft's most important connection, however, was with low magic, which could be used for either benevolent or malevolent purposes.[12] In the Middle Ages, malevolent magic was subsumed under the term *maleficium,* which could mean any kind of crime or evil doing, and in the early Middle Ages malevolent magicians were usually treated like any other criminals who cause harm to others. Whether I break your leg by pushing you down the stairs or by breaking a clay doll, my crime is similar and my liability comparable. Benevolent magic was often tacitly allowed to exist, but in theory the Church assumed that all magic drew upon the help of demons whether the magician intended it or not. The syllogism was: magic proceeds by compelling supernatural forces; but God and the angels are not subject to such compulsion; the forces compelled must therefore be demons. The Church consequently held that there was no good magic. Its position was not unreasonable since low magicians the world over often use appeals to spirits as well as allegedly mechanistic means of magic. In Europe these practices derived from appeals either to the old gods or else to local spirits such as elves and fairies, whom medieval Christianity came gradually to classify as minor demons in the same way it considered the great pagan gods major demons.[13]

The word "witch" or its equivalent in other languages was often used to mean "sorcerer" in the sense of "low magician." Many of the same motifs are found in both European witchcraft and the sorcery of other societies; the frequency of direct and even detailed parallels between the two overwhelms the argument that European witchcraft is exclusively theological in its origins and lacking in significant folklore connections. Witch motifs of other societies parallel to those of European witchcraft abound. Nearly fifty different motifs can be distinguished: the disturbance of the air by witches (by flight or weather-witching); riding out on bee-hives, brooms, fences, cats, or other vehicles; animals prowling by night in the witch's service; witches changing themselves or others into animals; the use of ointment to effect the changes; nocturnal gatherings (Hindu witches, for example, flew naked through the air at night and consumed human flesh); the witch meetings taking place on Christian holy days, themselves replacements of the old pagan holidays (Hallowe'en, for example, replaced the Eve of All Saints' Day, November 1, originally a Teutonic fire-festival day); the belief that bees are evil spirits; the association of black complexion, clothing, or other objects with witches or evil spirits; witches using boats; witches leaving their bodies to roam about; the use of brooms by the witches, against the witches, or as a test of witchcraft (witches in some places could not step across a broom); cannibalism by witches; the association of witches with animals, especially cats, dogs, frogs or toads, lizards, snakes, mice, owls, pigs, horses, and wolves; witches having special power over children, and especially their propensity for eating children; the circular dance, often naked; the fear of seeing the witch dance; the use of crossroads as a place where demonic powers are especially strong; conscious relationship with the Devil (much more emphasized in European witchcraft than in other cultures, which have little evidence of formal pacts with demons or worship of demons, though the Cherokees, for example, might sell themselves to evil spirits); the association of excrement with witchcraft; the evil eye; familiar spirits, often in the form of animals; exhumation of corpses by witches; green as well as black as a witch color (green was the color of the fairies); the use of hares or rabbits as familiars; the eating of human hearts; witches causing illness or death; the use of initiation rites (though here the variety of rites is so great that connections are hard to establish, and in any event the idea of formally giving oneself to the Devil and renouncing God is common only in European

14

witchcraft); sexual intercourse between demons and witches; witches' ability to become invisible; use of knots (ligatures) for various purposes including inducing impotence; the association of nakedness with witches; the idea that witches convene at night; that witches are usually old; that they hold orgies; the idea that salt can be used to combat witches' powers; the use of sticks (usually as magic wands—the notion of riding sticks seems to be fundamentally a European tradition); the sucking of blood; and finally the almost universal association of witchcraft primarily with women.[14]

Even in Europe itself, sorcery and witchcraft were continually confounded. A witch or a sorcerer might bear one of the following names: (1) *strix, stria, striga,* or *strigimaga* (originally a screech-owl, then a night-spirit and vampire, finally a witch); (2) *sortiarius* or *sortilegus* (i.e., a diviner, one who reads the lots [*sortes*]); (3) *masca* (occasionally *talamasca*), associated with the use of animal masks as festivals;* (4) *lamia* or *lama* (a vampire);† (5) *maleficus* (one who does evil magic, *maleficium*); (6) *scobax* (from Greek *scôps,* a screech-owl, or Latin *scoba,* a broom); (7) *gazarius* (from *Catharus,* a Catharist heretic);‡ (8) *waudensis*

---

* The origin of the word *masca* is uncertain. Jacob Grimm (*Teutonic Mythology,* III, 1082), derives it from *masticare* ("to eat") because the witches were believed to devour children or other illicit food.

† *Lamia,* another common name for a witch in the classical and early medieval periods, is derived from Lamia, the legendary queen of Libya who was beloved by Zeus. Hera, in jealousy, slew her children, and in wild revenge, she roams the world sucking the blood of children and babies.

‡ Though the popularity of this appellation dates from the time of the Catharists and owes its strength to the association with them, it has its roots in an older etymology—the Hebrew root *gaz,* meaning "to cut" and relating to the custom of cutting open animals in order to divine from their entrails. Thus the root came to imply magic of any kind. Papias glosses *"Gazarenus Hebraice, Latine Aruspex"* (see Du Cange, entry "Gazarenus"). The existence of this older tradition explains how the term *catharus* was corrupted into the particular form *gazarus.*

(from *Waldensis,* a Waldensian heretic); (9) *herbarius* (an herb-gatherer); (10) *pythonissa* (prophetess); (11) *factura* (which seems to derive from the Latin *factus* and to mean a "maker" of spells); (12) *divinator* (diviner); (13) *mathematicus* (diviner); (14) *necromanticus* (diviner by corpses, corrupted to *nigromanticus*); (15) *veneficus* (preparer of potions, usually poisons); (16) *tempestarius* (storm-maker); (17) *incantator* (enchanter, one who makes incantations); (18) Anglo-Saxon *wicce,* *wicca* (one who divines or casts spells; the masculine form *wicca* is more common than the femine *wicce;* (19) German *Hexe,* deriving from Old High German *hagazussa* (a night-spirit, cannibal, or sorceress).[15]

Clearly, European witchcraft is closely analogous to sorcery in other societies and deeply rooted in the traditions of low magic. Yet witchcraft goes beyond magic. One distinction between European witchcraft and low magic is that witches tended to rely upon the help of spirits. But even this distinction is blurred in two important respects. The evidence does not always show when and to what extent sorcerers or witches thought they were relying upon the help of spirits. In addition, theologians and Inquisitors, especially from the thirteenth century, were themselves increasingly unwilling to accept the distinction, preferring to subsume low magic under the rubric of witchcraft and accusing sorcerers of having a pact with the Devil that was if not explicit at least implicit, since in fact (they argued) no magic could be accomplished without the help of demons. Henry A. Kelly goes so far as to say that "in the context of Christian demonology, witchcraft means any human activity attributed to the help of evil spirits. From the theological point of view, there is no difference between witchcraft, sorcery, and magic."[16] This is not a true statement for most Christian theology, but it became substantially true for the theologians of the fifteenth and sixteenth centuries.

The degree to which demons were revered and Christ rejected

in European sorcery and in witchcraft provides a better distinction between the two. In this context their relationship can be illustrated by the accompanying diagram. From this one can perceive that European witchcraft is best viewed as a religious cult of the Devil, built on the foundations of low magic and folk traditions but formed and defined by the Christian society within which it operated. The action of Christianity on European witchcraft produced, among other characteristics, the sabbat, or witches'

Sorcery and witchcraft

meeting, usually under the presidency of the Devil and entailing some form of reverence to the Devil coupled with a renunciation of Christ.* The conception of witchcraft as an organized cult, as opposed to individual *maleficia,* is another product of the Christian environment that made of witchcraft a form of perverted religion.

The complexity of the witches' relationship with evil spirits is

---

* The derivation of the word "sabbat" is disputed. Some suggestions as to its origin include Sabazios, a Phrygian deity, and *esbat,* from French *s'esbattre,* to frolic (Murray's idea). Other possible derivations are from *sabbatarius,* "having to do with a feast," or even *sabaoth,* the host of heaven. But the simplest answer is that it derives from the Hebrew *shabbath* (Lat. *sabbatum*), the day of rest. The application of the term sabbath to the witch orgies is indicative of the loathing with which Christians in the later Middle Ages viewed the Jewish religion.

most characteristic of Christian witchcraft. Three kinds of evil spirits had to be dealt with: minor demons often taking the form of familiars and deriving from the elves, fairies, and kobolds of folklore; major demons, for example, Beelzebub, Ashtaroth, or Asmodeus, derived from Judaeo-Christian demonology; and the Devil himself. And there were at least five degrees of closeness in the relations that one might have with evil spirits: incantation, where they are called up and compelled to do one's bidding (this could be done with demons much more easily than with the Devil); an implicit pact with the spirits; an explicit pact promising something in return for their aid; sacrifice, homage, or other reverence; and finally worship.*

It was the idea of pact that seized the minds of the scholastics and the Inquisitors most firmly. Since *belief* in demons was always a strong element in the Judaeo-Christian tradition, it was never condemned, though before the thirteenth century theologians could be found who denied or modified the belief. From the thirteenth century and increasingly through the fifteenth and sixteenth such doubt was no longer tolerated, and to deny the power of demons was to incur accusations of heresy. Nor was *possession* by demons usually deemed witchcraft. Possession may sometimes have voluntary elements, as when one calls a demon into oneself in order to prophesy the future, but in the New Testament it is invariably involuntary and continued as a rule to be so considered during the Middle Ages. Pact, on the other hand,

---

* The term "demon" derives from the Greek *daimonion,* used in the Septuagint and the New Testament to denote an evil spirit, rather than from *daimôn,* a usually benevolent spirit or deity, like the one that attended Socrates. "Devil" derives from the Greek *diabolos* through Latin *diabolus.* In the Septuagint and the New Testament, as for most Christian writers, the *diabolos* (from *diaballein,* to slander), is the supreme spirit of evil. The term "devils" is sometimes used loosely as a synonym for "demons," but in this book "Devil" will denote the supreme evil spirit, and "demon" any other evil spirit.

was always condemned since it consisted of deliberate traffic with the Devil or demons. The idea of pact precedes Christianity—it is mentioned by the pagan Lucan, for example—but, although it was discussed by St. Augustine, it was not a widespread idea in the early Middle Ages. The earliest Christian legend involving pact is the story of St. Basil (c. 380); the most influential was that of St. Theophilus (d. c. 540), which was translated into Latin by Paul the Deacon in the eighth century and thereafter became steadily more popular. At first the pact was considered a legal contract in which each party had rights, and in this form the legend was used in connection with high magic, as with the stories of Gerbert (a tenth-century scholar and pope) and Faust. In the later Middle Ages pact included homage or other rever- ence to the Devil and was thus considered a form of apostasy and heresy.[17]

European witchcraft is best considered a form of heresy, for in order to worship the Christian Devil one must first be a Christian. Witchcraft is inseparable from heresy in at least two ways. In the first place, the scholastics and Inquisitors defined all de- monolatry as heresy. In the second place, as the sixteenth-century Thomas Stapleton put it, "Crescit cum magia haeresis, cum haeresi magia," heresy grows with witchcraft and witchcraft with heresy. Both experienced rapid growth in the thirteenth through fifteenth centuries, and in those places where heresy was strong, witchcraft also took hold.

Although the last two sentences clearly constitute something of a *petitio principii* in a matter of essential importance, the reality of witchcraft, in point of fact there is no doubt that witch- craft was a real phenomenon. It was real in the sense that large numbers of people—indeed at some points almost everyone— believed in it, and their belief itself constitutes an historical phe- nomenon. The degree to which people were obsessed by witch- craft, magic, and demons from the fourteenth to the seventeenth century is visible in almost every aspect of life in that period; witches were every bit as much a part of people's daily fantasies then as Communists are in the fantasies of modern conservatives or Imperialists in those of modern Guevaristas. Modern historians should not at the same time accept stigmata and appearances of the Virgin as expressions of wide popular belief and reject sabbats and appearances of the Devil as the narrow inventions of scholastics and Inquisitors.

But did an objective reality lie behind the phenomenon of belief? One difficulty in answering the question, aside from the fundamental philosophical difficulty of establishing objectivity, is in the antiwitchcraft bias of the sources. Even more important is the methodological bias of historians. If one defines European witchcraft in a way that excludes its roots in heresy, sorcery, and folklore but embraces all the supernatural elements assigned it by the Inquisitors, including flight through the night air and frigid intercourse with demons, one is likely to arrive at a negative answer. The question "Do you really believe in witchcraft?" usually means to inquire whether one subscribes to every folly that fiction and fancy have assigned to witches, and one is obliged to answer no. On the other hand if one places witchcraft in the context of the worldwide phenomenon of demon worship and witch belief, one will answer differently. As Arago observed, "Outside of pure mathematics, anyone who pronounces the word 'impossible' is lacking in prudence."

Within the framework of historical interpretations of European witchcraft, there are at least eight degrees of skepticism (in descending order). (1) Virtually no one in the Middle Ages believed in witchcraft, which was a vicious fraud perpetrated by the Inquisitors and their attendant theologians, who provoked witch scares in order to increase their own power and wealth. (2) Many people (including Inquisitors and theologians) were deluded by the superstitious atmosphere of the Middle Ages into believing that others were witches, but no one believed that he himself was a witch. (3) At least some people were deluded into believing themselves witches. (4) Some of what these witches believed and practiced was real, deriving from old pagan cults, folklore, sorcery, and heresy. (5) Witch beliefs and practices as described by the sources (mainly trial records) did exist to a substantial degree. Witches did worship the Devil; they did believe and practice what was attributed to them, though these beliefs and practices were constantly evolving. (6) A formal witch cult has existed virtually unchanged from ancient times (the argument of Margaret Murray and the modern occultists). (7) Weird phenomena, such as flying and shapeshifting, are themselves real. (8) The weird phenomena are not only real, but supernatural, and proof that the Devil and his minions live.

All of these positions, except the last, are historically feasible. The historian has no right to uphold (or for that matter oppose) the last, because he is concerned only with human events and causation; like the natural sciences, history by definition does not and cannot deal with the supernatural. The most useful approach to the other seven points is to follow the principle that the greater the unlikelihood of the alleged events in terms of general experience and other evidence, the more powerful the direct evidence in their favor needs to be in order to overcome the inertia of justified skepticism. On the other hand skepticism should never be elevated to dogmatism, and Alan Richardson's attack on Hume's tautological skepticism about miracles is persuasive: "There are not historical generalizations (or laws of history) which determine in advance of the historical enquiry whether an event may have happened or not; historical generalizations arise out of the evidence and are not *a priori* conditions of thinking which precede it."[18] The good historian always has his mind—and eyes—open.

On the basis of these general rules of skepticism, alternative seven can be eliminated; and the evidence, in spite of the quantity (not quality) of Murrayite and occulist assertions to the contrary, eliminates alternative six. A minimal understanding of medieval Christianity excludes alternative one, and the evidence severely limits the likelihood of alternative two. The most proper answer to the question of the reality of witchcraft lies in the range of alternatives three to five.

Even granting the fullest influence of scholastics and Inquisitors and accepting their fifteenth-century definition of witchcraft, we find ourselves dealing with realities. About 30 percent of the charges against the witches made by the Inquisitors at that time are associated with sorcery, about 25 percent with other folklore traditions, and about 25 percent with previous heresies. If one goes on to admit, as all historians do, that sorcery existed and was practiced in Europe as it has been in most societies and that heresies were believed and practiced, and if one admits, as all historians familiar with the evidence do, that magical folk beliefs and customs persisted in various forms through the Middle Ages, one must conclude that about 80 percent of the charges are associated with phenomena having existence independent of theological embroidery. The other 20 percent were introduced in the course of the development of the formal definition of witchcraft by its opponents. Some of these last are the elaborations of scholastics and Inquisitors concerned with the delineation of heresies, but almost all appeared, the sabbat being the only important exception, before the Inquisition intervened in witchcraft proper. Without denying that many of the traits ascribed to witchcraft are physically improbable or that many of the witches condemned were innocent,* one is obliged to regard witchcraft as a reality.

---

* The proportion of innocents sacrificed was greater in the sixteenth and seventeenth centuries, when the witch craze was at its height, than in the Middle Ages. As Lynn White observed (p. 23), "Innocent men and women

The definition of witchcraft that we use here is coherent, self-consistent, lacks self-contradiction, and permits investigation of the nature and development of witch practices in the Middle Ages. It does not beg questions by being too broad, equating witchcraft with all sorcery, or by being too narrow, limiting it to what was defined as witchcraft at the height of the witch craze. Witchcraft is a composite phenomenon drawing from folklore, sorcery, demonology, heresy, and Christian theology. The most useful heuristic is to accept the fifteenth-century scholastic and Inquisitorial definition of the witch as classical and then look back through the Middle Ages for the components of that definition, seeking their origins, their development, and the process of their eventual amalgamation. The best definition of witchcraft is one that recognizes change and development and is itself developmental. Witchcraft was what it was thought to be.

But what was witchcraft thought to be? The chief individual components defined as witchcraft in the classical period were: (1) those generally derived from sorcery (approximately 31 percent)—shapeshifting, riding or flying, cannibalism, child murder, the use of salves, familiars, invocation of demons, and the choice of night as the time for witch activities; (2) components generally derived from other folklore traditions (23 percent)—the goddess Diana, wild dances, the "Good Society," the wild man and the wild chase, incubi, and passing through closed doors or walls; (3) components deriving mainly from heresy (27 percent) —the definition of witchcraft as a sect, secret meetings, desecration of Cross or sacraments, formal repudiation of church, *synagoga*, sex orgies, and feasting; (4) components added for the most part by theologians (19 percent)—pact, Devil's mark,

---

have been persecuted for witchcraft, but it would appear from the records that many alleged witches have believed themselves in fact to be witches and have believed witchcraft to be effective."

worship of, sacrifice to, or homage to the Devil; the obscene kiss, and the sabbat. The sabbat appears in medieval witchcraft only at the end of the fifteenth century; the coven and the black mass simply did not exist and are in no way a part of medieval witchcraft.

Although the process by which these elements were assembled and welded into the phenomenon of witchcraft includes a gradual accretion of beliefs and practices, it is not as simple as a value-added process in which a result is produced by adding elements in a given sequence. The history of witchcraft is the history of an acculturation, where cultural elements are not only transmitted and accumulated but also syncretized and reinterpreted until they are transformed. In interpreting this acculturation, we shall ask where the elements of witchcraft came from, through what processes they were transmitted and how and why they were transformed, and what changes of meaning occurred behind the change of forms.

Our investigation is limited geographically to an area that possessed a relatively high degree of religious and social unity: those parts of medieval Christendom usually in communion with Rome.* It excludes eastern European as well as non-Christian sorcery on the grounds that developments in those categories were independent and quite different from witchcraft in western Europe, which is best understood as a variety of protest against Catholic society. It excludes high magic as almost wholly unconnected with witchcraft, and it excludes all cases of simple low magic or simple sorcery in which the element of protest is lacking. The many trials listed and commented upon by Hansen and Lea

* The degree of this unity should not be exaggerated. Local variations, often extensive, existed in medieval witchcraft as in medieval Christianity. Any history that is as geographically and chronologically broad as this one will inevitably cause some distortion in its collation of detail often widely dispersed in space and time.

24

that deal with simple sorcery alone will be omitted from consideration here. The chronological limits are at one end the establishment of Christianity as the legal religion of the Empire in the fourth century and at the other end the publication of the *Malleus Maleficarum* in 1486–1487, by which time the classical picture of witchcraft was complete. This is an inquiry into the origins of witchcraft in the context of medieval society and consequently cannot extend into the sixteenth and seventeenth centuries, when the witch craze was widest.

According to our theory a continuity of phenomena existed from ancient pagan beliefs and practices through the Middle Ages to the classical witchcraft of the fifteenth through eighteenth centuries. But this continuity was wholly unselfconscious, being without organization, institutions, or dogmas. Its elements were a magical world view, the practice of sorcery, folk traditions (especially those relating to agriculture and the hunt), and a willingness to ignore or oppose authority and public opinion by consorting with supernatural powers described by the Church as evil. Since the continuity fluctuated and was often only vaguely defined, it was much affected by prevalent opinion, both learned and popular. In other words, witches usually acted as they were supposed to act. The witchcraft of the earliest Middle Ages was partly a survival of pagan religion and magic and partly the product of their transformation by Christianity.

After about 700 the development of witchcraft was influenced by Reformist heresy. From about 1140 Catharism, with its emphasis upon Satan and its role in many places as successor to Reformism, helped transform it further. At the same time the growth of institutional organization within the Church, particularly the papacy, also added to the formation of the phenomenon, as did the rise of scholastic philosophy and the growth of popular fervor expressed in anti-Semitism, fanaticism, and crusade. The Inquisition was founded in the 1230s and from the beginning of the fourteenth century took a hand by enforcing scholastic definitions upon the accused by the use of torture. Antinomian heresy contributed to the formation of witchcraft in the thirteenth and fourteenth centuries, and from 1300 onward the increasing economic, political, and social crisis of medieval society created conditions in which various expressions of revolt occurred, witchcraft being among the most prominent. Finally, from the 1420s to 1487, the scholastic and Inquisitorial theorists of witchcraft fixed, by persuasion and force, the classical picture of the witch in the form it was to continue to have into the eighteenth century.

2

Witchcraft
in History

ITCHCRAFT, like any historical phenomenon, is a complex construct applied to events by the human mind. This construct develops in time in two ways: the idea of witchcraft held by its contemporaries developed—witchcraft was not the same in the sixteenth as it had been in the fourteenth century; and historians' conception of the development of witchcraft has itself developed. Only through an understanding of the varieties of vision and the diversity of definitions that have been applied to witchcraft will we be fully able to understand the phenomenon.[1]

The very weirdness of witchcraft has caused serious historians to skirt the subject with undue levity or undue skepticism in order to protect themselves from the importunities of thrill-seekers or the ridicule of their colleagues. Much of the writing on the topic is incompetent—no other subject in history has elicited so much drivel—and marred by lack of seriousness in treating an idea that killed hundreds of thousands. Curiously, the most serious and thorough works on medieval witchcraft were completed before 1905, by Henry Charles Lea in America and Joseph Hansen in Germany, neither, unfortunately, a professional historian with students to carry on his work.

The eighteenth century, when witchcraft ceased to be legally prosecuted, was also the century in which critical erudition and philosophy came together to produce modern historical thought. Consequently it was then that the first critical studies of witchcraft as a historical phenomenon, rather than as a current event, appeared. The rationalism of that time rejected the objective existence of sorcery and witchcraft, and the witch trials were attributed to the errors of superstition and fraud. The first critical historical work on the subject in English, by Francis Hutchinson, dismissed witchcraft as the product of "pagan and popish superstitions" inimical to the cause of true, rational Christianity.[2]

Hutchinson's work included a brief list of incidents of witchcraft from the time of the Old Testament to the present, but it was left to the scholarship of the Germans, already beginning to acquire a monumental reputation, to produce the most voluminous collections of incidents and bibliographies, collections that were used to excellent effect by George Lincoln Burr when in the early twentieth century he assembled the great White collection of witchcraft materials for Cornell University.[3] In France a general history of magic was essayed by Jules Garinet, but the best effort at a narrative history in this period was that of Johann Moritz Schwager, who unfortunately did not get beyond his first, essentially introductory, volume.

Beginning with the mid-nineteenth century, interpretations became diverse and can be classified according to their approach. One that is still very popular is the occult and esoteric. With its origins in the Romantic movement, occultism was reinforced in the later nineteenth century by diabolism, by the growth of interest in psychology and folklore, and by the general upsurge of interest in spiritualism and other esoteric pursuits. This interest is best understood partly in the context of the growth of irrationalism from the late nineteenth century, and partly as a search for some kind of supernatural experience on the part of people who had rejected conventional religion and somehow found séances more credible than sacraments. Writers of this school tend to believe in the objective reality of witchcraft and in its validity as a variety of occult worship. Their books, usually characterized by a cavalier attitude toward historical criticism and by the effort to accommodate witchcraft in a long and suppositious tradition of high and ancient wisdom, are as useless as they are numerous.[4]

A second school of thought is that of the conservative Christians, who are closer than any other modern writers to the tradition of the Fathers and the great theologians of the Middle Ages and Reformation. Their not unreasonable contention is that witchcraft must be taken seriously, not in the sense that the witches really possessed all the occult powers to which they laid claim, but in the sense that they were consciously and deliberately worshiping the power of evil. Many of these writers would go so far as to allow that the devotees were actively aided by the Devil. As early as the mid-nineteenth century, Catholic apologists were on this account defending the Church against accusations of brutality in its treatment of the witches, and the apologetic strain is still visible in works like those of Séjourné and Manser.[5] The Catholic Church has in modern times taken no official position in regard to witchcraft.

By far the most determined and informed modern defender of orthodoxy against the skeptics was Montague Summers, who explicitly believed the claims of the early witch hunters that the Devil actively and powerfully assisted the witches in the performance of all the evils ascribed to them. Summers, a notorious eccentric who died in 1948, claimed (but never proved) that he had holy orders. His numerous books all convey the attitude expressed in his introduction to the *Malleus Maleficarum,* the handbook of one of the most ruthless Inquisitors of the Middle Ages: "The *Malleus Maleficarum* is one of the world's few books written *sub specie aeternitatis."⁶* Summers' own works and his many editions and translations of classical witchcraft handbooks are marred by frequent liberties in translation, inaccurate references, and wild surmises; they are almost totally lacking in historical sense, for Summers saw witchcraft as a manifestation of the eternal and unchanging warfare between God and Satan. Yet Summers was well steeped in the sources, and his insight that European witchcraft was basically a perversion of Christianity and related to heresy, rather than the survival of a pagan religion as the Murrayites claimed, was correct. Summers' work was erratic and unreliable but not without value.

Far more influential than the previous two schools of thought is the late nineteenth-century liberal approach, rooted in scientism, optimism, and confidence in progress and human rationality. This approach is flawed by an essentially pre-Freudian and pre-Nazi lack of comprehension of the innate viciousness of man. Witchcraft, according to the liberal view, was a gross product of the superstitions of the Catholic Dark Ages, beyond which we have infinitely progressed and with which we have little in common. Because of this assumption, and also under the influence of the legal and political emphasis that dominated historical writing in the late nineteenth and early twentieth century, writers of this persuasion have focused their attention upon the witch trials, the Inquisition, and other mechanisms of repression. Emotionally committed to liberalism and viewing the Church as an obstacle in the road of progress, they reject the possibility of there being any real currents of witch belief and practice and insist that not the witches, but the Inquisitors, invented witchcraft.

This liberal, anticlerical point of view was expressed early by Garinet, Scott, and others, but its most learned and influential spokesman was Henry Charles Lea, the American historian of heresy, the Inquisition, and witchcraft. Lea, great scholar though he was, subscribed uncritically to the assumption of his time

30

that a historian could objectively describe human progress. Firmly believing that witchcraft was the invention of benighted Catholicism, Lea called it superstition to believe that anyone ever really worshiped the Devil, a strange position for a man who knew so much about medieval heresy. He admitted that some witches may have believed in their own powers, but only because the ideas propagated by the Inquisition had rendered them hysterical.[7] Although Lea contributed immeasurably to our knowledge of the repression of witchcraft, his dogmatic liberalism prevented him from seriously studying the witches themselves and thereby grasping that human irrationality and viciousness are not the monopoly of religious people or authoritarian institutions. This prejudice led him into further errors. Because he assumed that the Inquisition, not the witches, invented witchcraft, he insisted that the phenomenon did not begin until the mid-fourteenth century and so in the *Materials* ignores witch trials before 1321, the connection of witchcraft with earlier heresy, and its partial derivation from twelfth- and thirteenth-century currents of religious thought and social change.

This combination of scholarly erudition and thoroughness with philosophical and methodological narrowness characterized, to some degree, all those who followed in Lea's tradition. Partly because of Lea's example, the best work in English in the history of witchcraft continued to be done in the United States. The great president of Cornell University, Andrew Dickson White, aggressively scientistic and antireligious, proposed that witches were unfortunate wretches blamed by superstitious Catholicism for natural disasters like storms for which White knew the true, scientific explanations.[8] The Andrew Dickson White library at Cornell, still the finest collection of printed materials relating to witchcraft in the world, was mainly assembled by White's pupil and assistant George Lincoln Burr (1857–1938), whose influence in American witchcraft scholarship is second only to Lea's.[9]

Burr advanced the liberal-rationalist arguments as vigorously as White and more uncompromisingly than Lea. Witchcraft, never real, "was but a shadow, a nightmare: the nightmare of a religion, the shadow of a dogma";[10] it was invented by the Inquisition when its "ripening jurisprudence" needed to "find a place for this high crime."[11] Burr was contemptuous of the contentions of Summers and Murray that witchcraft must be treated as a real phenomenon.

Many other historians in Europe and in America shared Burr's view that the scholastics and the Inquisition caused the witchcraft epidemic. In the chapter "Magic and Witchcraft" of his great *History of the Rise and Influence of the Spirit of Rationalism in Europe,* W. E. H. Lecky attributed witchcraft to the superstition and terrorism of the Church and argued in Humian fashion that although the evidence for the reality of witchcraft is immense, it is inacceptable because it is rationally impossible.[12] Most historians of the Inquisition, focusing upon the institution rather than upon the heresies it was designed to deal with, tended to agree that the witches were innocent victims. One of the most influential liberal writers was the English anticlerical historian G. G. Coulton, who argued that the heresy of witchcraft was invented by the Inquisition in order to put an end to sorcery, which had existed for centuries but which the Church had just begun to be sophisticated enough to disapprove.

Wallace Notestein and the great Harvard literary scholar George Lyman Kittredge also stand within the liberal tradition; Kittredge, however, was more aware than most members of this tradition of the relevance of folklore and sorcery. Like Jean Marx and Fritz Byloff, he argued that there was a continuity of witchcraft from the simple sorcery of the early Middle Ages to the classical witchcraft of the sixteenth century. Although Inquisitors had invented the idea that witchcraft was a heresy, they worked with previously existing elements.[13] Marx states this point of view most clearly: "The scholarly and scholastic conception of witch-craft that the Inquisitors used contained a certain number of folk beliefs and traditions."[14] These beliefs and traditions, rather than the institutions of repression, became the center of attention for twentieth-century folklorists and anthropologists.

At the very end of the century the archivist of Cologne, Joseph Hansen, published the most important work on witchcraft in the Middle Ages: *Zauberwahn, Inquisition, und Hexenprozess*. This volume was followed by his collection of sources, many of which he himself discovered and edited: *Quellen und Untersuchungen zur Geschichte des Hexenwahns*. Hansen's contribution was the culmination of a tradition of careful scholarship in which polemic was muted and careful work in the documents was done to support generalization. The earliest of these works was that of W. G. Soldan, which originally appeared in 1843: *Geschichte der Hexenprocesse*. This first fully thorough book on the history of witchcraft was revised by Soldan's son-in-law Heinrich Heppe and again by Max Bauer, each revision incorporating new materials and constituting almost a new book. Soldan-Heppe-Bauer grasped the essence of the historical view of witchcraft, its development from ancient magic into something qualitatively different through the impact of theology and heresy. The emphasis of their work upon Roman antecedents of witchcraft redressed Grimm's over-emphasis upon the Teutonic and encouraged liberal writers to give attention to the influence of Roman and Canon law. But the Soldan-Heppe-Bauer work is lacking in factual accuracy and in adequate connections with the general history of the social en-vironment, and it shares the nineteenth-century liberal limitation of emphasis upon the machinery of repression rather than upon the phenomenon itself. Even the edition by Bauer in 1911 is vastly inferior to Hansen's work of a decade earlier.[15]

The fact that after seventy years Hansen still stands as the most thorough scholar of medieval witchcraft is indication enough of his stature. He had one defect—inability to escape the nineteenth-century emphasis upon institutional repression, which therefore occupies a disproportionate place in his work. The *Quellen,* for example, consists almost exclusively of records of later medieval witch trials rather than including documents of importance in folklore or social movements, and in Hansen's view, "the epidemic persecution of magicians and witches is a product of medieval theology, ecclesiastical organization, and of the magic trials conducted by papacy and Inquisition. These, under the influence of scholastic demonology, were conducted like heresy trials."[16] His strengths, on the other hand, sprang from his combination of erudition and philosophy. New materials have been discovered since his day, but the *Quellen* remains the most important treasure house for the historian of medieval witchcraft. Another of Hansen's virtues was his careful analysis of the trials themselves. Most important was his elaboration of the cumulative theory of witchcraft—the idea that it was a composite of many elements, including magic, folklore, demonology, and heresy as well as ecclesiastical repression. Though he did not develop the idea beyond a few suggestions, Hansen went farther than any previous historian in suggesting that the social context—plagues, for example, and wars—had to be considered in explaining the development of the witch craze. Finally, he set the precedent for the most useful method of exploring the origins of witchcraft, describing the elements of witchcraft as defined in the fifteenth century and then tracing them back to their origins. All scholarly interpretations of witchcraft today must be deeply indebted to Hansen's great example.

Though Hansen's was the best product of nineteenth-century liberalism, it was not the last. Nevertheless, the attention of the twentieth century turned increasingly to folklore and anthropology. Scholarly interest in folk traditions goes back to the work of the Grimm brothers in Germany early in the nineteenth century, but not until the end of the century did anthropology begin to have wide influence upon historical thought. As anthropologists illuminated the customs of the African, American, and Pacific peoples, they uncovered striking similarities to witch practices in Europe, and the Europeanists were quick to exploit these new approaches. It is difficult now for us to recapture the fresh bloom of enthusiasm for the study of ritual and myth that dominated much of European scholarship, literature, and art in the first few decades of the twentieth century under the influence of writers like Frazer, Lévi-Strauss, Evans-Pritchard, and Jessie Weston. Yet we are still in the debt of these scholars for directing us to a new road of approach, from which we can describe and map a terrain largely ignored by the liberals. This terrain is populated, not by the theories of philosophers or jurists, but by folk legends and tales, folk motifs in art and literature, popular feasts and festivals, the wild hunt and its hunters, secret cults, and sorcery. The folklorists' great contribution to the study of witchcraft is the recognition that the primitive elements in witch beliefs were not invented either by the scholastics or the Inquisitors but were handed down by folk tradition and varied from locality to locality.

Some folklorists have gone beyond the others to argue that the medieval witch cult was a survival of ancient Greco-Roman or Germanic pagan cults. As early as 1835 Jacob Grimm was already arguing the survival of the old Teutonic cults; Soldan argued for the Greco-Roman antecedents. A. A. Barb and Hugh Trevor-Roper have argued correctly that distinguishing between Teutonic and Greco-Roman pagan elements is difficult and in any event of little importance since our concern is with the general theory of pagan survival. The idea became quite popular in certain circles. Höfler argued that there was a long tradition of secret, demonic cults among the German peoples that persisted through the Middle Ages into the modern period, cults that included animal masquerades, orgiastic dances, and the wild hunt.

By far the most influential proponent of the secret survival theory was Margaret Alice Murray, anthropologist, folklorist, and Egyptologist. Murray's first work on European witchcraft was published in 1921, when anthropology, folklore, and myth were much in the air—Eliot's *Waste Land* would appear in 1922. Her two succeeding works were progressively more extreme and open to criticism, yet she, more than any other anthropologist, helped the folklorist displace the liberal view, and the *Encyclopaedia Britannica* used her article on "Witchcraft" until recently.[17] A full appraisal of Murray's work must take into account the vagaries of her later writings, where, for example, she argued that every king of England from the Conqueror through James I was secretly a high priest of the witch cult. But to be fair such an appraisal must also consider that those who knew her were convinced of her sanity, if not of her accuracy, and the most useful evaluation must rest upon her first, most moderate, and most influential book, *The Witch-Cult in Western Europe.*

Even in *The Witch-Cult* Murray's fundamental error is already evident: her assertion that an ancient fertility religion dedicated to the worship of the god Dianus (himself essentially a Murray invention) persisted as an organized and widespread cult from the later Roman Empire through the seventeenth century. This mistake bred others. Since, she argued, there was continuity in the cult's beliefs and rites, there was small change or development through the centuries; the witch cults were little influenced by ideas from Christianity or other aspects of medieval society. Consequently Murray read back into the entire history of witchcraft, wholly without justification from the sources, witch practices that were peculiar to certain times and places, such as the coven, a late development peculiar to Scotland, and the sabbat, which she

36

makes the center of her fertility cult but which is not mentioned in any of the sources before the late fifteenth century.

Indeed, Murray's use of sources in general is appalling. Not only did she force evidence to fit her theory, but she ignored vast bodies of materials, particularly for the Middle Ages, that were readily available to her and that, ironically, in some instances even would have fortified her position.[18] Yet her work advanced important anthropological ideas such as the connection between religion and low magic, and the derivation of certain witch beliefs—familiars, for example—from pagan folk customs. Murray's book emphasizes one essential point largely ignored by the liberals: pagan folk practices and beliefs, whether Greco-Roman, Teutonic, or Celtic, did not die out with the introduction of Christianity but rather remained and constituted the fundamental substratum of witchcraft.

The worst result of Murray's work has been the strength it has lent to charlatans and occultists. Although self-styled witches today can accept the liberals' belief that the witches were innocent of crime, they are hostile to the liberals' belief that the witches were innocent of witchcraft and insist instead that it is a valid and ancient variety of religion. Murray's theories support their contentions, they think, and they have consequently added a superstructure to her nonsense. Unfortunately, acceptance of many of the absurdities of Murray's position has not been limited to witches; some respectable modern writers have shown her influence all too strongly.[19] Other historians, like Byloff and Bonomo, have been willing to build upon the useful aspects of Murray's work without adopting its untenable elements, and the independent and careful researches of contemporary scholars have lent aspects of the Murray thesis considerable new strength.

The historical study of witchcraft has been enormously enhanced by psychologists and sociologists as well as by anthropologists. From the time that Freud began to explore the psychological foundation of magical and religious beliefs, notably in his *Totem and Taboo* and *Moses and Monotheism,* psychologists have been interested in the insights into psychopathology gained by the study of witch beliefs. The psychological approach reinforces the historiographical shift from the liberals' emphasis upon institutional repression to a more sophisticated understanding of the psychological reasons for the behavior of both the witches and their persecutors. Was the practice of witchcraft a form of rebellion against, or escape from, society? Did it provide fantasies of power for people who felt powerless or dispossessed in the world in which they lived? Can it be compared with other fantasy escapes into ritual, drama, heresy, mysticism, or pilgrimages? Is it an amalgam of ancient elements of folk panic, like terror of the woods and terror of animals? Is it a hideous kind of projection in which the twisted desires of the libido are projected upon witches by their persecutors? Did the witches induce hallucinations by the use of drugs such as aconite? These are some of the valuable questions discussed by the psychologists and psychologically oriented historians who have interested themselves in witchcraft. At least one psychiatrist, Nathaniel S. Lehrman, dissents. Following the skepticism of the liberal school and arguing that the witches were entirely innocent and perfectly sane, he attacks not only the psychiatric interpretation of witchcraft but the very bases of Freudian psychology itself. Rather than pursuing this debate, we should in the future use social psychology and social dynamics to attempt to understand the conditions of society that made the wide acceptance of witch beliefs possible. Michelet argued as far back as 1862 that witchcraft was a form of social rebellion rooted in the miseries of the fourteenth century, and since then other historians, some of them Marxists, have suggested that witchcraft, like heresy, was a manifestation of popular discontent with the rulers of society.[20]

Many of the most valuable contributions of the last century and a half have been scholarly accounts of particular cities, dioceses, or countries based on careful work in the archives. New material is occasionally still discovered in untouched archives by workers in local history who have recognized the importance of publishing documents relating to witchcraft. Most of the good particularist books and articles relating to medieval witchcraft have come from Germany, Austria, Switzerland, France, Italy, and England.

Understanding of medieval witchcraft has been advanced by works on closely related phenomena such as demonology, magic, and heresy, particularly in the last few decades. These have enhanced our grasp of how the dynamics of social change affected the development of witchcraft in itself and in its connection with beliefs regarding demons, magic, and heresy. The investigation of heresy is more important for understanding witchcraft than that of magic or even demonology, for witchcraft's opponents perceived it as a variety of religious dissent, and its roots tapped many earlier heresies.

One of the most influential contemporary writers on witchcraft has been Rossell Hope Robbins, whose strongly anti-Christian views make him one of the latest and most determined defenders of the nineteenth-century liberal position. Robbins' approach, beyond being a useful corrective to the excesses of the Murray school, has a number of virtues. His sense of moral outrage at a phenomenon that brought, at a reasonable estimate, two hundred thousand people to execution is in the best historical tradition, which perceives that the significance of events is not dimmed by the passage of time. His skepticism of records deriving from the Inquisitorial courts on the grounds that their confessions were often obtained under torture has been confirmed by the great historian of heresy, Herbert Grundmann.

But the argument that the Inquisition invented witchcraft because it had run out of heretics to prosecute cannot be accepted. In reality, heresy had never been so widespread as it was in the fourteenth and fifteenth centuries, when the Waldensians were actually increasing and great numbers of new sects were springing up. "And surely," as one historian observes, "for every heretic who fell victim to the Inquisition, twenty escaped it."[21] The history of witchcraft must be tied to that of heresy instead of to that of sorcery. For example, a geographical survey of the incidence of witchcraft would show that it was far more closely correlated with heresy than with the Inquisition. There were very few witch trials in Spain and Poland, where the Inquisition was powerful, whereas in England, where the Inquisition did not exist, trials were numerous. In those areas where heresy was strong, witchcraft too became important. This is true even for England. It was precisely in the fifteenth century, when England first felt the pressure of heresy, that witchcraft became a problem. Hence the idea that witchcraft is a Christian invention is true to only a limited degree.

Contemporary adherents of the anthropological and sociological approach have made many valuable contributions. Burstein investigates the phenomenon in relation to medical considerations, especially the psychopathology of old age. Runeberg, arguing from the strengths of Murray while setting aside her exaggerations, attacks the liberal school for dismissing the anthropological evidence in favor of the reality of witchcraft, evidence that phenomena very similar to European witchcraft exist in America and Africa among people untouched by Christian society. Like Hansen, Runeberg considers witchcraft a cumulative phenomenon, but he posited its elements as those of folk tradition at least as much as Christian theology. Witchcraft derives from ancient fertility rites handed down through the Middle Ages and modified, but not wholly transformed, by Christian thought. The old fertility cults were transformed into witchcraft by the pressures of persecution, which forced the cultists into close association with the heretics.

Enormous weight is lent to Runeberg's theory and the folklore interpretation in general by a brilliant monograph by the young Italian scholar, Carlo Ginzburg. Ginzburg became interested in the history of folklore through reading Murray, Runeberg, and Bonomo. After extensive work in the archives, he unearthed striking evidence to support their contentions. It is difficult, he argues, to prove a continuity of any organized cult from the ancient world, but it is possible to show a continuity of folk beliefs and practices of a fertility nature, overlaid through the centuries by "a cultural complex of very diverse components."[22] The proof Ginzburg offers is the existence of a fertility cult in Friuli as late as the end of the sixteenth century—the *benandanti* (those who walk well, or do good). The benandanti were fertility cultists and worshiped the goddess Diana. The firmness of the evidence for this strongly supports portions of the Murray-Runeberg thesis. Even more interesting is the curious transformation of the benandanti after the arrival of the Inquisition. The benandanti had previously explicitly rejected anything like worship of the Devil and had even gone out at night and fought pitched battles with the *strigoni,* members of the local witch cult. When the Inquisitors arrived, their rigidity did not permit them to see the difference between the two cults: the worship of Diana and the practice of non-Christian rites by the benandanti were enough to show that they were witches. Through trials and tortures the Inquisitors succeeded in forcing the benandanti to confess to the practice of witchcraft, and over a surprisingly short period of time they impressed their lie upon both the population in general and upon the benandanti themselves. As late as 1610 the benandanti were affirming their opposition to diabolism; by 1640 they had become convinced that they did worship the devil and went so far as to admit that they were in fact strigoni, members of the same sect against which they had previously fought so determinedly. "We can securely affirm," Ginzburg argues, "that diabolical witchcraft spread through Friuli in the shape of a deformation of an antecedent agrarian cult."[23] No firmer bit of evidence has ever been presented that witchcraft existed, that it was largely the product of elements of folk belief and practice, and that the role of the Inquisition was not to invent witchcraft, but to impose on others its own definition of witchcraft.

A variety of other interpretations has been offered by other serious contemporary scholars like Baroja and Rose. The most influential of the current interpretations will probably be that of Hugh Trevor-Roper, owing both to the eminence of its author and to its inherent good sense. Trevor-Roper argues that witchcraft was real in the sense that witches believed in it. It was neither an ancient fertility cult nor the product (except in part) of the theological imagination, but first and foremost an "articulation of social pressure."[24] Witchcraft was a craze in the sociological sense. The hatred of certain elements in society for certain other groups was formulated in a mythology of evil, which was at least in part accepted by those against whom it was created. Thus the witches, accused again and again of demonolatry, gradually came to fulfill the expectations of their accusers.

The trend of current historical thought is toward a widening of the spectrum of interpretation to take into account a number of diverse perspectives. No one interpretation is demanded by the sources, which are sparse, opaque, and difficult to penetrate. Almost all the documents we have relating to medieval heretics and witches were written by their adversaries—as treatises, descriptions in chronicles, or confessions forced on the heretics themselves. The Inquisitors in particular habitually used set formularies of questions and answers that determined in advance much of what they would "discover." These formularies were in Latin and could be "translated" for the accused in such a way that he would understand whatever the Inquisitor chose. Having received the answer he wished, he had only to record it as a response to the

Latin query, which might have a wholly different meaning from what the prisoner understood. If such devices failed, there was always torture, which was extensively, viciously, and persistently used and could break all but the most heroic spirits.

A more innocent but still dangerous difficulty in the sources is their medieval tendency to reproduce and repeat earlier materials without so indicating. Characteristics ascribed to any one group of witches may in fact be derived from descriptions of an earlier group or even from purely literary or theological sources. A final difficulty is the discrepancy in the number of sources available for different periods. Sources earlier than the thirteenth century are very sparse and in the earliest period, from the fourth through the seventh centuries, extremely fragmentary. It is possible that the assumption that witchcraft grew rapidly during the fourteenth and fifteenth centuries may be in part an illusion caused by the enormous growth of source material in that period. Some of the shortcomings in the sources are partly overcome by accepting, as we shall in this book, that what people thought happened is as interesting as what "objectively did happen," and much more certain.

3

The Transformation of Paganism, 300-700

THE foundations of medieval witchcraft consist of chthonic religion, folk traditions, and low magic, all three derived from the source cultures of Western civilization: the ancient Near East, especially Judaism, the Greco-Romans, the early Christians, and the Celts and Teutons. This oldest substratum of witchcraft was then progressively transformed by acculturation.

Christianity, acting as the great agent of synthesis that brought Judeao-Christian, Greco-Roman, and Celto-Teutonic cultures together and reshaped them into a new society, itself shared the magical conceptions of the time in which it arose, in spite of the fact that it deliberately rejected magic and in time became its chief enemy. The New Testament itself contains magical traces—for example, the exorcism of evil spirits—but it is in those apocryphal writings most influenced by gnosticism that magic is most evident, the child Jesus appearing as a magician capable of turning his playmates into goats or striking them dead.[1] Celsus, the great pagan opponent of Christianity, claimed that Jesus was a sorcerer. Simon the Magician with his false miracles and spurious charisma is, as Charles Williams illustrates in his novel *All Hallows' Eve,* a dark mirror image of the Christ. Christian leaders were not ignorant of these magical elements in gnosticism and popular Christianity, and magic was condemned by theologians and prosecuted by the Christian emperors of the fourth century. Only the conscious effort of its leaders kept Christianity from becoming another of the magical cults that were so popular at the time.

Christianity escaped this fate by assimilating the pervasive magical environment. To eradicate it was impossible even if it had been desirable. Christian people continued to practice ancient superstitions in a more or less disguised form, and pagan and magical elements entered the saints' cults.[2] The infinite resourcefulness with which the Church sought to destroy paganism by ingestion advanced the development of witchcraft, convincing those who remained attached to the old gods that they were really revering demons. By establishing that demons were evil by nature, theology lent an initial practical reality to the worship of evil. The fathers accused the pagans of demonolatry. Medieval writers, taking them literally, found it all the easier to believe that many people in their own day were worshiping Satan and his minions.

Christianity assimilated Mediterranean paganism. Then, as it moved northward from the fifth century through the eighth, it easily and rapidly absorbed those Celtic and Teutonic elements closely resembling Mediterranean paganism. Because these elements were more recent additions to the original witchcraft stratum, medieval witch practices and beliefs were more often expressed in Northern than in Mediterranean terms. But the beliefs and practices as a whole were, like medieval society in general, syncretic.

Of the pagan deities, Greco-Roman or Teuto-Celtic, that survived in Christian Europe, it was the chthonic rather than the heavenly gods that preserved the most vigor. The chthonic cults were more private and personal than the uranic, which tended to be politically established and publicly performed. Chthonic worship more easily evaded the political efforts of the Christians to suppress it, particularly in the society of the early Middle Ages, which lived by agriculture and the hunt. Finally, the Christians found it easier to demonize the chthonic gods than the heavenly ones, for the connection of fertility gods with the earth and hence with the underworld of ghosts and evil spirits was a venerable tradition in both Mediterranean and Northern cultures. The evil sorceresses of classical Rome, like Lucan's Erictho and Horace's Canidia or Sagana, were all closely associated with the underworld.

Many Mediterranean fertility rites exhibit characteristics of the later witch cult, though no demonstrable direct affiliation exists between them. The Dionysiac revels, for example, with their frenzied dancing and song, obscenity, and consumption of raw meat (including, at least legendarily, cannibalism), and the witches' sabbats, even if unaffiliated, were products of the same urge to ritual liberation. The theme of ritual liberation clearly continued into the Middle Ages in other forms, as in the Feast of Fools with its close resemblance to the Roman Saturnalia.

The most important explicit Mediterranean element in medieval witchcraft is the cult of Diana. Diana, or her Greek counterpart Artemis, was an unusually schizophrenic deity. Her best-known characteristics are those of the maiden huntress, the cold and pale virgin of the moon who transforms would-be lovers into animals and slays them. But, as those will recognize who remember St. Paul's encounter with Diana of the Ephesians, the many-breasted fertility goddess of Asia Minor, Diana did not always choose to be maidenly. The virgin huntress was also the protector of animals (or was sometimes even the animal itself, an archetypal identification vividly recalled by D. H. Lawrence in *The Fox*) and consequently the guarantor of their fertility. It was Diana's proclivities for procreation that made her the goddess of the moon, whose crescent phase symbolizes increase, and whose horns in that stage symbolize (among other things) the strange lunar pull upon animals; the moon was also associated with the monthly period of human females, and hence Diana was a guardian of the fertility of women as well as that of animals. As Lucina, she was the patroness of childbirth.

At once a goddess of sky and earth, Diana's chthonic characteristics brought her into close association with the underworld, where she was identified with the three-faced Hecate, dread pale goddess of hell, fertility, and death, patroness of evil magic and transformations, and the mother of lamias. Hecate was worshiped at the crossroads, and her three faces signify power over earth and sky as well as in hell. This dark Diana of fertility appears frequently as a leader of witches in the early Middle Ages and even in sixteenth-century Italy; there her followers went out in procession Thursday nights to a meeting where they feasted and danced in her honor in order to insure the fertility of their fields. They also put out food and drink for wandering night spirits and could depart their bodies to journey in their souls. The same characteristics are associated with the cults of certain Teutonic and Celtic deities, and it was probably the pedants, learned in classical literature, who introduced the name and figure Diana into these essentially Northern rites.

These Northern cults of vegetation and venery left the clearest mark on later witchcraft. The Valkyries shifted their shape, rode out at night, and met at the *trolla-thing*, where revels anticipatory of the sabbat occurred. The god Odin could transform himself too, as could the goddess Freya, who hunted nightly astride a boar. "Down to the latest period we perceive in the whole witch-business a *clear connexion with the sacrifices and spirit-world of the ancient Germans*," Grimm observed, and his point was anticipated by early Christian Roman law, which in the sixth century equated the Teutonic fertility deities with demons.[3]

The Teutonic tradition most influential in witchcraft was the wild rout, or *wilde Jagd*, in which a procession of beings, led by a spirit, roamed through the countryside reveling, killing, devastating, or eating whatever they found in their path. Both the

48

name and the nature of the leader of the hunt varied according to locality—sometimes it was a vegetation, and sometimes a huntress, deity. Almost always it was a female spirit, rather than a male, and it was most commonly named Perchta or Hulda. The usual translation of this deity's name by Latin writers was *Diana*, but *Herodias* was a curious common variation. Explanations of the name cannot stop at indicating that Herod's bloodthirsty sister was a natural villainess for Christian writers to introduce, for they might as readily have used others. The choice was more likely dictated by the fact that the leader of the *wilde Jagd* so often had a name beginning with *Ber* or *Her,* like Berhta.*

The *Her-* name is even more clearly associated with the male leaders of the wild chase, whose identity is even stranger than that of the female deities.† These beings, originally fertility spirits, were known in the Middle Ages as "wild men" or "men of the

* The variations are important because so many appear in the early records of witchcraft. In southern Germany the name was usually Perchta, Berhta, or Berta; since this deity was called "the bright one," was a huntress, and so a natural counterpart of Diana, it seems probable that chroniclers and theologians often translated her name by that of the Roman goddess. In central Germany the goddess was more closely associated with agriculture than the hunt, and her name was Holt, Holle, or Hulda. About 1100, the name Pharaildis came in—almost certainly a muddling of Frau Hilde with a St. Pharaildis, who had nothing to do with fertility cults. Other names were Faste, Selga, Selda, and Venus (the last another result of classical pedantry). In France the names Abundia and Satia appear, attesting to their fertility-cult origins; and in Italy Befana, Befania, or Epiphania (see also "Bezezia," DuCange, I, 647), the name probably deriving from the ancient New Year's rites that took place at the same time as the new Christian feast of Epiphany. The Icelandic sagas, which in many respects preserve ancient Teutonic traditions, speak of shapeshifting and of riding out at night on beasts, on roofs, or even (in *Burnt Njal*) on brooms. See Walter Jaide, *Wesen und Herkunft des mittelalterlichen Hexenwahns im Lichte der Sagaforschung* (Leipzig, 1936).

† Such as Herne the Hunter, Herlechin (whence Herlequin, Harlequin, Hellequin, Hillikin), Herla, Berchtold, Berhtolt, Berndietrich, and others; though Hackel and Odin or Wuotan also appear. Their wild men were called *sauvages, selvaggi, selvatici,* and *homines selvatici.*

forest," and their existence was taken seriously enough to make them prominent figures in many legends, stories, and artistic representations.[4] The wild man, both brutal and erotic, was a perfect projection of the repressed libidinous impulses of medieval men. His counterpart the wild woman, who was a murderess, child-eater, bloodsucker, and occasionally a sex nymph, was a prototype of the witch.

These entities—gods, spirits, or demons—had gradually to be transformed into the witch, who was a human being. Even their followers in the wild chase were at first envisioned as spirits. Often as ghosts they rode in the procession of the dead, which became a motif of medieval literature. Sometime during the early Middle Ages the new idea arose that those who followed the wild cavalcade were not spirits but human beings, particularly women. The history of the growth of the witch belief is, in this instance as in many others, the story of the gradual humanization of the demonic.

Of pagan survivals, nothing was more appealing to the popular imagination than the ancient festivals, and nothing persisted longer. These were largely seasonal festivals, responding to the failing of light in winter and its renewal in the spring, the growth and harvesting of crops, and the fluctuation in the supply of animals for the hunt.[5] The later fixing of the witch rites on Christian feast days, such as November 1, February 1, May 1, and August 1, was less an effort to parody Christianity than a consequence of the fact that those Christian feasts fell upon the same days as the old pagan festivals. There is no reason why the feast of All Souls, let alone that of St. Walpurga or the Circumcision, should have attracted the mockery of the witches more than Easter or any of the numerous feast days in the Christian calendar. From November 1 to February 1, the pagans made special ritual efforts to restore the vigor of the sun. Long before October 31 became Hallowe'en, the Eve of All Saints' Day, it was Winter Eve, when the *nod-fyr* ("needfire") was kindled to provide hope of the rebirth of the light after the winter darkness to come. Guy Fawkes' Day is a secular replacement of this old fire festival. Between Christmas and Epiphany the medieval Feast of Fools was often held, where a ritual return to chaos was enacted in the form of licentious reveling; this was essentially a winter solstice rite signifying the beginning of a new year and a new life. The Roman Saturnalia of December 17–24 was such a cosmic renewal rite; the birth of Mithra occurred on December 25, and that of Osiris on January 6, later the Christian Epiphany. On the first of January northern Europeans in the early Middle Ages practiced paleolithic rites designed to preserve and augment the supply of beasts for the hunt during the coming year, rites that called for the wearing of animal skins, horns, or masks. Another ancient fire festival that occurred on February 1 was transformed into the Christian Candlemas. April 30, which happened to be the eve of St. Walpurga, an inoffensive eighth-century Anglo-Saxon missionary to Germany, was more significantly the eve of May Day, which the Romans had celebrated (from April 28 to May 3) as the fertility festival of the Floralia, while in the north it was greeted by the renewal rites associated with the maypole and the "green man." June 23, which happened to be the eve of St. John the Baptist, was Midsummer Eve, the climax of the fire and fertility rites celebrating the triumph of the sun and renewed vegetation.

These festivals were significant because they were high days to other gods than Christ or Jehovah. From this Runeberg concluded that "the witches' sabbath may thus be explained as an esoteric form of those pagan fertility rites which survived in Western Europe centuries after the official introduction of Christianity."[6] But the historian must limit this unequivocal plea for the fertility-cult origins of witchcraft. In the first place it is doubtful whether the dates of the witches' sabbat were ever standardized, so that it is impossible to prove a calendar continuity through the Middle Ages into the sixteenth and seventeenth centuries. The "fact" that some later witch practices occurred on seasonal festival days may have been, like Diana's appearance in Northern rites, a figment of the pedantic imagination. On the other hand, some pagan festivals, such as the Feast of Fools, the hunting masquerades of the first of January, and weekly revels on Thursday (*dies Iovis*), did persist into the Middle Ages and bring with them certain elements that would be connected with the witch cult: dancing, eroticism, banquets, animal disguises, and the leading of the festival by a ritual king. The fertility festivals were only one element in the foundations of witchcraft, but a very significant one.

In addition to the chthonic deities and the fertility cults, many undefined and constantly shifting folk traditions lay at the root of witchcraft. As Wayland Hand has said, other beings did what witches were later supposed to do, and strange spirits that walked the night were transformed by the more mundane imagination of the later Middle Ages into human hags.

Among the most important folk elements in the witch idea were familiars, shapeshifting, and flight. The small demons that became the witches' familiars of the later Middle Ages were originally dwarves, trolls, fairies, elves, kobolds, or the fertility spirits called Green Men, any of whom could be either frightening or funny. The dwarves were spirits of darkness and the underworld and were often equated with ghosts or other malignant spirits. The elves were originally spirits of light and goodness. Tolkien's *Lord of the Rings* recently restored the high elves to their rightful place, but throughout the Middle Ages they were usually confused with lesser and more mischievous spirits such as the Scottish brownies. Robin Hood may have originally been a Green Man, and his hood not an article of clothing but a bull's head or half. Kobolds brought good luck to houses and even helped with household chores so long as they were given food and drink. If refused, they might turn nasty. In these qualities they resembled the *bonae mulieres,* who demanded food and drink in return for their patronage of a household. Such spirits were equated by the Church with minor demons, and though they could be made fun of and tricked on occasion, their powers were taken seriously. They were given amusing or diminutive names that were retained when they became witches' familiars, names like Heinnekin, Rumpelstiltskin, Haussibut, or Robin Goodfellow.[7]

These demons could take the form of animals or of little men or render themselves invisible. In the later Middle Ages they became witches themselves or witches' familiars. Often little distinction was drawn between the two, witness the many stories in which a sinister animal is hurt or killed in the night and on the following morning a witch is found with wounds in the corresponding parts of her body. This variation of shape was perfectly acceptable to a world view in which apart from this material world there was a real, spiritual world where a man and an animal—or God and a piece of bread—could have the same essence.

A favorite activity of these malignant entities was to ride out at night bent on revelry, mischief, or blasphemy. They rode out as spirits, for example, as Valkyries or lamias; as beasts like werewolves, vampires, or strigae; and on beasts or objects like fences, sticks, or brooms. Several rationalistic explanations of the witch flight have been offered. Hansen surmised that the witches claimed to have flown long distances to the sabbat in order not to incriminate their friends who lived nearby. Robbins suggests that the concept of flight was a necessary consequence of the dishonesty of the trial records: if a defense witness swore to have seen the accused witch at Valenciennes on the same night she was supposed to have taken part in a sabbat at Arras, the Inquisition assumed, not that there was any doubt that she had been at Arras, but that she had been at both places, having flown from one to the other. Some historians of medicine argue that the witch induced sensations of flight by rubbing herself with a salve containing aconite and nightshade. The aconite depresses the cardiovascular system and produces sensory semiparalysis, while the nightshade induces delirium, excitement, and sometimes unconsciousness.[8] These theories may have a limited validity in explaining why the idea of flight persisted. But its origins are in the ancient traditions of the people of the Near East, the Greeks, and the Teutons. Continuing through medieval folk tradition, the idea was reinforced by the Christian idea that the demons, cast down from heaven, would abide in the air until the day of judgment (Ephesians, 2:2).

Some of the ancient ingredients of witchcraft had been considered magical rather than religious by the pagans themselves. Jewish magic, derived from Babylonian and Persian sources, was occasionally devoted to maleficium but much more often to divination; it was universally condemned by the religious leaders of the Jews. Almost every Old Testament passage dealing with magic or "witchcraft" is really concerned with divination. The "witch" of Endor was really a seer, and in the passage of Exodus 22:18, used to horrible purpose by the Inquisitors and translated in the King James as "Thou shalt not suffer a witch to live," the Hebrew for "witch" is *kasaph,* connoting a diviner rather than anything like a later witch.[9] The magicians of the New Testament, Simon, for example, were also diviners.[10]

Greco-Roman magic and that of the Celts and Teutons were more varied. In addition to divination they included shapeshifting,* and weather-witching; they were used to prevent sickness or

* The identification of men or gods with animals is one of the most common elements of religion and myth. Totemism, in which the members of a social group identify themselves with a particular animal, is a familiar phenomenon. The gods of Egypt, of Greece and Rome, and of the Celts and Teutons were often theriomorphic. The idea is that something may have all the appearances of an animal yet really be a person or god. Though menbeasts appear throughout mythic literature, Harry Levin in the *Gates of Horn* (New York, 1963) demonstrates the distinction between great, wild,

cause it and to attract or turn away love. It was this kind of magic that supplied medieval witchcraft with the tradition of the incantation, the belief that one could force a spirit to appear by naming him. Horace's witches called upon Night and Diana. Virgil described Dido's anguish over the loss of Aeneas:

> Ter centum tonat ore deos, Erebumque Chaosque
> Tergeminamque Hecaten, tria virginis ora Dianae.[11]

Roman law tended to ignore magic unless it caused harm to person or property. In that event it was prosecuted and punished like any other harmful crime, an attitude that carried through the early Middle Ages.

In the period A.D. 300–700, the classical Teuto-Celtic, and early Christian elements of witchcraft were assembled and then synthesized, creating an initial stream of witch beliefs which was fed and augmented in the succeeding century by Reformist heresy and other elements of maturing medieval society. Our concern here is not with all the magic and pagan cults and practices that survived, but only with those that were formative in the development of witchcraft.

In the fourth and fifth centuries paganism was still very much alive in the Mediterranean world and dominant in the North. The Christian synods and writers of the period condemned pagan religion and pagan magic in the same breath, including sacrifices to the old gods, the veneration of sacred trees, rocks, and springs, and the use of charms and ligatures.[12] The repression of magic and

---

and holy animals like lions or wolves and tame, weak animals like cats or toads. Witches dominated weak, familiar spirits in the form of domesticated animals; but when they changed their own shapes, they chose the forms of wolves or other fierce animals in order to increase their own powers. This is the origin of the werewolf motif. The werewolf is literally a man-wolf (AS. wer: man). The concept is more Teutonic than Mediterranean, and the Latin gerulphus derives from werwolf. Modern French loup-garou is a pleonasm literally meaning "wolf-man-wolf."

witchcraft was not then in the foreground of the Church's vision, since its attention was focused to such a great extent upon its own organization, the solution of essential doctrinal questions, and the reduction of heretical dissent. From the end of the fifth century, as Christianity turned its attention to the conversion of Northern paganism, it took more pains with problems of magic and superstition. The Church's hand in dealing with magic was strengthened by two processes that began in the sixth century and culminated in the fifteenth: the gradual dissolution of the distinction between the attitudes of religious and civil law toward magic, and the assimilation of maleficium, originally purely a secular crime, to idolatry, apostasy, and paganism.

By the fifth century only a few of the elements of classical witchcraft had materialized. The attitude of the early Middle Ages toward these beliefs was ambivalent. The classical idea of the night-flying, bloodsucking striga persisted, but an Irish synod of the mid-fifth century condemned such belief as unchristian.[13] The ancient idea of shapeshifting was also still powerful—the wily Devil had transformed himself into an angel of light in order to deceive St. Simeon Stylites.[14] This was a transformation of a supernatural being, but the belief that men too change their shapes was encouraged not only by the classical legends of Circe and the *Golden Ass* of Apuleius, but also by the rites of the Kalends of January at which men dressed as beasts in order to guarantee an abundance of animals for the hunt.[15]

St. Augustine, whose influence on subsequent Christian thought was unequaled, affirmed the reality of magic, which he argued could be performed only with the help of demons, who, having been cast out of heaven, wander through the air, pale with envy of God and seeking the ruin of men. Augustine argued that demons, as spiritual beings, could take many forms, but that men on the other hand were unable to change their forms either by themselves or through demoniacal intervention. God does not grant power to demons to make things what they are not. He does allow them the power to delude men's minds, however, and shape-shifting may be considered this kind of illusion.[16]

The persistence of pagan revels, with sexual licence and indulgence in food and drink, are described in the fifth century by St. Maximus of Tours and Severian, and both indicate that at least some of the revels were dedicated to the worship of the goddess Diana.[17] The idea of pact, which would later become central in the classical definition of witchcraft, had no place in popular thought or practice at this time. It originated in the minds of theologians, and a passage in St. Augustine's *On Christian Doctrine* laid the basis for the belief in pact that would be established in canon law by Gratian's *Decretum* in the twelfth century.[18]

The sixth century witnessed a continuation of the confrontation of paganism by Christianity, particularly in the new kingdoms of the Franks, Burgundians, Visigoths, and Lombards, where the ruling Teutons had acquired their Christianity even more recently and absorbed it less thoroughly than the Latin peoples they had conquered. The sources for the history of witchcraft in this period include Gregory of Tours' *History of the Franks* and some saints' lives, but the most significant materials are the letters of popes and bishops concerned with residual paganism, the decisions of ecclesiastical synods, and the laws of the new Teutonic kingdoms.

These laws reveal the amalgamation of traditional Teutonic custom and codified Roman law under the influence of Christian morality, the product being, with respect to the history of witchcraft, the amalgamation of the sin of paganism with secular crime. Pagan rites and customs were confronted by the most formidable forces then in existence: the Christian kings of the Germans, backed by the authority of the Theodosian Code, the Fathers, the New Testament, and the Old Testament. By the sixth century little organized paganism remained in the Christianized Teutonic countries (the situation in the unconverted Anglo-Saxon kingdoms, German Saxony, and Bavaria was different). Yet ancient rites and customs only thinly veiled with Christianity persisted, and in some places the open worship of idols still continued.[19]

To educated Christians the most repulsive aspects of the worship of the old gods were the sacrifice of animals and the ritual eating of the consecrated food (idolothytes); they brought to mind the great persecutions by the pagan Roman emperors during which Christians were forced to eat the sacrificial meats or face death. The sixth-century laws against sacrifice illustrate the Church's success in transforming pagan deities into demons, for though some of the condemnations refer to gods or spirits, others call these spirits demons. This transformation is particularly clear in the *Lex romana Visigothorum,* or *Breviarium,* of King Alaric II of the Visigoths, who in 506 adapted the Theodosian Code to the needs of his people. The Theodosian injunction against sacrifice was carefully changed by the Visigothic king to specify sacrifice to demons. Since pagan sacrifice was common in both sixth-century Spain and Gaul,[20] the change is more than academic.

Pagan festivals persisted as well as isolated offerings to the spirits. The festivals most important for the development of the witch idea were the fertility rites associated with Diana or Hecate, the festivals on Thursday, which later became a favorite day for witch meetings, and the hunting celebrations on the first of January. That some regarded the hunting festival not merely as a ritual masquerade but as a real transformation of man into beast is clear from Caesarius' condemnation: "What rational person could believe that he would find men of sound mind who would wish to change themselves into a stag or other wild beast?"[21] The synods and Caesarius also bear witness to the custom of transvestitism at the same New Year's festival, where men dressed as women, a masquerade probably originating in a fertility rite of some kind. The orgiastic banquets accompanied by song, dance, and sexual revels were both continuations of the ancient bacchanals and precursors of the witches' sabbat.[22]

Other components of the witch idea appear in the sixth century. According to Jordanes' *History of the Goths,* the original Huns were the offspring of women and incubi, a story that was often repeated in the Middle Ages. Incubi, lustful angels who sleep with women, appear in many works of the Church Fathers, and their ultimate origins are in the numerous stories of the Greeks, Romans, and postexilic Jews about intercourse between men and spirits. In the Teutonic laws of the sixth and seventh centuries, the striga and lamia, those wandering and bloodsucking night spirits of the ancients, are always completely distinguished from the maleficus or herbarius, indicating that sorcerers were infrequently associated with evil spirits. This is true in Spain, for example, where lamias, far from being considered human, are identified with nymphs and even with Minerva. Yet the distinction is already beginning to break down. "Lamia" is sometimes used as a translation of the Teutonic *hagazussa,* which is a person, and in some of the laws striae and strigae are classified with other evil women such as prostitutes.

A hint of the idea of flight also appears in the Salic law, where "striga" is glossed as *fara* ("one who goes").[23] Through their association with the bloodsucking strigae witches became identified with cannibals. This identification became one of the most important elements of witchcraft. The Salic law, in what is surely a legal understatement, established a fine of two hundred shillings as the punishment for a witch's eating a person. It also imposed a fine upon men who brought the cauldron to the place where the witches cooked.[24]

The final contribution of the sixth century to the lore of witchcraft was the Greek story of the pact of Theophilus with the Devil. Although the story, until it was translated into Latin two centuries later, had no effect upon the development of the Western European idea of witchcraft, it does illustrate that the notion of pact was established in the popular, as well as in the theological, tradition of the early Middle Ages.

In the seventh century the number of documents on witchcraft as well as other phenomena declined, particularly in northern Europe. The Anglo-Saxon kingdoms were still in the process of construction, and the Merovingian state and church were in a state of severe dislocation and decline that would not be reversed before the early eighth century. Even in the south, Italy was still suffering the consequences of the disastrous wars between the Byzantines and the Lombards, and the papacy had not recovered its independence from the emperor at Constantinople. Consequently the greatest activity on the part of secular and ecclesiastical lawmakers was in Spain, where the Visigothic kingdom was at its height until its collapse and conquest by the Arabs in 711–713.

Exceptions to the dearth of sources are the Penitential Books. Originating in Ireland and rapidly spreading in influence, they soon appeared in various forms all over Europe. These books, which describe sins in detail and establish the penance appropriate for each, usually deal with sorcerers as *malefici* in much the same way that the civil laws did: their sin is usually considered to be the physical harm they have done to others or to the property of others rather than their dealings with demons. In general, the survival of pagan practices is still the primary concern of all the sources, and the transformation of the old gods and spirits into demons is still in process.

Consequently the most common condemnations of practices relating to witchcraft have to do with idolatry, often identified with the worship of demons, as in the Penitential of Columban, c. 600, which forbids feasting at pagan shrines, taking communion at the table of demons, and worshiping demons. The reverence of Diana and comparable chthonic deities does seem to have had special significance, but there is no evidence of any Murrayite Dianist cult. The important twelfth synod of Toledo (January 9–25, 681), which voted approval of the laws of the Visigothic King Erwic against Jews and magicians, treats Jews and magicians in conjunction. Although it does not identify the two, the condemnation of the Jewish "sabbat" in this context may have provided a precedent for the tendency of the later Middle Ages to bestow names like sabbat and synagogue upon the witch assemblies.[25]

Again, closely associated with the survival of idolatry are the notions of invocation and sacrifice, now almost exclusively considered to be offered to demons rather than to gods. Most of the condemnations of such practices in penitentials, laws, and synodal decrees are borrowed from earlier laws, particularly the *Breviarium,* and do not indicate the existence of a widespread cult of demons at this time.[26] Fertility festivals and orgies are condemned, usually those of shepherds and hunters on the first of January. A seventh-century sermon attributed to St. Eli also refers to the feast of St. John the Baptist (later a traditional witches' festival), forbidding dancing, leaping, and diabolical chants on that day.[27]

In the seventh century the stria and lamia motifs were subjected to some skepticism, because the characteristics formerly attributed to spirits now seemed less credible when assigned to humans. The *Pactus Alamannorum* (613–623) imposes a fine on those accusing innocent people of being witches, and the passage is especially interesting because it contains a prohibition against the seizing and harming of witches by individuals, the first indication of mob violence against witches. An edict of Rothari (643) forbids the burning of women for the crime of cannibalism on the grounds that the crime is impossible. But Isidore of Seville was, as usual, more credulous. For him, lamias and *larvae* lived, as child stealers and incubi. Isidore makes the first mention in witch literature of a "society," but the context makes it almost certain that he is referring, not to a witch cult, but to commerce between demons and men.[28]

At the end of the seventh century the synthesis of the Teuto-Celtic and the Mediterranean in the new medieval civilization was incomplete, and the concept of witchcraft still consisted of traditions that had not yet been fully united. Nonetheless, the figure of the witch was beginning to assume at least shadowy outlines. Already the witch was more a human being than a spirit, and more often a woman than a man. She invoked demons, occasionally—but still rarely—had sexual intercourse with them, made sacrifices to them, and through their powers could take the form of a beast that ate human flesh and drank human blood. She celebrated nocturnal feasts and orgies in honor of chthonic demons or deities, most commonly Diana or Hecate. The transition in the legal status of witchcraft from secular crime, simple sorcery involving hurt to others, to supernatural trespass had begun. Unattached to the idea of the witch, but already existing in the background to be used later by theologians and Inquisitors, was the notion of pact, the concept through which witchcraft would be assimilated to heresy and made an ecclesiastical crime. From the beginning of the eighth century, the new, popular heretical movements that appeared had an increasingly important influence upon the idea of the witch.

4

Popular Witchcraft and Heresy, 700-1140

Y the end of Charlemagne's reign in 814 overt paganism had almost ceased to exist except along the eastern marches of the Frankish empire, where the Slavs remained unconverted. Subterranean paganism was also withering. The chief difficulty that Catholicism would now face, other than the renewal of severe assaults from without by Magyars, Vikings, and Muslims, was no longer paganism but heresy.

Unlike ancient heresy, medieval heresy was for the most part concerned with moral and human, rather than metaphysical, problems. From the eighth to the twelfth century the dominant variety of heresy was Reformism. Although seldom organized into widely spread or highly organized sects, Reformism often attracted wide support among both laymen and clergy. It demanded a return to the purity of the primitive Church and in an age when ecclesiastical organization and order were growing, reaffirmed the prophetic tradition, rooted in the Gospels, that the values of this world are in constant need of being overthrown so that the kingdom of God may replace the kingdom of this world.

Reformist heresy encouraged the development of witchcraft by its antisacerdotalism and overt willingness to oppose the Church and society, and by the presence on its fringes of a large number of eccentric heresiarchs whose doctrines drew upon popular sorcery, paganism, and superstition. From the early eleventh century both heresy and withcraft increased markedly. One reason for this increase was the Church's new and vigorous policy of reform and renovation, which touched the monasteries, the bishops, and eventually the papacy itself. The reform popes sought to rebuild all of Christian society in terms of a new order of justice. To achieve this new order, they constructed a more efficient ecclesiastical organization. This new efficiency led to an increase of papal and episcopal activity in the detection and the repression of dissent. As the Church became purer it became more intolerant of what it considered impurity. Accompanying and encouraging the growth of ecclesiastical renovation was a great movement of popular enthusiasm for reform. But this enthusiasm proved a mixed blessing: it sometimes degenerated into a fanaticism that produced crusades, pogroms, and lynchings. In this atmosphere of suspicion and tension both popular mind and Church authority began to equate sorcery and heresy with witchcraft.

Moreover, reform enthusiasms produced not only excesses of orthodoxy but also Reformist heresy itself. To many laymen and priests the Church seemed to proceed with lamentable slowness toward the new Jerusalem. Disillusioned, they took up antisacerdotalism and preached that the kingdom of God was in the hearts of the saved and that there was no need for priests or Church. For the first time in the history of Western Christendom dissent became widespread and pervasive. And as heretical dissent flourished, witchcraft, that most extreme of all heresies, began to take a more defined form.

The organization of the new Western European civilization in the eighth century through the labors of missionaries like St. Boniface, rulers like Charles Martel and Charlemagne, and popes like Gregory II made the Church's efforts to eliminate paganism ever more effective. As paganism's influence on witchcraft was reduced, that of heresy increased.

There were two especially significant changes in the phenomenon of witchcraft during the eighth century. The first was the spread of the idea of pact. The story of Theophilus, the sixth-century priest who had made a pact to renounce Christ and honor the Devil in order to obtain the episcopate (he repented and was saved by the intercession of the Blessed Virgin), was translated into Latin by Paul the Deacon and began by the end of the century to enjoy widening popularity and many imitations.

The second significant change was that the idea of maleficium was increasingly attached to the older, pagan elements of witchcraft, so that eventually, in the later Middle Ages, *malefica* became one of the two most common names in Latin for "witch," the other being *striga*. In the previous century the idea had been established that the striga was a human malefactor rather than a spirit. Now her maleficence began to be more clearly dissociated from other crimes. Whereas the word "maleficium" had formerly meant any kind of crime, it now came to denote witchcraft in particular.[1] When during the succeeding centuries the idea developed that the witch, besides worshiping demons and going on wild rides with them, also practiced evil magic with their help, large portions of low magic could be assimilated to witchcraft and sorcerers could be prosecuted for what now was no longer considered a simple crime against society but a heresy and a crime against God.

The missionaries, kings, and popes who labored to build a Christian society were concerned not only with the conversion of still pagan peoples like the German Saxons but even more with the regularization of barely Christianized paganism in the more settled areas. Priests as well as laymen continued to practice rites little removed from heathenism. Gregory II was shocked at the reports of barely disguised idolatry that Boniface sent him from

Germany; he found them hard to believe and ordered the missionary to check their authenticity.[2]

Kings and councils joined the struggle against the continuing idolatrous worship of pagan deities in the guise of saints or martyrs. Idolatry was outlawed by the Bigotian penitential. Magic, idolatry, and all dealing with demons were outlawed in the great collection of canons made by Dionysus Exiguus and in its revision by Pope Hadrian I (772–795). Charlemagne incorporated this into law at the council of Aachen in 802, and the law subsequently had considerable influence among the Franks.[3] The attention that secular law would henceforth pay to witchcraft had already become apparent in the *admonitio generalis* issued by Charlemagne to his *missi dominici* in 789. The relevant passages condemn *malefici* (evil sorcerers) as distinct from magicians. In addition they warn against using any angels' names other than those having scriptural justification. The confusion of pagan deities and spirits with Christian angels is another indication of the persistence of paganism and gives a glimpse of a nascent popular demonology.

Invocation of, and sacrifice to, demons (as the pagan spirits were increasingly known) were considered especially evil. This was the view of St. Boniface and the great popes who supported him. Boniface found a priest sacrificing to Jupiter, and Gregory III forbade sacrifice to demons at fountains and trees. These and other early eighth-century writers distinguished between sacrifice to demons in small matters and sacrifice in great matters.[4] Pope Zachary comments to Boniface that superstitious priests "gather about them a like-minded following and carry on their false ministry, not in a Catholic Church, but in the open country in the huts of farm laborers, where their ignorance and stupid folly can be hidden from the bishops."[5] The *indiculus superstitionum* attached to the canons of the synod of Leptinnes in 744 prohibits sacrifice to saints instead of to God, an indication that the saints were being confused in the popular mind with the old deities. A baptismal formula attached to the same council indicates that the old gods still lived:

Do you renounce the demon?
I renounce the demon.
And all relations with the demon?
I renounce all relations with the demon.
And all the works of the demon?
I renounce all the works of the demon, and all his words, and Thor, and Odin, and Saxnot, and all evil beings that are like them.[6]

The only comment on human sacrifice in this century comes from the capitulary that Charlemagne issued for the control of the newly conquered and forcefully converted province of Saxony. The ninth chapter says: "If anyone sacrifices a human being to the Devil and offers sacrifice to demons as is the custom of the pagans, let him be put to death." Chapter 6 assigns a like punishment to those eating the flesh of witches. This one reference is no justification for assuming that the sinister practices existed elsewhere in Europe.[7]

The chief pagan festival that continued to exercise the attention of the authorities was the beast masquerade at New Year's, with its accompanying belief in shapeshifting. Condemnations of this festival became so standardized that it is difficult to know how much they represented current problems and how much they were merely repetitions of past condemnations. The most common accusation is that people went about on New Year's dressed as stags or calves, though an interesting variant is "in a cart." Other kinds of disguises are suggested by a Spanish penitential that condemns wearing skins or disguising oneself as a woman. The *indiculus superstitionum* mentions a rite whose particulars include dressing as women or in torn clothes or skins to represent animals.[8]

In addition to the New Year's feasts, festivals honoring Wuotan or Mercury on Wednesday, and Thor or Jupiter on Thursday, are also condemned, as were the Spurcalia, an old German feast sacrificing pigs in honor of the vernal equinox, and the Brumalia, a Bacchic feast on December 25. A verb used occasionally for the celebration of these old festivals was *sabbatizare,* which may have influenced the later development of the term "witches' sabbat." The only evidence for shapeshifting apart from these penitential and synodal condemnations is Boniface's condemnation of the Saxon belief in werewolves and strigae as superstitious.[9]

A transformation in the dissenters' festive orgies began in the eighth century. To the old pagan revels with their feasting and dancing the element of sexual license was now introduced from the heresies. It derived in part from the heretics' need for secrecy and from the excesses of pneumatic antinomianism; it was also partly a projection by the orthodox of their own libidinous desires upon the dissenters. Orgiastic feasts occurred in the festivals of the Spurcalia and Brumalia, but the specific accusations of sexual license that were to become standard in the later witch trials were leveled for the first time in the 740s against the heretic Aldebert.

Aldebert was a preacher in northern France who, affecting apostolic humility in speech and dress, wandered through the towns and countryside calling for a reform of the Church under his leadership. He claimed that Jesus had sent him a letter from heaven patenting his claim to be the equal of the apostles; he was widely venerated as a saint and distributed his nail parings and hair clippings to the faithful. Many of his followers were women, and in a letter to St. Boniface, Pope Zachary accused him of immorality with his female followers.[10]

Other aspects of his ministry also connect Aldebert with the tradition of witchcraft. He set up crosses at fields and streams, indicating a willingness to capitalize upon popular devotion to the old pagan spirits. Most curiously, he composed a prayer to the angels Uriel, Raguel, Tubuel, Michael, Adinus, Tubuas, Sabaoc, and Simiel. The authorities, assuming that these were the names of demons whom Aldebert worshiped, made the first specific accusation of the worship of demons derived from the angels of the Judeo-Christian tradition rather than from pagan deities. The two demonic traditions were woven together into the fabric of witchcraft, but they never became one. Generally, the Judeo-Christian fallen angels became the greater demons, the pagan gods lesser demons, and a third group—fairies and kobolds—the least important demons. It is unlikely that Aldebert considered the objects of his prayer demons, but his choice of angelic names is odd. Michael is of course quite orthodox, and Uriel, Raguel, and Tubuel have some standing in the Jewish apocalyptic tradition if not in the Old Testament, but Adinus, Sabaoc (Sabaoth), and Simiel are names strongly associated with gnosticism. The choice does indicate that ancient though muddled ideas survived upon which new unorthodox traditions could be based. The inclusion of Simiel in the prayer is specially curious, for Simiel was identified with Samael, the rebellious throne-angel, one of whose other names was Satan.

The tradition of the cannibal strigae continues into the eighth century. The new version of the Salic law, published 751–764, repeats the old injunction against those who falsely accuse others of partaking in a witches' cuisine or of bearing the cauldron to the places where they cook.[11] The capitulary of 775–790 for Saxony enjoins against both belief in cannibalism and cannibalism itself: "If anyone, deceived by the Devil, believes after the manner of the pagans that any man or woman is a witch and eats men, and if on this account he burns (the alleged witch) or gives her flesh to be eaten or eats it, he shall be punished by capital sentence." Such a strange gastronomic predilection can be attributed to the belief that one assimilated the powers of one he consumed. One Cathwulf wrote to Charlemagne about 775 urging him to prose-

cute strigae and other evildoers. Earlier in the century St. Boniface had warned against belief in strigae. In these ambiguities we
sense that the transition of the striga from a blood-sucking spirit to
a human malefactor had not yet been fully completed but was
well under way.[12]

The synod of Rome in 743 provides a glimpse into the derivation
of the bonae mulieres of later witch legend from the earlier local
spirits: if anyone prepares tables, makes incantations, or leads
dances, he shall be anathema. The custom of leaving food for the
band of people en route to their secret meetings and orgies came,
as did the practice of votive offerings to saints, from the ancient
custom of setting out offerings for spirits. Here again the transition
from pagan spirit to demon to wicked human malefactor is under
way.[13]

Until about 850 the Frankish empire continued vigorous, but in
the hundred and fifty years that followed, western Europe suffered
fragmentation from within and assault from without. The effort
to survive left little energy to expend upon intellectual, doctrinal,
or even disciplinary considerations. Literary activity of all kinds
declined markedly, and source material for almost all aspects of
European civilization, including material relating to heresy and to
witchcraft, is rare. This paucity of material does not prove that
there was little heresy or witchcraft, but there was less concern
about them than either before or after.

Mentions of the striga, the incubus, and shapeshifting increased
through the ninth century; then, at the beginning of the tenth,
the concepts of nocturnal flight, sexual debauchery, and pact became widely significant for the first time. High magic enjoyed
great strength. In the reign of Louis the Pious (814–840), every
great lord had his own astrologer, and by the end of the tenth century the influence of Muslim science and magic through Spain had
become so great that one pope, Sylvester II (Gerbert of Auril-

lac), who had studied in Spain, was widely supposed to be a great magician.[14]

Reformism continued to dominate such heresy as was recorded in this period. Though the imprint of heresy upon witchcraft was still light, the two were being brought closer by the growth of the idea of pact. This important development was in large part the result of the increase of ecclesiastical responsibility for the repression of sin as a consequence of the breakdown of the secular power and of the close Church-state relationships that characterized the Carolingian empire. The Church was less inclined than the secular authorities to accept the idea that maleficium was simply a secular crime and tended more and more to equate it with treating with the Devil, sin, and heresy.

Since in the later Middle Ages the repression of witchcraft had so much influence upon the development of the phenomenon itself, it is useful to discuss the means of repressing witchcraft up until 1000. The earlier Middle Ages were relatively lenient toward heresy and sorcery; maleficium was still considered primarily a secular crime, and the punishment for even those beliefs and actions defined as heresy was not severe. The first official execution for heresy did not occur until 1022, and usually heretics were corrected and reprimanded many times before receiving even the lightest punishments. The Church was lenient because it was not as yet secure or well organized enough to undertake a full campaign against the rebellious.

Yet the groundwork for later severity was being laid. Maleficium was gradually being wed to heresy and diabolism, and the machinery of repression was gradually being tuned up.

Although maleficium was rarely considered more than a secular crime, the synod of Tours in 813 had already revived the warnings of Jerome and Augustine that all magic was a snare of that "Ancient Enemy," the Devil. The synod of Paris on June 6, 829, for the first time cited the stern passages of Leviticus 20:6 and Exodus 22:18 enjoining that a sorcerer should not be permitted to live, and it went on to say that the king had the right to punish those who, by transferring their loyalty to Satan, were doing harm. The punishment for this crime was to be severe but was not specified. In the same year the bishops reported to King Louis the Pious at Worms that evil people of both sexes had sought the Devil's help in working evil upon others. At the beginning of the tenth century the former abbot of Prüm, Regino, wrote that the wicked were practicing magic by diabolical incantations. These examples, which could easily be multiplied, demonstrate how the practice of magic was slowly beginning to be identified with diabolism.[15]

This identification made it easier, when ecclesiastical power and organization were improved, to prosecute witches severely. Before 1000, however, severity was not yet the established pattern. The Roman Empire's laws against the practice of harmful magic had been strong, but they ignored most of the other aspects of what came to be the witchcraft of the later Middle Ages. Yet the precedent for harshness had been set, and the Theodosian and Justinian codes could prescribe death as the punishment for malefici without departing from Roman tradition. Christianity, in its extraordinary amalgamation of Greco-Roman with Jewish thought, blended the strict Roman view of magic with the harsh Jewish view found in Exodus, enabling St. Jerome, for example, to refer to both traditions in putting forward his view that malefici ought to be executed. When Alaric II summarized and adopted the code of Justinian in his *Breviarium* for the Visigoths, he assumed that the Visigothic state, like the Roman, had jurisdiction over maleficium and could punish it severely, and this tradition was followed by the Frankish state under the Carolingians. Yet neither the Visigoths nor the Carolingians moved very far away from the Romans in their view that maleficium should be punished much the same way as any harmful act against others. The idea that it constituted a pact with Satan and therefore required special treatment was as yet embryonic.

Consequently the attitude of the various legal authorities was in this period quite variable. The very first indication of the use of torture in dealing with sorcerers appears in a capitulary of Charlemagne's in 805, with the caution that it not be carried so far as to cause death. Typically, the penitentials of the seventh to ninth centuries seldom imposed penances of more than three years for maleficium, incantations, and idolatry. The harshest penalties for maleficium in this period seem to be those issued by Bishop Remedius of Chur (800–820), who ordered that the first offense should be punished by shaving the offender's head and parading him around the countryside on a donkey; the second by cutting out his nose and tongue; and the third by placing him at "the mercy" of the judge, who might even declare him worthy of death. The capitulary of Quierzy, January 4, 873, indicates that the secular law could be severe. It ordered that each count should take care to hunt down suspected malefici and bring them to trial and, if convicted, to death.[16]

The laws of Alfred the Great in England, in accordance with his policy of remaking the codes in conformity with Christian law, threaten witches with the death penalty enjoined by Exodus. Alfred's successors on the throne were also harsh. Edward the Elder ordered exile as a punishment for *wiccan* (magicians) and *wigleras* (soothsayers), and Ethelstan ordered execution for *wiccecraeftum* if it resulted in death. The only indication of mob action against suspected witches appears in the *Pactus Alamannorum* of 613–623, which forbade the lynching of witches.[17]

The practice of overt paganism seems to have almost completely vanished throughout most of Europe, except when new inroads of pagan invaders occurred, as the Danish invasion of England and the Slavic rebellions in the eastern marches of Germany during the tenth and early eleventh centuries.[18] Even the assaults of the Magyars and the Vikings (except in Danish England) did not seem to produce any wide revival. Most condemnations of paganism appearing in penitentials, synodal decrees, and letters are merely repetitions of earlier materials. A residue of paganism in Christian Europe remained. Pope Formosus wrote in 893 to Archbishop Hermann of Cologne that the Church of Christ was being persecuted by the "wiles of pagans and false Christians," and Bishop Hervé of Reims had some correspondence about relapsed pagans, but he was almost certainly referring to the difficulty of keeping the converted Northmen in Normandy from their old ways.[19]

The most impressive evidence is from Benevento, where later in the Middle Ages some of the greatest witch assemblies supposedly took place (though there is no evidence of a link). In the ninth century, St. Barbato had to struggle against the residual paganism of the Lombards, who at Benevento revered a snake and a sacred tree, around which they rode, keeping their backs turned toward it. This difficult feat of equitation is most interesting in its relevance to later accounts of witches dancing back to back or in a circle facing outward. In any event, Barbato, in the manner of all good missionary saints, ordered the sacred tree felled, thus putting an end to the practice.[20]

The equation of pagan practices and magic with demon worship had now become the rule, witness a letter of the scholar Raban Maur specifically stating that magic is the equivalent of idolatry and demonism.[21]

Condemnations of pagan festivals, like injunctions against paganism in general, were usually repetitions of the old rules against dressing as a stag or a calf on the first of January. Some penitentials mention other practices, including dances in which the revelers are disguised as women, and the drinking of a potion on the first of May.[22] For almost the first time, some instances of shapeshifting occur independent of the kalends of January festivals. In the Eddas there are charms of uncertain date against witches "playing their game in the air" and changing their shapes.[23] About 900, the monk of St. Gall relates a story of a pact in which the Devil changes himself into the form of a mule.

One of the few instances in which the terms "lamia" and "striga" appear at this time is an Irish synod of about 800 that declares any Christian who believes in such things anathema. Hincmar of Reims, on the other hand, believed in strigae and identified them with incubi.[24]

The dancing, reveling, and night flying that characterize medieval witchcraft at its height began to take firmer form around the end of the ninth century, though their shadowy origins lay in the old pagan festivals and in the kind of irreverent behavior condemned by the synod of Rome in 826, which noted with horror that "many people, mostly women, come to Church on Sundays and holy days not to attend the Mass but to dance, sing broad songs, and do other such pagan things. Therefore priests ought to admonish the people to come to church only to pray." The tenth-century Anglo-Saxon *Leechbook* prescribes a salve against spirits that walk about at night and against "women with whom the Devil has sexual intercourse." Writing about 936, Rather, bishop of Liège and then of Verona, condemns those who believe that Herodias rules one-third of the world. This is the earliest mention of Herodias as a leader of evil spirits of persons, and though Rather explicitly identifies her with the murderess of John the Baptist, he may unwittingly have been accepting a popular transformation of the unfamiliar name of Hecate into a Biblical name known to every Christian.[25]

The most important tenth-century text relating to Diana's troop of women is the famous *Canon Episcopi*. This document appears first in about 906 in a book written by Regino of Prüm.[26] Regino, who became abbot of Prüm in 892, was expelled from his

monastery in 899 and went to work for Archbishop Radbod of
Trier, for whom he wrote this book—a compilation of regulations
drawn from earlier synods, penitentials, and capitularies—to guide
bishops in the visitation of their dioceses. Among the materials
given is the *Canon Episcopi,* so called from its opening word,
episcopi. Throughout the Middle Ages the document was believed to be a canon of the council of Ancyra in 314,* but in fact,
it did not derive from Ancyra and is not a canon at all. It is almost
certainly a Carolingian capitulary of the turn of the century.[27]
The following are the essential passages of the canon in its fullest
form:

Bishops and their officials must labor with all their strength to uproot
thoroughly from their parishes the pernicious art of sorcery and malefice
invented by the devil, and if they find a man or woman follower of this
wickedness to eject them foully disgraced from their parishes. . . . It
is also not to be omitted that some wicked women perverted by the devil,
seduced by illusions and phantasms of demons, believe and profess themselves, in the hours of night to ride upon certain beasts with Diana, the
goddess of the pagans, and an innumerable multitude of women, and
in the silence of the dead of night to traverse great spaces of earth, and
to obey her commands as of their mistress, and to be summoned to her
service on certain nights. But I wish it were they alone who perished
in their faithlessness and did not draw many with them into the destruction of infidelity. For an innumerable multitude, deceived by this
false opinion, believe this to be true and, so believing, wander from
the right faith and are involved in the error of the pagans when they
think that there is anything of divinity or power except the one God.
Wherefore the priests throughout their churches should preach with all

* This notion, disproved in the seventeenth century, derived from a misreading of the manuscript. Regino had cited the previous canon as deriving
from Ancyra, and later scribes assumed that that derivation applied to the
Canon Episcopi as well. The mistake was of great importance, for the
antiquity and venerability attributed to the canon by assigning it to the
prestigious council of Ancyra helps to explain why it was given such weight
throughout the Middle Ages.

insistence to the people that they may know this to be in every way false and that such phantasms are imposed upon the minds of infidels and not by the divine but by the malignant spirit. Thus Satan himself, who transfigures himself into an angel of light, when he has captured the mind of a miserable woman and has subjugated her to himself by infidelity and incredulity, immediately transforms himself into the species and similitudes of different personages and, deluding the mind which he holds captive and exhibiting things, joyous or mournful, and persons, known or unknown, leads it through devious ways, and while the spirit alone endures this, the faithless mind thinks these things happen not in the spirit but in the body. Who is there that is not led out of himself in dreams and nocturnal visions, and sees much when sleeping which he had never seen waking? . . . Whoever therefore believes that anything can be made, or that any creature can be changed to better or to worse or be transformed into another species or similitude, except by the creator himself who made everything and through whom all things were made, is beyond doubt an infidel.[28]

The *Canon Episcopi* is important both for what it tells us about ninth- and tenth-century beliefs and for its influence upon the later Middle Ages. It was reproduced in the tenth-century penitential, the *Corrector,* again in the *Decretum* of Burchard of Worms, and then received as authoritative by canon lawyers and theologians throughout the Middle Ages.[29] Believing that the canon dated back to the venerable synod of Ancyra, later medieval theologians had to justify their own acceptance of witchcraft by arguing that the canon applied to old pagan beliefs but not to contemporary witch practices. The liberal historians have argued that the need for this sophisticated reversal demonstrates first that there was no belief in witches in the early Middle Ages and second that witchcraft did not exist until the Inquisitors invented it; if it had, those who reported it would have provided their own details rather than merely repeating the canon.*

* Against this one may argue that ancient canons were not usually tampered with when reproduced, but if thought important they might be

On the contrary, the unusual amount of attention that this particular "canon" received indicates a real concern with witchcraft. Those emphasizing the skepticism of the early Middle Ages miss the most important point: the very pains that Regino and Burchard took to condemn belief in most of these phenomena indicate that many people really did believe. In the same way that synodal and penitential condemnations of pagan idolatry indicate that pagan idolatry existed, the mere fact of the canon indicates that there were some—indeed the canon itself says that there were an innumerable multitude—who believed what it condemns. Far from demonstrating skepticism, the canon and its attendant injunctions are important evidence that witch beliefs were already highly developed in the early Middle Ages.

In analyzing the beliefs condemned by the canon, it is necessary to distinguish carefully among the versions: first, Regino's short version; second, his longer one; third, the new versions introduced by Burchard of Worms.

In Regino's short version,* bishops were asked to detect certain crimes in their dioceses, crimes bringing the punishment of expulsion from the diocese. First, they were to inquire whether there were any women who through incantations provoked love, hatred, or harm to persons or property. Then they must determine whether there was any woman claiming to ride out at night on a beast accompanied by a throng of demons transformed into women, and asserting that she had become a part of their band. The first part of the instruction deals with simple sorcery but indicates that already the Church was beginning to attach sorcery to more serious charges of witchcraft and heresy. The second part is more im-

---

glossed or discussed. The *Canon Episcopi* was frequently glossed and discussed by the canon lawyers and theologians of the eleventh through fourteenth centuries.

* It is probable, though not certain, that the short version is an abridgement and amalgamation of *two* previous capitulary instructions, of which the longer version of the canon was one.

portant: it contains both shapeshifting and a full reference to the wild ride of folk tradition.

Here, at the turn of the tenth century, we see the amalgamation of several traditions. The oldest is the ancient idea of the strigae, night vampires who flew out to drink human blood. The second is the Northern tradition of the Valkyries, who give rise to the Eddic notion of witches "playing their game in the air." The third is the old fear of ghosts walking about at night. The fourth, and most powerful in folk tradition, is that of the wild ride or *wilde Jagd*. The four traditions are fused in the notion of the woman who flies out at night to the worship of strange gods. If the blood drinking and cannibalism of the strigae is not yet present in the canon, it soon will be, as will the idea of flight on animals or fences or sticks. In the canon itself, the ride takes place on animals and evidently is terrestrial rather than aerial.

This short version of the canon attaches double importance to women. Not only do the demons transform themselves into female form, but it is clearly women who believe that they can ride out and join them.

The longer version of the canon is similar in essentials to the shorter. Bishops are to drive out of their dioceses those who believe in and practice the wild ride, and they are to preach seriously to all their people so that these beliefs may not spread. The sentence of exile was justified on the grounds that those who practice these things have implicitly cut themselves off from God and become heretics and servants of the Devil. Though this sentence is light compared with the harshness of later penalties, it is already menacing, for it contains, first, one of the earliest direct linkings of witchcraft to heresy and, second, a strong statement of the diabolical nature of heresy. As in the short version, women are considered to be specially involved: an "innumerable multitude" have been deceived by these women into believing that what they say is true. Thus the condemnation is on two levels: it is forbidden to believe that you yourself ride out, and it is forbidden to believe that others do so. The second position is more skeptical than the first, but even there it is not forbidden to believe that other people *believe* that they themselves ride out, for that is the position of the author of the canon himself. This version is no more a monument to skepticism than the other.

The longer version is more explicit as to the activities of the night riders. Not only do demons assume the shapes of women and ride out on beasts at night, but they ride as followers of "Diana, the goddess of the pagans." We have found the worship of Diana or related fertility goddesses one of the pagan practices most resistant to Christianization in the seventh and eighth centuries. Now she appears again, as the leader of the *wilde Jagd,* as a goddess, and, most significantly, as the leader of demons, for her followers are partly human and partly demons in the shape of women. The canon thus firmly links both the fertility rites and the related wild chase to demonism. As chief of a demon horde, Diana can now be equated with Satan, and her followers with worshipers of Satan. In this regard, the further additions of the canon are of great importance. Not only do the women ride out with her, but they obey her as their lady (*domina*) as opposed to their true Lord, Jesus Christ (*dominus*). And they meet secretly on specified nights to worship her. We are still far from the sabbat of the fifteenth century, but now for the first time many of the major elements of later witchcraft have been brought together, amalgamated, and labeled as heresy and diabolism.

Next to Regino's *Canon Episcopi,* the most important witchcraft document of the tenth century is the *Corrector* of Burchard, a deacon who became archbishop of Worms and about 1008–1012 wrote his *Decretorum Libri XX* (*Decretum*), one of the greatest collections of canon law before Gratian. Book 19 is a most useful guide to the beliefs of the tenth century, for it presents Burchard's systematization of penitential materials, some very old and some dating from the tenth century.[30]

The most important witchcraft texts given by the *Corrector* are versions of Regino's canon that differ from the earlier mainly in a shift of emphasis from the events themselves to belief in the events. It is forbidden to *believe* that there are women who claim that they go out: where Regino condemned separately the general belief and the women's own belief, the *Corrector* repudiates the *general belief in the women's belief* and thus is essentially more skeptical. The other important innovation is that the *Corrector*'s shorter version of the canon calls the leader of the band of riding women "the witch Holda." Holda is a north German fertility goddess and leader of the wild chase. Here is further, conclusive evidence that a Germanic fertility deity whom the canonists identified with Diana was worshiped and that the idea of strigae had been linked to that of the wild ride.[31]

More of the lineaments of later witchcraft are found in the pages of the *Corrector*.[32] All are condemnations of beliefs in practices rather than of the practices themselves. One must not, for example, believe that there are beings who transform men into wolves or other shapes, for only God can change one thing into another. Neither must one believe that there are wild women of the wood who appear in bodily form to men, seduce them, and then disappear into thin air. Here the wild women are identified with succubi and consequently with demons. One must not believe that there are women who believe that they sneak out at night while their husbands are asleep, pass through closed doors, and travel long distances to kill Christians and eat them or else cut out their hearts and replace them with straw. This is the first mention of cannibalism since the injunctions of Charlemagne against the newly converted Saxons at the end of the eighth century and the first mention anywhere of the passage through closed doors while husbands sleep, an activity that was to be a cliché of later witchcraft. Finally, one is forbidden to believe that some women claim that they go out at night through closed doors and fly up into the clouds to do battle.

This passage is of particular importance. It is the first mention of flight through the air, rather than simply on beasts, in the history of witchcraft proper.[33] Also, it will be echoed centuries later in the strange beliefs of the benandanti, though whether there is any connection between the two is doubtful. The benandanti rode out at night to do battle with the *strigoni* or witches, but the *Corrector* does not state with whom the tenth-century ladies made war.

The *Corrector* offers a glimpse into another of the earliest known manifestations of the idea of the *bonae mulieres,* the spirits, fairies, little men, or, sometimes, mortal women, who went out at night to bestow favors or fertility or goods and in return to claim gifts of food or clothing from the households they visited. This motif became entrenched in folklore and still persists in children's stories. "Hast thou made," the *Corrector* inquires, "little boys' size bows and boys' shoes, and cast them into thy storeroom or thy barn so that satyrs or goblins might sport with them in order that they might bring to thee the goods of others so that thou shouldst become richer?"[34]

As in the previous century, Reformist heresies continued to provide a background of dissent, and the strange beliefs of some heretics blended heresy with witchcraft. The capitulary of Aachen in 802 forbade the veneration of false angels, and in 827 the capitulary of Ansegis inveighed against credence placed in letters allegedly sent down from heaven via angel-mail, and against the invocation of false angels.[35]

Agobard, archbishop of Lyon (814–849), noted for his credulity regarding the evilness of the Jews, unfortunately reserved his skepticism for the less dangerous idea that men could change the weather by magic. Among the beliefs upon which he pours scorn is that there is a land called Magonia from which cloud ships float, bearing rain and hail. The weather sorcerers cause storms by calling upon the cloud sailors to discharge their cargo, and reward them by gifts of grain and other food. This was accepted to the point that the populace set upon three men and a woman whom they claimed were cloud sailors who had fallen off their airships. They put the wretched victims in chains and were scarcely restrained from stoning them to death.[36]

In 847 or 848 a self-proclaimed prophetess named Theuda appeared near Mainz, preaching that she knew the secrets of the divine heart, including the exact date of the end of the world, and attracting many of the common people of both sexes to follow her. In the reign of Archbishop Frotaire of Bordeaux (860–876), one Burgand persuaded a large number of followers to break into churches and steal chalices, patens, and holy oil. Large numbers of people could evidently be won over to beliefs and practices that were condemned by the Church as superstitious.[37]

It was always the concept of pact that gave the most explicit impetus to the wedding of witchcraft to heresy, and two stories of this time indicate that that concept was developing and gaining popularity. In 860, Archbishop Hincmar of Reims wrote a treatise on the power of magic to destroy marital affection. In his essay, the term "striga" is used to denote a worker of maleficium, evidence of the assimilation of sorcery to witchcraft while both were being associated with heresy.[38]

In the same treatise, Hincmar tells of a young man who went to a sorcerer in order to procure the favors of a certain young girl. The magician asked him whether in return he would renounce Christ in writing. The young man agreed, and the magician wrote the Devil a letter expressing his hopes that he would be contented with this new recruit. The magician handed the boy the letter and told him to go out at night and thrust the letter into the air.

The boy did so that same night, lifting up the letter and calling upon the Devil for help. The Prince of the Power of the Shadows appeared and led him into the presence of Satan, who asked in a parody of the baptismal formula of renunciation:

"Do you believe in me?"

"Yes, I believe," replied the boy.

"Do you renounce Christ?"

"I do renounce him."

"Well, you Christians always come to me when you need help and then try to repent afterwards, seeing that Christ is merciful. I want you to sign up in writing so that there will be no possibility of your escaping me."

The boy did as he was told, and the Devil, fulfilling his part of the bargain, caused the girl to love the young man. She asked her father to give her to him in marriage, but the father, who purposed that his daughter should become a nun, refused. The girl, realizing that she was in the power of demons but unable to stop herself, replied that she would surely die. At last the boy, burdened with guilt, confessed his pact with Satan, and with the help of St. Basil, the girl was released from his evil power. This story, adapted from St. Jerome, introduces for the first time in the Middle Ages the formal renunciation of Christ, a standard element of later witchcraft.

The second story was told in 883 by Notker Balbulus.[39] An Italian bishop was greatly covetous of material things. The Devil, eager to cast down a clergyman, found a poor man in the road and told him that he would make him rich if he would deliver himself over. The man agreed.

"Fine," said the Devil. "I shall now change myself into a splendid mule. Mount me and go to the bishop. When he stares covetously at the mule, refuse to sell it. Draw off as if in anger and pretend to leave. He will send messengers after you offering you many rich things in exchange for the animal. At length you will pretend to be moved by their pleas and agree, grudgingly, to let their master have the mule. Then run away and find a place to hide."

All this was done, and the bishop, inflated with pride over his new possession, rode out in pomp through the city, into the fields, and down to the stream for refreshment. As he approached the water, the mule went into a frenzy, kicked, snorted, and ignoring all efforts to stop him, rushed into the river and sank, drowning the greedy prelate with him.

Both these stories are exempla, told didactically, the latter with the "vanity of vanities" moral typical of medieval writing. Both are indications of the increasing popularity of the idea of pact.

As Europe recovered from the period of internal decay and external assault that stretched from about 850 to 1000, attention could be turned away from mere survival back to questions of religious expression and ecclesiastical organization. Powerful movements of reform began to spread through the Church, generating both dissent and the ecclesiastical efficiency that repressed it.

Reformist heresy continued to dominate the West until the coming of Catharist dualism in the 1140s.[40] The connection between nascent witchcraft and Reformism was limited: after all, diabolism had little in common with apostolic purity. They were both, however, willing to defy Church and society, especially when that defiance was expressed in contempt for the priesthood and sacraments. Also the dark and twisted ideas of the eccentric fringes of Reformist heresy had parallels with emerging witchcraft.

The concept of witchcraft was now forming more rapidly. Historians have often mistakenly dismissed accounts of witchlike practices in this period as meaningless clichés. But charges of witchcraft were seldom couched in polemical terms such as the terms "Communist" or "Fascist" that are used in today's name-calling. When, for example, during the struggles between emperor and pope, Gregory VII was accused of sorcery and necromancy, the intention was to link him with the same tradition of high magic and divination from which his forebear Sylvester II had allegedly sprung, not with diabolism, the sabbat, or other characteristics of classical witchcraft. Furthermore, many of these characteristics— such as the use of ashes of murdered children to make communion bread—were now appearing for the first time, and, though they may later have become clichés, they should not be dismissed as such in the eleventh century when they had no immediate precedent. Nor, finally, was sorcery identified as witchcraft. In this period many · accusations of simple sorcery or maleficium bear little trace of witch ideas. Such characteristics were not being assigned wholesale by careless or malicious chroniclers.

At the beginning of the eleventh century two eccentric heretics appeared. Leutard, who lived near Châlons-sur-Marne, was, like Aldebert earlier, an ignorant peasant with peculiar ideas who attracted a considerable following among his peers. In most respects a Reformist, Leutard also expressed even less conventional ideas, such as the notion that a spirit had lodged in his belly in the shape of a swarm of bees.* Thereafter he smashed the crucifix and sent away his wife. The other heretic, Vilgard of Ravenna, advocated the veneration of the ancient poets and was accused of having been visited by demons in the forms of these writers. Then in 1018–1028 a group of heretics appeared in Aquitaine who were accused of spurning the cross and holding sex orgies.[41]

A trial for heresy was conducted by King Robert II at Orléans in 1022.[42] The Orléans heretics were essentially Reformists, but the sources assign them a number of witchlike characteristics:

---

* Bees are among the animals most frequently associated with witches in Wayland Hand's collection of witch characteristics. It is impossible to say where Leutard got this particular notion, though there was a remotely similar event in sixth-century Gaul, where a woodcutter became a heretic after having been surrounded by a swarm of flies (Gregory of Tours, *History of the Franks*, X, 25).

some of these were new in the history of witchcraft; others were more clearly delineated than before. The first charge was that they held sex orgies at night in a secret place, undergound or in an abandoned building. The devotees appeared bearing torches. They chanted the names of demons until one evil spirit did appear, after which the lights were put out. The extinction of the lights re-appears repeatedly in the later trials, as does the allegation that the sectaries seized for their lewd purposes whoever lay closest to hand, whether mother, sister, or nun. The children conceived at the orgies were burned eight days after birth, a grotesque echo of the eight days that in Christian practice elapsed between baptism and the doffing of the neophyte garments of purity. Their ashes were made into a substance that was used in a blasphemous parody of Christian communion.

The heretics said that when they were filled with the Holy Spirit, they had angelic visions and could be transported immediately from place to place. This is the earliest reference to demonic (or, as the heretics would have it, angelic) transportation attached to heresy and consequently an important stage in the development of the witchcraft phenomenon. The sectaries were alleged to have adored the Devil, who appeared to claim his homage in the form of a beast, an angel of light, or a black man. Adhémar's reference to the angel of light is not unusual, as the *Canon Episcopi* had warned of the Devil's angelic power to shift shapes and to take on this pleasing form. But this is the first appearance of the Devil as a black man, a form that in later trials became almost *de rigueur*.

The heretics were also supposed to have recited a litany of demons (unnamed in the sources). It is possible that these demons may have had a gnostic origin, but the practice described recalls much more directly Aldebert's litany and synodal condemnations of the veneration of false angels. Formal renunciation of Christ and expectoration upon his image, presumably the corpus of the crucifix, is a theme of later witch trials, usually in conjunction with the accusation that the sacraments have been desecrated for the gratification of the Dark One. The minor, frivolous charge made by Adhémar that the Devil daily gave the heretics money found few later echoes and may be dismissed except as an illustration of what materially immediate solidity Satan might exhibit.

Of the witch charges at Orléans the four most significant are the sexual orgies, the sacrifice of human beings, specifically children, the burning of the children, and cannibalism. Of these only one is new—the burning, testified to by two of the most reliable sources. The heretics themselves ended in the flames, and the charge may have been invented by the orthodox to justify this mode of execution, unusual for the time. Or the reverse may be true: the punishment may have been designed to suit the actual crime. The other charges are all ancient in origin. Since they figure so prominently in all the later literature of witchcraft, their origins must be discussed in detail, and then the question must be raised whether the accusations at Orléans were merely the product of ancient literary tradition or whether they had some basis in fact.

Human sacrifice, cannibalism, and sexual orgies had played an important part in religious ritual the world over.[43] Among the Greeks, legends of cannibalism were common: Thyestes' children were served to him at dinner by Atreus; Pelops was eaten in part by Demeter; and, at the very beginning of the world, Kronos attempted to devour all his own divine children. It is not clear whether any orgies were practiced at Eleusis, though the early Christian writers thought so, but it is certain that such orgies occurred in the cults of Demeter, Attis, and Dionysos.[44] Human sacrifice was offered to Dionysos in Boeotia, Lesbos, and Chios, and sexual orgies were common in the rites of Sabazios, a divinity identified with Dionysos. Those who refused to worship Dionysos were driven mad, sometimes tearing people to pieces and eating them, as in Euripides' *Bacchae*.* In the *Nichomachean Ethics* (VII, v. 2), Aristotle lists among other unnatural criminals "those who provide children for one another to eat." Human sacrifice, including the burning of children, is mentioned frequently in the Old Testament, though the symbolic meaning of fire there is often purificatory.[45]

That cannibalism, sacrifice, and orgies were not uncommon in religious practice, indicates that they can happen anywhere and at any time. But they were never widespread, and it is more to the point that those who found them unsavory seized upon them as weapons against their religious opponents. When we encounter accounts of orgies we cannot be sure whether we are dealing with reality or merely with polemics.

The Romans, whether sincerely or not, lodged accusations of ritual sacrifice first against the Jews and then against the Christians. The charge against the Jews seems to have originated at the court of Antiochus Epiphanes of Syria (125-96 B.C.). Josephus in his tract *Against Apion* refutes as a typical pagan slander Apion's belief that each year the Jews ritually sacrificed and ate a Greek.[46]

The Romans pressed even more lurid charges against the Christians. In the first century the Christians were already commonly accused of ritually sacrificing and eating humans, usually children. The old idea was reinforced by the pagans' fuzzy understanding of Christian communion: some apparently believed that the Christians dipped the host in the blood of a sacrificed child. The idea that the Christians commonly committed incest may have drawn some of its strength from their use of the terms "brothers" and "sisters" and from the kiss of peace.[47]

---

* It is also relevant to the development of the witch cult that Dionysos and his subsidiary god Silenus usually rode on asses, which were sometimes deemed sacred to the witches. In Apuleius, Lucius' transformation into an ass is accompanied by references to the unusual sexual powers of that animal.

In any event, the Christian writers began early in the second century seriously to refute these accusations, often turning them back against the Romans. Aristides (c. 145) argued that it was the pagans, not the Christians, who held ritual sex orgies. Justin Martyr (c. 150) defended Christianity against accusations of incest, promiscuity, and the consumption of human flesh. Like Origen later, he accused the Jews of being chiefly responsible for the spread of these calumnies. Justin was also the first apologist to suggest that Christian heretics were instrumental in bringing down these libels on the orthodox: he claimed that the Marcionites did in fact practice cannibalism and incest. And, in the *Dialogue with Trypho,* he uses a phrase, "aposbennyntes tous lychnous (with the lights extinguished)" in his description of the sex orgies. This phrase reappears in the writings of Michael Psellos, the Byzantine statesman and theologian, in the eleventh century, and, in one form or another of Latin translation, in Western descriptions of orgies beginning at Orléans and persisting through the history of witchcraft in the Middle Ages.

Tatian (c. 170) and Athenagoras (176) defended Christianity against the calumnies of incest and cannibalism, and in the same century Irenaeus claimed that certain heretical sects had brought down these slanders upon Christians by actually practicing such perversions themselves. Theophilus (c. 190) wrote against the idea that Christians ate people and lived promiscuously, and Tertullian (c. 197) wrote at great length in his *Apologia* on this subject. Tertullian argued that the pagans practiced vicious acts and then blamed the Christians for incest and the sacrifice of babies.

In their refutation of pagan allegations, Tertullian and his contemporary Minucius Felix introduced a detail that would reappear in numerous witch trials in the Middle Ages. The pagans had claimed that at the Christian orgy the lights would be extinguished in an extraordinary fashion: dogs were tied to the lamps and then tempted away with bits of meat so that, rushing to get the food, the animals would upset the lamps, upon which the orgy would proceed. Later witch literature reproduced this scenario with either a cat or a dog, which was assumed to be a manifestation of an evil spirit.

Tertullian cites three secret crimes alleged against the Christians, as apart from the public and indisputably actual crimes of refusing adoration to the pagan gods and *lèse-majesté* against the emperor: ritual infanticide, incest, and a variety of cannibalism in which the host was dipped in children's blood before being consumed. As in the witch literature later, it was the neophyte who was required to practice these abominations. Minucius Felix, however, reports pagan assumptions that the cannibalism included the actual consumption of human flesh, and that the loathsome rites were practiced indiscriminately by all Christians.

The Christian writers were not merely paranoid. Both Tertullian and Minucius were influenced in their ideas of what Romans believed of Christians by an actual event: the persecution of Christians at Vienne and Lyon, reported in a letter from those churches in 177. There, the slaves of Christian masters were tortured in order to procure the admission that the Christians practiced ritual "Oedipal incest" and "Thyestean feasts" where they consumed grown men or children. This letter seems to contain the first reference to children in particular as food: in the later witch trials they were almost the exclusive fare.

In the third century, Christian writers were more aggressive in carrying the war to the enemy camp. Clement of Alexandria (c. 200) turned the charges of perversion back upon the pagans, detailing the bloodthirsty nature of their rituals and myths. It was Clement who also established the accusations against heretics as standard procedure. The Carpocratians, he argued, were licentious, practicing incestuous orgies after having their lamps overturned. The Montanists used the blood of children in their unholy sacrifices. The gnostics cooked and ate embryos for their Passover meal, and they partook of a horrible Eucharist confected of semen and menses.

Clement's pupil Origen ridiculed the pagan Celsus for his absurd beliefs that Christians sacrificed and ate children, invoked demons, and held revels at night when, after the lights were extinguished, each would seize in his carnal lust whoever lay nearest. Eusebius of Caesarea (c. 350) defended the Christians against the accusations of incest and eating their own children, adding that the blame should be fixed on the Carpocratians. Medieval witches were occasionally supposed to consume their own children, but the witch tradition, like that of the early Christians, usually assumed that they stole the offspring of others. Epiphanius of Salamis (374–377) argued that the gnostics ate semen and that the Montanists sacrificed children. St. Jerome said that the Montanists baked a bread made out of children's blood and flour. St. John Chrysostom (398–404) insisted that the Jews sacrificed their own children, and in the fifth century Salvian the Presbyter blamed the gnostics for bringing down upon the Christians the charges of incest and child murder.

In his *On the Customs of the Manichaeans,* St. Augustine comments upon the sexual irregularities of that sect, to which he had once himself belonged. Here Augustine reports that a woman went to a Manichaean meeting, trusting in the good faith and holiness of the people. But when the elect entered, one of them put out the lamp and in the dark would have forced her to sin had she not driven him away by screaming. Indeed, all the elect wished to have the light extinguished for such pleasurable purposes. Other sexual irregularities of the Manichaeans are described by Augustine in the same treatise and in his *On the Heresies.*[48]

Clearly, in the writings of the Fathers there was ample material to feed the imaginations of the medieval polemicists against heresy and witchcraft. Charges of perversion were brought in the East against the Euchites, Messalians, Paulicians, and Bogomils over a time span stretching from the seventh into the eleventh century.[49] About 1050, the Byzantine theologian Michael Psellos argued that the Euchites or Messalians murdered children and prepared food from their ashes, that the heretics revered Satanael, a son of God who fell from heaven, and that the heretics practiced sexual orgies. Psellos' description is similar to those of Paul of Saint-Père de Chartres and Adhémar de Chabannes, both of whom dealt with the events at Orléans.[50] In both Psellos and the Western accounts, the children conceived during the orgies are cremated and made into food; in both, the orgies follow the extinction of the lights.*

Thus the charges made against the Orléans heretics were to a large extent literary clichés, yet they cannot simply be dismissed. Although such charges later became standard in witch trials, this is their first appearance in the medieval West. Why should the Fathers' ancient descriptions of heretical debaucheries have been revived now? Even more to the point, why should Paul of Saint-Père and Adhémar have chosen these particular details from among all the lurid accounts available? The imitation of the Fathers may not have been wholly literary. The Orléans heretics themselves, who were literate clergymen, may have read Augustine or the other Fathers and determined to emulate what they had condemned. Like the Euchites in the Balkans, these heretics may indeed have practiced some secret and not wholly proper rites, which the sources then fit into the preexisting literary tradition. The essential point is that the *idea* of the heretical orgy was now introduced into medieval Europe. Whether or not these particular heretics practiced these witchlike rites, their presence in the writings of contemporaries is proof that the *phenomenon* of witchcraft—human perception of, and presumably belief in, witchcraft —had developed to this level.[51]

Later heretics of the eleventh and early twelfth centuries showed

* Paul's phrase "omnibus extinctis luminaribus" is "tous te lychnous aposbennyntes" in Psellos, almost exactly the phrase employed by Justin Martyr.

some of these characteristics, but seldom in the variety and detail of the Orléans incident. At Monforte in 1028 Reformist heretics were accused by the unreliable Glaber of worshiping pagan idols; and in 1043–1048 heretics at Châlons were accused of holding secret conventicles and engaging in "filthy rites." A more serious case was that of Alberic of Brittany in 1076–1096, a priest who smeared the crucifix with excrement and poured animal blood over the altar, then caught it in vials and sold them as relics to the credulous. Alberic doubtless had little to do with witchcraft proper, but that such things could occur indicates the superstition, crudeness, and blasphemy that existed, from which witchcraft could draw strength. At Ivois near Trier in 1102–1124 basically Reformist heretics were accused of holding secret conventicles.[52]

The most important event of the first decades of the twelfth century was the career of Tanchelm in the Low Countries from 1110 to 1120. Tanchelm was an eccentric Reformist who allegedly distributed his bath water to the people as a holy relic and who prefigured the later antinomian heretics in his insistence that he was filled with the Holy Spirit. That Tanchelm presided at sexual orgies, deflowering virgins in the presence of their mothers, is doubtful, but the charge was made and believed. Again, perhaps the most remarkable aspect of his career is its testimony to widespread superstition, for Tanchelm was enormously popular and even for a while had some political influence.[53]

It was at Bucy-le-long, a village near Soissons, that around 1114 the fullest account of witch attributes since Orléans occurred, and the sources are clearly dependent in part upon the Orléans account. These heretics held their secret meetings in caves (a favorite rendezvous of the later Luciferans) where the sacraments were desecrated and where, after the ceremonies, the lights were turned out (*hisque extinctis*), and the devotees seized whomever was nearest. The men had intercourse with the women *a tergo* (a position which was later to be much favored by the Devil at the

Sabbat), and men lay with men and women with women.* Finally, as at Orléans, the heretics took a child, burned it alive, and made from its ashes a bread which they consumed ritually. Later, in 1116, the Henricians were accused of sexual immorality with women and little boys. In these cases, the mythology of orgies and cannibalism expressed at Orléans was retained and elaborated.[54]

At Sint-Truiden in 1133–1136 there was a strange episode involving a huge shiplike object. Peasants, resentful of the weavers who had immigrated into the neighboring towns, forced a group of them to tow the strange vehicle around the countryside for miles. Many who joined the crowd in tormenting the weavers made the boat the object of a possibly jesting but certainly blasphemous adoration, and when the strange ritual was over, they slipped off into the darkness for sexual revelry.

The best source for the heresy of Pons, whose doctrines in 1140–1147 were similar to those of the Henricians, says that he practiced magic and worshiped the Devil. Both he and Peter of Bruys ordered the destruction or rejection of crosses. Eudo of Brittany, condemned in 1148 as a madman and heretic who claimed to be God the Son, is alleged to have worked diabolical incantations and spells.[55]

There is no way of being certain how many of these accusations had a basis in reality, but they do show that in the period 1000–1150 heresy and witchcraft were increasingly identified with each other and both of them associated with diabolism.

Into this period too some of the older pagan traditions persisted, especially in recently converted areas of Europe. Olaf Tryggvason of Norway had to struggle against residual paganism; Archbishop Unwan of Bremen (1013–1029) complained of continued superstitions in his diocese, and as late as 1075 similar complaints were

* This, the first explicit allegation of homosexuality, also became a commonplace in later trials: variations on the phrases "vir cum viris" and "femina cum feminis" appear again and again.

being lodged there. Continued Slavic rebellions on the eastern marches of Germany usually entailed revanchism against Christianity, and in 1092 Duke Bratislav II of Bohemia was obliged to destroy groves and trees where people still worshiped and offered sacrifices to demons. The concept of magic as a form of idolatry was reaffirmed by the Spanish synods of Coyaca in 1050 and Santiago in 1056. And Radulf Glaber, for what his testimony is worth, declaimed in mid-eleventh century against the persistent worship of idols.[56]

The most important channels of old ideas in the eleventh and twelfth centuries were the *Canon Episcopi* and related texts. Book 10 of the *Decretum* of Burchard of Worms, which closely follows the work of Regino of Prüm and repeated Regino's version of the canon almost exactly, was extensively adopted by later writers such as Ivo and Gratian, and thus passed not only into canon law but also into the thought-treasury of the scholastic philosophers. Book 10 summarizes all the old attacks upon idolatry and paganism, including the revels at New Year's, warns against calling upon the Devil for assistance, and prohibits both sacrifices to demons at night and diabolical songs and dances at funerals. Regino's fuller version of the *Canon Episcopi* is repeated and the name of Herodias added in conjunction with that of Diana. Ivo, Gratian, and the other great canonists followed Burchard's version of the canon, with the occasional addition of Minerva to Diana and Herodias.[57]

Independent references to the wild chase at this time are not plentiful, but Orderic Vitalis reported that in January 1091 while walking at night, a priest of Bonneville was horrified to be accosted by a huge giant who summoned him to stop and look about. To his mounting terror, the clergyman saw approaching a vast procession of those suffering in purgatory, each person being tormented in a manner appropriate to his sins; an adulteress, for example, rode on a saddle spiked with nails. The story as Orderic offers it is a fairly typical exemplum, a tale told to inculcate morality, but it has several interesting elements. The giant may be a manifestation of the Wild Man. Then, the clerks and bishops in the procession wore black caps, and among those who passed by were Ethiopians who bore with them a trunk on which a man was crucified, another example of the black man associated with evil and hell. All these elements seem related to the wild chase, and the connection is firmly demonstrated by the fact that the leader of the procession was Herlechin. Orderic's procession resembles both the wild chase and the Dianic riding-out at night.[58]

The old tradition of the lecherous, bloodsucking strigae seemed to have faded in most of Catholic Europe, but it produced a lively debate in eleventh-century Hungary. The laws of King Stephen I (997–1038) distinguished strigae from malefici, asserting that the former ride out at night and fornicate. On their first offense, they are to receive a penance, but the second offense will merit branding and the third death. King Ladislas (1077–1095) grouped them with whores, indicating that his conception of them was primarily as night-going succubi. That both Stephen and Ladislas definitely had a supernatural view of strigae is proved by the unusual reversal of policy during the reign of King Coloman (1095–1114). King Coloman's attitude toward strigae was wholly skeptical. He argued that, though malefici should be appropriately chastised, strigae should not be punished for the simple reason that it is impossible that they should exist. This is one of the few instances of growing rather than decreasing skepticism about witchcraft in the Middle Ages.[59]

Vampires were rare in Europe at this time, although according to Walter Map, a wizard in Wales reportedly returned from the dead and dined habitually on his neighbors' blood. In England, earlier, King Ethelred II in 1008–1011 and King Cnut (1016–1035), following Edward the Elder, condemned wiccan and wigleras; the meanings of these terms, however, had probably remained unchanged: magicians and soothsayers.[60]

The lurid tales of witchcraft that had begun to appear in the ninth and tenth centuries now became a common element in sermons and chronicles. An eleventh-century story used later by Vincent of Beauvais tells how St. Peter Damian interceded with Pope Leo IX to condemn witches who had turned a young minstrel into a donkey and sold him.[61]

An old story of uncertain date, possibly originating in the ninth century, was fully developed by William of Malmesbury, who claimed unconvincingly that he heard it from someone who had witnessed the episode in Berkeley in 1065. According to William, there was a woman living at Berkeley who was a sorceress. She had a familiar in the shape of a jackdaw who warned her of approaching danger by chattering. One day he told her of the accidental death of her son and his whole family. Fearing that the wrath of God was being visited upon her in punishment for her sins, she summoned her remaining children, a monk and a nun, and confessed her sins. Warning them that there was no hope that her corrupted soul could be preserved from hell, she besought them for the love they bore her that they would help preserve her body. This would be possible, she said, if when she died they would sew up her corpse in the skin of a stag and then lay it on its back in a stone coffin. They were then to place atop the coffin a heavy stone bound with thick chains and to order that psalms be said for her unremittingly for fifty nights and masses for as many days. If the body lay undisturbed in the tomb for three days and nights, they might be reasonably assured of its safety and bury it in the ground.

The witch died, and the children followed her bidding. But her sins were too great. The very first night after the body had been laid out, a tall demon and his accomplices burst into the church, ripped the chains apart and pushed the huge stone away, commanding the body to rise. They hustled her out of the church, forced her to mount a black horse with spikes on its back, and rode away with her. This is a typical medieval morality story in which sins—in this case witchcraft—are graphically punished by demons. The most interesting elements are the tallness of the chief demon and the blackness of the horse, tallness and blackness being characteristics that later became typical of the Devil at the Sabbat; and the sewing of the corpse in the skin of a stag, recalling the alleged shapeshifting powers of the witches and harking back to the ancient prohibition against masquerading as a stag at New Year's. Though it is unlikely that anyone was still practicing ancient pagan rites, clearly their memory remained alive in folk tradition.[62]

The witch story became very common in the thirteenth century; in the twelfth it was still a bit unusual. William of Newburgh, however, tells one about the reign of King Henry I. A country fellow was walking alone at night past an ancient burial mound, from the depths of which he heard talking and singing. He found a door hidden in the side of the mound and entered. Inside was a cave, brightly lit with lamps, where men and women sat at a solemn banquet. One, who was standing at the entrance, bade the farmer enter, and when he had done so, offered him a cup. The peasant pretended to drink but instead surreptitiously poured out the liquid and hid the cup in his clothing. Making his way out with his prize and examining it, he found it to be of beautiful design and unusual material. He took it to the king, to whom he gave it in exchange for a great reward. The most interesting aspect of the tale is the secret meeting at night in the cave, so common in stories of witchcraft and heresy and here revealed as a vivid element in folklore.[63]

In many respects, the period 1000–1150 is of unusual importance in the history of witchcraft. Ancient paganism finally died out as an independent force and remained only in Christianized forms; popular heresy acquired considerable force; and witchcraft, increasingly separated from simple magic and sorcery, began to be more and more closely bound to heresy, a process that would culminate in the fifteenth century.

Through its connection with heresy, witchcraft in this period witnessed the addition of new elements and the further development and definition of older ones: the sex orgy, the feast, the secret meetings at night in caves, cannibalism, the murder of children, the express renunciation of God and adoration of demons, the desecration of the cross and the sacraments. All these had now become fixed elements in the composition of witchcraft.

Finally, the sweeping changes in medieval society beginning in the eleventh century provided a richer soil for witchcraft to grow in. The time of troubles was followed by an increasing prosperity that in turn produced population growth and movements, and encouraged the development of towns, industry, and commerce. The shifting population and employment produced an *interior* instability in medieval society, as opposed to the external threats that had plagued it earlier, and this internal instability caused widespread disequilibrium and discontent, resulting in pressures for political and religious change. The Crusades, the pogroms, the strife between papacy and empire, the development of new monastic orders, the rise of mysticism, the growth of heresy and of intolerance toward heresy, and, finally, the growth of witchcraft itself were all symptoms of this discontent. When a society is pressed from without, it unites, and strains are minimized; when it is secure and triumphant, as medieval Christendom came increasingly to be after 1000, forces of destruction from within are released. The crisis continued and deepened as the twelfth century proceeded, and social discontent and fears made it possible for two more important elements to be added to the cauldron of witchcraft: demonology and Catharist dualism.

5

Demonology, Catharism, and Witchcraft, 1140-1230

T H E essential element in Christian witchcraft is defiance of Church and society on behalf of the power of evil. Witchcraft and hatred of witches both grew in the twelfth and thirteenth centuries as the power of evil became more vivid in the minds of men. Satan had been considered a real figure even before Christian times. But now, through the influence of Catharist dualism, he was no longer merely a rebellious though powerful creature with a faulty will. He became an eternal, cosmic principle, little below God in power and glory, and beginning to approach the majesty he was to attain in *Paradise Lost*. Yet, paradoxically, as his heavenly might increased, so did his worldly immanence. The everyday fairies, elves, and kobolds of folklore had become demons, and through an extension of the magical principles that controlled them, even Satan might, though with danger, be constrained.

In yet another way Satan was drawing nearer. Ever more robustly he stalked a world subject to increasing change and dislocation: rapid population growth, immigration to the cities, changes in economic patterns, shifts in politics, and disturbing movements of reform and counterreform in the Church. Society longed for order and found its quest thwarted by forces it could not understand. Amid such insecurities, spiritual realities seemed all the more immediate. As people moved from villages to the towns, where for the first time in their lives they had to live among strangers, they came to dread impersonality and sought increasingly to personalize spiritual entities. Under these conditions, European society underwent a massive shift in taste, characterized in the graphic arts by the transition from Romanesque to Gothic, but equally powerful in theology, literature, and every aspect of medieval life.

The result was a great transformation in man's view of the supernatural. The saints, the Virgin, and God himself were progressively humanized. The stiff, composed, majestic Christ of the Romanesque crucifixes yielded to the suffering, compassionate Christ of Gothic art. Christ the awesome and remote Creator was replaced by the brother and lover of men, and his new gentleness was supplemented by the tenderness and warmth of the cult of the Virgin. The very same impetus humanized Satan. Christ, the Virgin, Satan—all three were no longer remote principles but immediately present, every moment, in the bustle of the day and in the stillness of the night. The eternal Principle of Evil walked in solid, if invisible, substance at one's side and crouched when one was quiet in the dark recesses of room and mind. With such a sense of immediate and terrible power, courts could convict hundreds of thousands of worshiping him, and of these some at least could be guilty.

Demonology

It is necessary to go back beyond the origins of Christianity to understand how medieval people could become so obsessed with the Devil and his demons. The notion of demons requires not only a recognition of evil in the world but a sense of this evil as a personal force that can be feared, placated, even worshiped. It is possible to guess, though not to demonstrate, the paleontology of this belief in demons. Originally they may have been hostile spirits of the dead, or the spirits of animals or humans outside the primitive community, personalizations of the harmful or destructive powers of nature, or, most importantly, projections of the destructive and uncontrollable forces within the self.

This last element became in historical times the most pervasive, for there is a curious relationship between our will and the demon that we have projected from our darkest desires. The ultimate origins of the evil tendencies inherent within men may be literally demonic, or the result of original sin, or the remnants of our animal nature, or forces of the Freudian id, or whatever you like. Whatever their origin, one of the silliest follies of modern man is to deny that they *are* inherent in men or to suppose that either "progress" or revolution is going to eliminate or control them. On the one hand, we humanize the Devil, not only by portraying him in human form but by allowing him to exercise his powers through human weaknesses; on the other hand the Devil dehumanizes us, shattering our fantasies of order and security, and the illusion that we can control our environment or even ourselves. Satan's destiny and ours are linked.

In the Middle Ages, the power of evil was manifested both in a supreme spirit of evil and in numerous, lesser spirits derived from the old gods or from fairies, kobolds, or other such beings. The supreme evil spirit was called the Devil or Satan; the lesser spirits were called demons. The distinction between the Devil and the demons was usually maintained.* It is a good distinction, because

---

* The Devil is from Latin *diabolus*, Greek *diabolos*, from *diaballein*, to slander—there is no connection with the Indo-European root *div*, whence *deus*, "divine," etc. Satan is the Hebrew *satan*, an enemy, from the root *satan* to persecute. "Demon" is from the Greek *daimonion*, usually connoting an evil spirit, from *daimon*, a god or a spirit. A few writers use the term *kakodemons*, from Greek *kakos*, evil, in order to emphasize their distinction from good spirits like Socrates' *daimon*. The Fourth Lateran Council made the distinction between *diabolus enim et alii daemones*. But some writers use the terms interchangeably.

the origins and functions of the Devil were eventually clearly separated from those of the lesser demons.

The Christian demonology of the Middle Ages is rooted in Jewish conceptions of evil, which in turn are derived from the traditions of the ancient Near East. Before the Exile, Jewish ideas closely resembled those of the Sumerians, Babylonians, Canaanites, and to some extent the Egyptians. In all of these cultures, a clear distinction existed between the principle of evil (the ontogeny of evil in a world created by a good God) and the idea of demons, lesser spirits, good or evil, who are produced by the animism that perceives in every thing a being with thought and will.

The Sumerians and Babylonians usually explained evil in terms of an alienation myth. God made the world good, but man rejected the goodness. The evil resulting from this rejection is in part man's creation and in part, if evil is taken to mean that which is harmful to man, the manifestation of God's righteous punishment.

Sometimes, however, the question arose whether God might not in some way be the ultimate creator of evil, and evil gods as well as good consequently appeared in the pantheons. The idea of evil in both Mesopotamia and Egypt was invariably identified with disorder, with the shattering of the world of peace and harmony which was the ultimate will of the Creator. Evil was accordingly often associated with darkness and the underworld, where death, gloom, and the extinction of the harmony of life occurred.* The underworld had associations with fertility as well as with death (for crops rise up from the earth), and from the conjunction of

---

* Our word "hell" derives from the Scandinavian *Hel,* the dark underworld to which the shades of the dead repaired. Like Hades, it was not originally a place of punishment. *Hel* was also the name of the female deity, sometimes described as the daughter of Loki, who presided over the underworld.

the two concepts came the dying-and-rising gods like Attis, Adonis, and Osiris. For the Canaanites, good was represented by the god of fertility, Baal, who struggled against the god of sterility and death, Mot.

But the attitude of the Semites toward fertility gods was ambivalent, and there appears to have been a deliberate effort to discredit them, particularly the Great Mother, whose cult is as old as the origins of agriculture. Thus certain forms of the fertility deities, notably the pig (associated closely with the Great Mother, Adonis, Attis, and Osiris) or the serpent, came to be considered evil. Animistic spirits, some good and some evil, dwelt everywhere and in everything, in trees, at tombs, at springs, in rivers, and in the mountains. But animals, the most lively, unpredictable, and humanlike of nonhuman creatures, were endowed with the most vivid spirits. Originally, these might be friendly, hostile, or morally neutral. As the spirits were increasingly identified with evil demons, their animal forms were also associated with evil, particularly those considered ugly or frightening. The serpent, the crocodile, the pig, and the goat were already linked with evil in the ancient Near East.* But there was as yet no idea that these still minor demons were forms of the hostile gods, far less that any of them was the substantial representation of the principle of evil. They partook of evil, but they were not evil's very essence.

Preexilic Jewish thought was of this pattern. The fierce monotheism of Jewish religious leaders had dimmed the vividness of animistic spirits to a greater degree than was true among their neighbors, but spirits still existed in various forms: angels (messengers between God and man), and lying spirits like Lilith, the

---

* In medieval art, common animal forms of the Devil, besides these, were the lion, griffin, basilisk, horse, eagle, crow, raven, bat, fly, worm, black bull, donkey, salamander, phoenix, dog, wolf, cat, hare, unicorn, cock, and dragon.

night monster, and the Se'irim (hairy demons). These evil spirits were not yet identified with the principle of evil, for the early Jews, like their Semitic neighbors, had no conception of a Principle of Evil independent of the Deity and explained evil in terms of the alienation myth.

The conquest of the Jews by the Babylonians and the subsequent exile of large numbers of the Jewish people in Babylonia from 586–538 B.C., followed by two centuries of often harsh Persian rule, produced in Jewish thought a deep transformation that was nowhere more thorough than in its conception of evil. This transformation resulted in part from the influence of Zoroastrian dualism, which was strong in Babylonia, but even more from the Jews' need to satisfactorily explain to themselves the wretched fate that had befallen them.

Persian dualism had a great influence upon the Jewish and, later, the medieval concept of evil. The creation of Zarathustra in the seventh century B.C., it passed through many changes in its centuries of development and fathered related religions like Mithraism and Manichaeism. The essential principles of Zoroastrianism were always dualistic. The universe was ruled by Ahura Mazda (later Ormazd), the god of light, who alone was eternal and all-powerful. But on only a slightly lower level an ancient cosmic war raged between the Spirit of Truth (a manifestation of Mazda, or his son) and the Spirit of Falsehood or Evil, Angra Mainyu (later Ahriman). Though in the end Ahriman would be defeated, he struggled incessantly to tempt and subvert man's loyalty to Goodness.

Through its influence upon the Jews of the Exile, and later upon the Essenes, Persian dualism entered into Christian thought at birth. It was in the atmosphere of the Babylonian captivity that the conception of Satan appeared among the Jews. The word *satan* had appeared in the preexilic Old Testament, but only with the connotation of an adversary, not necessarily supernatural and not necessarily evil. But in Zechariah 3, I Chronicles 21, and Job, all postexilic, Satan has become a distinct personality. In their agony, the Jews no longer found it tolerable either to assume human responsibility for the wretchedness of the human condition or to attribute it directly to God. Yet in these books Satan was by no means an independent power of evil; rather, he was God's agent for temptation and for retribution.

As the Jews increasingly understood the essential goodness and power of God, they shrank from making him even the indirect source of evil; and the influence of Persian thought caused them to advance the idea that Satan was the adversary, not only of man, but of God. Judaism never taught that Satan was a spirit independent of, and coeval with, the God of Goodness. But the idea grew that he was a spirit who, created good by God, then fell through his own fault into evil. This quality of being a creature infinitely inferior to God, though powerful in evil, was the chief distinction between the Jewish Satan and the Persian Ahriman. Otherwise they were similar: both were accusers, seducers, and destroyers; both were associated with the serpent; both would be destroyed at the end of the world; and both were the rulers of hosts of evil spirits. Earlier Jewish demons had been independent of Satan, but now he became for ever after head of all the hosts of hell.[1]

The second great influence upon postexilic Judaism was Hellenistic. Greek demons were in origin animistic, but as early as Hesiod, they were conceived of as messengers or mediators between gods and men, an idea developed by Plato and his pupil Xenocrates, who distinguished between good and evil demons. Philo, the great Hellenistic Jewish philosopher, identified the good demons with the Hebrew messengers of God. The Judaism and Christianity of the first centuries A.D. followed Xenocrates in distinguishing between good and bad spirits. Further, they treated the Greek deities, especially the chthonic gods, as they had those of the Philistines and Canaanites, classifying them as evil spirits. Another important element of Greek thought entering into late Judaism and early Christianity was Platonic dualism, derived from Orphism, in which matter was less real and consequently less good than spirit. The evil giants of Orphism were identified with the evil spirits begotten by the fallen angels.

The apocryphal and apocalyptic literature of the Jews from the second century B.C. to the first century A.D., and the literature of the gnostics thereafter, was strongly influenced by these Greek ideas, an influence that can be seen clearly in the most important of the apocryphal works, the books of Enoch. The elaborate demonology of these works had little influence upon medieval Christianity, but their idea of Satan and the fallen angels became entrenched in the Christian view of the world. They traced evil to a war in heaven in which the good angels rebelled against God. One explanation for the rebellion was that it occurred after the creation of Adam, when the angels, lusting after the daughters of men, came down, fornicated with them, and engendered a race of evil giants or demons. The second idea, most common among Christians, was that the angels fell before the creation of man, the cause being a pride and lust for power that led them into jealousy of God.

In I Enoch (second century B.C.), there seem to be a group of satans, leaders of the fallen angels, but by the beginning of the Christian period it was more generally believed that there was *one* Satan who led the rebellion. The angels are identified with the stars, and Lucifer, the light-bearer, was the greatest star who fell. Though orthodox Jews and Christians, unlike the extreme Messalians, Bogomils, and Catharists, never held that Satan was a son of God, the conception that he was the source of all evil was already established in Jewish thought when Christianity made its advent.

Early Christianity was the heir of all these traditions. Like the contemporary Jews and gnostics, the early Christians had a detailed demonology that increasingly equated demons with fallen angels and identified pagan gods with both. Possession by evil spirits, a phenomenon later closely tied to witchcraft, had a firm place in the New Testament and the Fathers, as did the idea that all magic was worked with the aid of demons.

Most Christian writers, like Tertullian, argued that Satan had been the wisest, highest, or most glorious of the angels, and Lactantius even insisted that he had been created (though not begotten) before the beginning of the world, putting him in an ontological category above all other spirits save God. Some Fathers dissented, holding that Satan and his followers were from the baser orders of angels, but general opinion throughout the Middle Ages made Satan's angelic nature, though morally low, ontologically high. The majority opinion about the fall of the angels, held by St. Augustine and therefore accepted in the Middle Ages, was that it had occurred before the creation of Adam, but some of the old notion that the angels had fallen through lust for the daughters of men persisted to reinforce antifeminine prejudices. The Antichrist of the Book of Revelations and subsequent Christian thought was the human general of Satan's armies at the end of the world; sometimes he was identified with Satan himself.

According to St. Paul and most of the Fathers, the Devil and his minions have aerial bodies like those of the angels,* but can take on the appearance, though not the substance, of animals or men.

Satan and his angels dwell in the underworld, as the ancient chthonic deities did; or in the air, with the angels; or right upon earth. One of the curious paradoxes of Christian teaching is that though Satan had been cast out of heaven and into hell by St. Michael, and though his grip on men had been broken by the Passion of Christ, he and his demons still have power to roam the

---

* I.e., refined bodies that occupy little if any space and are in their natural state sensorily imperceptible.

world seeking the destruction of souls. Christianity had established that evil has two roots: one the twisted will of Satan and the angels that followed him, and the other the twisted will of Adam and of mankind. God does not will this evil, but he tolerates it as a retribution for, or at least a consequence of, man's primordial sin. Satan thus has the power to tempt and to punish Christians. Over non-Christians or bad Christians his power is much greater. Infidels, mortal sinners, heretics, and, eventually, witches, cut off from the mystical body of Christ, were conjoined to that of Satan.

St. Augustine's ideas of demonology were little modified by theologians before the eleventh century. But in the meanwhile, popular thought became increasingly dualistic. The refinements of theology limiting the powers of Satan were lost on the people, who dwelt in awe and terror of the Lord of all evil. This terror increased as time went on. There had been few representations of Satan in earlier medieval art, and when he did appear it was with a face more sad than monstrous. But as the idea that Satan was the author of all evil grew, his malevolence and that of his demons reached out to embrace the entire range of human unhappiness. If one fell ill, it was the work of demons; if one felt lust, it was the Devil tempting him or even, in the form of a succubus, seducing him; if rains failed, wells dried up, or crops suffered, it was the work of demons. Marital incompatibility was caused by the jealousy of demons. Insanity and fits were the result of demonic possession. The entire earth was populated by an invisible but intensely real host of fiendish spirits undyingly hostile to human happiness and welfare.

The ubiquity of the demons was enhanced by elements added to demonology by Teutonic and Celtic influences. Neither Celts nor Teutons had any idea of a supreme principle of evil, but the Christians identified their gods and lesser spirits with demons and condemned their worship as idolatrous and superstitious.

The gods survived in the popular imagination, sometimes with dignity, sometimes degraded, as demons, sprites, or even sometimes saints. Many of the Northern spirits were theriomorphic and reinforced the imagery of demons as animals. The Devil's horns, rooted in the heads of Mediterranean fauns and satyrs, most notably in that of the great god Pan, also sprouted from the foreheads of the gods and totems of the North, notably the Gallic horned god Cernunnos. The most visible and direct contribution of the Northern myths to the witch phenomenon was the host of lesser spirits—fairies, kobolds, gnomes, leprechauns, or elves—which the Church assiduously attempted to assimilate to the army of demons. The assimilation was never complete, for the creatures preserved something of their original identity in folk tradition. Even as demons, they were never nearly as powerful or terrible as the Judaeo-Christian fallen angels. Though a stupid person could be badly hurt by underestimating them, a clever one could trick, cajole, and exploit them. The most important function of the lesser demons in witchcraft was as familiars. Many was the person who, in the old folk tradition, believed that he had commerce with the little folk, and a Church that was convinced that all nonangelic spirits were evil assumed that the diminutive spirits helped the witches perform their evil deeds. Hence the pet names given to the witches' familiars, which in no case ever bore the nomenclature of the fallen angels. Names like Hämmerlein, Haussibut, or Hinkebein attest the droll, if mischievous, nature of these spirits.

In the eleventh century, and even more in the twelfth and thirteenth, the power of Satan and his demons continued to expand. This was owing to the growth of dualist thought spurred by the introduction of Catharism in the 1140's, to the humanizing effect of the revolution in taste, to the influence of the Jewish cabala, and in great measure to the triumph of Aristotelianism over Platonism and Neoplatonism among the intellectuals. Aristotelianism, with its conception of a narrowly ordered rational universe, placed all irrational forces in the realm of evil, as opposed to the more tolerant loosely structured Platonism and Neoplatonism.

Peter Lombard's *Sentences,* the most influential textbook of theology in the central Middle Ages, did not concern itself at length with demonology but argued in the old tradition that the angels were cast down from heaven into the air because of their pride. (See Ephesians 2:2, where Satan is described as the prince of the power of the air.) In the air they will reside until cast into hell at the Last Judgment. William of Conches, taking a Neoplatonic position, argued that there were two orders of good demons (*kalodemones*) who lived in the ether and upper atmosphere and one order of evil demons who lived in the air close to the earth and who had partly aerial and partly watery bodies. William of Conches was sharply attacked by William of St. Thierry and other Aristotelians, and arguments like his were seldom heard again until the revival of Neoplatonism in the Renaissance.

In art (including windows, painting, illumination, stories, and sermons), evil spirits now appeared more frequently and became more horrible, monstrous, and grotesque. The Devil's most common appearance came to be a deformed but recognizably human shape, for in these distortions of the human body men could see, as in a mirror, the distortions that sin worked in their souls. The didactic lessons of the monstrous reached their most grotesque later in the artistic tradition of which Hieronymus Bosch is the most famous example. Nowadays we treat monsters as a joke or, stupidly, as entertainment for children, but in the Middle Ages the monstrous was understood as a graphic symbol of the ontologically and morally real dislocation of the universe by sin.

Demons were assumed to be omnipresent and menacing. From the twelfth century, scenes of the Last Judgment became popular in art, almost always including a representation of monstrous demons carrying off the souls of the dead into hell. Demons as well as angels clustered round the bed of a dying man, hoping for the opportunity to snatch his soul away. Popular tales and ecclesiastical exempla of the powers of evil abounded. St. Romuald was haunted by a demon who came to him at night and lay heavily across his legs, paining him and keeping him from turning over. The demon endeavored to tempt the saint with visions of the pleasures of this world, and when all else failed, appeared to him as a monster and threatened to kill him. But the good Romuald was able through prayers and sharp reprimands to withstand the assault. Pope Gregory VII told from his personal experience the story of a monk in a monastery near Aachen who was visited by the Devil in his dreams at night and in hallucinations during the day, so that even during the singing of the office the Devil was by his side, whispering and distracting him.[2]

Though the Devil's form was usually human—even occasionally a handsome young man or a pretty seductress—he continued to have many animal attributes deriving from the theriomorphic character of his forebears. The human and animal qualities began to be combined, and the Devil began to appear as a human with horns, cloven hooves, and a tail, black in color (less commonly red or yellow), and often hairy. Horns were also associated with the Devil because of their significance in the fertility cults, and possibly in part from the Greek tradition of endowing Zeus with horns as a symbol of power.[3] Paradoxically, Satan can appear either as an attractive "White Devil" or an ugly "Black Devil." Sometimes he appears as a degenerate or deformed person with a physical ugliness that inspires terror.[4]

The origin of the Devil's blackness is a subject of importance not only for the history of symbolism but also as a partial explanation of the ancient fear of the black man that disturbs race relations today. Carmelina Naselli's explanation that the fear of blackness arises from the struggle of early Christianity with the blacks for the control of Northeastern Africa is implausible, but she is correct in maintaining that it precedes the Crusades. The

Ethiopian as the Devil, far from being new with *Othello* or even with the *Song of Roland*, is found in the writings of the Fathers (for example, "The Black One" of the Epistle of Barnabas). Sin and hell are dark, and St. Jerome said: "Born of the Devil, we are black."[5] There is a deep psychological terror of blackness associated with death and night. The "black man" is also a Jungian archetype of the brute or of the lower nature or drives and is found in this capacity long before there was any considerable contact between Europeans and Black Africa. Some of the characteristics assigned to (especially male) blacks by white racists today, such as animal strength, hairiness, and great sexual potency, including outsized organs, were applied more than half a millennium ago to the black Devil. The features of the Black One of medieval symbolism are not always negroid. Naselli herself cites a description of a black devil having a sharp face and fine hair. Nor is the Devil usually described as negroid in the later witch trials. Rather, he is often dressed in shaggy animal skins, suggesting a closer connection with chthonic deities than with African blacks.

The Devil is sometimes both pallid and black in the same document. His paleness is the product of an ancient tradition. Hecate herself was pale, for one naturally associates pallor as well as blackness with the lightless underworld and the chalky countenance of death. St. Augustine refers to the demons as pale with envy of God. Pallidity was a characteristic often attributed to heretics. As early as the fourth century the Priscillianists were detected by their color, and from the eleventh century heretics were commonly supposed to be pale, one explanation being that they had lost their color through excessive fasting and abstention from meat.[6]

Satan and his demons sometimes appeared armed with spears in order to torment the souls of the damned.[7] The medieval Devil was sometimes furnished with a hammer or thunderbolt, attesting the influence of the Northern gods. The three-faced Devil of

Dante seems without extensive precedent in medieval witch literature; the literary and mythological precedent is the three faces of
Hecate, the chthonic counterpart of Diana. Stories of incubi,
succubi, and possession were legion. Demons cannot stand the
light of day, according to some writers, and hence must be called
up either at night or underground, a belief that reinforced the
idea that heretics met secretly after dark or in caves. In such an
atmosphere, where demons were efficacious and ubiquitous, witchcraft acquired new vigor.

Intellectual and Popular Bases of Witchcraft

Nascent scholasticism began to offer complex intellectual justifications for witch beliefs. Nonetheless, although high magic, including astrology and divination, began in the twelfth century to
attract increasing attention among the intellectuals, witchcraft did
not enter into their consideration nearly to the degree that it did
in the following century. John of Salisbury, for example, contents
himself with repeating the prohibitions of the *Canon Episcopi*
against belief in the night ride with Herodias and Diana.[8]

The intellectuals proved willing to accept the idea that the
witches had sexual intercourse with the Devil, for they could
draw upon the old tradition of the fallen angels lusting after the
daughters of men. They had more difficulty with shapeshifting
and flight. John of Salisbury's suggestion that demons could pro-
voke delusions, although they could not alter the substance of
things, was in a tradition generally accepted by the scholastics.
Since sorcerers had long been associated with such illusion, they
could in this way be tied ever more closely to diabolism. Abelard
followed the Fathers in arguing that magic employed both natural
forces and demons to obtain its ends. Hildegard of Bingen was
more innovative. Reflecting the increasing strength of Aristotelian
thought, she argued that Satan's power pervades nature, drawing
it in the direction of nothingness or ontological evil. The neat

Aristotelian universe in which evil is ontologically associated with nothingness, and both in turn associated with moral evil, provided a category in which to put the witches: they were Satan's helpers in his efforts to obliterate the Good.

There were still traces of ancient skepticism, particularly in the peripheral regions of civilization, witness the law of Westgotland about 1170 making it a punishable act to defame a woman by accusing her of riding out on sticks or of being a *striga, masca,* or *herbaria.* A penitential of Bartholomew Iscanus, bishop of Exeter, 1161–1184, repeats the ancient condemnations of the belief in riding out with Herodias or Diana, the practice of throwing a gift in the granary for the demons called fauns in the hope that they would bring more grain, and the belief that the shape of another animal can be changed into that of a wolf.[9]

Popular tradition was more influential than intellectual debate. There was a continual demand on the part of the clergy for more stories to edify congregations or to deter them from evil, and didactic popular tales begin to creep into literature. It was in these popular stories that the characteristic ideas of witchcraft were spread most widely and most fully developed.[10]

One of the most famous collections of gossip, lore, and satire in the twelfth century was Walter Map's *On the Folly of Courtiers.* Written about 1180, it contained tales of diabolical pact, incubi, the wild rout, shapeshifting, and child murder. One tale is told of the reign of William the Conqueror. A rollicking knight called Edric the Wild was coming home one night from his carousing, when he happened in a lonely place to see a dwelling in which pretty girls were singing and dancing. Bursting in, he seized one of the young ladies, carried her off by force, and made love to her. He discovered then that she was a succubus (a predecessor of Keats' *belle dame sans merci*). She bore him a child, whom they named Alnod, and who, unlike most of the offspring of such unions, grew up to be a holy man.[11]

116

In another story, a young man named Eudo lost his fortune. While he was bewailing his lot, a huge, ugly man appeared and offered to restore Eudo's wealth in return for his allegiance. At first Eudo resisted, but after a long, persuasive speech on the part of the tempter he assented and soon was restored to his pristine affluence. Later, however, he repented and confessed his sins to the bishop of Beauvais. The good prelate told him that only by hurling himself into the fire to die could he do appropriate penance and so escape the pains of hell. Eudo followed this sage advice and, we may hope, regained eternal grace.

The Devil could appear in many forms. In one tale he undertook to murder the child of a good knight and his wife. This he accomplished by cutting its throat on its first birthday. The couple had another baby, and then a third, but these also he slew on the first anniversaries of their birth. The knight was blessed with a fourth child, and in order to protect it, a holy pilgrim lay awake in its chamber all through the night of its birthday. Before dawn, the form of a lovely and famous lady of the city appeared in the room with a knife and advanced on the sleeping infant. Leaping to his feet, the pilgrim accosted her with surprise and horror. Yet the lady was innocent and at that very moment asleep in her own bed. The murderess was the Devil, who had taken the lady's shape in order to accomplish his evil purposes. When confronted by the pilgrim, he flew shrieking out the window.

Yet another story tells of an orgy held in the caverns of gnomes by an ancient British king named Herla, who must have been related to the *Her-* leaders of the wild hunt.

Other stories of shapeshifting, riding out, and incubi are offered by Gervaise of Tilbury, who dedicated his work to the Emperor Otto IV about 1214. Gervaise combines bonae mulieres, lamias, strigae, mascae, incubi, sylvani, and panes (plural of Pan), with liberal sprinkles of the *Canon Episcopi* to create a composite idea of the witch's flight that later became standard in witch-hunting literature. Influenced by the canon, Gervaise expresses some reservations as to the reality of what he describes, quoting Augustine and other authorities to the effect that these things are either accomplished by demons or are simple illusions. But he dismisses his doubts with reports that he has obtained from "eyewitnesses." Witches are men and women who ride out at night over long distances. Gervaise knows of certain old women who have seen with their own eyes the flight of witches over land and sea, and he is sure that in this way they can span the entire globe, as long as in their flight none of them mentions the name of Christ. If that happens, they will immediately plummet to the ground. At Arles, Gervaise saw a woman who in this fashion had been plunged into the Rhône and soaked to her navel; either the river was very shallow at that point or the lady was exceptionally buoyant. Riding about in this fashion, they enter people's houses, disturbing sleepers by sitting on their chests and causing nightmares of suffocation and falling. As incubi, they have sexual relations with women. They suck blood, steal children from their beds, light lamps, and rummage through baskets, bins, and jars to take whatever food they please. At their will they take the form of cats, and Gervaise knows of a case in Auvergne where men have taken the form of wolves.

Here, then, in Gervaise, many elements are united: the good women (or elves or fairies) for whom one sets out food and drink in order to insure fertility; the bloodsucking strigae, the lustful and sleep-disturbing lamias, the wild chase and its riders of ancient folk legend, the shapeshifting associated with the hunters' cults. All these have now become one.[12]

Caesarius of Heisterbach, who wrote his *Dialogue of Miracles* about 1220, though not as creatively synthetic as Gervaise, had an even larger collection of witch stories.[13] Pact, which did not impress Gervaise, interested Caesarius more. A knight of Liège, having lost his money, was persuaded by one of his peasants to

118

call up Satan. In return for the improvement of his fortunes, the knight formally renounced God and rendered feudal homage to the Devil. When further pressed to renounce the Blessed Virgin, however, he recoiled and was saved from damnation by our grateful Lady's intervention.* Or again, another young man was persuaded by his steward to make "the legal sign of repudiation (of Christ) with his hand and forthwith do homage to the Devil." As in nightmares when our closest friends suddenly change into something strange and threatening, Caesarius' spirits were present in almost every conceivable human (seldom animal) form: incubi, women, servants, a nun, a man dressed in white, a respectable young man, a priest, and a pretty girl.

Henry of Falkenstein, a knight who did not believe in demons, one day encountered a priest named Philip who was reputed to have the power of invoking evil spirits. Henry challenged him to show his powers. One day at noon (when demonic power is high) Philip took the knight to a crossroad, drew a circle round him with a sword, placed him within it and explained the magical properties of a circle within a circle. Then he said, "If you put forth any of your limbs outside this circle before I come back, you will die, because you will immediately be dragged forth by demons and torn in pieces." As the knight stood within the charmed circumference, horrible manifestations occurred around its borders, culminating in the appearance of a demon "like a gigantic man, very huge and very black, clothed in a dark robe, and so hideous that the knight could not look upon him." Never again did Henry deny the existence of demons.

According to Hansen, the idea that things and persons could be bodily transported by spiritual agencies, as St. Paul was snatched up to seventh heaven, was one of the foundations for the idea of witches' flight.[14] Though this may be exaggerated—

* This indicates the strength the cult of Mary was gaining in the thirteenth century.

certainly Hansen's idea that mystical *raptus* or ecstasy is a source of the phenomenon of witch flight is unlikely—the connection is there, and it appears in Caesarius, where God or, more frequently, the Devil transports people through the air over vast distances, in one case from India to Germany.

One of the strangest stories in Caesarius contains elements repeated in the later witch trials. Two men in simple dress came to Besançon feigning poverty and asceticism. By walking upon water or through flames and performing other wonders of this sort, they convinced the credulous populace to follow them in spite of the vigorous opposition of the bishop. At last the prelate, not knowing what else to do, summoned a priest known to be an expert in necromancy and ordered him to call up the Devil and inquire who these men were. The Prince of Darkness replied that they were his servants. "The indentures under which they have become my vassals," he said, "have been sewn in their armpits just under the skin." When these diabolical contracts were found and removed, the heretics could be put to death.[15] This story, probably wholly fictitious, is the first of its kind. Later the witch hunters habitually searched the armpits and other secret places of the body for such contracts or other diabolical amulets having the supernatural virtue of preserving the wearers from punishment. It is doubtful that they took their ideas from Caesarius, but the tradition from which they were drawing stretched as far back as the thirteenth century.

Witchcraft and Heresy, 1140–1230

In his emphasis upon the assimilation of sorcery to heresy, Lea exaggerated the decline in the number of cases of sorcery in the central and later Middle Ages.[16] Actually there were many trials for maleficium throughout this period, trials in which there was little reference to witchcraft. It was heresy, not sorcery, that now shaped the witch phenomenon.

From 1140 to 1230 the heresy of Catharism was the single

greatest influence upon demonology and witchcraft. The intrinsic similarities of Catharism and Christianity explain the success of the former among Western Christians. Persian dualism, with its struggle between the spirits of good and evil, and Greek dualism, with its antithesis between matter and spirit, united in influencing Jewish and Christian thought in the first century A.D. From this nexus arose both heretical dualism and a strong dualist element in Christian orthodoxy.

The main strength of Western dualism before the twelfth century was within orthodox Christianity itself, manifesting itself in (1) the belief that the reality of God's world was greater than that of the material world; (2) a certain distrust, in some writers reaching extreme distaste, for the flesh as opposed to the spirit; and (3) varying degrees of asceticism in order to free the spirit from too much concern with the body. These ideas were sometimes aggravated by gnostic influences, as with the followers of Priscillian in the fifth and sixth centuries, or simply exaggerated by Reformist enthusiasm, as was true for most of the heresies before 1140.[17]

The Reformist exaggeration of the dualist tendencies in orthodox Christianity prepared the way for the advent of Eastern dualism in the 1140's.[18] At that time a mitigated dualism—holding that Satan, though immensely powerful, was a creature of God— appeared in southern France and along the Rhine, possibly imported by Crusaders returning from the Holy Land. By 1150, absolute dualists who argued that Satan's existence preceded the creation of the universe were replacing the mitigated dualists. By 1170, aided by Bogomil missionaries from Bulgaria who came to Southern France and Italy, the absolute dualists had become dominant. By the beginning of the next century, Catharist power was widespread in Lombardy, the Rhineland, and particularly in southern France.

So great was the appeal of Catharism to all ranks and orders of people that the Church considered it as serious a threat as Islam, and, aided by the king and nobility of northern France, Pope Innocent III in 1208 preached a Crusade against the Albigensians, as the Catharists of southern France were known. By 1230 the Albigensians had been conquered.

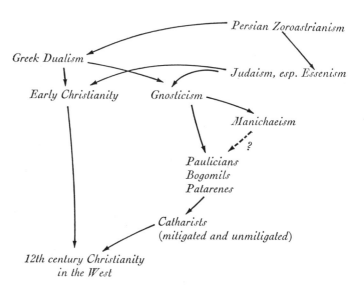

*The development of dualist ideas**

Catharism persisted after the Crusade, but it was further weakened by the Inquisition, which followed on the heels of the Crusaders. Isolated pockets, however, continued to exist throughout the fourteenth and fifteenth centuries, sometimes in close association

---

* The lines of influence shown here are extremely schematized, and the relations between these vaguely defined systems were much more cómplex. Gnosticism, and probably Manichaeism, influenced later dualist sects, among others the Paulicians of Asia Minor, the Bogomils of Bulgaria, and the Patarenes of Illyria, but the lines of filiation among these groups have never been clearly established.

with witchcraft, and the last mention of active Catharism (before its self-conscious revival in the twentieth century) occurs as late as the sixteenth century.

Many essential Catharist doctrines encouraged the development of witchcraft.[19] The Spirit of Evil (whether a creature, as the mitigated dualists taught, or coeval with God, as the absolute dualists maintained) created the material world for the purpose of entrapping spirit in matter. He imprisoned the human soul in a cage of flesh. The creator of the world, the God of the Old Testament, is the lord of matter, the prince of this world, and the Devil. All the personages of the Old Testament, and John the Baptist in the New, are demons. Christ was a pure spirit sent down by the good God into this world in order to teach man how to escape from the matter that confines him. By the practice of Catharism, man might follow the teachings of Christ and so liberate himself; but the Catholic Church was established by the Devil in order to delude people. Of all sins, the worst was pro-creation, since the conception of a child imprisoned a soul in flesh. Since Christ was pure spirit, he did not suffer on the cross, and the cross could not be venerated; since the Eucharist and baptism employ material substances, they too were condemned.

The Catharists rejected all the Catholic sacraments, substituting rituals of their own. Their chief sacrament was the *consolamentum,* conferred by the laying on of hands and cleansing the recipient of all guilt and sin. It could be administered only once to each person, except in special circumstances. Only those fully instructed in the religion and proven in virtue would receive the *consolamentum* in the midst of life (others received it on their deathbed), and thereafter these were known as *perfecti,* dedicated to a life lived wholly without sin. Those who had not yet received the *consolamentum* were called *credentes* (believers), and these were urged to study and practice asceticism until they too were worthy. In practice, however, some *credentes* chose to live as libertines in the expectation that the *consolamentum,* when taken later, would free them from guilt.

At first glance, it is difficult to see how the Catharists, who feared and hated the Devil even more than Catholics did, should have had anything to do with witchcraft. Yet the connection is firmly established. It was from the time the Catharists arrived in Western Europe that concern with witchcraft greatly increased. Although Catharism reached its peak at the beginning of the thirteenth century and witchcraft only began to take on epidemic proportions a century later, the Inquisition turned the accusations it had previously made against the Catharists against the witches. It was precisely in those areas—the Low Countries, Germany, France, and northern Italy—where Catharism had been strongest that witchcraft was most widespread. In Spain, Scandinavia, and southern Italy, where Catharism was weak, so was witchcraft.

These external connections are in themselves no conclusive evidence, but they are reinforced by internal considerations, primarily the underlining by Catharism of certain ideas already present, though less prominent, in orthodox Christianity. The most important of such considerations is this: The Catharists taught that the God of this world is evil—he is the Devil. The true good God is the lord of spirit and is hidden from our souls, encased as they are in matter. Now, if the Devil is indeed Lord of the World, his powers nearly equal to God's, and his presence vividly and everywhere felt, many will choose to propitiate and worship such a power, rather than rigorously to struggle against it with almost superhuman asceticism like that of the *perfecti.* The dark and chthonic powers had always been placated by the worship of the pagans, and there is no reason why medieval people under the influence of Catharism should not have done the same. Moreover, if one accepted the identification of the Devil with the God of the Old Testament, but had been brought up as a Christian to venerate that God, it would actually be consistent to worship the Devil. The mighty struggle between God and Satan impressed itself on many a mind, and some forgot that Catharism promised the ultimate victory of God and hoped instead for the triumph of Satan.

The kind of thinking, twisted from the Catharist as much as from the Catholic point of view, that might come to such conclusions appears in this statement of Catharist beliefs written about 1208–1213. Some of the heretics say

that the malign god exists without beginning or end, and rules as many and as extensive lands, heavens, people, and creatures as the good God. The present world, they say, will never pass away or be depopulated. . . . God himself, they say, has two wives, Collam and Colibam, and from them He engendered sons and daughters, as do humans. On the basis of this belief, some of them hold there is no sin in man and woman kissing and embracing each other, or even lying together in intercourse, nor can one sin in doing so for payment. . . . (They) await the general resurrection which they shall experience, so they say, in the land of the living, with all their inheritance which they shall recover by force of arms. For they say that until then they shall possess that land of the malign spirit and shall make use of the clothing of the sheep, and shall eat the good things of the earth, and shall not depart thence until all Israel is saved.[20]

All the associations that the orthodox opponents of heresy had made between the older heresies and witchcraft were now made with the Catharists, particularly desecration of cross and sacraments, cannibalism, secret conventicles at night, formal renunciation of Christ, and sexual orgies. St. Augustine (*The Nature of Good*, XLVIII, 47) argued that the Manichaeans ate their babies in order to free their spirits from the flesh.

Ultimately, the most important coincidence between witchcraft and Catharism was ideological. The cultural revolution of the period produced the rise of what Ladner calls eros, a restless striving now more than ever concentrated upon the desire for material pleasures, whether sexual or monetary.[21] This striving came into conflict with traditional Christian values and caused a condition of psychological dissonance resulting in widespread alienation. To some extent these longings could be sublimated, and the Franciscans and similar orthodox reform movements could absorb them. But the same force that drove the new monastic movements also generated the rebellion and deviation of the flagellants, the heretics, and the witches. Ladner argues that the alienation so produced was qualitatively different from that of the earlier Middle Ages, when man felt alienated from God, or deliberately alienated himself from the world for the sake of God. Now man felt alienated from man, from the established institutions of men, and most particularly from the Church. Goliardic poetry, secular literature, courtly love, popular or even learned irreverence, all these created a milieu in which ideologized irreverence such as heresy and witchcraft could flourish.

Discontent was variously expressed. A priest in the diocese of Aquileia during the pontificate of Alexander III (1159–1181) was suspended for two years for calling up a demon.[22] Caesarius reports of heretics in Verona about 1175 that they congregated in a large hall underground, heard a blasphemous sermon, put out the lights, and held an orgy, allegations clearly in the old tradition dating back to Orléans in 1022.[23]

Already the strange connection between Waldensians and witches was being made. Alan of Lille accused the Waldensians, whose real heresy consisted of excessive asceticism, of being "incontinent . . . for in their assemblies they indulge in gluttony and devote themselves to excesses."[24] Similar charges were made against the Waldensians in a treatise ascribed to David of Augsburg.[25] They meet secretly at night and freely perform their evil rites while others sleep, David tells us. The other crimes with which they were commonly charged, namely kissing cats and frogs (the first hint of the *osculum infame,* later a standard witch crime), calling up the Devil, and fornicating in an orgy with the lights turned out, aroused David's doubts. These charges, he noted, are usually made against the Catharists, and are not properly assigned to any other sect.

Of all the charges linking witchcraft with Catharism, that of libertinism is the most common. The Catharists denied it, and at least one orthodox writer agreed with them. About 1240, a Franciscan friar named James Capelli wrote: "The rumor of the fornication which is said to prevail among them is most false. For it is true that once a month, either by day or by night, in order to avoid gossip by the people, men and women meet together, not, as some lyingly say, for purposes of fornication, but so they may hear preaching and make confession. . . . They are wrongfully wounded in popular rumor by many malicious charges of blasphemy from those who say that they commit many shameful and horrid acts of which they are innocent."[26]

Most modern historians have agreed with James and dismissed the charge as unfounded, in spite of the fact that the sources almost unanimously support it. Of late some have begun to reconsider their opinions. Evidence has grown that many of the early dualist and gnostic sects encouraged libertinism, and Nygren even argued that some of the pagan Roman accusations of immorality among the primitive Christians may have been valid, not for ordinary Christians, but for Christian gnostics. Antoine Dondaine and Ernst Werner have both argued that otherwise reliable medieval sources cannot be dismissed on this one point, and Werner has shown conclusively that the Bohemian Adamites of the fourteenth and fifteenth centuries did indeed follow immoral practices. The late Gottfried Koch, with Werner one of the best Marxist historians of medieval heresy, suggests that libertinism springs naturally from the contempt in which dualism holds matter: despising matter and material pleasure, one either eschews them entirely or engages in them promiscuously and contempt-uously. The body should not be rendered undeserved respect, and sexual aberrations can be dismissed as unimportant.[27]

Libertinism was real, and it was a trait logically connecting Catharism and the later antinomian sects. Far from being op-posites, Werner argued, dualism and pantheism had the same basic religious motivation: "Escape from the bonds of worldly un-righteousness and inadequacy, in order to attain godly purity. . . . Libertinism is the clearest way of taking a stand against the standards of this world and a drastic assertion of the holiness of the sectaries. The full meaning of the break with the old eon on the part of the heretical community is best grasped in the libertine consequences of that break. An act such as the desecration of an altar, which the older generation regarded as a blasphemy, was considered by the heretics a sign that a new Era had begun."[28]

The ideal of spiritual liberty was of great importance to John of Salisbury and other twelfth-century thinkers. The emphasis upon the "law of love" helped to produce mysticism and millennarian-ism as well as a certain amount of antinomianism. This kind of libertinism was not a product of lust, but a direct consequence of the dualist, the pantheist, and even the orthodox Christian drive to freedom from this world. This being so, it is all the more likely that the charges of libertinism leveled against the heretics were substantially true. Kurze argues that even a *topos*—a cliché—may contain a "kernel of historical individuality." All myths are in one sense or another true; the question is why these particular myths were so widespread.[29]

In any event the license ascribed to the Catharists could easily be transferred to the witches. Geoffrey of Auxerre wrote about 1150 that the Catharists taught free sex; and the Council of Reims in 1157 condemned sexual orgies on the part of the heretics. About 1180 Joachim of Flora, describing heretics he called Patarini, implies that they had orgies, and this judgment on the "Patarenes" was confirmed by Walter Map, writing about 1182.[30] The sectaries, Map claimed, put out the lights and after an obscene rite proceeded to indiscriminate intercourse, each person seizing the one next to him. Alan of Lille makes the connection between dualism and immorality explicit. The dualists say, he reported, that a person must use every means at his disposal to cleanse himself of everything earthly or diabolical clinging to him. In order to rid themselves of concern for the body, they engage in random sexual intercourse. Thus, as Koch points out, they abused the body in order to show their contempt for it, and the Catharist dislike of marriage was the result, not only of their horror of imprisoning souls in bodies, but also of the respect that marriage accords the body.[31]

In the 1150's or 1160's heretics in Germany were practicing rites of exceptional strangeness. At dawn, at noon, and in the evening, these heretics offered solemn sacrifices to the Devil, whom they allegedly called Belphegor (a pagan god of love and fertility appearing in the Old Testament). In his honor they held revels in which the lights were extinguished and everyone committed incest. On Christmas Eve, while others were celebrating the birth of Christ, they performed rites that mocked the solemnity of the Nativity. The priest of their cult, in mockery of the Christian kiss of peace, touched the altar with his bare backside. The oblations are brought out befouled by human sperm. The chronicler has himself seen in Regensburg an episcopal chapel that had been profaned by this blasphemous cult. Heisig argues that this is a gnostic cult of Basilidean origin, and that the heretics must have identified their sperm with the Giver of Life, i.e., the Holy Spirit, who was identified by some early Christians with the *logos spermatikos* of the Neoplatonists. It is unlikely that the sect was really gnostic, for there is no evidence anywhere else in medieval

Europe of such practices. Perhaps Gerhoh was embellishing with his own pedantic knowledge of Augustine the ideas of a group infected with Catharist libertinism.[32]

Next to libertinism, the most common witch trait attributed to Catharists was their tendency to adore the Devil. Ralph the Ardent says that because the "Manichaeans" of the Agenais believe that the Devil was the architect of the material world, they secretly adore him as the creator of their bodies.[33] One of the more curious tales of medieval heresy is reported at Reims in 1176–1180. There a handsome young clergyman propositioned a peasant girl, and when he was refused on the grounds that she believed it a sin to lose her virginal purity, she was charged with being a Catharist heretic. She was alleged to be a member of a group of heretics in the city who believed that a fallen angel named Luzabel was the creator of the world and had power over all things in it. They met in subterranean caverns, offered sacrifices to Lucifer, and engaged in sacrilegious practices. The story also includes one of the first specific links of heresy to flight: the chaste girl, who was, incidentally, finally burned as a heretic, confessed that she had been led astray by a certain old woman, who was brought into court and accused. It proved impossible to bring the crone to her just punishment, however, for as she was seized in order to make her ready for the stake, she produced a ball of thread from her bosom, and, holding onto one end, threw the ball out the window, crying out "Catch," in a loud voice. Immediately she was lifted up by the thread and flew out the window, never to be seen again. Doubtless, as Ralph of Coggeshall argues, this was accomplished through the intervention of demons.[34]

Walter Map's heretics worshiped the Devil immediately after the lights were extinguished and before engaging in their sexual revels. It is in this account of Map's, dating from about 1182, that a precise mention of the obscene kiss occurs:

130

About the first watch of the night, when gates, doors, and windows have been closed, the groups sit waiting in silence in their respective synagogues, and a black cat of marvelous size climbs down a rope which hangs in their midst. On seeing it, they put out the lights. They do not sing hymns or repeat them distinctly, but hum through clenched teeth and pantingly feel their way toward the place where they saw their lord. When they have found him they kiss him, each the more humbly as he is the more inflamed with frenzy—some the feet, more under the tail, most the private parts.[35]

This is an important description, for it is the first time the witches' conventicles are called *synagogues* and one of the first times the Devil appears to his worshipers in the form of a cat. These heretics were also alleged to make converts of innocent people by serving magical food that turned their minds. Map edifies his readers with the story of a noble prince of the region near Vienne who protected himself by carrying round some salt previously consecrated for baptismal purposes. The nobleman's own nephew attempted to entrap him with demon food, but the good prince protected himself by sprinkling the salt upon the succulent dishes, which immediately turned into rabbit dung.[36]

Alan of Lille's Catharists, like Walter Map's, adored the Devil in the form of a cat, whose posterior they kissed. In one of the more amusing etymological blunders of the period, Alan suggests that the Catharists' name might be derived from the *cattus* they worshiped.[37]

The Catharists, like the witches and most heretics, were supposed to have secret meetings or conventicles, often undergound.[38] Before the twelfth century, these meetings had been given no special name, but now, both Map's heretics and Joachim of Flora's were said to assemble in "synagogues." By the fourteenth century this was the commonly accepted term for the witches' assembly, and continued to be so until the middle of the fifteenth century, when "sabbat" began to be used. The use of either term in this context is evidence of the increased anti-Jewish feelings of the later Middle Ages, and it may be that the absurd stories of Jewish ritual sacrifice of Christian children did much to re-enforce the old tradition of the blood-sucking strigae with their cannibalism and child stealing.[39]

The century of Catharism and growing popularity of tales of diabolism thus introduced into the phenomenon of witchcraft the obscene kiss, the synagogue, and ritual adoration of the Devil under a variety of forms. It strengthened and added new dimensions to the notions of ritual murder, witches' flight, and sexual orgy. Most important, it confirmed the relationship between heresy and witchcraft, which was now to be further developed in the succeeding centuries.

6

Antinomianism, Scholasticism, and the Inquisition, 1230-1300

N the mid-thirteenth century, the papal Inquisition was founded, and Aristotelian scholasticism was firmly established as the dominant method of thought. As witchcraft seemed an invention of the scholastics and Inquisitors to Lea, Hansen, and other liberal historians, they argued that witchcraft began at this time. They alleged that the classical charges of witchcraft were first allowed by the Inquisition and that other courts did not participate in witch trials to any great degree until the fifteenth century. In fact, episcopal and secular courts were very much involved in the formulation of the witch phenomenon in the thirteenth century and in the fourteenth nearly equaled the Inquisition in the vigor and ingenuity of their prosecution of witches. Had we as many records from the secular and episcopal courts, we should probably find that they actually exceeded the Inquisitorial courts in the number of witch prosecutions they conducted. The greatest number of witch cases did occur in areas where the Inquisition was active: France, the Low Countries, Germany, and Lombardy.

But these were also areas where social change and dislocation were especially prevalent and where heresy had always been most active. It is with heresy that the geographical, chronological, and ideological ties of witchcraft were strongest, and these ties had begun to be formed centuries before the advent of either scholasticism or the Inquisition. Though the development of witchcraft was encouraged by scholasticism and hastened by the Inquisition, it was in heresy and popular culture that it was rooted and from which it continued to draw most of its nourishment.

Popular Culture

The tales most commonly spread by popular writers during this century concerned either pact or the "good women." The Theophilus story received wider circulation than ever after it took popular form in Rutebeuf's vernacular *Miracle de Théophile,* written about 1261. This is the old, Faustian story retold, except that Rutebeuf was, unlike earlier writers, less concerned with the miraculous intervention of the Virgin than with the original trespass of Theophilus.[1] This emphasis is an example of the process of humanization that had begun in the previous century. It was rife with dangers: if the evils formerly attributed to demons were now attributed to men, the alienation of man from man could advance the more rapidly. In the graphic arts, depictions of pact begin to be popular in the thirteenth century, as does another important ingredient of witchcraft, the theft of children by demons. This theme was brought even closer to witchcraft when people, often the parents themselves, were shown delivering children to the Devil.[2] In 1258, Thomas of Cantimpré told a story involving both pact and flight. In a tavern a group of men sat round a table having a drink, and one was arguing that there is no life after death. At that moment, a large, strong man entered, asked for a drink, and inquired what the other guests were discussing. "Souls," replied the skeptical toper. "Anyone want to buy mine for the price of a round of drinks?" Silently, the big man bought drinks for the assembled company and asked them whether he had paid well.

134

Receiving their assent, he seized the boaster and flew off with him into the air, so that, "as is certain, he might take him with him to hell. For the big fellow was the Devil in the form of a man."[3]

Another popular story relating to witchcraft has to do with the wild ride and the bonae. A typical version from about 1254 is told by Jacques de Vitry in his *Golden Legend*. One evening, St. Germain of Auxerre was dining at the home of a friend. After they had risen from the table, the hosts began, to Germain's astonishment, to set the table again. When asked why, they said that they were preparing for the good ladies who ride out at night. Curious, Germain stayed awake all night in order to find out what might befall. After waiting a long time, he saw a crowd of demons in the shape of men and women enter the house and sit down at the table to supper. Jumping up, the saint forbade the guests to leave and ran to awaken the entire household, inquiring whether they recognized any of those at the table. "Yes," replied his hosts, "they are all our neighbors." Once again the saint forbade the demons to leave and persuaded his hosts to go out and visit their neighbors' houses, where they found everyone tucked safely in bed asleep. Thus St. Germain proved to his friends that they had been entertaining demons in disguise.[4]

Writing about 1270, the author of the second part of the *Roman de la Rose,* Jean de Meun, expressed his skepticism in such matters. Many people have the illusion that they ride out at night to roam with Dame Habonde, Jean wrote; they even claim that a third of the world joins them. Three times a week their souls leave their bodies, pass through doors or other barriers, and, riding far and wide with the good women (*bonnes dames*), penetrate into other people's houses. Here the wild chase is unquestioningly identified with the activities of the sprites (bonae) who go into houses to get food and clothing: Abundia, the Gallic fertility spirit, here replaces Diana or Herodias, and she, like one of the three faces of Hecate, rules a third of the world.[5]

Heresy

Heresy continued to be encouraged by the dissonance caused by population growth and its consequent social change, though the reversal of these trends in the following century by plague and famine would be even more dislocating. The thirteenth century, far from being either a time of "medieval synthesis," the "greatest of centuries," as devout Catholics have called it, or "the stupidest of centuries," as hostile rationalists have deemed it, was actually torn by doubts and tensions.[6] These tensions were often expressed in popular movements of grotesque violence. The Crusades against Albigensians or Muslims were diverted abroad to the pillage of Constantinople and at home to the persecution of the Jews. The exaggerated enthusiasm of the best of Christians is demonstrated in the improbable voyage of St. Francis to Egypt in an effort to convert the Sultan.

In lesser men than Francis such zeal took frightening forms. One of the earliest movements of social protest was the passage through France in 1251 (it was repeated in 1320) of the *Pastoureaux,* peasants and urban workers who wandered about pillaging, burning, and demanding betterment of their condition.

Even more grotesque were the dance manias. Though these proliferated after the plagues of the next century, they commenced early in the thirteenth. At Erfurt in 1237 more than a hundred children attempted to jump and dance all the way to Armstadt, and many were killed.[7] The mania was a reality. By the end of the thirteenth century the dance of death began to be a popular moral theme in art and literature and reached its height in the fifteenth century along with the obsession with grisly *memento mori*. Though the *danse macabre* was originally a dance of the dead, it soon became a dance of living people who were reminded of the nearness of death and the vanity of the world. In the typical dance-of-death story, revelers would be checked in the midst of their dance by the appearance of a spectral figure which caused them to stop still in terror and grief. The dance of death was to a large extent a literary and artistic invention for moral purposes.[8]

Ritual flagellation, on the other hand, was widely practiced in reality. It began in Perugia in 1260—a date about which the millennarian speculations of Joachim of Flora had already aroused expectations, as we shall see. It spread to Germany in 1261, subsequently affecting much of Europe. The movement was sporadic until the Black Death in 1347–1349 gave it new vigor and occasioned a vast outbreak; it persisted with recurrent vigor into the late fifteenth century. Preaching that the end of the world was at hand, and that salvation could come only to those who joined them in the practice of the most extreme asceticism, the flagellants attracted great followings in times of distress. They would arrive at a town or village in procession, wearing white robes decorated front and back with red crosses. Coming to the church in the center of town, they would stand in circles and strip to the waist. In turn, each would lie flat on the ground, his head at the feet of the one ahead of him, while the one behind struck him with a whip, during which others in the group stood in the midst of the circle, leading the people in hymns and prayers. After this, each beat himself with a scourge in which iron hooks were imbedded until he lay bleeding on the ground, unable to rise. This was done twice a day and once at night. Such hysterical fanaticism released the wildest passions of pious violence in the onlookers, and many joined in. The madness was not easily restrained: when the clergy attempted to check these excesses, the flagellants and their followers turned anticlerical and antisacramental, burning churches and killing priests or anyone else who opposed them, their cruellest slaughters being reserved for the Jews. All these fanatical movements, along with orthodox mysticism and the multiplying variety of heretical sects, were manifestations of revulsion against the increasing institutionalization of the Church and against its inability to protect them from plague and other disaster.[9]

The thirteenth century saw a continuation of the Catharist and Waldensian heresies, and in 1233 Inquisitor Konrad of Marburg was already accusing the Waldensians of participating in sex orgies like those of the Catharists.[10] But the most important heresies of the thirteenth and fourteenth centuries, both because they were new and because they were relatively widespread, were antinomian.[11]

The great antinomian heresies of the later Middle Ages began quietly in the lecture halls of the University of Paris. There, a scholar named Amalric of Bena (d. 1206), under the influence of the writings of John Scotus Eriugena, taught an intellectually refined pantheism that included the assertion that "God is all things in all things."* About 1190 an Italian named Joachim of Flora enunciated a millennarian theology: there were three ages of the world—that of the Father, that of the Son, and that of the Holy Spirit. The last he predicted would come in 1260 and would revolutionize the world, bringing the Kingdom of God into the hearts of men. The first age had been the rule of law, the second age was the rule of faith, but the third age was an age in which God would reveal himself directly to each man. Since all men would be transformed by God, there would be no need for law, governments, or the Church; there would be no need even for food, for men's bodies would be spiritually transformed. Seeing God face to face, men would spend their lives in endless joy.

The pantheism of Amalric and the hopeful millenarianism of Joachim were combined from about 1205 to about 1230 in the doctrine of a group called the Amalricians, who, unlike the professor from whom they derived their name, were largely unlettered. If God is all things, they argued, then I am God, unable

* Different from the Arab-Aristotelian–derived pantheism of his contemporary David of Dinant, who had little influence upon heretics.

to sin. I can do wrong only when I forget that I am God. They advanced the date for the coming of the Third Age to 1210, presumably so that they could be assured of enjoying it themselves. At that time, they said, all men would be converted to their sect, outside of which there could be no salvation.

In addition to Joachism and Amalricianism, new apostolic groups similar to the Waldensians in their emphasis upon interior justification were founded. The thrust toward pious communal living that had led to the foundation of new monastic orders, the canons regular, and the friars, affected women as well. Many women entered convents, but convents were too strict for some or too expensive for others (a novice entering a covenant often had to pay a dowry). Some poor women, especially in the cities, united to live in foundations called Beguinages, where religious rules were lax and where they pooled their economic resources by doing weaving and other work for the cloth industry. Their own poverty, coupled with their resentment of the rich, especially the cloth manufacturers, caused them to emphasize the same virtues of apostolic poverty that both St. Francis and Valdes had professed. In the meanwhile, the Fraticelli, a group of Franciscans dissatisfied with the laxity of the order, also began to uphold apostolic piety against the established Church, which they believed had defaulted on its spiritual obligations. Some Beguines, Beghards (their male counterparts), and Fraticelli became involved in heretical (usually antinomian) activity by the end of the thirteenth century as a consequence of their resistance to the Church.

These movements shared a dislike of the power and wealth of those in authority. Although present-day protests demand a larger share of the pie, movements of poverty in the Middle Ages, whether orthodox or heretical, all took quite another position: they argued that the Christianity of the Bible and of the Apostles had pointed out that one could not serve God and Mammon and that a rich man was unlikely to be saved. Consequently they insisted, not that they should become rich, but that everyone should become poor.

Beginning about 1210 a number of heretics appeared in Germany, the Low Countries, and Italy. In Germany they were called the Brethren of the Free Spirit, in Italy the sect of the Freedom of the Spirit. Unlike the Catharists, they had no ecclesiastical organization, but, loosely bound by common views deriving from Joachism, Amalrician pantheism, and apostolic poverty, they constituted an important complex of heretics that persisted into the fifteenth century.

A concept of internal justification united these traditions. The mystics and the Reformist apostolics argued that the infusion of the grace of God into all men who would accept it justified each individual by the light within and released him from the need of church, government, or laws. The Joachites argued that in the third age man was transformed and became a spiritual being wholly filled with God. The Amalricians insisted that all men *were* God. The Brethren of the Free Spirit accepted the premises according to their preferences, but they all accepted the conclusion, arguing that they were themselves the Holy Spirit or Christ. Since all things are God, there is no evil. Evil, like good, comes from God and is God. Since we are ourselves God, they argued, we need obey no law. Priests, scholars, and lawyers read what is written on paper, but we see the truth from within ourselves. Urges to lust, greed, or other so-called sins should be fulfilled as soon as possible, since they come from God: the only evil is to *resist* these feelings, which are those of Christ himself. The language, but not the sentiment, seems strange today, when people are again arguing that there is no guide to conduct but feelings.

In a curious reversal of Catharist custom, the Brethren often practiced asceticism as neophytes, but when fully initiated as "men of freedom" they became the same as God, were incapable of sin, and were permitted all things. According to the confession of one of the Brethren they believed that the practice of incest was permissible even upon the high altar, that homosexuality was licit, and that it was possible to restore virginity by sleeping with one of the sect. It was even alleged that if a group of Brethren fornicated with a woman, the holiest would sleep with her last so that she might crown the activity by the restoration of her maidenhead.[12]

A meeting of the Brethren at Cologne in 1325 bears many similarities to the witches' sabbat, including a sexual orgy.[13]

Another group, more attached to the Reformist tradition than the Brethren but nonetheless antinomian in spirit, arose in Italy under the name of Apostolici.* One Gerard Segarelli began preaching in Parma in the year 1260 that the Kingdom of the Spirit had arrived, as Joachim of Flora had predicted. After his death, Segarelli was replaced as leader of the sect by a Brother Dolcino. The Apostolici met in secret conventicles and believed that since they were filled with the Holy Spirit they were incapable of sinning and were not obliged to obey the laws. Fornication and all other supposed sins were not only permissible but desirable so long as done in the name of love—again, the modern ear detects a curious resonance. Another sect, arising in Milan in 1271, was led by a prophetess named Guglielma who claimed to be the incarnation of the Holy Spirit.

The Luciferans who appeared in Germany from 1227 and the Adamites of fourteenth- and fifteenth-century Bohemia also held, it is reported, sexual orgies in subterranean places and argued that it was permissible to do there what was sin above the ground. Developing the premise that all things are God, the Luciferans argued that the Devil was therefore God. He was unjustly cast down from heaven, and he would one day be restored to his rightful place. Now, on earth, it is he who should be worshiped.

* Or Pseudo-Apostolici, or Dolcinists. Salimbene contemptuously notes in his Chronicle, MGH SS, XXXII, 255: "They call themselves apostles. But they are not: they are the synagogue (*synagoga*) of Satan."

These heresies were clearly influential in the formation of the witch cult. Just as the Catharists had encouraged witchcraft by magnifying the awesome power of the Devil, the antinomians, by arguing that all action was virtuous and that Satan was God, advanced the cause of rebellion, libertinism, and Satanism. But so close to classical witchcraft did the Luciferans, the Adamites, and some of the Free Spirit heretics come that they not only influenced witchcraft but were in a sense witches themselves.

Scholasticism

Scholastic influence upon witchcraft has been greatly exaggerated. The witch ideas were evolved in popular culture and only afterward were picked up by intellectuals. The idea that intellectuals are always ahead of popular culture is one of the more pervasive, and less persuasive, self-delusions of the intelligentsia. The scholastics made few innovations in magic, demonology, or witchcraft. They accepted the reality of maleficium in the tradition of Augustine. They were much concerned with the problems raised by high magic. This was the century of the Jewish cabala, the century when *grimoires* (manuals of magic) were being published, when works of astrology and alchemy with their philosophical justifications were being translated from Arabic and Greek. But few of the scholastics showed any concern with classical witchcraft. Vincent of Beauvais, Alexander Neckham, Bartholomew of England, Michael Scot, Albertus Magnus, all these and most others—the only major exception being William of Auvergne—had virtually nothing to say about it; and what they did say was much in the tradition of the earlier Middle Ages.

Nonetheless the scholastics did provide an authoritative intellectual structure that was later used to bad effect by the witch hunters. In the first place, they reaffirmed and buttressed traditional Christian demonology and maleficium. Just as important, they generally adopted an Aristotelian world view favoring the development of witchcraft as opposed to a Neoplatonic world view favoring the development of high magic and not as conducive to witch beliefs. Neoplatonism, vigorously combated by most scholastics, did not regain its position until the Renaissance. The Neoplatonic view was that a world soul united the universe in one system of microcosm-macrocosm, sympathy-antipathy, so that all things were interrelated and mutually responsive. In such a universe any marvel could be effected through natural magic without recourse to the supernatural. Such a view was adopted by Neoplatonist Renaissance magicians like Giordano Bruno and by most of the modern occultists that succeeded them. This adherence to natural magic is part of the explanation for the traditional antipathy of occultists toward supernatural religion.

Natural magic, as Sir Walter Raleigh, one of its advocates, put it, "Bringeth to light the inmost virtues, and draweth them out of Nature's hidden bosome to humane use: *Virtutes in centro centri latentes:* Virtues hidden in the center of the center." As opposed to this approach, "St. Thomas' view was set within a fundamentally Aristotelian framework, that is, a framework which assumed contact-action as the basis of efficient causation, ruled out action at a distance through sympathy-antipathy and the world-soul, and was inhospitable to the notion of marvelous effects being produced through 'natural' means. The Aquinian view, in other words, had the corollary that the extraordinary use of 'natural' laws to produce extraordinary effects in nature was only possible through demonic intervention."[14] The Aristotelianism of the scholastics was a narrowly rational system, so that irrational events were seen as supernatural and often demonic. This was opposed to the more supple, mystical Neoplatonic system, which was broader in its acceptance of what was natural. Scholastic Aristotelianism was accordingly bound to reinforce the trend, already begun within the Augustinian tradition, toward driving magic in the direction of witchcraft.

The chief means of uniting sorcery and witchcraft was the idea of pact. Though Aristotelians first and foremost, some scholastics were willing to admit that some magic was accomplished naturally. They believed, however, that most magical operations required the aid of demons. But if one calls upon demons to help perform magic, one must offer the demons something in return. Hence, one must have an implicit pact with them. The distinction between implicit pact and explicit pact was clearly made by Albertus Magnus: in explicit pact one literally made a covenant with the Devil, face to face, à la Faust; in implicit pact one takes an action that could not be accomplished without demonic aid and therefore without in some way rendering service to demons. William of Auvergne argued that all magic derived from implicit pact, and Aquinas extended this argument to include even astrology. Demons are evil; magic entails implicit pact with them, and consequently all magic is evil. For this reason, medieval and modern Christianity has never accepted the distinction between "white" and "black" magic and has declared all magic demonic.

Under popular influence, the scholastic view of pact began in this period to undergo an important modification. Previously men had bargained with demons on a relatively equal basis. The old ideas lingered both in the Faustian tradition of compact and in the tales of men's efforts to outwit lesser demons. But in his relationship to the Devil, to Satan himself, the human contracting party is no longer an equal making a bargain, but a subject doing homage to his master. This new dimension made possible the further development of the idea of Satanic worship and classical witchcraft.

Another area in which scholastic thought was influential but only slightly innovative was sexual commerce between men and demons. Hansen exaggerates when he says that there is no trace of sexual relations between witches and demons before the thirteenth century.[15] What did happen, however, is that the idea of such sexual union acquired a new coloration. The idea that

144

demons in the form of incubi and succubi had intercourse with humans is of ancient origin. The idea that the heretics or witches had sexual orgies in their nightly conventicles went back to the eleventh century. But the idea that the witch united herself with the Devil in ritual intercourse at the witches' synagogue was new. Like all the new ideas of witchcraft, however, it originated in popular legend, and the scholastics for the most part kept to the earlier tradition of incubi, debating only whether demons materialized their aerial bodies to have sex or whether they stole human sperm as succubi and emitted it as incubi.

The new dimension of ritual intercourse had further significance. Though demons could act at will as either incubi or succubi, ritual coupling was usually ascribed to women rather than to men. This is because the popular imagination made the Devil, like God, masculine, although Christian philosophy considered demons, like angels, sexless; and because the ancient Pauline-patristic tradition judged the female sex to be weaker than the male physically, mentally, and morally. William of Auvergne argued that it was women rather than men who deluded themselves into believing that they rode out at night because their minds were feebler and more subject to illusion.[16] Abelard blamed Eloise for leading him into ruin through carnal temptation, as Eve had led Adam and as women had led men since the beginning of the world. The *Malleus Maleficarum* of the fifteenth century considered women peculiarly susceptible to demonic temptation through their manifold weaknesses. This tradition was responsible for placing the chief blame for witchcraft upon women.

Curiously, this view was contemporary with that of courtly love, which elevated women to the level of beings more lofty and spiritual, finer and less coarse, than men. The ambivalence between these opposite conceptions of women has remained with us into the twentieth century. The irrationality of both traditions is at last being recognized, so that women may be treated as no better than men and no worse. If there had been no exaggerated contempt for women's morality and perhaps no exaggerated respect for her magical powers, the burden of the witch delusion might not have fallen upon the female sex.

The approach of the scholastics to shapeshifting and flight was also traditional and resembled their attitudes toward ritual sex. Demons can employ natural processes to cause certain wonderful results, or they can delude the senses into perceiving false wonders, but they cannot really change shapes. Demons can move people through the air, but only rarely and only under the orders of God. The most important Biblical justification for this belief was the Devil's removal of Jesus to the high place during the Temptation in the wilderness. As Hopkin argues, however, there is no real connection between the idea of *raptus* and bodily flight. Far from being innovators in these ideas, the scholastics, including Alexander of Hales, Aquinas, and John of Freiburg, all subscribe to the *Canon Episcopi* and argue that the rides with Diana are illusion.[17]

The two scholastics who had most effect upon the development of witchcraft were Aquinas and William of Auvergne—Aquinas because of the general weight of his authority, and William because he was the most concerned with these problems.[18] The night rides are real, William argued, but they are made, not by people, but by demons. These are called the ladies of the night or "Hellequins" and are led by Domina Abundia or Satia. They fly through the air and invade people's cellars, where they eat and drink the provisions set out for them and in return bring prosperity upon the house. Other demons are permitted by God to kill children in order to punish their parents. These strigae or lamias eat the children they steal; but they too are demons and not, as some people believe, women. There are people who use these demons in magical rites and who consequently are guilty of making pact with them and worshiping them. This worship, at its

146

worst, is conducted in subterranean caverns where idolaters worship Lucifer in the form of a black cat or a toad. As an act of homage, they kiss the cat's buttocks or the toad's mouth.[19]

Like those of most scholastics, Aquinas' views of magic, heresy, and demonology were much in the Augustinian tradition, and in no way approached the witchcraft found in popular writings. Those who have attempted to make Thomas responsible for the witch craze neglect this fact and fail to consider that his influence was limited in his own time and for almost two hundred years after his death. In the mid-fifteenth century he at last was considered authoritative, but by that time the witch craze was already in full spate. It is true that the Catholic witch hunters of the fifteenth and later centuries drew justification for their activities from the writings of Thomas, but this was natural in view of the fact that anything they could cull from respected theologians was fuel for their fire.

Aquinas argued in traditional fashion that demons could only act under the permission of God. People who worked magic did enter into an implicit pact with Satan, but Thomas was skeptical that anyone ever made an explicit compact. Like everyone else, he believed in the reality of maleficium, but he in no way departed from the skepticism of the *Canon Episcopi* and insisted that the night flight was an illusion. He believed in incubi: demons were intellectual substances dwelling in the air and permitted by God to take dense shapes and in those shapes perform sexual acts. But this has nothing to do with the heretical sexual revel and even less with the ritual intercourse of the sabbat. On these four essential points, pact, flight, maleficium, and ritual intercourse, the great scholastic can in no way be held responsible for the witch phenomenon except in the general sense that the Aristotelian system he used was conducive to support of the craze that was beginning to grow.

Repression and Inquisition

From the eleventh century till the mid-thirteenth the strongest source of pressure on witches was popular hysteria, which was expressed both in influence upon the law and in violence outside the law. The hatred of dissenters and infidels that produced the Crusades and the pogroms also brought about a number of lynchings of alleged witches, and on the other side there is no evidence in the Middle Ages of any popular resistance either to lynchings or to judicial procedures against witches.[20]

Because of popular pressure and because of the revival of Roman law, legal proceedings against heretics, sorcerers, and witches became increasingly harsh. This harshness and inflexibility in turn fixed the common image of the witch all the more firmly, so that legal cruelty and mass hysteria reinforced one another. Before the thirteenth century, moderation in the legal repression of dissenters was the rule, so that in 1080 Pope Gregory VII could write to King Harold of Denmark to beware of blaming unfortunate women for sickness, frosts, and other untimely events.[21]

In the eleventh century, and even more in the twelfth, punishments and procedures on the part of both secular and religious courts became more severe. Theologically the position of the dissenter was weak. To most medieval theologians, no illegitimate violence was being done to the Jews, infidels, and heretics put to the sword at the behest of the Church: these people had no rights to be violated. Although theology recognized that all men were made in the image of God and even that Christ had died for all men, the infidels by virtue of their deliberate choice of error had cut themselves off from humanity. St. Augustine believed that the individual had no right to dissent. He and those who followed him insisted that error had no rights and that ignorance of the law of God was no excuse.[22] St. Thomas Aquinas leaned at one point in the direction of the rights of conscience but then went on to argue that heresy must be a sin because such a degree of ignorance must be the result of criminal negligence. Abelard's insistence upon the absolute right of the informed conscience of the individual was almost unique in medieval moral philosophies.

The Church's most common justification for its use of force, one congenial to the medieval spirit, was the argument that it was legitimate to force to salvation those who would otherwise reject it. The passage of Luke 14:17–24, "Compel them to come in," was frequently cited as authority for the idea that torture or threat of death might bring about a salutary repentance. If all else failed and the accused had to be executed, the hope remained that in his last moments he might repent and reconcile himself to God. Another common argument was that heresy was treason. The *crimen laesae majestatis* was a crime punishable by death in the Roman Empire, and the Christian emperors and their lawgivers early associated religious dissent against Christ with political dissent against the emperor. The Theodosian Code (IX, xiv, 3) and the *Corpus Juris Civilis* of Justinian (IX, viii, 5), themselves based upon preceding imperial constitutions, affirmed that heresy was *lèse-majesté* against Christ, and therefore was as much more worthy of death than was treason against the emperor as the majesty of Christ was greater than that of any earthly lord.[23]

The revival of Roman law in the late eleventh and twelfth centuries generally produced heavier punishments for crime, and sorcery was no exception. In the *Treuga Henrici* of 1224, burning is decreed for all sorcerers and relapsed heretics in the Empire.[24] Both the *Sachsenspiegel* (1225) and the *Schwabenspiegel* (c. 1275), with the city laws that followed their examples (like those of Hamburg in 1220, Bremen in 1303, and Lübeck in 1400), decreed burning for magic, including invocation of the Devil. From the late thirteenth century, royal courts, particularly in the France of Philip IV, were very active in using sorcery and witch trials to political advantage. The contention of Lea and Hansen that the secular courts never prosecuted for witchcraft before 1400 is absolutely erroneous unless witchcraft is defined in such a way that it did not exist before 1400.[25]

But the prosecution of witches was based upon the heresy trials rather than upon those for sorcery, and burning was increasingly used as a punishment for relapsed heretics from the beginning of the eleventh century, first by the secular courts and then by the Church. The choice of fire as the preferred means for extirpating dissenters is explained on the deepest levels by the purificatory power attributed to that element in most mythologies, and in Christianity the choice was reinforced by the analogy with hell and by the numerous examples of purificatory fire in the Old and New Testaments.[26] The Jews, Greeks, Teutons, and Romans all used burning as a punishment for certain serious crimes, and the non-Christian Romans set at least one precedent for the burning of dissenters in Diocletian's edict of 297 ordering death by fire for the leaders of the Manichaeans.

The most direct reason for the adoption of the stake in the Middle Ages, however, was that it provided a substitute for the ordeal by fire which was gradually abandoned in the course of the twelfth century. Ordeal by fire was used by almost all the Indo-European peoples, including the Teutons and the Greeks, the idea being that fire, a manifestation of divine power, will be prevented by that power from harming the innocent. The ordeal was in common use in early medieval courts, and both Rufinus and Gregory of Tours indicate that it was at least occasionally used to prove heretics or infidels wrong—if they shirked the test or were hurt in it, God was not with them. The ordeal was finally banned by the Fourth Lateran Council in 1215: Roman law, its influence on the rise, was skeptical of the value of ordeals; other alternatives, like the jury system, began to be used in some countries; and canonists and theologians were increasingly in-

150

clined to argue that the ordeal was superstitious and a violation of the injunction of Deuteronomy 6:16, "Ye shall not tempt the Lord your God." No such pall of superstition hung round execution by fire, which was no temptation of God but a straightforward delivery of the wicked into his hands.[27]

The first burning for heresy in the Middle Ages is hinted in the case of Vilgard of Ravenna, c. 1000, but the first fully attested incident was at Orléans in 1022, followed by Monforte in 1028. Through the eleventh and most of the twelfth century, burning was unusual, being unprovided for in the law codes. This defect was remedied at the end of the twelfth century. Pedro II of Aragon in 1197 ordered the burning of heretics who relapsed and reentered the country after banishment, and Innocent III in 1198 called for the execution of heretics whenever the ban of excommunication was ineffective against them. Pressed by the successes of the Catharists in southern France, Innocent in 1198, using the phrase, "treason against Christ," called for exile and confiscation of property as just punishments for dissenters. Frederick II's strong measures against heretics in 1224, 1231, 1238, and 1239 were endorsed by the Church. As early as 1184, Lucius III had hinted at burning for heretics by referring to the passage of John 15:6, "If a man abide not in me, he is cast forth as a branch, and is withered; and men gather them, and cast them into the fire, and they are burned." Honorius III (1227), the council of Toulouse (1229), and Gregory IX (1231) endorsed Frederick's policies, and the endorsement became canon law when published as part of Gregory's Decretal collection of 1234. The tradition of burning heretics was of course turned against witches to the degree that witchcraft was assimilated to heresy. From the fifteenth century onward, witches were treated even more severely than heretics, being burned upon first conviction rather than upon relapse.

The increasing use of force, involving crusades against both heretics and infidels, and pogroms against the Jews, as well as the legal execution of heretics and witches, was also manifest in the increasing use of torture by both secular and ecclesiastical courts. Torture—the use of coercion to extract confession or the implication of others—played an enormous role in the development of witchcraft from the thirteenth century onward. We are aware of how "courts of justice" proceed in some countries today and how innocent men will confess to monstrous crimes once they have been broken by prolonged torture. Men were no hardier in the Middle Ages. After days of unrelenting torment, coupled with the despair of knowing how few people ever escaped death by maintaining their innocence, it was a rare defendant who could continue to resist.[28]

Unfortunately for theories of progress, torture derived less from the "primitive barbarism" of the so-called "Dark Ages" than from the refined law of the later Roman Empire, and it grew during the Renaissance and Reformation, beginning to decline only in the seventeenth century before its reintroduction in the twentieth. It is no coincidence that the witch hysteria was at its height precisely in the period when torture was most widely used. Torture did not create witchcraft, for witchcraft already existed, but it was responsible for fanning the flames of popular hysteria into the holocausts of the sixteenth and seventeenth centuries.

Under the Roman Republic, slaves and foreigners had been subject to judicial torture under certain circumstances, but under the Empire it was first introduced for treason and then extended to poisoning, adultery, sorcery, and other serious crimes. It appears in the *Digest* (XLVIII, 18) of Justinian, whence it passed into medieval practice at the time of the revival of Roman law. Teutonic law generally did not permit torture, though some Teutonic codes influenced by Roman law did allow it on a very limited basis, usually only for slaves. In the early Middle Ages its use was very limited and almost always illegal, but with the rediscovery of the *Digest* in the late eleventh century, it was revived. Still restricted in the twelfth century, it was extensively adopted in the thirteenth by the secular powers, the kingdom of France for example, as well as the kingdom of Jerusalem and many of the Italian cities, and it continued to spread in the fourteenth and fifteenth.

The attitude of the Church changed at much the same time. Torture was universally condemned by the earlier theologians and canonists (for example, St. Augustine) as well as by popes like Gregory the Great and Nicholas I. As late as Gratian's *Decretum,* canonists opposed torture, but even as Gratian wrote, it was increasingly, if illegally, used in many episcopal courts. In the course of the thirteenth century, it obtained general ecclesiastical approval. The reasons for the change are unclear, but some may be surmised. First, the Church was following the example of the secular courts; second, it was influenced by the *Digest;* third, it was increasingly tightly organized and intolerant of deviation, while at the same time the number of dissenters was growing at an alarming rate; fourth, it used torture to some extent as a substitute for the ordeal (the idea still being that God would protect the innocent from false confessions); and fifth, the procedures enjoined upon the Inquisition induced that body to favor the use of torture, for under Inquisitorial rules no one could be convicted without a confession, which was usually not obtainable except under duress. Though the authorities tried to limit the use of torture within strict boundaries, it soon became a monstrous blot upon the record of the medieval Church. In 1252, in his bull *Ad Extirpanda,* Pope Innocent IV ordered civil authorities to apply torture in cases of heresy so long as it did not take life or injure limb. Alexander IV and his successors authorized the use of torture by the Inquisition directly.

As long as heresy remained a minor threat, responsibility for the correction of dissent was left in the hands of the bishops. But with the growth of both heresy and ecclesiastical efficiency, the popes began to press for firmer measures. At the council of Verona in 1184, Lucius III left the prosecution of heresy in the jurisdiction of the bishops but required them once or twice a year to visit, or to cause their officials to visit, any parish suspected of being infected with heresy. This episcopal inquisition was simply a variety of the regular episcopal visitation in which the bishop sought out and prosecuted all violations of canon law, and analogous to the inquests of civil law and administration by the secular authorities.

A further step was taken by Innocent III. Previously, canon law, including the codifications of Ivo and Gratian, had forbidden one and the same person to act as both prosecutor and judge, but in a number of bulls Innocent allowed a judge to try a defendant for a notorious crime even when there was no accuser, and to act as both judge and prosecutor, this procedure being confirmed by the Fourth Lateran. In certain serious matters, including heresy, the prisoner was now obliged to answer the judge's questions on oath, this being termed a procedure *per inquisitionem*. The inquisition became standard procedure in canon law. Such inquisitions were directed at all ecclesiastical crimes and misdemeanors, such as simony or blasphemy, but it was against heresy that they were most widely used.[29]

The inquisition remained under episcopal control even after the Catharists and Waldensians had alienated much of southern France from the Church, and in 1209 at Avignon and at Montpelier the arrangements of 1184 were confirmed. Before contemplating the establishment of a papal Inquisition the papacy in its efforts to repress dissent turned first to the preaching of the mendicant orders and then to the Crusade. Even the great Fourth Lateran Council of 1215 did not take this step, although it for the first time established papal legates with special commissions to investigate heresy.

Gregory IX (1227–1241), terrified of heresy, step by step initiated the procedures that created the centrally directed Inquisition. In 1227 he sent Konrad of Marburg as legate with a commission to investigate heresy according to the provisions of 1215. After the end of the Albigensian war in 1229, the pope took further measures to make sure that the defeated heresies would not revive: in 1231 he issued a bull defining ecclesiastical legislation against heretics more carefully and entrusting the execution of this legislation to the mendicants, especially the Dominicans; in the following year and again in 1233 their authority was confirmed and extended. In 1233 Konrad of Marburg was established as papal Inquisitor in Germany, and in 1235 Robert le Bougre became his counterpart in France. Thus the papal legislation of 1227–1235 established the Inquisition as a centralized institution staffed by the Dominicans and, to a lesser extent, by Franciscans, and directed from Rome.

The power of the Inquisition was repeatedly corroborated in subsequent decades by papal bulls such as *Ad extirpanda* of Innocent IV, issued on May 15, 1252, a terrible measure against heretics in Italy, authorizing seizure of their goods, imprisonment, torture, and, on conviction, death, all on minimal evidence. This appalling document was reconfirmed, though with some revisions, by Alexander IV and later by Clement IV (1265–1268).[30]

As the Church fortified itself against heresy, it also moved further in the direction of assimilating sorcery to heresy. The statutes of the Cistercian order in 1240 declared that "the crime of sorcery is a kind of heretical depravity," by that time a commonly accepted opinion.[31] The manuals that began to appear in 1230, advising Inquisitors how to proceed, often included questions on witchcraft as well as on more conventional heresy. A formulary from Southern France in 1270 tells the Inquisitor to ask the accused whether he has done anything that pertains to the worship of demons, whether he has invoked demons to help him foretell the future, or whether he has offered them sacrifice. Another French formulary of 1280 inquires whether the prisoner has called up demons in his chambers or at crossroads.[32]

The efforts of the Inquisitors to increase their jurisdiction by extending it to sorcery became quite open, and they endeavored to persuade Pope Alexander IV (1254–1261) to remove sorcery from the jurisdiction of the bishops and turn it over to them. Though he firmly refused to do so, he allowed them a hole in the dike which they quickly enlarged.[33] The Inquisition, Alexander said, was too occupied with more important matters to be able to busy itself with sorcery, but in cases where the sorcery clearly involved heresy (*sapere heresim manifeste*), it would be under their jurisdiction. From that moment, the Inquisitors exerted themselves through use of the theory of implicit pact and all other means at their disposal to identify sorcery with heresy whenever it was to their advantage.

The attitude of the Inquisition in the 1250s is typified by the work of Stephen of Bourbon, Inquisitor in southern France from 1235. Demons ride out in the shape of wolves and kill children, Stephen asserts. Or they appear in the nursery in the shape of women and suck the children's blood. The wild chase appears in Stephen's *Anecdotes* in several forms: A rustic sees a pack of hunting hounds running after the prey and followed by a crowd of foot and horse soldiers who told him they were the retinue of King Arthur. Old women believe, though falsely, that they fly out at night on sticks with Diana and Herodias. They call themselves the *bonae res* and assemble at night to worship these goddesses.[34]

Stephen was able to follow the skepticism of the *Canon Episcopi* about the reality of the flight and at the same time to believe that there were indeed women who worshiped false deities. In one of his stories, an old woman, wishing to please her priest, said to him one day in church: "Sir, you ought to be very grateful to me, for I have saved you from death. For when I was riding out with the *bonis rebus* we entered your house with torches in the middle of the night. Seeing you lying naked asleep, I covered you up quickly so that our ladies (Diana and Herodias) might not see your nakedness, for if they had done, they would have whipped you to death." When the priest asked how they had entered the house when it was locked up, she replied that they had no difficulty passing through walls or locked doors. The priest was less impressed by her powers than by her credulity, called her a sortilega, and beat her soundly for her folly.

Stephen also tells of male roisterers in another place who like to dress themselves up as women. Entering the house of a rich farmer, they danced about, singing, "We take one and give back a hundred," referring to the powers of the bonae to confer prosperity upon a house in which they have been given presents. The farmer's wife appeared and tried to put an end to their revel, but they began carrying all the goods out of the house, saying to her: "Be quiet and close your eyes. You shall be rich, because we are the *bonae res*, and your goods will be multiplied."

Far worse than the bonae were the women near Clermont, Lyon, and in the Auvergne, who met at night, held orgies, and had ritual intercourse with the Devil. Stephen himself interviewed a woman who told him that she lived in a house where people were accustomed to assemble for a feast at an empty table. When they sat down at their places, a small black cat appeared, climbed up to the table, and walked around it in a circle. Immediately the table was spread with dishes of various fine foods, and the people fell to with gusto. Stephen doubted the veracity of the tale. The curious thing is the appearance of the black cat, which form the Devil habitually took at the witch assemblies.

On another occasion, a woman who had been arrested for maleficium told Stephen the following story. She had a mistress who frequently led her to an underground place where a crowd of men and women assembled with torches and candles. They gathered round a large vessel full of water into which a rod had been thrust (a fertility rite?). The master then called upon Lucifer to come to them. Thereupon a cat of hideous appearance descended the rod into the room. Dipping his tail into the water, he brought it out wet and used it as an aspergill. Then the lights were all extinguished, and each person seized his neighbor in promiscuous embrace. The woman expressed her willingness to identify those whom she had seen in the cavern and promptly accused others who had been arrested at the same time. This case is typical of Inquisitorial proceedings not only in content but in procedure. Here, for the first, but scarcely the last, time in the history of witchcraft the accusation is lodged by one of the accused against the others, either as the result of torture or in the hope of obtaining mercy.

For it was Inquisitorial procedure even more than Inquisitorial beliefs that helped create the witch hysteria. The Inquisition readily adopted torture, now sanctified in canon law, and justified it as a weapon against the snares of the Devil. The Inquisition was fighting the dark lord far more than the witches who lay under his power, and, however weak *they* might be, *he* had the power and guile to resist all normal means of getting at the truth. More practically, the Inquisitors favored torture because canon law required a confession for conviction, and torture could produce a confession when all else failed.[35] The principles by which the Inquisition would operate for centuries were established in the thirteenth: torture; the protection of the identity of accusers and of witnesses from the accused; the use of informers, paid or unpaid; the refusal to hear defense witnesses; the lack of counsel for defendants; the reading of the charges to the defendant in a vernacular deliberately translated faultily from Latin so that the replies could be entered against the original Latin, sometimes to exactly the opposite effect of what the prisoner had actually said; and denial of appeal.[36]

The Inquisitors were taught what to look for, and they almost always found it, whether it existed or not. The madness reinforced itself, for each conviction crystallized the image of the witch in the popular consciousness and convinced with its resonance generations of future Inquisitors that the crime of witchcraft was real.

The Heretic Witches

The first papal Inquisitor in Germany, Konrad of Marburg, did not take long to produce a crop of witches more diabolical than any that had before been seen.[37] That Konrad did not invent the heresies out of whole cloth is made evident by their alleged doctrines, which are partly Catharist and partly antinomian in nature. In 1224 there had already been a synod at Hildesheim in which a Premonstratensian named Heinrich Minneke was condemned for having written that matrimony was useless and that the Devil would one day be restored to grace. In 1231 three different groups of heretics were reported at Trier. Two were in the Reformist or Catharist tradition, but the third was alleged to have stranger rites, including kissing the face of a pale man or the anus of a cat. Bishop Thierry II held a synod and on the basis of the evidence condemned three women to the stake, one of whom, named Luckard, claimed that Lucifer had been unjustly cast down from heaven and would ultimately, she hoped, regain his rightful place. Here is the Catharist hidden God identified with Lucifer.[38]

Whatever initial justification there might have been for Konrad's Inquisition, he did more to cause than to dissipate trouble. Shortly after he arrived in the Rhineland, the archbishop of Mainz and a Dominican, Bernard, himself a papal official, wrote to Pope Gregory IX that Konrad had been forcing innocent people to confess by threatening them with the stake if they refused. According to his critics, he had claimed that an image of Lucifer at Cologne gave out oracles, and they themselves had with incredulity heard the confession of a man who had been subjected to his intimidations. The man confessed to having given the kiss of peace to a cat, a pallid man, and other diabolical monsters. Both the writers of the letter and the chronicler who reports the incident expressed their doubt that such things really occurred.[39]

Yet the historian is obliged to be skeptical even of skeptics. In the first place, the bishops were envious of the power bestowed upon the Inquisitors by the pope. Konrad, not a tactful man, was naturally opposed by the bishops; eventually they obtained his recall. Alberic, the chronicler, violently hated Konrad and was happy to discredit him in any way he could. And Alberic even qualifies his own skepticism, admitting that not all that Konrad reported could be illusion, for Luciferan ideas had indeed been imported into the Rhineland by a teacher from Toulouse.

Unfortunately Pope Gregory IX was less skeptical. Obsessed as he was by his fear of heresy, he was willing to believe any allegation and to accept any method. On March 13, 1233 he wrote to the Rhenish bishops urging that they support Konrad with greater zeal. Then, on June 13, 1233, he issued his bull *Vox in Rama*, warning the archbishop of Mainz and the bishop of Hildesheim of the terrible beliefs and practices reported to him by the Inquisitor.[40]

The heretics, Gregory told his bishops, have secret meetings. When a postulant wishes to become a member of their congregation, he is led into the midst of the meeting, whereupon the Devil appears in the form of a toad, goose, or duck, as a black cat with erect tail which descends a statue backwards to meet his worshipers, or as a thin, pale man with black, shining eyes. The postulant kisses the apparition either on the mouth or on the anus. When he has done, the master of the sect, and then the other initiates, also give the obscene kiss. After songs and a short liturgy, the lights are extinguished in order that a bisexual orgy may more comfortably occur. When everyone has been satisfied, the lights are relit, and thereupon a man emerges from a corner. From the waist upwards he shines like the sun; below the waist he is covered with hair. The master hands him part of the new initiate's clothing and then retires.

Among the doctrines of these heretics is that they must go to communion every Easter, keep the host in their mouths until they return home, and then spit it out into the privy. God has unjustly cast Lucifer down into hell, they maintain. Lucifer is the true creator, and one day he will cast the usurper God out of heaven and return to his pristine glory, leading all his followers with him to perfect happiness. Consequently his worshipers render all obedience to him and totally renounce the false God of the Christians.

Similar to the tradition of *Vox in Rama* is a confession by a heretic named Lepzet.[41] The initiate to the sect, he reports, must formally renounce the sacraments of the Church. A pale-faced man in black, of terrifying appearance, appears, and the postulant kisses him. Then a huge frog, as big as a pot, with a gaping eye, materializes, and this also he kisses. He is then considered initiated, and he returns to the house of the master of the sect. When the sectaries wish to practice their religion, they go secretly into a cave beneath the master's cellar. There their bishop (the master?) bares his buttocks, into which he inserts a silver spoon with which he offers an oblation. Then the congregation kiss the master's backside. After this, they all stand or sit around a pillar, up which a huge cat climbs until he reaches the top, where a lamp has been placed. There the animal clings, lifting up his tail so that everyone may kiss his anus. Then the cat puts out the light and each person carnally embraces the one next to him, "masculi in masculos et feminae in feminas."

These heretics, who are named "Cathari" in the manuscript, believed that the God of heaven is the evil god who unjustly cast Lucifer out of heaven. They called Lucifer their father and said that he was the creator of all visible things, including human bodies (scarcely an orthodox Catharist point of view). At the end of the world, Lucifer would regain his power with the help of the Antichrist, who would be engendered by the carnal union of the sun and the moon.

Lepzet confessed publicly that for five years he had worn a hair shirt in mourning for Lucifer's exile. He received communion three times a year, hiding the host in his mouth and taking it home and burning it. He had personally killed thirty people in accordance with the teaching of the sect that murder is a sacrifice pleasing to their God, Lucifer. He and his friends also accepted as virtues other deeds that Christians call sins. They condemned marriage as fornication but approved incest. If a man wished to sleep with his mother, he must pay her 18d. according to the rules of the sect: 6d. for having conceived him, 6d. for bearing him, and 6d. for nursing him. A man might sleep with his daughter for 9d., but the best bargain was a sister, who cost only 6d. Sodomy was perfectly acceptable. In addition to these tenets, Lepzet's group held some beliefs that were much closer to orthodox Catharism, including the abstention from meat, milk or other products associated with reproduction, the conferring of grace by the imposition of hands, and the use of endura if they wished to become martyrs.

The confession of Lepzet and the charges reported by *Vox in Rama* could be dismissed as fabrications extorted by the Inquisition. However, Lepzet's confession was made to a secular court. Moreover, much of what he said shows the influence of Catharism and antinomianism. We are, then, probably dealing with real heretics. But what is believable in the charges? The apparition of huge toads and obscene cats can scarcely be accepted, but not much else is wholly unbelievable or even, within the context of the heretical background, improbable. Even the pallid or hairy men can be explained without recourse to the supernatural if one remembers the long-lived custom of dressing in the clothes of animals for ritual purposes. A manuscript of 1280 (like one of about 1325) shows pictures of maskers dressed as stags, donkeys, hares, or bulls.[42]

The rest can easily be explained as offshoots of heretical tradition, Catharist or antinomian. Discontented individuals coming under the influence of heretical teachings might well agree that this world was created by an evil God, and that God's enemy, Lucifer, is consequently good. They would accept with the greatest pleasure the idea that Lucifer would triumph at the end of the world and lead them with him to eternal bliss. And they would then quite naturally decide that in order to obtain this reward they must worship him here on earth in the way he wishes. Much of what was alleged against these heretic-witches had been thought or done by earlier heretics, and very little was not done later by modern Satanists of one kind or another. The most important point is that the phenomenon of witchcraft, the idea of witchcraft, had grown and was reinforced, but the further likelihood that the phenomenon existed in the minds of the accused as well as in those of the accusers cannot be dismissed.

No other witchcraft cases that we know of in the thirteenth century were as rich in detail as those just considered. At Maastricht in 1234 a *nigromanticus* from Toledo taught the citizens how to practice magic and invoke the Devil. At Mont-Aimé in 1239 there was a trial of Catharists in which one of the accused said that she was carried through the air to Milan on Good Friday in order to wait upon the Catharists at a banquet.

She could go without fear of detection because she had left a demon in her shape in bed with her husband. Imprecise reports of witchcraft come from Pistoia in 1250. At Toulouse in 1275 Angèle de la Barthe, a 56-year-old woman of moderate wealth, was tried by the Inquisition. She was accused of having intercourse every night over a period of years with an incubus. Of this unholy union was born a child who was half wolf and half snake: for two years he feasted on small children and then disappeared. It is doubtful that such peculiar silliness was suggested to Angèle by the Inquisition; far more likely, she was mad. In any event, the pitiless institution delivered her to the secular arm to be burnt.[43]

The old notion of the witch's flight was not only retained but began to make its appearance in art, the earliest picture of a witch riding a broom being in the cathedral at Schleswig and dating from about 1280.[44] At Conserans in 1280, Bishop Auger II ordered that no woman should be permitted to maintain that she rode out at night with Diana, Herodias, or Bensoria.[45] This is a significant change from the *Canon Episcopi*, for it clearly places the blame on the women themselves, not on those who believe them.

One of Margaret Murray's favorite tales was the story of John, priest of Inverkeithing, who in Easter week 1282 went about to the villages of his parish summoning little girls to a celebration. At the church, he led them in a circular dance around an image of fertility, carrying about a representation of a phallus upon a pole in order to excite them. On another occasion, he ordered penitents to perform their penance by stripping and whipping one another with goads. John was eventually murdered by an irate parishioner. His murder is certainly not surprising, and the theory that it is proof of the persistence of a fertility cult in Scotland, as Miss Murray would have liked, is supported by no other evidence. John, like Angèle de la Barthe, evidently had a not entirely balanced personality. Nothing in the Inverkeithing case makes it a part of the tradition out of which classical witchcraft was formed.[46]

The fourteenth century would now see the further development of that tradition, which was still being built on the basis of antinomian heresy and Inquisitorial pressures. The extremely acute social pressures of that century, famines, plagues, and wars, would provide increasing fuel for the Inquisitors' fires.

7

Witchcraft and Rebellion in Medieval Society, 1300-1360

ONDITIONS in the fourteenth century continued to encourage the development of witchcraft. The centralization of ecclesiastical government proceeded at Avignon as it had at Rome, and canon law, ever more detailed, still followed the harsh example of Roman law in regard to heretics and witches. The power and scope of the Inquisition expanded, especially in France, Germany, the Netherlands, and northern Italy, areas where heresy and witchcraft continued to be strong. Heretical movements, especially of the antinomian variety, became increasingly popular. On the other side of the coin, so did violent repression of both heretics and infidels.

Not only heretics but also Jews were sometimes identified with witches in the popular mind. The terms "synagoga," and later "sabbat," were applied, as an indictment of Judaism, to the witches' assembly. The kidnapping and ritual murder of Christian children and the desecration of the Eucharist were ascribed to both Jews and witches. In 1322, a woman of Ehingen, in Swabia, stole the Eucharist from the altar and hid it so that she might use it in her incantations. When the townspeople discovered the crime, they immediately assumed the Jews were guilty and killed eighteen of them. Only belatedly was the real culprit, who was a Christian, found and burned.[1]

Yet, curiously, the identification of the witch with the social outcast did not go as far as it might. The supposedly Jewish custom of blasphemously stabbing the Eucharist was never alleged against the witches. Witches were seldom accused of poisoning wells, though the crime was frequently charged to Jews, lepers, and other hated minorities. It is amazing that the Inquisitors never identified witchcraft with leprosy. The disease was commonly believed to be a product of moral decay, and lepers were spurned not only because of fear of contagion but also because they were considered evil. Fear of contagion may have kept the Inquisitors from prosecuting lepers. Or it may be that the Inquisitors preferred not to limit their supply of victims by identifying them with a readily recognizable group. They may even have been restrained by pity and Christian mercy. It is even more astonishing that the mobs who persecuted and lynched lepers never thought to view them as witches, especially since the whiteness of the lepers' skin might have seemed a manifestation of the pallidity associated with heretics and demons.[2]

As the conditions producing witchcraft in the thirteenth century grew more pronounced in the fourteenth, the phenomenon itself grew in magnitude. There were new circumstances as well. For the first time, the witch phenomenon was deliberately encouraged by leaders of Church and state for the simple political reason that one could accuse one's enemies of witchcraft almost with impunity. Not everyone could be credibly accused of being a Jew or a leper, and to force elaborate confessions of doctrinal heresy was exceedingly complicated. But almost anyone could be made to appear to be a witch. The secrecy of procedure permitted accusations of witchcraft to be made without much fear of retribution. Thus public policy and private spite exacerbated popular fear of witchcraft until almost any accusation could immediately gain wide credibility.

Political cynicism and totalitarian measures were manifestations of the deterioration in medieval society that began in the four-teenth century. The increase in witchcraft is best understood in the context of this general deterioration.

The changes that began around 1300 were so fundamental that many modern historians have chosen this date to mark the end of the Middle Ages and the beginning of the age of transition known, depending on one's point of view, as the "Renaissance" or the "Autumn of the Middle Ages." Politically, the notion of a united Christian society was shattered in the course of the ensuing century. The power of the Empire was enormously reduced. The papacy became subject to pressures on the part of the national states, and by the end of the century a schism had reduced respect for the institution throughout Europe. Empire and papacy, though often mutually hostile, had both stood for a united Christian society. Now the kings of France and England, the Italian cities, and the German princes were establishing sover-eignty at a local level and all but forgetting the old ideals of unity. Rational scholasticism had lost its dominance of intellectual and religious life: undermined by the skepticism of Ockham, it yielded in prestige on the one hand to empiricism and on the other to mysticism. Both politically and intellectually, the individual was losing his well-defined place in the scheme of things, and the resultant feelings of anomie made it much easier for kings, Inquisitors, or, for that matter, heretics and witches to manipulate him.[3] Later, kings and princes would have the will to compel resistance to the Church, as well as compliance with it; the result would be the strong national heretical movements of Hussitism and, eventually, of the Reformation.

Underlying the political and cultural dislocations of the four-teenth century were the terrible economic and social crises caused by unusually severe wars and famines, and the long series of plagues, of which the Black Death of 1347–1349 was only the most famous and severe. The population, which had been growing rapidly for three hundred years, was now suddenly reduced. This caused a restructuring of the economy and of the social institutions, such as feudalism and manorialism, that had operated within the framework of the old economy. Farms, villages, and manors were abandoned, but many towns actually increased their population through immigration, and the merchant and industrial classes began to acquire the power and wealth that would eventually lead to their domination of a more urbanized world. All these changes, shocking to a society that had been relatively stable for centuries, combined to create a new sense of alienation, an alienation that included a loss of faith in a Church that had failed to protect its people from these terrors, an alienation that increased the power of blackness over the minds of the people.[4]

One difficulty with explaining the rise of the witch craze in terms of the crises of the fourteenth century is that witchcraft continued steadily to expand its grip on the human spirit for another three hundred years. One might cite the troubles of the fifteenth, sixteenth, and early seventeenth centuries as further indications that witchcraft thrived on social dislocation, and one might then go on to argue that the relative calm of the period 1650–1750 put an end to witchcraft. Or one might attribute the decline of witchcraft to a decline in religious fervor, which reduced the zeal of both witches and witch hunters. But the most fundamental reason for the longevity of witchcraft may be that, after the terrors of the fourteenth century made the image of the witch more vivid than ever before, the political power of the princes and the popes, the procedures of the Inquisition, the harsh strictures of canon and civil law, and the opinions of the theologians united to fix that vivid picture in the European mind almost indelibly. In the fourteenth century the reality, and the dangerous power, of witchcraft became a *communis opinio theologorum*. It was also the common opinion of all mankind, scarcely

170

more to be questioned than the reality of the Incarnation or of the house next door. Indeed, the Reformation questioned the power of witchcraft far less than it did the efficacy of the sacraments, the communion of saints, or the authority of the pope.

Intellectual Judgments and Juridical Repression

Under these conditions intellectual justifications for the rapprochement of sorcery and heresy became general, although the old distinction between sorcery and witchcraft was still maintained. The great scientist Nicholas Oresme distinguished in good Aristotelian terms between natural and demonic magic, insisting that strange events were better explained in natural than in supernatural terms. Demons are active in the world, he argued, and those who follow them are witches, but in fact demonism is relatively uncommon, and we must treat the confessions of witch activities with some skepticism because they are often obtained under torture or the threat of torture. Such distinctions were not confined to intellectuals but were preached from the pulpit. Nor was witchcraft itself always identified with heresy. Sometimes it was, as it had been in the early Middle Ages, simply considered a sin. This was the opinion of the preacher Robert Brunne. "If ever you . . . have offered sacrifice to the Devil through witchcraft," he said, "you have sinned."[5]

The central question was still how to deal with witchcraft, under what rubric to prosecute it and to whose jurisdiction to entrust the prosecution. Alexander IV had forbidden the Inquisition to deal with sorcery or witchcraft unless it was clearly heretical. As the fourteenth century began, secular and episcopal courts were active more frequently than the Inquisition in sorcery cases, their zeal for the faith whetted by their hope for profit through sentences of confiscation. Philip IV of France in 1303 forbade the Inquisition to deal with sorcerers, usurers, and Jews so that he might himself profit by the actions, and Philip and most of his successors found not only economic but political profit in the sorcery and witch trials.[6]

In this the French rulers had before them the example of Pope John XXII, whose cynical, or fanatical, use of the Inquisition for political purposes was unparalleled. Trials specifically involving witchcraft will be dealt with at length later, but they must be understood in the context of even broader irresponsibility. John used the Inquisition, not only in sorcery trials, but in every way his ingenuity could discover. Again and again he accused his enemies of plotting against his life with incantations and wax dolls. The madness was checked only some years after his death: his successor Benedict XII in 1337 acquitted the Bishop of Béziers of having purposed the death of good Pope John.[7]

The trial of the Templars by Philip IV is one of the most notorious in history, but that king's example was assiduously followed by his successors. The reign of his son Louis X (1314–1316) was short but terrible: Enguerrand de Marigny, Pierre de Latilly, Jeanne de Latilly, and Francesco Gaetani were each accused of plotting at one time or another the magical destruction of the king, his brother Charles, or other members of the royal entourage. Nor was the noxious cloud generated at the court of Louis X contained there. It spread throughout the country, where rival noblemen accused one another of maleficent magic. It continued into the reign of his brother Charles IV (1322–1328), who tried Countess Matilda of Artois for magically poisoning his predecessor and then in 1326 went on to conduct trials in Toulouse against priests accused of plotting against his own life by magic. When the throne passed to the Valois, this lunacy became real insanity. In 1331 the first of the Valois kings, Philip VI, protected himself against a magical plot on his life, and the real terror of sorcery shown by his later successors, Charles V, Charles VI, Charles VII, and Louis XI drove them to the bounds of madness or beyond.[8] Other countries did not fear to imitate France, and Edward II used his French cousins' methods in 1324, when over twenty persons were tried for having attempted to bring about the death of the English king and his favorites by magic.[9]

While popes, kings, and nobles were using the courts for their own purposes, the Inquisition was trying, with some success, to extend its own jurisdiction over sorcery by identifying it with heresy. On August 22, 1320, John XXII had the cardinal of St. Sabina write the Inquisitors of Toulouse and Carcassonne, ordering them to prosecute sorcerers as heretics. The cardinal described the behavior of the alleged heretics in the old language of maleficium, charging that they used invocation and wax dolls, but adding the charge that they sacrificed to demons, paid homage to them, and, by giving a written contract or some other sign, made with them an express pact. On November 4, 1330, Pope John wrote the archbishops of Narbonne and Toulouse, their suffragans, and the Inquisitors of Toulouse and Carcassonne desiring all witch cases presently in court to be swiftly concluded and no new ones begun. The pope was not withdrawing the Inquisition's authority over witchcraft, as Lea suggested, but rather trying to get the Inquisition and the bishops to proceed in unison so as not to divide and weaken their efforts.[10]

John's successors, Benedict XII (1334–1342) and Gregory XI (1370–1378), followed him in encouraging Inquisition and bishops to press on together against the witches and the heretics. The idea of pact was the shallowest part of the stream that separated sorcery from heresy and witchcraft and the place where it could be most easily forded by the eager witch hunters. The canon extravagante, *Super illius specula,* issued by Pope John in 1326 or 1327, authorized the Inquisition to proceed against sorcerers since they had "made a pact with hell," sacrificing to demons and adoring them.[11]

The distinguished lawyer Oldrado da Ponte, defending an accused heretic before Pope John, argued that heresy, being a very serious crime, demanded both sure proof and initial careful definition. Simple sorcery, including love magic and abortion magic, is not heresy. The invocation of demons may be. If one calls up demons to *use* them, it is not heresy; if one adores them or offers them sacrifices, it is. Those who strove more assiduously to please the pope were stricter. About 1330 the Inquisitor Zanchino Ugolini wrote a treatise *Super materia haereticorum,* which brought sorcery much closer to heresy than Oldrado had done. Anyone who is excommunicated is a heretic cut off from the mystical body of Christ. Consequently anyone not in communion with the pope, including schismatics, Jews, or even pagans, is a heretic. John XXII had excommunicated all sorcerers; therefore all sorcerers were heretics. Another treatise written anonymously about 1330 by a supporter of the pope declared that sorcery was an exception to the rule that heresy is an intellectual error. The essential point is pact: if a pact, either implicit or explicit, has been made with demons, he who made the pact is a heretic. The canonist Johannes Andreae wrote, "Those are to be called heretics who forsake God and seek the aid of the Devil."[12]

There was no great distinction at this time between the procedures of the episcopal or secular courts against witchcraft and those of the Inquisition, and the popes made efforts to minimize even those distinctions that did exist. Nonetheless the Inquisition did try more cases and in a more standardized fashion, so that it must bear the prime responsibility for binding the crime of witchcraft to that of heresy. The formularies in the *Practica* (the influential Inquisitors' manual written about 1320 by Bernard Gui) mention, aside from such ordinary sorcery as the use of images or herbs, the abuse of the sacraments for magical purposes, the invocation of demons, paying them reverence or homage, and offering them sacrifice. Any kind of worship paid the Devil or demons, Gui said, constitutes idolatry and heresy.[13]

The Bonae and the Wild Ride

Gui also suggests that Inquisitors investigate the "women who are called the *bonae res* and who ride out at night," though it is not wholly clear from the context to what degree Gui believed in the reality of these good folk.[14] The *Fasciculus morum*, written by an English Franciscan at about the same time as Gui's work (1320), a treatise that became very popular among fourteenth-century preachers, devotes the chapter *De fide* to various forms of magic, among them the wild ride. Here we find, essentially, the *Canon Episcopi* under the influence of romantic tradition and folklore:

But, I ask, what is to be said of those wretched and superstitious persons who say that by night they see most fair queens and other maidens tripping with the lady Diana and leading the dances with the goddess of the pagans, who (i.e. maidens?) in our vulgar tongue are called *Elves,* and believe that the latter transform men and women into other shapes and conduct them to *Elvelond,* where now, as they say, dwell those mighty champions, Onewone and Wade, all of which are only phantoms displayed by an evil spirit? For, when the Devil has subjected the mind of anyone to such monstrous beliefs, he sometimes transforms himself now into the form of an angel, now of a man, now of women, now on foot, now as knights in tournaments and jousts, now, as has been said, in dances and other sports. As the result of all these things a wretch of this kind deludes his mind, when thus in manifold ways made captive by religious scepticism, into believing or narrating.[15]

The ride and the revels are illusions, to be sure, but they are illusions provoked by the Devil in the minds of those who believe they participate.

This is an important transition in the tradition of the wild ride, for though the old, simple skepticism of the canon is repeated in the fourteenth century, the illusion is now less often considered the belief in such belief, but the belief itself, which is much closer to an acceptance of the reality of witchcraft.[16] John Bromyard, a preacher who also associated the wild ride with fairyland, tells a story that illustrates the point. A priest found a woman in his parish who claimed that she could transport herself at night to join in these revels. He dared her to do it, and when she failed, he gave her a sound beating. Both Bromyard and the parish priest are skeptical, but the woman herself believes.

Another fourteenth-century story is ambiguous as to the reality of the bonae. Ribald peasants dressed as women came to a house at night, dancing and repeatedly chanting, "Take one and give back a hundred." Going through the house, they removed all that they wished but promised to return what they had stolen a hundredfold. The victims of the masquerade must have been ready to be convinced of the fairy powers of the bonae; still, these particular bonae were perpetrating deliberate fraud. An Italian treatise by Giacopo Passavanti (d. 1357) takes a further step away from skepticism. It asserts not only that the night riders themselves believed that they participated in the revels but that they identified their companions as witches. They boast, Passavanti says, "of going out at night and riding through the air with the witches."[17]

Heresy and Witchcraft

While popes and Inquisitors were solidifying the legal and theoretical amalgamation of witchcraft with heresy, the witch phenomenon continued in practice to draw upon actual heresy. The susceptibility of fourteenth-century society to strange ideas is illustrated by the wide outbreak of ritual flagellation following the Black Death. From 1349 till at least 1357 flagellants ranged through the Low Countries, Germany, and northern France, attracting large numbers of followers by preaching that through the penance of self-torment the wrath of God might be turned away. The authorities managed temporarily to repress the sect, but it sprang up again around 1400, following another severe outbreak of plague.[18]

The most important group of proto-witches in the fourteenth century were the Luciferans, whose doctrines were derived from Catharism and antinomianism, and who were sometimes even confused with the Waldensians. Luciferans were found in Austria, Brandenburg, and Bohemia, and their influence in the last country lingered on to affect the Adamites of the next century.[19]

The Luciferans are heard of for the first time in Austria between 1310 and 1315. Though they made no secret of worshiping the Devil, the name "Luciferan" had probably been invented by their enemies. Some have argued that the appearance of these witch-heretics in Austria and Bohemia, and also toward the end of the century in Switzerland and Savoy, shows that witchcraft developed from mountainous folk-origins. But the Austrian heretics appeared along the Danube in precisely the least wild part of Austria; and the other contemporary center of heretical and witch activity was in the populous area of Toulouse and Carcassonne. Witchcraft arose where heresy was strong and spread into the mountains on the heels of the Inquisition. In Austria, Luciferanism arose after the arrival in the country of antinomian Beghards from the west. In order to combat these Beghards, Bishop Bernhard of Passau (1285–1313) introduced the Inquisition into Austria, and it was his Inquisitors who rooted out the Luciferans.[20]

The Inquisitors found heretics in Styria in 1310 and tried them the following year. The doctrines of these heretics are not known, but those discovered in 1315 at Krems, down the Danube from Vienna, are Luciferan par excellence. These heretics had a bishop named Neumaister, who claimed to have functioned in that office for fifty years.* This might be an exaggeration, but the longevity of the sect is also attested in the confession of a young man named Andreas, who was burned with Neumaister and who claimed to have been brought up in the sect since childhood. The heretics boasted thirteen apostles, two of whom each year were taken up to heaven—possibly as some kind of ritual sacrifice or *endura*. Their authority derived in succession from the prophets Elias and Enoch, a curious elaboration which could indicate that the heretics had been at least indirectly exposed to the apocalyptic ideas and demonology of the ancient books of Enoch.

The heretics believed that the Catholic clergy was corrupt and faithless to the true God, arguing that the Jewish prophets were the true priests of the Church, a belief that is best explained as a curious perversion of Catharism. Evidently these heretics followed the Catharist argument that the God of the Old Testament was different from the God of the New Testament and that he was, in effect, the Devil; but they diverged sharply from the Catharists by arguing that this Old Testament Devil-God was to be worshiped. These beliefs were in fact a heresy of a heresy.

The heretics celebrated rituals in honor of Lucifer and argued that one day he would be restored with the other fallen angels to his rightful place in heaven while Michael and the archangels took his former place in hell. The heretics' hope was that they would accompany Lucifer when he took rightful repossession of his kingdom, and they hailed one another by saying: "May the injured Lucifer greet you." In another apparently direct slap at Catharist orthodoxy, they ate meat every day. They practiced sexual orgies underground at night, and they argued that whatever you do underground was permissible. A girl confessed to the Inquisitors that though she was a virgin above ground, her con-

* Is the name symbolic—New Master? Few heretics and fewer witches had bishops: this is probably a Catharist element.

dition below the earth was otherwise. Rejecting Catholicism as violently as Catharism, they dismissed as worthless the mass, the Eucharist, baptism, penance, matrimony, and prayers to the saints.

The Styrian heretics were numerous. At the stake, Neumaister claimed that he had 80,000 followers, and one of his disciples said that he had adherents in thirty-six villages and towns. Either these were gross exaggerations (Neumaister's figure is of course ridiculous) or the Inquisition was singularly lax, for in all it burned only about thirty—sixteen at Krems, eleven at St. Pölten, two in Vienna, and several at Hinnisperg. However, many others were tried and escaped the stake by recanting, and the testimony that the sect had existed for a long time reinforces the supposition that there were a good number of Luciferans at large. One of the sources indicates that there were many in Austria, Bohemia, and neighboring lands, and incidents continued to occur down to mid-century.[21]

In 1318 a Dominican prior named Arnold may have been assassinated by Austrian heretics, but the evidence is not clear; it is certain, however, that in 1315 the heretics were active in Prague. In that year a canon of St. Vitus Cathedral reported to Rome that the bishop of Prague, John of Drázik, had through laxity permitted heretics to spread throughout his diocese. The Bohemian Luciferans were similar to the Austrian: they had, however, an elaborate hierarchy, with an archbishop and seven bishops, each of whom ruled 300 heretics. They rejected the Church, the pope, and the idea of the Resurrection. They argued that Lucifer would one day triumph and lead them into heaven with him. They met at night and, with lights extinguished, the bishop led them in sexual orgies.[22]

In 1336 other heretics, who were called Waldensians but held the beliefs of Luciferans, appeared in Austria. At their meetings in caverns, Lucifer appeared to them as the king of heaven, arrayed in splendid crown, sceptre, and shining clothes, and followed by many retainers. After they had practiced a kind of blasphemous communion, the lights were extinguished and each took the one next him, "vir in virum, foemina in foeminam."[23]

In 1340, heretics were found in Salzburg who rejected the Church, the sacraments, and the Trinity. They argued that nothing done underground was sin, and they held orgies on Catholic feast days. They revered Lucifer, hoped for his restoration to heaven, and greeted one another with the words: "May he who has been cast down greet you; hail to you to whom dominion has come." In the same year at Salzburg, another incident occurred, possibly related to the above. A priest named Rudolf cast down a cup of consecrated wine on the floor, a sacrilege he had already committed once before at Halle. When apprehended by the officials, he argued that Jews and pagans might be saved without baptism, that Christ was not present in the Eucharist, and that the fallen angels would one day be restored to heaven because their sin was in thought rather than in action.[24]

As in Austria and Bohemia, so it was in Brandenburg. In 1336, the bishop of Magdeburg, with the help of the Inquisition, burned fourteen men and women of Angermünde as *Luciferiani*. Information about the heretics at Prenzlau in Brandenburg in 1384 is more precise: a clergyman there read a sermon to his congregation accusing them of believing that Lucifer was God or the brother of God. They held that in the beginning there had been war in heaven, and God had cast out his brother; later, Lucifer would cast God out, and his followers would join him in heaven. The heretics rubbed from their children the salt bestowed at baptism as protection against evil spirits; they denied that the host is Christ; they met at nights in cellars and made love promiscuously. They believed that the Devil transported them over long distances. The wild ride had for a long time been tied to maleficium. Now, for the first time since the Orléans trial of 1022, it is clearly conjoined with heresy, and in the form of flight.

Another step toward the amalgamation of heresy and witchcraft had been taken.[25]

In 1335 two trials for heresy, sorcery, and witchcraft occurred, at Toulouse and Carcassonne, in the area in which Catharist influence had been strongest. By this time Catharism had been almost entirely destroyed, and the Inquisitors were with papal encouragement widening the horizons of their attention. The account of these trials, the most extensive dealing with witchcraft up to that time, should expunge Lea's idea that John XXII intended by his bull of 1330 to prevent the Inquisition from investigating heretical witchcraft. The trials have always attracted the attention of historians of witchcraft because they are allegedly the first in which the term "sabbat" was used. Because the materials are known only in translation, the use of the name is uncertain, but new elements of the witch phenomenon appear for the first time in this, the most detailed description of the witch cult in the fourteenth century.[26]

The first of the two trials was held at Carcassonne on May 16, 1335, when seventy-four persons were accused before the Inquisition of magic or heresy, of whom fourteen were eventually executed by the secular arm.[27] Most of the charges dealt with old-fashioned maleficium, but some included witchcraft. A shepherd named André Cicéron said Mass naked so as to invoke the demonic powers necessary to prepare a magical compound from the bread and wine, arguing that this was the way our father Adam sacrificed. The Inquisitors took this statement as a heresy, for Adam did not of course say mass. To the historian the interesting aspect of the accusation is its prefiguration of the doctrines of the fifteenth-century Adamites in Bohemia. Two other shepherds, Catala and Paul Rodier were accused of calling up the Devil at crossroads and obtaining poison from him to use in the wells, a charge that was often lodged against Jews and lepers but was unusual in a trial for witchcraft. The two shepherds also sacrificed a black hen to Satan in order to bring the scourge of war upon the country.

Four women, Paule Viguier, Armande Robert, Matheline Faure, and Pierrille Roland, were accused of having boasted that they had once gone at night to a sabbat that had taken place atop Mount Alaric between Carcassonne and Narbonne. Although they denied this before the court, they were overwhelmed by the testimony of witnesses who claimed to have heard the boast. The women saved themselves from the stake by repeatedly professing their loyalty to the Church and their hatred of Satan and all his works.

The next month, June, a trial was conducted at Toulouse by Pierre Gui, Bernard's brother, and two general vicars of the archbishop of Toulouse, in line with the pope's wish to have the Inquisition and the bishops cooperate with one another. Sixty-three cases were heard, most of them having to do with sorcery, and eight persons were sent to the stake. The most interesting cases are those of Anne-Marie de Georgel and Catherine Delort, middle-aged women of Toulouse who were tortured and eventually burned as witches. They confessed that for twenty years they had been "members of the army of Satan" and that they had given themselves to him in this life and in the next. Their confessions are similar, but close to identical only in the parts dealing with doctrine rather than with practice, an indication that there may be reality here beyond the Inquisition's ability to elicit desired answers through torture. This is, however, one of the first witch trials in which torture is known to have been employed, and as such it was an evil omen for the future.

Both Anne-Marie and Catherine confessed that they had often attended the sabbat, which was held either Friday or Saturday night, sometimes in one place and sometimes in another, and that there were many people, both men and women, at the meetings. Anne-Marie said that she had entered the cult only through accident and fear. One Tuesday morning while she was alone doing the family washing, a gigantic man came walking on the surface of the water towards her. He had black skin, eyes that burned like coals, and he wore an animal hide. The thing asked her to give herself to him, and she replied, from fear and awe, that she would. Thereupon he blew into her mouth, and from the following Saturday onward she had the power of transporting herself to the assembly by a simple act of will. At the assembly, she would encounter a huge goat, to whom she would submit sexually in return for practical lessons on how to work maleficium of various kinds. This is the first ritual copulation with Satan on record. Previous witch accounts frequently mention sexual orgies among the worshipers, but here the diabolical president of the assembly himself engages in intercourse with the witch. Though both men and women attended the assemblies, accusations of witchcraft now begin with increasing frequency to be made against women in particular. This tendency was strongly reinforced by the idea of ritual copulation with the Devil, whose sex was usually supposed to be male. Demons could still take the shapes of either men or women and serve as both succubi and incubi, but the lord of the sabbat, the Devil himself, was almost always male. As a corollary, the female Diana and Herodias now appear less frequently as the leaders of the witch ride.

Among the skills that Anne-Marie learned was how to make different kinds of poisons and ointments, whose ingredients she obtained by digging up bodies from cemeteries and going to gallows to obtain clothing, hair, nails, and fat from the bodies of hanged criminals. This sort of activity also appears for the first time here.

The Inquisitors then went on to ask her the doctrinal basis of her beliefs. She replied, in terms that she had either adopted from Catharism or from the Inquisitors who forced her to confess to Catharist ideas, that God and the Devil were completely equal,

God ruling in heaven and the Devil ruling on earth. The souls who followed the Devil remained on earth after death or else in the air, supposedly as companions of the demons, who by current theology lived in both places. These ghosts wandered about, especially near the places where they had once lived, and tried to suggest to children that they follow Satan instead of God. God and the Devil would struggle for all eternity, but at this time Satan was in the ascendant. Anne-Marie hoped to share in his triumph. She now claimed to be penitent and pleaded to be reconciled to the Church, but her pleas were in vain, for she was delivered over to the secular arm to be burnt at the stake.

Catherine Delort confessed that ten years previously she had had an affair with a shepherd who had persuaded her to make a pact with Satan. He took her at midnight to a crossroads at the edge of a forest. There they built a fire, putting on it the remains of human bodies they had taken from a cemetery. She cut her left arm and let a few drops of her blood fall onto the burning mess, while speaking strange words which she did not now remember. Thereupon a demon named Berit appeared in the shape of a purplish flame, which evidently conferred upon her the power to do all kinds of maleficium.[28] Following her pact with Berit, Catherine would fall into a deep sleep every Saturday night, during which she would be transported to the witches' assembly, which was held in various locations in southern France. There she adored a goat, to whom she submitted sexually, and participated in a general orgy with the other members of the group. Together they ritually devoured the bodies of children stolen from their homes and drank loathsome potions. But they eschewed all salt. The lack of salt, mentioned for the first time in a witch ceremony, is of course a product of the ancient tradition that it could dispel evil spirits, a tradition long accepted by the Church in its use of salt at baptism. The ancient cannibalism of the strix or striga apparently here caused the idea of eating the children conceived during the sex orgies, as at Orléans, to develop into a general paedophagy. The belief in child eating must naturally have increased the general fear and loathing of the populace for the witches.

Another aspect of the case that became standard procedure in the later witch trials was the pressure placed upon Catherine to implicate others. Under repeated torture she was asked to name the people whom she met at the assembly, and she ended by yielding. Some of those she named were subsequently arrested and tried. When forced to explain the doctrines behind her beliefs, Catherine (whose story was otherwise quite different from Anne-Marie's) replied in singularly similar terms, adding only that the kingdom of Christ was drawing to a close and would soon be replaced by the kingdom of Antichrist, an idea that might have derived from a distorted view of Joachite millenarianism. Like Anne-Marie, Catherine was delivered to the secular arm to be burned.

The zeal of the Inquisitors of Toulouse and Carcassonne against the witches continued to the end of the century. Most of the cases dealt with ill-defined sorcery, but some included witch characteristics. In 1352, seven persons were condemned for beseeching a goat to take them to the witches' assembly. Although they had not succeeded in obtaining their wish, they were sentenced to twelve years in prison. At the same trial, eight others who had sold their souls to the Devil and taken part in magical ceremonies were sentenced to life imprisonment, while eight who had killed children with the evil eye or with incantations were sent to the stake. The following year, sixty-eight persons were arraigned before the Inquisition at Toulouse for magic and heresy. They had done acts of sorcery, danced in a magic circle, and parodied the ceremonies of the Church. In the second-hand form of the source which we have, there is no precise description of the dance, but if the story of the priest of Inverkeithing is dismissed as irrelevant, this is the first report of a ritual dance at the witch assembly. The influence of the sect of the dancers may have been stronger than has been imagined.[29]

One of the few trials associated with Italy during this century was conducted by the papal Inquisition in Lombardy with the cooperation of the bishop of Novara. At this trial a number of sorcerers were prosecuted, one of whom was a woman from Orta, a village in the diocese. She confessed that she had abjured Christ and baptism, that she had trampled on the cross, prayed to the Devil on her knees, and killed children with magic. The bishop and the Inquisitor, uncertain as to what they should do to her, referred the case to the great lawyer Bartolo of Sassoferrato, who judged that her actions betokened heresy and that she was worthy of death.[30]

Most of the trials for sorcery and witchcraft in the fourteenth century arose directly or indirectly from the Inquisition's efforts to bind sorcery to heresy. For the most part they contained no elaborate descriptions of witches' assemblies such as those found in the trials at Toulouse and Carcassonne in 1335. Indeed, there were numerous trials at both Carcassonne and Toulouse which had much to do with maleficium and invocations but involved little of a more specific nature regarding witchcraft.[31] In some cases the charges were closer to, though still distinct from, real witchcraft. At Carcassonne in 1329 a Carmelite monk named Peter Recordi was condemned by the Inquisition for having made images of wax, toads' blood, and spittle, consecrating them to the Devil and then hiding them in the houses of women with whom he purposed sexual intercourse. He was also accused of having called up Satan in person and sacrificed a butterfly to him; the reason for this particular choice of victim is unclear. In 1322, a woman at Ehingen in Swabia performed magic with the aid of a consecrated host. Her crime was not unusual, but the punishment indicates the hardening attitudes toward sorcery: she was burned at the stake for a heretic. On April 7, 1338, Pope Benedict XII ordered Guillaume Lombardi, provost of Bariol in the diocese of Fréjus, to investigate two women who had given themselves "souls and bodies" to the Devil and who in word and deed had done many "vicious and damnable things with him." In 1340, at one of the many trials for sorcery at Toulouse, a priest named Lucas de Lafond of Grenade (a village nearby) was tried by the Inquisition in 1340 for practicing necromancy and other magical ceremonies in which he performed blasphemous rites and desecrated the sacraments and sacramentals. He was sentenced to life imprisonment. In 1347, a *nigromanticus* went to the town of Torrenbüren, where he deluded people into believing that he could turn things into gold. He raised the bodies of the dead for his magical purposes and got a village woman with child, promising her that her offspring would be holier than John the Baptist. Such were the permutations of demonic absurdity in the fourteenth century.[32]

At the height of the controversy between King Philip IV of France and Pope Boniface VIII, the king held an assembly at the Louvre (June, 1303) in which Boniface was declared deposed. Among the oddly assorted charges brought against the pope was that of being a sorcerer. Even odder was the accusation that he had a familiar spirit.[33] Though sorcerers had long been supposed to have commerce with demons, the idea of a witch's familiar, a spirit that lives with him, follows him, and gives him advice and magical aid, became popular only in the fourteenth century. The concept of the familiar is closely related to that of the pet demon. It is no coincidence that the familiar and the pet name for the demon—Berit, Robin, and so on—appear at the same time. The fairy or kobold of folklore had become demonized, and sometime in the course of the late thirteenth century the popular imagination attached the folk demon to the witch. By the fourteenth century, as the action of King Philip attests, witchcraft's enemies had taken up the idea and attached it to the witch phenomenon.

By the end of the century it had become one of the important standard accusations deriving from folklore rather than heresy.

Often the familiar was supposed to exist in a purely spiritual form. But sometimes it was given a material shape, almost always the form of an animal. The roots of this notion are two: the animal forms that the Devil and demons had always taken, forms probably derived from the old hunting cults; and the even more ancient idea, found in the sorcery of many societies, that the sorcerer himself can change his shape. All these diverse ideas were now brought together.

In 1323, a priest at Château-Landon in the diocese of Sens promised a Cistercian abbot that he could recover lost property for him. He obtained a black cat, fed it bread dipped in holy water and chrism, and shut it up in a cage for three days. His intention was to kill the animal, cut its hide up into strips, and use the strips to make a magic circle into which he could summon the demon Berit or Berich in order to inquire as to the whereabouts of the treasure. Unfortunately, dogs found the cat in his cage and set up such a clamor that the contraption, and subsequently the entire plot, was discovered. The archbishop and the Inquisition held a joint trial and sentenced the priest and one of his helpers to the stake; the abbot and several canons regular who had been involved were degraded from their ecclesiastical offices.[34]

In 1325–1326, when Duke Frederick III of Austria was a prisoner, his brother Leopold summoned an expert nigromancer to summon up a demon to help. The spirit appeared as a poor, bleary-eyed traveler, with tattered shoes and a peasant's cap. His name was Truwesniet. He agreed to set Frederick free and straightaway transported himself, appearing to the prisoner as a poor scholar with a shawl wrapped round his shoulders. Frederick asked him who he was. "Never mind," Truwesniet replied. "Just come with me and I will take you to your brother." But Frederick, preferring prison to the company of even fraternally provided demons, made the sign of the cross and caused him to vanish.[35]

An interesting fourteenth-century case involving familiar demons, that of Alice Kyteler in Ireland, is well known.[36] Lady Alice, a wealthy woman of Kilkenny, had had four husbands, who had left all their property to her and to her eldest son, William Outlaw. The younger children, wishing to break the will, accused her before Bishop Richard Ledrede of Ossory of having bewitched her husbands. Richard condemned her as a heretic and a magician. One of her comrades, Petronilla of Meath, was flogged six times and then burned at the stake, the first burning for heresy in Ireland. Subsequently others of Alice's comrades, named by Petronilla under torture, were also punished, by burning, branding, beating, exile, or excommunication. A few hid and escaped punishment.

Alice's own case was appealed to Dublin, where considerable skepticism was expressed about her guilt. Bishop Richard, a Franciscan from London, was known to be arrogant and quarrelsome, and later he spent nine years in the prisons of the archbishop of Dublin for an unspecified heresy. During the appeal of Alice Kyteler, the seneschal Arnold le Poer, observing that until then no heresy had ever been found in Ireland, accused Ledrede of being a meddlesome Englishman who found heretics under every bed, and some of the other bishops grew so angry at Ledrede that they struck him. In the end, however, Alice and her companions were found guilty and her goods confiscated. She herself had meanwhile escaped to England, never to be heard of again.

The political ramifications of the trial are complex: Alice's son William Outlaw was a man of considerable guile and wide political connections, and though he had originally been one of the accused, he managed to escape simply by agreeing to do penance for having abetted heretics. No one knows who eventually acquired Alice's considerable properties, but she and her friends were clearly the victims of complex machinations prompted by politics and greed.

But politics do not explain all the remarkable features of the case. At the very least, we need to know why certain peculiar charges, heretofore unknown in the history of witchcraft, were made against a woman in a country where trials for heresy and sorcery had been nonexistent. Alice's was the first trial for heresy and sorcery in Ireland; and there was not to be another until the seventeenth century. In 1317–1320 Bishop Ledrede had called a synod which condemned a "new and pestilential sect in our parts," threatening priests and showing contempt for God and Church.[37] We have no further details on this sect, and, as Arnold le Poer suggested at Dublin, the bishop may have been too susceptible to finding a heretic in anyone who opposed him. It cannot be assumed that Alice's witchcraft derived from these alleged heretics. But then whence did it derive? Even if Ledrede was credulous, greedy, politically motivated, or all of these, and pursued Alice purely from spite, why were these particular charges made? Richard Ledrede was from London; political trials for sorcery and witchcraft were going on in England at this time, but none of them was as lurid as either the trial of Alice or the contemporary witch trials on the Continent. Could Bishop Ledrede have heard of some of these trials and used them against Alice? Possibly, but the Kyteler case contains not only elements that the Continental trials of the fourteenth century lacked, but, very curiously, some that would become common in the fifteenth century or later. Yet little suggests that the Kyteler case ever became a model. Perhaps, then, the charges were true; perhaps Alice was the head of a witch-cult whose activities were going on all over Europe and the British Isles in secret and here at Ossory uncovered by the diligence of Bishop Ledrede. For this Murrayite conclusion there is no substantial evidence whatever. The Kyteler case is a mélange of ideas, some derived from Bishop Ledrede's knowledge of the English and Continental trials, some from Irish folklore, and some, probably, from the ingenious imaginations of the bishop and his men, or even of Alice and her friends, for it is perfectly possible that Alice Kyteler dabbled in sorcery and other eccentric practices.

According to the *Narratio*, Alice had completely renounced Christ and the Church in order to obtain magical powers. To the same end, she sacrificed to demons (not the Devil), cutting up live animals and offering them up at crossroads. So far these are common charges of sorcery and pact. But now the new element of the familiar is introduced. These sacrifices were offered up to a demon named Robert or Robin Artisson, "Son of Art," whom the *Narratio* describes as one of the lesser demons. Almost certainly, Robert (Robin was a common nickname for Robert) was an Irish folk spirit. His name is exactly parallel to the names like Pierrot or Hennekin given in France and Germany to such minor sprites. As much like a fairy as a witch's familiar, Robert appeared in a number of shapes: a cat, a shaggy dog, or an Ethiopian. In this last the borrowing from the Continental heresy and witch trials is obvious, but even here there is a new element. The Ethiopian appears with two bigger or taller comrades, one of whom bore an iron rod in his hands. This iron rod, though possibly phallic, is more likely the sceptre of power sometimes borne in the fifteenth century by the Devil that later becomes the trident (the pitchfork of modern Halloween costumes), symbol of power over sky, earth, and underworld. The association is made firmer in the account of the confession of Petronilla of Meath, who said that she acted as a go-between for Alice and Robert Artisson, and that she often saw the demons in the form of three black men, *each* bearing an iron rod.

These demons taught Lady Alice her magic arts, and she learned under their instruction to make ointments of loathsome composition as well as other magical concoctions. To them she gave everything that she had, and they straightaway returned it to her for her use, a procedure probably attributable to the eagerness of Alice's prosecutors to find every possible justification for confiscating her property. But her relationship with the demons did not stop at these business transactions. She used Robert Artisson as her incubus, and with her associates she held secret candlelit conventicles at night. When the candles were blown out, she and her comrades cried "Fi, fi, fi, amen," and fell to a sexual orgy.* Again we have the first appearance of a trait that would later become common but that is strange to find isolated here in fourteenth-century Ireland. Even stranger is that the number accused was twelve, so that with Robert Artisson, Alice and her friends constituted a group of thirteen, a fact that inexplicably escaped Miss Murray in her fanatical search for covens. The *Narratio* makes no point of the fact either, and it certainly does not mention a "coven," so the number is probably coincidental. Perhaps the author meant implicitly to indict Alice and her group for blasphemously imitating the apostolic number, a charge brought in some previous cases of heresy—Manasses the blacksmith, the supporter of Tanchelm in the twelfth century is said to have sacrilegiously enrolled a following of twelve. Later untrustworthy chronicles allege that Alice used a salve to anoint a stick on which she rambled about (she did not fly), and that she possessed a host on which was inscribed the monogram, not of Christ, but of the Devil.

One of the most fully documented witch cases of the Middle Ages thus remains one of the most difficult to place in its context. What is puzzling is not so much its mixture of heretical, folk,

---

* The meaning of this cry is uncertain—it may be the *Narratio's* translation into Latin (*fi*) of something like "Do it," or "Go to it," which would put it in the spirit of the fifteenth-century injunction "Meclez" favored at the witches' sabbat.

and idiosyncratic elements, a mixture not unfamiliar in other trials, but its prefigurement of later cases on which it could have had little direct influence.

A few witch stories appear in the literature of the fourteenth century: in a version of Wolfram von Eschenbach's *Parzival* by Klaus Wisse and Philipp Colin, written between 1331 and 1336, the authors insert some of their own passages into the tale of King Karade of Nantes, who marries Isève (Iseult), a niece of King Arthur. Isève has a lover named Elyaphres who "can turn animals into human beings, chop off their heads, and replace them without injurious consequences." Elyaphres transforms a dog, a pig, and a filly into three pretty girls, with whom he replaces Isève on the first three wedding nights. Isève bears her lover a son, Karados, who when older avenges his putative father Karade by causing Elyaphres to mate with a dog, a pig, and a filly in their real forms.[38]

Even more boisterous is Boccaccio's "Ninth Tale of the Eighth Night" of the *Decameron,* written about 1350. It tells of a secret society that met twice a month for feasting and sexual revels; later in the same tale the rogue Buffalmaco instructs a physician how he may join the "Society of Rovers." A "Beaste, blacke and horned, but of no great stature," will come to fetch him. The physician is to mount the Beast's back, and he will be borne off to the meeting of the company. This is, in Boccaccio fashion, a trick of Buffalmaco, who disguises himself as the Beast the better to make a fool of the doctor. Boccaccio's skeptical laughter at the wild ride did not prevent the Inquisitors from sending thousands of people to the stake during the next three centuries for having participated in it.[39]

Political Trials for Witchcraft

The early fourteenth century was the golden age of the political trial for sorcery, heresy, and witchcraft. Though political exploitation of alleged spiritual crimes continued into later centuries, it was never more manifest than at this time, when its effectiveness had newly been discovered and put to good use by such unscrupulous politicians as Philip IV, John XXII, and Edward II. The defendants were wholly, or at least largely, innocent.

There were ten politically motivated trials between 1300 and 1360 involving charges related to the witch phenomenon: those of (1) Walter, bishop of Lichfield and Coventry and former treasurer of King Edward I, which concluded in 1303; (2) Bishop Guichard of Troyes, which lasted from 1308 to 1313; (3) John Tannere alias John Canne, who was hanged for treason in 1314 or 1315; (4) a doctor, a barber, and a clergyman at the court of John XXII in 1317–1319; (5) Bernard Délicieux, a Franciscan minorite with millenarian and mystical leanings, tried at Toulouse in 1319 by the bishop and the secular authorities; (6) the enemies of John XXII in the mark of Ancona in 1320–1325; (7) Matteo Visconti (d. 1322), tried by the archbishop of Milan for plotting against John; (8) Count Robert of Artois, accused in 1327 of plotting against Philip VI; (9) Edmund, Earl of Kent, accused of witchcraft by Roger Mortimer in 1330; (10) the Templars, the bulk of whose prosecutions occurred between 1306 and 1314 in England and France.[40]

The trial of the Templars was extraordinary and must therefore be treated separately, but the accusations associated with the other trials were drawn from the treasury of already existing witch beliefs and used as weapons with which to destroy the accused. The most common charge was invocation of the Devil (four trials); then there was homage or service rendered to the Devil (three), adoration or veneration of the Devil (three), pact (one), and the obscene kiss (one). That pact is mentioned only once is worth noting; it is also absent in the trial of the Templars, a curious fact, since Hansen, Robbins, and others have made so much of its use as the most effective way of linking sorcery with heresy. Though linking the two was not the purpose of the prosecutors, it is strange that they did not elect to use some of the strongest charges available to them.

The prosecution of the Templars is one of the longest and most complex of medieval witch actions: the first accusations were made in 1305, and the trials continued through 1314; the kings of France and England and the pope were all involved. The eventual condemnation of the Templars and their suppression as an order has been thoroughly investigated. It was first and foremost a measure taken by Philip IV, Edward II, and Clement V to destroy an organization whose great political power threatened them and whose immense wealth they needed to fill their coffers at a time when the costs of government were increasing much more rapidly than the available revenues. Our concern is not with the political complexities of the intrigues but with their implications for witchcraft.

The trials of the Templars were numerous and varied considerably in their particulars but are nonetheless susceptible to summary. In the initial order for their prosecution, it was charged that as a condition of membership postulants were obliged to deny God, Christ, and the Virgin, and to assert that Christ was a false prophet. They had to spit upon the cross three times, trample on it, or urinate upon it. This formal renunciation of Christianity, which we have found in previous witch trials, derives directly from old heretical tradition. The other thing demanded of the initiate—that he kiss the mouth, navel, and buttocks of the prior and caress him obscenely—is in the tradition of the *osculum infame,* but it is peculiar in that the kiss, rather than being offered directly to the Devil, was instead bestowed upon a man. This variation probably represents an attempt by their enemies to reinforce the sexual charges being made against the Templars, namely that they practiced homosexuality.

The initial order of arrest stated that the Templars did not consider sodomy a sin. This allegation may have derived from corrupt Catharism, or Philip may simply have thought that it could believably be lodged against male convents. It may even have had its roots in some of the earlier witch orgies, though these were more often bisexual than homosexual. In addition, the initial order said that the Templars kissed and adored an idol that most often was in the form of a golden calf or of a human head with a long beard. They were alleged to have worn round their necks a cord or amulet that had been consecrated by having been placed round the neck of the idol. Their priests, it was also said, never consecrated the host at mass.

The accusations of explicit idolatry and paganism were meant to tell heavily against an order that had spent much time in the East and might be supposed to have been contaminated by Islam. Nothing could be further from true Muslim practice than idolatry, but the point is that Western Christians believed that Muslims worshiped idols. In later accusations the connection with Islam was made more explicit by giving the idol the name Baphómet, a corruption of Mahomet (Mohammed). The only surprising thing about the allegations of Islamic practices is that they were not elaborated. Surely the corruption that might most plausibly taint an order that had operated for a century and a half in the Middle East would be acceptance of Islamic ideas. The great idol of Baphómet was kept at the temple at Montpelier, and there were lesser representations of the idol in every chapter house. Some had three faces (like Hecate or Dante's Satan); others consisted simply of a human skull.

The Templars invoked the Devil, and demons appeared to them in various forms, for example, as succubi with whom they had intercourse, or as a huge black cat, which they worshiped and to whom they gave the obscene kiss. They made powders out of the ashes of dead Templars or out of their own illegitimate children, whom they had murdered. All these accusations are, with variations, familiar from current witch charges. Another allegation was that the Grand Master and others gave absolution even though they were not priests. This charge is in a sense more credible: the Templars' enemies may have been confounding disciplinary pardon, which would be proper to the Grand Master, with sacerdotal absolution.

From this mélange of heresy, paganism, and witchcraft, a number of allegations are conspicuously absent: pact, familiars, night-riding, the sorcerers' salve. Their absence is more than a matter of mild interest. It means that the kings, eager as they were to find any charge against the Templars that could stand, did not simply seize upon any allegation that came to mind. This raises the important question why they chose the particular charges that were in fact made. And this in turn raises the question whether there may not have been some truth in them.

The question of the Templars' guilt has been discussed at length by so many writers and so inconclusively, that nothing would be gained by repeating old arguments and speculations. The doubts are still outstanding and are better left in the form of questions. Were the Templars guilty or not as charged? Were they guilty of some of the charges, such as those of homosexuality? Were they guilty of having strange initiation rites? Were they really heretics, idolaters, or even in some sense witches? Gmelin's contention that the Templars were undoubtedly "as pure as the Holy Father himself" is questionable.

But that the charges were at the very least exaggerated is scarcely open to doubt. The kings' desire for power and wealth and the pope's interested connivance in their prosecution entitle us to initial skepticism, and when the methods of the trials are examined, the doubt becomes massive. Torture was widely used to elicit the confessions, and at the trial at Paris the royal court steadfastly refused to hear the depositions of no fewer than 573 witnesses for the defense. At the time, and for years after the trials, Philip carried on extensive propaganda in an effort to persuade the world of this justice in destroying the order. The king could afford to show no mercy, for if only individual Templars were found guilty of these sins, they could be punished and the order still survive. Consequently he was obliged to pursue his persecutions until the entire order was shown to be corrupt and vicious. The only recourse for the pope was to dissolve it, a measure finally taken at the council of Vienne in 1311–1312, after which the Templars' property was distributed to the Knights Hospitaler, sums having first been withdrawn by the kings and the pope to offset the expenses they had incurred in the course of the prosecution.

Although there may well have been—indeed there probably were—some guilty Templars, the whole order could not have been tainted with diabolism. The persecution of the Templars was, like the contemporary persecution of the Jews, a device: religious hatreds and fears were used to enable royal power to confiscate the wealth of a prosperous and powerful group.

The importance for the history of witchcraft of the action against the Templars is that its extent and political importance fixed its characteristics in the public consciousness for generations. The charges used against the Templars were drawn for the most part from the tradition of heresy and witchcraft, and the trial itself, like the trials in Austria at the same time or those at Toulouse and Carcassonne two decades later, was used as a model in the later development of the witch phenomenon.

8

The Beginning of the
Witch Craze, 1360-1427

N the period 1360–1427 witchcraft had not yet reached craze proportions, but with the increasing disintegration of medieval society, the prince of disorder, the Devil, haunted the popular and artistic imagination ever more darkly.[1] The great era of the political trial for witchcraft concluded about 1360; there were some such trials later in the period, but the enthusiasm with which Philip the Fair and his contemporaries had staged them as state policy had apparently dimmed. On the other hand, the Inquisitors were ever more energetic in connecting witchcraft with women, Jews, and heretics.

The long accepted argument first advanced by Joseph Hansen is that the witch craze began in Alpine regions, where scholastic and Inquisitorial doctrines of witchcraft first penetrated the secular courts in the early fifteenth century. Until that time no trace of the witch's flight, sexual orgies, or cannibalism had appeared in the trials. But this explanation is incorrect. The secular courts were involved in witch cases well before 1400 and to almost as great an extent as the Inquisition itself. Nor were cannibalism and flight introduced into witchcraft from the folklore of the conservative and superstitious mountain people. They had been a part of the witch tradition at least as far back as the trial at Orléans in 1022. Hansen went astray in his assumption that the history of witchcraft is an extension of the history of sorcery. Indeed, this assumption is a logical contradiction of his own contention that witchcraft was the creation of scholastics and Inquisitors. The concern of the Inquisitors was to emphasize the heretical nature of witchcraft through pact; they had no reason to introduce concepts derived from sorcery. Sorcery and folklore had considerable influence upon European witchcraft, but in its essence it was an extension, not of sorcery, but of heresy.

This misunderstanding of Hansen's led him to the false conclusion that the witch craze swept down from mountain redoubts upon the plains and valleys of unprotected Europe. It is true that an exceptional number of witch cases occurred in the Alps during the fifteenth century, but the chief reason is that for centuries the mountains had been the refuge of the Waldensians, Dolcinists, and other heretics of the sort. Hansen's scenario is the reverse of what is true. Some of the most important witch trials took place long before the outbreak in the mountains, and in such unmountainous locations as Toulouse and Paris. Witchcraft first flourished in the wealthy lowlands where heresy was strong, and spread with heresy *into* the mountains, not the reverse.

Yet Hansen was right in asserting that the period around 1430 was crucial. What did happen, beginning in 1427, was the publication of quantities of theoretical discourses devoted exclusively to witchcraft, and a vast increase in the number and scope of the witch trials. The growth of witchcraft from 1360–1427, which prepared the enormous expansion of the succeeding period, was encouraged by closely related phenomena such as the frenzies of the flagellants and the dancers. Far from diminishing after the first shock of the Black Death of 1347–1349 had worn off, these psychic epidemics increased in numbers and frenzy as the fourteenth century went on, an indication of widespread "social and cultural maladjustment."[2] These movements, which swept the

Low Countries, Germany, and northern France in 1374 and continued at least until 1420, were more than responses to plagues and famines; they were manifestations of the misery and fear caused by uncontrollable and unpredictable change in a Christian society in which change was not valued.[3] The flagellants were active into the fifteenth century. The dance craze had appeared in the thirteenth century, but the first wide outbreak occurred in 1374, at which time it spread rapidly throughout northwestern Europe. Called St. John's Dancers or St. Vitus' Dancers* in the north, they were paralleled by the Tarantella dancers of Italy, whose mania apparently began about 1350 in Apulia and spread by 1400 to northern Italy. The peak of the dance craze in the north was about 1430, but outbreaks continued through the next century and even into the sixteenth. Typically, the dancers would gather in the town or village, strip half naked, and dance in a circle until they fell from exhaustion. Over the prostrate bodies of the fallen the other dancers would continue until all were exhausted. Sometimes their gyrations were frighteningly grotesque. As they danced, they would call out the names of demons. Probably they believed themselves possessed and were imploring the demons to cease tormenting them; usually they were treated with kindness as needing a cure, though some authorities took a dimmer view and believed that their cries were meant to invoke demonic assistance.

The dancers were for the most part poor and illiterate people; in addition, a large proportion of them were, it seems, unmarried women. Part of the explanation for this may be individual hysteria, but there have always been eager virgins and frustrated

---

* St. John's Day, June 24, fell on the same day as an old pagan festival (James, *Seasonal Feasts*, pp. 225–226). A chapel of St. Vitus stood at Strasbourg during the dancing outbreak there in 1418. The frenzied dancers were brought there by the authorities and cured of their mania through the intercession of that saint, a fourth-century martyr.

old maids, and such ladies do not always join in hysterical mass demonstrations. Witchcraft was increasingly being associated with women, and the special position of the female sex in these movements must be considered. The plagues and famines, with their concomitant shifts in population distribution—the countryside being in some measure abandoned for the prosperous towns—may have put women in a peculiarly difficult position. Women tend to outlive men; often the old or even middle-aged mother, aunt, or grandmother may have been left at home and alone in the village while the family went off to town to get better work. Perhaps the plague had carried off most of her contemporaries, increasing her sense of isolation and bitterness. Reliable demographic statistics are lacking, but men may conceivably have suffered greater mortality in the plagues, increasing the number of women that were left alone.[4] If women did in fact feel particularly anomalous and helpless in the changing society of the fourteenth and fifteenth centuries, they might well have tended more readily to participate in the antisocial frenzies of the dancers or the rites of the witches.

Repression of Witchcraft

Toward the end of the fourteenth century, the fear of magic, witchcraft, and heresy was increasing. On September 19, 1398, the University of Paris affirmed that magic was efficacious and expressed its alarm that ancient errors were regaining their sway over the minds of men. It announced that there was a distinction between natural magic and magic going beyond natural means; the latter always involved a pact, explicit or implicit, with demons.[5] Largely through the idea of pact, sorcery was increasingly identified with heresy, for example at trials at Lucerne in 1419 and at Interlaken in 1424, where the term *Hexerei* was used for the first time for sorcery.[6] Accompanying greater suspicion of magic was a harshness in the prosecution of witchcraft that became marked around 1400. This was not only the result of the increased organizational efficiency of the Church and the growing political power of the Inquisition. It was also a desperate effort to preserve society on the part of people who felt (accurately, as it turned out) that the very existence of Christian society as it had been known throughout the Middle Ages was threatened. As in present-day America, it is not always easy to appraise accurately the real threats to society. Consequently the authorities lashed out at those to whom they could most easily attribute hostility and menace: witches, Jews, and heretics. The orthodox believed that Christian society constituted almost an institutionalization of God's will for man; therefore hostility to that society could only proceed from the Devil, and all those presumed to pose a threat to society must be considered limbs of Satan.

Thus to envision the witch persecution solely as a variety of frenzy or hysteria is to miss the point, though it certainly became that on the level of popular action. The persecution is rather to be compared to the action taken in modern America against supposed Communists or in modern Russia against supposed social fascists: organized, self-righteous repression, rational within the narrow bounds of what current orthodoxy considers rational, of elements believed to be representative of the Ultimate Enemy. Sometimes coldly, sometimes with regret, sometimes even with compassion, the Inquisitors proceeded without mercy against the agents of the Ultimate Enemy of Christ. If the witch obdured under torture, professing her innocence while urged by the most terrible agonies to do otherwise, her captors assumed that the Devil was assisting her, perhaps through the use of magical amulets or charms concealed upon her body. If the witch's helplessness in captivity seemed to belie the hideous powers ascribed to her, this too was a trick of the Devil's to disarm the Inquisitors, or else a miracle of Christ's enacted to preserve his champions from harm. Once a woman had been arrested for witchcraft, there was very little that could save her from a harsh sentence.

The more seriously witchcraft was taken and the more powerful the Inquisition became, the more naturally witch cases were referred to it, although throughout this period the secular and episcopal tribunals continued to be as active as the Inquisition itself. Indeed, disputes as to jurisdiction over witch cases were not uncommon. On August 14, 1374, Pope Gregory XI issued a letter to the Inquisitors of France in which he took issue with those who had argued that the Inquisition had no right to intervene in trials for magic. Most magic, the pope argued, was worked with the aid of demons, and any invocation of demons was justly within the limits of Inquisitorial jurisdiction.[7] The pope's judgment was not accepted without demur by the French courts. Parlement considered magic a civil crime, and throughout the period most sorcery trials were conducted in secular courts. In England attitudes were similar. It was Parliament that in April, 1376, heard accusations of witchcraft lodged against Alice Perrers, the mistress of Edward III.[8] In 1401, Parliament approved the statute *De haeretico comburendo,* specifying the stake for all convicted heretics who would not recant or, having recanted, became recidivists. In Hungary, the law code of Kulm, drawn up about 1390, ordered that magicians offering themselves to the Devil must be burnt at the stake, and at Buda in 1421 it was ordered that at the first offense, witches (or sorcerers—the meaning is not clear) were to be tied to a ladder with a Jew's hat placed upon their heads, there to be exposed to the scorn and revilement of the populace; on the second offense they were to be burnt as heretics.[9]

Diocesan statutes also took cognizance of witchcraft. The synod of Benevento in 1378 forbade all magic, especially the misuse of the sacraments; at the synod of Langres in 1404 Cardinal Louis of Bourbon forbade both the use of sorcery and belief in its efficacity.[10] Pope Alexander V, mistrusting the leniency of episcopal courts, wrote to the Inquisitor of Avignon on August 30, 1409 and ordered him to take charge of all those who were sorcerers (sortilegi) and invokers of demons. This bull was reiterated by Martin V on February 3, 1418.[11] Such wrangling over jurisdiction reached its height during the activities of Heinrich Institoris, the Inquisitor and author of the *Malleus Maleficarum,* which were deeply resented by the bishops. But whatever the disputes among themselves, all authorities were agreed that witchcraft must be eradicated in whatever form it took and wherever it appeared.

While courts grew harsher, the theoretical treatises that dealt with witchcraft were noticeably more liberal. They were certainly much more lenient than the tracts that began to appear in 1427 and that dominated the rest of the fifteenth century. Looking back, the historian can hail them as documents of relative skepticism and enlightenment. Or, if he chooses a wider philosophical vision, he can be skeptical of the skeptics. There is ample evidence that witch beliefs and practices did exist and that the same elements of social insecurity that exacerbated repression also worked to increase the actual level of witch activity. But, as well as these impulses to *believe* in witchcraft, there were also societal impulses to *disbelieve.* Neoplatonic resistance to Aristotelian witchcraft, materialistic biases, even simple personal jealousy of successful witch hunters might have induced some of the writers of these tracts to take an unduly skeptical position, a position which they often justified as traditional by citing the *Canon Episcopi.*

I do not mean to make any prejudgments here—indeed what I want to do is precisely to remove a prejudgment common in existing histories of witchcraft. Much of the skepticism of these writers was probably justified, but their disbelief does not disprove the existence of witch practices any more than the belief of later theoreticians proves them. For our purposes, the development of the phenomenon is of prime interest. In the overview the significance of these theoreticians is limited to the slight extent to which they slowed the development of that phenomenon.

Of these writers, Raymond of Tarrega must be treated apart, for the position he took was so permissive that it was itself condemned as heretical. A Spanish Dominican, he wrote a book called *On the Invocation of Demons* about 1370 in which he argued that we are permitted to adore creatures as long as we keep in mind that we are adoring what is Godlike in them. Consequently, we are permitted to offer dulia or even latria to demons so long as we adore, not their evil, but their existence, which was given them by God. It is not desirable to sacrifice to demons, but to do so is no more serious than adoring an image of Christ or of the saints. The book was understandably not well received by the Inquisition in Spain, and it was formally condemned and burnt by Eymeric in the presence of the archbishop of Tarragona.[12]

Eymeric (1320–1393), a well-known Inquisitor in Aragon and at Avignon, himself produced a treatise, *Against Those Who Call Up Demons,* in 1369. Around 1376, he published his famous *Directorium,* a manual for Inquisitors based in large part upon the earlier work of Bernard Gui. The *Directorium* is divided into three parts, the first offering definitions of orthodox beliefs, the second defining various heresies, and the third detailing how to deal with them.[13] Nicholas von Jauer, a professor at Prague from 1395 to 1402 and then at Heidelberg from 1402 to 1435, wrote *Treatise on Superstitions* in 1405. Around 1400, a Dominican named Johann Herolt wrote a sermon in which he discussed witchcraft. At Pavia, Antonio Guaineri (fl. 1410–1440) wrote a medical treatise that touched on witchcraft, and a professor of theology at Heidelberg, Johann von Frankfurt, composed in 1412 a still unedited treatise with the title "Whether Demons Can Be

Coerced through the Use of Characters, Figures, and Incan-
tations." Another unedited treatise on demons, probably from
Cologne, appeared about 1415; the great French conciliarist Jean
Gerson wrote, about the time of the council of Basel in 1415,
Treatise Proving Spirits; in a similar tradition was the work of
Sozzini (Socinus) of Siena.[14]

These theoreticians argued that demons had considerable
powers, but that they could operate only with God's tolerance and
permission. Although they had no power to transform reality, they
could cause illusions by changing appearances. They could not,
for example, transform a man into a wolf but could cause him
to take on the appearance of a wolf; they could cause their own
spiritual bodies to take on the illusion of various shapes: it is in
this way that they could act as incubi. The women who ride out
at night are but demons in woman's shape. The putative women
who take part in the games in the forest are likewise demons, as
are those who stage the illusions of battles in the forest.[15] The
strigae and lamias who come to molest children are not old women
as they seem, but demons, and it is a sin to believe that women
change into cats or come to suck the blood of children. Setting
out gifts for Habundia and Satia is foolishness and sin, since
these alleged goddesses are really demons.

Skepticism was sometimes carried even further. The Cologne
treatise suggests that some of these illusions proceed directly from
disturbed minds rather than from demonic influence. This is
particularly true in the case of women, whose flighty minds are
more susceptible to delusion than those of men. Guaineri agreed
that an incubus was merely a psychological illusion caused by
some kind of physiological disorder. For him, the idea that women
called *strigae* or *zobianae* could really change into cats or other
shapes was simply absurd.[16]

All agreed in condemning the veneration of demons, though
Johann insisted that it was impossible to call them up without

the consent of God, and that even if one did succeed in doing this with God's permission, the answers the demons gave to the questions of the diviner would be ambivalent and of very little value. Nicholas von Jauer agreed, affirming that demons could not know the future. Hence divination was an impossibility. Eymeric was more firm than any in his condemnation of demonolatry. He distinguished carefully between "simple sorcerers" who worked through natural forces and "heretical sorcerers" who employed demons. To do simple magic is a sin; to call upon demons is apostasy and heresy. Von Jauer and Gerson agreed with Eymeric on this point, insisting that any invocation of demons involved pact and was therefore heretical. Eymeric went on to distinguish two degrees of seriousness in the heresy. Dulia, for example placing the names of demons among the names of saints in the liturgy or in prayers, was naturally less serious than latria. Latria of demons—demonolatry proper—included sacrifice, prayer, the promise of obedience, a specific offer of services to them, or in their honor wearing white or black clothes, cutting oneself and bleeding, observing chastity or fasting, or lighting torches.

The meaning of some of these activities is somewhat vague. The cutting and bleeding may refer to the idea of explicit pact, in which contracts with Satan were supposed to be signed in blood. The lighting of torches is doubtless a reference to the practice of holding revels in secret places at night and the concomitant procession with torches, often followed by sexual orgies of the sort that were associated with heretics as far back as Augustine's treatise on the morals of the Manichaeans. The observation of chastity and fasts for hell's sake is probably a not very subtle effort to attribute the virtues of the Catharist perfecti to love of Satan rather than to love of Christ. The skepticism of these writers was patently not strong enough to provide much resistance to harsh judicial procedures or to discourage the development of credulity on the part of later theoreticians.

Minor Cases, 1360–1427

There were a number of cases in which accusations relating to witchcraft were sparse, imprecise, or merely conventional. A man and a woman were tried for witchcraft, charges unspecified, at the village of Halfedanges in 1372;[17] in 1388 Sir Robert Tresilian was reported to have used diabolical names and a demon's head in his magical activities.[18] On February 23, 1399, witches (their crimes unspecified) were burnt at Portagruaro in Friuli, and Filippo da Siena (1339–1442) tells of parents who gave their child to an enchantress who in turn handed it over to the Devil to cure. The Devil healed the child temporarily, but six months later it mysteriously died.[19] In May, 1401, at Geneva a woman named Jeannette was tried by a secular court (it was an area where the bishop had secular jurisdiction) for maleficium and magic. The Devil, who came at her call, took the form of a man dressed in a tunic of black velvet.[20] In 1404 the *prévôt* of Paris announced to Parlement that the bodies of children were disappearing from their graves and the corpses of criminals being stolen from the gallows, the purpose being to use the remains in maleficium.[21] In 1410 the notary Géraud Cassendi was prosecuted by the Inquisition at Carcassonne for invoking demons, and in the same year idolatry of a spring and a stone was discovered in Turnstone parish in the diocese of Hereford.[22]

Mention of pact in these trials is rare, a fact that remains curious in the light of the assertions of the liberal historians that it was used so intensely by the Inquisition to link sorcery with heresy. But a carpenter who died in 1366 was said to have made a pact with the Devil in order to succeed at his trade.[23]

Worship of demons or sacrifice to them was apparently considered more significant than pact. An old woman named Gabrina Albetti, who came from a relatively prosperous family in the village of San Prospero in Emilia, was brought to trial at Reggio in

July, 1375. She had taught a number of other women how to sacrifice to the Devil. One of them alleged that Gabrina had instructed her to go out at night, take off her clothes, and kneel nude, looking up at the largest star in heaven (evidently an allusion to Satan's identity with Lucifer), crying out "I adore thee, o great Devil." In this, one of the first clear witch cases in Italy, Gabrina was judged, not by the Inquisition, but by a secular tribunal. She was condemned to be branded and to have her tongue excised.[24] A woman named Marta was tortured in Florence about 1375: she was alleged to have placed candles round a dish and to have taken off her clothes and stood above the dish in the nude, making magical signs.[25] At the village of Rugomago near Siena in 1383, the country people adored and called up Satan and Beelzebub, made sacrifices to them, and worshiped idols, or so it was said by the Inquisition. "They call upon all the princes of darkness, and through malice and through the power of these, they are able to kill a man" and to accomplish other evil things.[26] Hans Vintler, a Tyrolese poet who wrote about 1410, said that there were people who prayed to the Devil.[27] Franciscan monks were tried in Venice in 1422 in a process conducted jointly by the Inquisition and the secular courts for having sacrificed to demons.[28]

Another aspect of witchcraft that was taken seriously was the ride with Diana, which was often combined with the expeditions of the bonae. The Inquisition at Milan in 1390 indicted a woman for having said that she was a member of the society of Diana and that she went out at night in that company to eat, drink, and thieve from the houses of the wealthy. At Valpute near Isère in 1395 it was reported that a festival was celebrated in the village every three years, in which *ribauds* ("revelers") would get together, elect a king, and then go out doing mischief, a custom related to the Feast of Fools and possibly to the bonae. Vintler reported that some Tyrolese women claimed to have attended a great assembly called the *Var* (*varen:* to ride), where at least twenty people rode out together at midnight on calves, goats, cows, pigs, stools, or even cabinets, in the company of Herodias, Diana, or Percht (Perchta or Bertha) "with the iron nose." Vintler is inclined to believe that the ride was really undertaken by demons in the form of women. In 1423, at Nieder-Hauenstein near Basel, a woman was sentenced to death for witchcraft by the secular court because she admitted to practicing maleficium and to having ridden out at night on wolves.[29]

Major Witch Trials Not Connected with Other Heresy

In the years 1384–1390, two cases were tried before the *podestà*, the secular court of Milan, and then referred to the Inquisition.[30] Basically they were trials for maleficium, but they also showed traces, not only of association with some of the older witch traditions such as the wild hunt, but also with the benandanti found in sixteenth-century Italy by Carlo Ginzburg. The first of these trials, that of a woman named Sibillia, opened on April 30, 1384. The charge was heresy. It was alleged of Sibillia that every Thursday night she went out with "Signora Oriente" and her *società*, and paid homage to her. The gradual amalgamation of the wild hunt to witchcraft is illustrated in the homage, the first on record rendered the chief of the wild hunt. Oriente taught the society how to divine the future. At the meetings, they consumed every sort of animal except the ass, which was exempted because of its long association with Jesus; he had been carried by an ass into Egypt and had ridden one in triumph into Jerusalem. Oriente then resurrected all the animals that had been consumed. Sibillia's claim that these rites were no sin was rejected, and she was condemned to wear two red crosses as a penance. Six years later, on May 26, 1390, Sibillia was tried again as a recidivist, and she readily admitted that since her previous conviction she had been twice to the assembly. She further admitted that her association with the games of Diana and Herodias went back to her childhood. Again she acknowledged that she did homage to Diana. She continued to aver that what she did was no sin, though she admitted that the members of the society dared not use the name of God for fear of offending Oriente.

In the first trial, with the exception of the act of homage, diabolism does not appear. Though animals are present, they are real beasts; there is no suggestion of shapeshifting. There is no mention of flight on the animals' backs, and no sex orgy. Here, simply, is the old folk tradition of the wild hunt. In the second trial, the Inquisitors have fitted that tradition more closely into their conception of witchcraft by identifying Oriente with Diana and Herodias (most likely, they put these names into Sibillia's mouth, for in her first confession she never referred to Oriente by any other name), and by introducing the suggestion that the name of God was offensive to Oriente. In the first trial, the ass was not eaten, but that prohibition can be taken in three ways. To be sure, it might mean that an animal beloved by Christ was distasteful to Oriente, but it might also mean that the society revered Christ and abstained in his honor. A wholly different explanation is that the donkey or ass is often considered sacred to Satan as well. Sibillia was undeniably involved in strange, even heretical, practices. But the Inquisition was clearly imposing its own assumptions about witchcraft upon people who probably did not consider themselves worshipers of Satan.

The second case, that of Pierina de' Bugatis, was also first heard by the podestà, but from the beginning it showed more of the influence of witch stereotypes. Pierina's first confession to the podestà was in 1390. She described much the same activities as Sibillia, though in her account of the animals who came to the society she excluded the wolf as well as the ass, adding that should any other animal be absent from the meeting, the world would be destroyed. Both living and dead people attended the society, but those who had been hanged or beheaded were excluded because, their necks having been broken, they were unable to make the bow of reverence to Oriente! The members of the society ate the animals who came, but they replaced the bones in the skins, and Oriente resurrected them with a touch of her magic wand. The most likely origin of this belief is that it is a remnant of an ancient fertility cult. The connection of the wild hunt with the bonae mulieres was made on this basis. That connection is here made specific. For the society, Pierina confessed, went round at night to the houses of the rich, from which they stole food and drink, though they passed the dwellings of the poor with a blessing.* Oriente taught her followers the magic arts but warned them to keep the doings of the assembly absolutely quiet for fear of persecution. Oriente, Pierina said, rules the society as Christ rules the world.

Pierina's case was referred to the Inquisition, to whom she made a second deposition on July 21, 1390. Here the intention of the Inquisition to understand the society of Diana in terms of witchcraft is even clearer than in the case of Sibillia. Pierina confessed that she had been attending the revels of the society since she was sixteen, having been forced at that age to take the place of an aunt who, had she not found a substitute, would never have been permitted to die. Whenever Pierina wished to attend a meeting, she would call upon Lucifel,† who appeared to her in the form of a man. He instructed her and bore her (presumably aloft) to the meeting. At the age of 30, Pierina had drawn a spoonful of blood from her body and with it signed a pact with the Devil.

These trials are the best example before those of the benandanti of how the Inquisition interpreted strange fertility rites as witch-

---

* An indication of some degree of social consciousness and of a possible influence of the cult of poverty associated with the Fraticelli and other fourteenth-century heretics.

† The Devil's name here appears in the trial for the first time: there is no indication from her previous deposition that Pierina identified Oriente with diabolical activity.

craft and by threat insured that the accused added elements of diabolism to their confessions.

In 1390–1391, about the time that the trials of Sibillia and Pierina were going on in Italy, there were two of significance at Paris.[31] The Paris trials, unlike the Italian, were centered on maleficium rather than on the wild ride, but similar efforts were made to transform magic into something more hideous. At Paris, these labors were carried out entirely by the secular authority, the cases being heard by the court of the provost and then appealed to the Parlement. The Inquisition was in no way involved. The first trial was held July 30, 1390. In the dock were two women, Margot de la Barre, called Coingnet, a woman of the lowest class who wandered from village to village with prostitutes and was reputed to have magical powers; and Marion la Droiturière, a woman of somewhat higher station. Marion had been jilted by her lover, who had gone off to marry another woman, and Marion called upon Margot to help her get revenge by magically rendering the man impotent with his wife. This was simple maleficium, but after they were tortured, both women were more forthcoming: Margot admitted calling up the Devil with the words, "Enemy, I conjure you, in the name of the Father and the Son and the Holy Spirit, that you come to me here.* Thereupon a demon appeared "in the shape that demons take in Passion plays," except that he did not have horns. Both Margot and Marion were burnt at the stake by order of the provost.

The second trial, which lasted from October 29, 1390, to August 19, 1391, was even more significant. Here again the provost tried two women, Jehanne de Brigue, called La Cordière, and Macète de Ruilly. Jehanne, who had a reputation as a diviner and who had previously been imprisoned for a year by the Bishop

---

* The idea that the Devil or demons could be conjured by the name of God is very old. It was considered one of the most effective, if one of the most blasphemous, ways of doing so.

of Meaux for practicing magic, was indicted first on the charge that she had bewitched Hennequin de Ruilly in order to cause him to marry Macète. This plan succeeded, but it came to pass that Macète was not satisfied with the treatment she received from Hennequin. She consulted Jehanne again, and with wax figures and toads they did magic together that caused Hennequin to suffer a grave illness. In the course of the proceedings Jehanne implicated Macète by claiming that it was she who actually had performed the magic. Perhaps this was true; perhaps Jehanne hoped to get off with a lighter sentence; or perhaps she yielded to the torture that was administered to her.

With such inducements Jehanne told the provost's court what it wanted to know. She confessed that as a child she had been taught by her godmother, whose name was also Jehanne, how to divine the future. This was accomplished by calling up a demon named Haussibut. To summon him, she had to refrain from crossing herself, from using holy water, and even from washing her hands for a day before. When the appropriate time came, she called upon the Trinity to force the demon to come, drew a circle round herself, and called out, "Haussibut, come to me." Her godmother invited her to offer one of her arms to the demon, but Jehanne demurred. Later she refused a reasonable compromise whereby she was to leave him an arm and a finger upon her death. Macète was not brought to trial until August 4. After torture, she admitted that she had called upon Lucifer while saying three times each the Gospel of John (presumably the opening passage), the Our Father, and the Hail Mary. Both women were condemned. Jehanne appealed her case to the Parlement of Paris, but that court upheld her conviction, and she and Macète were burnt at the stake on August 19. Here the secular courts were responsible for transforming maleficium into heresy.

At Simmenthal near Bern, a series of witch trials were held from about 1395 to 1405, and a number of people were convicted of witchcraft and burnt.[32] The trials were conducted by the secular courts and the fact that they specify witch characteristics in great detail suggests again that of the Inquisition's responsibility in the development of the phenomenon was proportionately less than some have suggested. The witches at Simmenthal were accused of constituting a sect that met at Church on Sunday morning, not for mass, but to worship Satan. There they performed rites including homage to the Devil. They stole children, killed them, and then cooked and ate them, or else they drained them of their juices in order to make ointments. With the ointment, they changed themselves into animals, rendered themselves invisible, or rubbed their bodies in order to obtain the power of flying through the air.

In 1424 a witch named Finicella was burnt at Rome by the secular authorities. She had with the Devil's help slain children and other creatures. One day in the shape of a cat she attempted to kill a neighbor's child, but the child's father succeeded in driving off the cat and wounding it with a knife. Later Finicella was found with a wound in the corresponding part of her human body. Here it seems that the popular stories of shapeshifting purveyed by Caesarius of Heisterbach and other such writers played a larger part than the traditions of heresy and witchcraft found in most of the trials.[33]

A series of cases were tried by the Inquisition from 1421 to about 1440.[34] The accused were for the most part poor people—peasants or shepherds. The standard accusation was that they had invoked demons, but the form in which the demon appeared varied greatly from case to case. He was a black rooster, a black dog, a black cat, a black crow, a pig, or a dog. More frequently, he appeared as a person. He was a pale young man with clothes of white and red or with a long tunic and a harsh voice; or a ruddy man with clothes of red and black. He was a knight in black armor or a huge man in black with eyes as big as a steer's. Most often he was a Negro—once an old and ugly one, dressed in black and with a red mouth. In the fifteenth century, Portuguese, Spanish, and Italian traders were coming into contact with African blacks, and the slave trade, suspended in Europe for over half a millennium, was now being revived with the Africans as victims. Given the ancient fear of darkness, it was natural that the European mind should associate the black Africans with the Devil and his demons. The difficulty today of escaping from this ancient tradition sometimes seems ludicrously clear, as when a recent candidate for the position of mayor of New York, addressing a crowd of blacks in a friendly fashion, announced that "My heart is as black as yours." The idea that "black is beautiful," however true it may be, has not centuries but millennia to overcome.

Frequently, however, in these Dauphiné trials the Devil appeared as one of the little people of folk legend—the leprechauns, kobolds, and gnomes of folklore who have been transformed by Christian theology into demons. Hence he is a *little* dark man, or a small man who stammers. He is a little boy dressed in black, or with pale face, long tunic and black belt, or of lascivious appearance. The small-animal forms taken by the theriomorphic demons are part of the same tradition of pet or familiar demons. The names bestowed upon the demons at these trials are usually consistent with this tradition. Though Lucifel appears once, and there is a Barrabarri, whose name may well be a corruption of Barrabas (transformed in the popular mind, like Herodias, from a person into an evil spirit), the other demons are called Brunet, Corp-diable, Griffart, Guillaume or Guillemet, Pierre, Borrel, Jean, Tartas, Revel, Guli, Juson, and Ginifert: mischievous, but hardly awful names.

The accused, it was said, had paid homage to the Devil, made pact with him, and offered him the osculum infame. They sacrificed black cats and first-born children (sometimes their own) to him. Afterward they cooked the children in order to obtain ingredients for their magic powders. The Devil forbade them to kiss the cross or make the sign of the cross, to adore the host, or to go to mass. To demonstrate their pure loyalty to him, they must trample upon the cross. Sometimes he placed a mark on his followers.* The witches of Dauphiné constituted a sect, and they assembled at sabbats, usually on Thursdays, but sometimes on Tuesdays or Saturdays. They were transported to the sabbat by the Devil over long distances, often riding upon black horses, red mares, or sticks they had anointed in order to cause them to levitate.

At the sabbat, the witches danced, held sexual orgies, and frequently had intercourse with demons or even with the Devil himself. Though the appearance of the Devil at the witches' revels had heretofore been hinted at, it only now in the fifteenth century was clearly and consistently assumed. In Dauphiné, he appeared to his worshipers as a black cat or as a man with terrible, shining eyes, wearing a crown and black garments. There he received the witches' homage and sexual favors. If the witches were arrested, he would visit them in prison to strengthen them against the efforts of the Inquisitors or, if all else had failed, to help them commit suicide and so escape execution.

These Dauphiné trials encouraged the expansion of the concept of witchcraft in the succeeding period, during which classical witchcraft would be defined.

---

* The Devil's mark does not appear before the fifteenth century and then only rarely. It became extremely common in the sixteenth and seventeenth centuries, when witches were stripped and shaved in order to examine them for the mark, which was taken as absolute proof of guilt. The Devil's mark was a small scar, birthmark, or other discoloration presumed to have been left upon the body by his talon. Its etiology is uncertain, though it may be a parody of the Christian popular tradition that God marks his own (symbolically to be sure) at baptism. The Devil's mark is sometimes confused with the witch's mark, a protuberance on the skin thought to be a small teat used for suckling familiars, and which is not mentioned before 1480.

Heresy and Witchcraft

That witchcraft was a heresy had already been established by the theoreticians of the previous period. Now the witch hunters wished to give this new, diabolical sect a name that would make clear that the witches were neither simple sorcerers nor the mere figments of the imagination presented by the *Canon Episcopi*. The new names explicitly asserted the heretical nature of the witches: *haeretici fascinarii, sortilegi haereticales,* or *secta strigarum*. Often such appellations, more congenial to the ears of theologians than to those of ordinary people, were replaced by names like *waudenses* or *gazarii,* which tied the witches to the Waldensians and the Catharists, or other easily recognized heretics.

The insistence upon the witches' heretical nature often caused witches and heretics to be put on trial together, as in Carcassonne where from 1387 to 1400 more than two hundred persons were condemned and sixty-seven burnt for crimes of magic, or for being Waldensians, Beguines, or Albigensians. At Toulouse in 1412 sorcerers and so-called Beguines were tried together and sentenced to unusually light punishments—life imprisonment, pilgrimages, or fines—whereas others were condemned to death for "sorcery and sodomy." The crime of sodomy may have been introduced against the witches here by analogy to the trial of the Templars or with reference to the supposed homosexuality of the Catharists. Homosexuality was not a deviation ordinarily alleged against the witches. In 1423 several sorcerers suspected of heresy were condemned to death or life imprisonment at Carcassonne.[35]

A treatise of the early fifteenth century, the *Errores Valdensium,* claims of the Waldensians that they kissed the posterior parts of a demon in cat form and that they flew to their meetings in a twinkling of an eye on a staff rubbed with magical salve.[36] The problem of why the apostolic-minded Waldensians should have become associated with diabolism has long interested historians. Apparently the identification of witches and Waldensians was first made in Alpine regions, where heretics had been accustomed to retreat from orthodox persecution, and where the Waldensians were numerous enough to cause the orthodox inhabitants to refer to all heretics by that name, just as earlier the Germans had come to refer to all heretics as *Cathari,* from which the German *Ketzer* ("heretic") derives. The confusion was so pronounced that often, as at a trial of "Waldensians" at Fribourg in 1399, it is difficult to say whether the accused were really Waldensians, other heretics, or witches.[37] Again like the Catharists, the Waldensians were supposedly sexually depraved, and by the beginning of the fifteenth century a sex fiend was often termed a *Vaudois.* From the Alps the identification spread through southern and then northern France, though it was seldom used beyond French-speaking lands. The term was finally adopted formally in a bull issued on March 23, 1440, by Pope Eugenius IV.[38] It was justified by theologians on the grounds that the Waldensians, though originally devoted to poverty and asceticism, had gradually become committed to witchcraft, and the distinction between *Waudenses* (witch Waldensians) and *Waldenses* (old-fashioned Waldensians) was soon lost. The identification was so firmly fixed that *vauderie* came to be a synonym for the sabbat, and *aller en vauderie* meant "to go to the sabbat."

Witches were also still identified with Catharists. The term *Gazarii* (from *Cathari*) was applied to the witches in Savoy in the 1420s and 1430s by the Inquisition, and the usage gained wide currency thereafter. Hansen and Runeberg have overemphasized the importance of the mountains in the formation of witchcraft.[39] What occurred in Switzerland and Savoy was merely that heresies long established in those regions were now wedded to witchcraft in both the official and the public mind.

At Pinarolo and Turin in Lombardy, Antonio da Savigliano, a

Dominican Inquisitor, conducted in 1387–1388 a series of trials extraordinarily significant for the way in which Waldensianism, Catharism, and witchcraft became inseparably blended. An initial group of heretics, apparently all of modest social status, were tried, tortured,* and thereby induced to implicate others until most of the town was involved. Though their doctrines were a mélange, they were explicitly identified as a sect or society of Waldensians and linked with the heretics of Dauphiné who were described as "the Poor of Lyon."[40] Their doctrines do in fact bear some similarities to Waldensianism. They believed that their sect was of such moral excellence that no one could be saved without belonging to it. The Catholic Church and its sacraments were useless, being an invention of priests to obtain money; and any member of their sect could consecrate the Eucharist himself. Pilgrimages, the veneration of the cross, almsgiving, and hagioduly were all superstitions of the Catholic Church, which had been corrupt from the time of Constantine. The heretics had their own pope in Apulia.† All oaths are mortal sin.

---

* For the first time, a phrase now appears that in one form or another will be repeated at witch trials for the next two centuries. The accused at Pinarolo were said to have confessed their crimes *sine tortura et extra locum torturae*: "without torture, and even out of sight of the instruments of torture." This phrase, suggesting that the confessions were freely obtained, is a statement that, though literally true, is morally deceptive. Those "free" confessions were obtained by first threatening the victims with torture or actually torturing them and then taking them into another room where they were offered the choice of "freely" confessing or being returned to the torture chamber. From the mid-fourteenth century torture was ever more frequently employed by both the Inquisitorial and the secular courts, and the historian may be fairly sure that wherever the implication of large numbers of people in a community occurs, it is the result of forcing the prisoners to implicate others (whether guilty or innocent) in order to obtain the surcease of their torments.

† The meaning of this passage is obscure. The heretics of Monforte in 1028 had claimed to have their own pontiff, but in the context it is clear that they had the Holy Spirit in mind. The context at Pinarolo would admit this explanation, but it is not clear why, if this were so, he should be thought

Other doctrines are more Catharist in flavor: Christ was not really God, for God is incapable of dying, nor would he wish to humiliate himself by taking on flesh.* There is no resurrection of the body. The Devil is the lord of this world, who made all material things. When a woman is pregnant, therefore, she is filled with the Devil. Her child is encased in diabolical matter and cannot be saved until he is received into the sect. The Old Testament and the Mosaic Law are the creations of the Devil. The heretics had "masters" who bestowed upon them consecrated bread called the *consolamentum* (a departure from ordinary Catharist practice, where the consolamentum was bestowed by the laying on of hands). They osculated this bread as a sign of reverence, and when they received it they took it with folded hands.† If they had not received the consolamentum by the time they died, their spirit would transmigrate into a lower form of life. When offered the consolamentum at any time before their natural death, they might choose either to die by practicing the endura or to live and be a "confessor," which they called a "magister" or a "perfectus." Thus far, their doctrines are representative of a somewhat deviant, but in no sense diabolist, Catharism. The

---

of as inhabiting Apulia. It is remotely possible that this is a confused memory of the prophet of Calabria, Joachim of Flora, or, much more likely, a reference to the proximity of Apulia to the Balkans, whence came the Bogomil missionaries. It is barely possible that this "pope" was a high-ranking Catharist, but there has never been any evidence that the Catharists had a supreme leader.

* Yet at least one of the sectaries confessed to a corollary that would have been shunned by any ordinary Catharist: Jesus was, therefore, not God, but the offspring of the carnal union of Mary and Joseph. His body, in other words, was real indeed, as opposed to the Catharist belief that it was an illusion only. This may represent a deviation from Catharism in the direction of witchcraft.

† *Manibus junctis:* hands pressed flat together and pointed upwards in an apex. This was the traditional Catharist sign of greeting and prayer, derived from the Hindus and in the twelfth and thirteenth centuries adopted by Catholic Europe.

teaching that they were the true sons of God or that it was all right to eat meat on fast days are not Catharist doctrines and might have derived from antinomianism.

Their other ideas were close to witchcraft. They held a synagogue at various places once or twice a month; usually ten or eleven people attended, both men and women. There they made a formal renunciation of the Catholic faith and adored Satan as their God, for, they claimed, he was more powerful than the Christian God and would one day overcome him. They promised that they would never leave the sect and that they would never reveal its secrets to anyone; this they swore upon a red book, possibly a volume of magic or one containing the names of the evil angels. At the synagogue, they heard sermons, received the heretical sacraments, and then feasted and drank. Some of the drinks were of loathsome composition. They had the virtue of rendering it impossible for those who partook of them ever to abandon the sect, but if imbibed too freely they might kill. After the feast, the lights were extinguished* and there followed a revel in which everyone seized whom he might. One of the accused, a woman named Bilia, admitted to having a familiar toad to which she fed meat, bread, and cheese, and out of whose feces, together with human body hair, she made a powder from which she confected the potions drunk at the synagogues.

The familiar and insoluble problem is how much of this may be believed. The use of torture and the eagerness of the Inquisitors to implicate as many people as possible does not inspire confidence in either the honesty of the proceedings or in that of the official account of the trial. Yet the Inquisitors did not pull out all the

---

* This element appears frequently in these trials and is derived from the ancient tradition stretching back to Orléans in 1022 and ultimately to the Fathers. It must have been introduced into the confessions by the Inquisitors, but this is proof, not that rites were not practiced (though that is certainly possible), but merely that the Inquisitors were interpreting the rites in the manner to which they had become accustomed.

stops: there was no mention of flight, shapeshifting, pact, incubi, child murder, magical salves, or the personal appearance of the Devil at the synagogues. The sources yield an understanding of the state of the concept of witchcraft at this time, but they do not show what the accused really believed. That at least some of them were heretics and may have practiced strange rites is no doubt true, but the undiscriminating zeal of the Inquisition has made further resolution of the problem impossible.

Other manifestations of antinomian heresy during this period helped to construct the phenomenon of witchcraft. At Cambrai, a sect called the "Men of Intelligence" was condemned in 1411 by the famous bishop of Cambrai, Pierre D'Ailly.[41] The movement may have gone back to the teachings of Sister Bloemardine who preached the freedom of the spirit in the Low Countries in the 1330s; in any event it had close connections with the Beghard movement and with the Brethren of the Free Spirit, for the Men of Intelligence preached a doctrine of internal pneumatic illumination and justification. The two leaders, Giles Cantor, an illiterate layman of about sixty, and William of Hilderniss, a Carmelite, confessed that they believed that in the third age, the age of the Spirit, all men, including Jews and pagans, would be saved, and with them the demons and the Devil himself. Their group was defined as a "sect," and it met in "conventicles." The Holy Spirit dwelt within them and justified their every action. Often they went naked to show that they were as innocent as Adam in paradise before the fall. They practiced free love at the urgings of the Spirit, holding the sex act to be a religious act of a value equal to that of prayer. William recanted and was suspended from his priestly functions and sentenced to three years in the bishop's prison.

In 1421, a group of heretics called Adamites were exterminated in Bohemia by John Žižka. Although no relation to the second-century Adamites who condemned marriage, advocated free love as a means of liberating the flesh, and went naked in order to symbolize their equivalence to Adam in his antelapsarian innocence, they were given the name of the earlier heretics because of the similarity of their practices. The Adamite heresy was introduced into Bohemia by Beghards emigrating from the west, probably because of religious persecution like that at Cambrai, and the basis of their teaching was pneumatic antinomianism.* They taught that nakedness was essential to purity, for this was the only way to restore antelapsarian innocence. They preached free love, and groups of men and women lived together in sexual promiscuity. Žižka's crusade against them was in retaliation for alleged attacks they had made upon the neighboring peasants, killing those who would not join them, but it is not clear whether this atrocity was an invention of their enemies used to justify their extinction, or, if not, from what kind of doctrine it sprang. It was not commonly alleged, curiously enough, against either medieval heretics or witches that they used force to attempt the conversion of their enemies.[42]

With the 1420s closes the long period of centuries of restraint. By 1430 the witch phenomenon had achieved almost its final form; in the following half century it would become a frenzy.

* The sources call them *Pichardi, Pickardi, Pickhardi,* or *Picardi,* which poses an etymological problem somewhat similar to the use of "Vaudois" for "witch." *Picardus* is a corruption of *Beghardus,* but that the corruption took this particular form probably relates to the origin of the emigrants in the region of Flanders and Picardy.

9

The Classical Formulation
of the Witch Phenomenon,
1427-1486

THE fifteenth century witnessed a vast expansion of witch literature and witch trials. In part this geometric progression of the witch phenomenon can be attributed to the decay of those ideas and institutions that had held medieval society together. Deprived of the old securities, people responded in panic that at that particular time found vent in terror of witchcraft. In other ways, witchcraft was the result of those aspects of the period that have generally been considered positive and are collectively known as the Renaissance.

The Renaissance revival of the classics and of Neoplatonism caused a vast reawakening, first in intellectual circles, and then at large, of the magical world view. This in turn greatly augmented the intellectual respectability of belief in witchcraft, until eventually it became difficult to argue against it. Trevor-Roper argues that witchcraft and high magic are totally different, the former springing from Aristotelianism, the latter from an antithetical Neoplatonism. Theoretically, he is right. But Trevor-Roper may here be treating the minds of the fifteenth-century Inquisitors as if they were as capable of making intellectual distinctions as his own. No matter how unrelated the two phenomena were in essence, they were related in that they presented a similar appearance, both to the popular and to the ecclesiastical mind. It is no more a fortuitous coincidence that the outburst of the witch hysteria in the fifteenth century is contemporaneous with the revival of high magic than that the ecclesiastical authority severely punished both the magicians and the witches as heretics.

From 1427, when publication of discourses on witchcraft began to proliferate, to 1486, the date of publication of the sinister *Malleus Maleficarum,* the witch phenomenon became thoroughly articulated. Ideas that had previously remained distinct were now joined in a whole. Maleficium was sometimes still treated independently, sometimes in conjunction with witchcraft, but in witchcraft proper, the heretical had merged completely with folklore elements such as the wild ride, so that it is no longer sensible or even possible to differentiate witch cases in which heresy was prominent from others. The degree to which Alpine superstition influenced the witch belief has been exaggerated.[1] The articulation of classical, heretical witchcraft originated in the lowlands where heresy was strong and only then moved into more remote regions like the Alps.[2]

Repression

The sheer number of witch prosecutions and executions increased enormously over the previous century.[3] Canon law had yet clearly to establish procedures in cases of witchcraft but permitted both bishops and Inquisition to proceed against witches either separately or jointly. The episcopal courts had been more concerned with heresy trials than any other institution, and their involvement with witch trials had up till now been preponderant. In the fifteenth century, however, the activity of the Inquisition in witch cases became so vigorous that the number of cases tried by bishops' courts and synods became relatively, though not absolutely, much smaller.[4] The secular courts were in an anomalous position. They had always had jurisdiction over maleficium,

228

but their rights over witchcraft were questionable since it was considered a branch of heresy. Most secular courts continued to prosecute sorcery without reference to heresy, but some followed the ecclesiastical courts in equating the two.[5] On the continent, the secular courts frequently used torture, and the sentences they handed down were as severe as those of the Inquisition. In England, though torture was sometimes extralegally applied, it never became standard procedure.[6]

The Inquisition, under the protection of canon law and the papacy, dominated trials in the fifteenth century to a degree that it had not done before. Precisely because canon law was unclear on provisions for procedure in witch trials, the Inquisition expanded its activities as rapidly as the resistance of the local authorities, episcopal or secular, could be overcome or bypassed.[7] This expansion of power would not have been possible without the support of the papacy. The activity of the fifteenth-century popes in bolstering the Inquisition finally fixed the crime of witchcraft in canon law, removing it from the realm of superstition and magic and placing it in the much more serious category of heresy.

In a number of bulls, Pope Eugenius IV (1431–1447) ordered the Inquisition to proceed against magicians and diviners, whose crimes he defined in terms of classical witchcraft: they sacrificed to demons, prayed to them, and rendered them homage; they desecrated the cross and made pacts with the Devil.[8] Eugenius' were the most explicit of any papal condemnations in the fifteenth century, though his successor, Nicholas V (1447–1455) made it clear that the Inquisition could prosecute sorcerers even when their connection with heresy was dubious.[9]

The next important papal contribution to the witch phenomenon was made by Innocent VIII (1484–1492), the great patron of Renaissance arts and letters, who published his infamous bull *Summis desiderantes affectibus* on December 5, 1484.[10] This letter was issued at the request of Institoris and Sprenger, the future authors of the *Malleus Maleficarum,* who needed the support of the Holy See against the opposition to their activities mounted by the local authorities in the Alps. The importance of *Summis desiderantes* has always been understood: included as a prefatory justification in the *Malleus,* it established once and for all that the Inquisition against witches had full papal approval and thereby opened the door for the bloodbaths of the following century. Yet it was less influential in the formation of the witch phenomenon itself than the *Malleus* or even the pronouncements of Eugenius IV. Other than incubi, incantations, and maleficium, there is little trace in the bull of the classical manifestations of the witch phenomenon, including the sabbat and its appurtenances. In his other letters, Innocent established the definition of witchcraft as heresy, but nowhere did he explicitly define witchcraft with reference to its component parts.[11] The importance of Innocent VIII's witch pronouncements lay chiefly in his support of Heinrich Institoris and Jakob Sprenger.

The careers of these notorious Inquisitors are well known.[12] Their great work, the *Malleus Maleficarum,* the "Hammer of Witches," derives its title from one often bestowed upon Inquisitors: "Hammer of heretics." It was written in 1485 or 1486, printed in the latter year with the *Summis desiderantes* of Innocent VIII as a preface, and immediately achieved broad popularity among Inquisitors and throughout the Church. Institoris was the chief author of the *Malleus,* Sprenger's role being relatively minor. Institoris was born at Schlettstadt near Strasbourg about 1430, and there entered the Dominican order. A staunch defender of papal privilege and a persuasive speaker, he had influential friends among the Dominicans at Rome and eventually obtained the patronage of the papacy. He was named Inquisitor for southern Germany in 1474 and became involved in witch trials as early as 1476. Institoris was an arrogant, ambitious, and ruthless man who made many enemies in and out of his own order (he was accused in 1482 of embezzling Dominican monies intended for the war against the Turks), and opposition to his activities in the mountainous regions of Germany on the part of the local episcopal and secular authorities was considerable.[13] Eventually Sprenger himself turned against him, and Institoris was condemned by the Dominican order in 1490 for the irregularity of his procedures, though this did not put an end to his activity, for Pope Alexander VI sent him in 1500 to fight heresy in Bohemia and Moravia.

Sprenger's career, on the other hand, indicates how enthusiasm for the purity of the Church and the defense of the Christian religion could produce sincere loathing of witches. Sprenger was born around 1436–1438 in Basel, where he entered the Dominican order, then went on to study at Cologne, where he eventually became a professor of theology. He became an Inquisitor in the Rhineland in 1470 and cooperated with Institoris both in action and to a small degree in the composition of the *Malleus,* until he at last sickened of his colleague's excesses.

The *Malleus Maleficarum* was modeled on the Inquisitorial handbooks of Eymeric and others and used a scholastic organization and method, proceeding with *quaestiones,* opposing arguments, and conclusions. It contributed little original to the witch phenomenon, but its careful organization and argumentation, combined with the papal approval that accompanied it, fixed the whole system of witch beliefs firmly in the mind of Inquisition and society in general. The authority of the *Malleus* placed those who would oppose the idea of witchcraft at a disadvantage for centuries, and its ideas were eagerly borrowed even by Protestants who wholeheartedly rejected other aspects of Catholicism. Witchcraft continued to develop in the following two centuries, but departures from and additions to the phenomenon as set forth in the *Malleus* were minor.

The purpose of the *Malleus* was systematically to refute all arguments against the reality of witchcraft. The authors maintain that many of the crimes alleged against witches are objectively real; others are illusions, but illusions provoked by the Devil at the behest of the witches. The *Malleus* circumvents the skepticism of the *Canon Episcopi* with the argument that modern witches are different from the women whose wild ride the canon declares fantasy (a conclusion that, curiously, is quite true in the light of the development of the witch phenomenon since the tenth century). Three elements are necessary for witchcraft: the evil-intentioned witch, the help of the Devil, and the permission of God, who though he hates evil allows it to occur, since without freedom with its potential for evil men would have no potential for good. Witchcraft is the most evil of all crimes, and worthy of the most severe punishment, for it is immediate and direct treason against God himself. The particulars of witchcraft enumerated in the *Malleus* include almost all the characteristics associated with classical witchcraft, insuring that they would thereafter be accepted as authoritative.

In view of the fact that the authors were spreading their nets so wide, it is curious that they made no mention of familiar spirits, of the obscene kiss, or even of the feasting and orgies of the sabbat. Nor is there any reference to the witches' or Devil's mark, both of which became so common in the trials of the next two centuries. The *Malleus* authorized stripping and shaving witches, but the purpose was to determine whether they had any amulets or magical charms hidden on their bodies, not to search for the distinguishing marks.

The *Malleus* defined witchcraft as the most abominable of all heresies, its four essential characteristics being the renunciation of the Christian faith, the sacrifice of unbaptized infants to Satan, the devotion of body and soul to evil, and sexual relationships with incubi. Witches have become servants of the Devil by making a pact with him and engaging in ritual copulation with Satan. They render homage to the Devil. They use incantations, effect apparent changes in their shapes by means of diabolical illusion, practice various forms of maleficium, are transvected through the air from place to place by the power of demons, and use the Christian sacraments in their vile rites. They cook and eat children, either their own or those of others; and they use the children's flesh and bones to obtain a salve or ointment which they then employ in their magical operations.

Monstrous as these ideas are, they were not original to Institoris, but proceed out of the long tradition of witch theory. That theory continued to develop in the fifteenth century.[14] Beginning in 1430, there was a marked increase in the quantity of treatises dealing with witchcraft. Whereas witchcraft had heretofore been considered an aspect of the broader problems of magic or heresy, it now itself became the center of attention. The quantum jump in theory is bound to the swift increase in the number of witch trials, but the relationship of the two phenomena in terms of cause and effect is impossible to fix. Both proceed from the fact that fifteenth-century attitudes had become far more receptive to the idea of witchcraft than ever before. This receptivity had been in part prepared by previous witch trials and treatises. It was also supported by the growing popularity of the comprehensive magical world view of Renaissance Neoplatonism. This, no matter how different from the Aristotelian framework into which witchcraft had originally been built, reinforced in the scholarly, and eventually in the popular, mind credence in a cosmic system of spirits more populous and active than commonly allowed for in the older Christian tradition.[15] The theorists of witchcraft were most of them not feeble in either intelligence or moral sense. They were among the intellectual and ecclesiastical leaders of their time and believed firmly in the horrors about which they wrote. Most, like the authors of the *Malleus,* were concerned with proving the reality of witchcraft against both rational skepticism and that based on the *Canon Episcopi.* As Robbins has rightly argued, the intellectuals were more responsible than the ignoramuses for the witch hysteria that gripped Western Europe in the three centuries from 1400 to 1700.

The fact that the printing press could now disseminate the works of the witch theorists in a quantity hitherto undreamed of added enormously to the growth of the witch craze. The first printed book on witchcraft, the *Fortalicium Fidei,* was issued in 1464, only about ten years after Gutenberg had produced the first book printed with movable type. It was an unfortunate coincidence that printing should have been invented just as the fervor of the witch hunters was mounting, and the swift propagation of the witch hysteria by the press was the first evidence that Gutenberg had not liberated man from original sin.

A distinct shift in attitude occurs among the theorists of this period. Many are still conservative, following the skeptical tradition of the *Canon Episcopi* to the extent that they deny the reality of shapeshifting and flight, though most insist that people are really deluded by the Devil into believing that they do such things. This skeptical attitude was maintained most firmly by humanists opposed to low superstition and attracted by the new Neoplatonism. Yet an increasing number bypassed or even refuted, though few dared ignore, the *Canon Episcopi.* Their gathering fear of witchcraft reflected the deep though implicit terror of medieval society in the process of seeing its values deteriorate. It is not a coincidence that many of the theorists were present at, or at least in some direct way connected with, the council of Basel, in which the concern with schism, heresy, and conciliarism indicated the extreme peril in which the medieval Catholic Church lay and from which it was never wholly to escape.

The names given the witches by the theorists indicate that the folk traditions lingered among the newer heretical definitions.

Though the witches were most often called *Vaudenses, Gazarii,* or simply *haeretici,* old names such as *lamiae, mascae,* and *striae* or *strigae* lingered on, the last commonly incorporated into the name of the "sect": the *secta strigarum.*[16] Some names are translations by the theorists of local, vernacular names such as the Spanish *bruxe (bruja)* or *xurguine.*[17]

The theorists are in a quandary about Diana and the night rides. On the one hand, they are impressed by the traditional skepticism of the *Canon Episcopi,* which some accept outright, some rephrase in scholastic tradition by assuming that the women are themselves deluded, and some accept in part.[18] Nider, credulous though he was in other respects, backed the canon, recounting the story of a woman who claimed that she rode out with Diana in a large basket. She was watched, and witnesses reported that she really remained in the room but fell into a trance, from which she awakened convinced that she had been on long travels. The spectrum of credulity is subtly shaded. Those who believed that the women were deluded in their belief that they rode out generally held that the delusion was brought about by the power of demons. From there it is a short step to arguing that although the canon was perfectly right in denying that women rode out with Diana, they did indeed ride out with demons who deluded them by posing as Diana.* Other writers insisted that the *Canon Episcopi* was irrelevant to these new heretics, whom the Devil's wiles had but lately stirred up.[19] Unlike the women of the Dianic ride, these new heretics meet for the express purposes of working *maleficium* and worshiping the Devil. Vineti and Jacquier

---

* Torquemada's *"Diana est diabolus"* is an unusually strong statement, for Diana was usually equated only with a demon. The masculine gender of *diabolus* here accentuates the position that we are dealing with *the* Devil. Visconti speaks of her as a demon who presides over the assembly. His genders appear mixed: he says that the heretics adored *"dominam ludi tanquam dominum et deum suum,"* an indication that this lady was more than an ordinary demon.

warned that it is therefore dangerous, even foolhardy, to lull oneself into a sense of false security by relying upon the canon. In the sixteenth century, the extension of this argument placed those who supported the canon in mortal peril: they might be accused of attempting to impede the prosecution of the guilty.

The majority of the writers now accepted an actual flight through the air, some specifying that the witches rode on brooms or sticks or on beasts, usually cats or goats.[20] Of these fifteenth-century theorists, only Tinctoris argued that the witches obtained the power of flight by anointing themselves with the magical salve.

Related to the tradition of the Dianic ride is the rout of the bonae mulieres.[21] A number of the theoreticians argued that the witches went into people's houses to obtain food and drink, and Bernard of Como calls their revels the *"ludi bonae societatis."* The persistence of this tradition in the fifteenth century makes it easier to comprehend the presence in sixteenth-century Italy of Carlo Ginzburg's benandanti, who fought battles at night with the witches. Both Nider and Alfonso de Spina argue that the witches, or their accompanying demons, fight battles or make a noise like armies marching.

In order to penetrate into people's houses to obtain their food, or to steal their children, or for other evil purposes, Vignate claimed, witches might pass through closed doors. This idea was vigorously denied by most of the other writers, but many of these argued that witches appear to go through closed doors because demons open and close them rapidly to permit their entry and departure; or else the witches themselves have the supernatural power of opening and shutting the doors faster than the eye can see. To avoid the superstition of believing that witches could pass through solid substances, Mamoris adopted instead the rational explanation that they obtained entry by flying down the chimney.[22]

Most of the theoreticians follow the scholastics in asserting the reality of incubi.[23] It is significant that they feel impelled to discuss the incubi in connection with witchcraft, but only Jordanes de Bergamo makes the explicit statement that at the revels the witches have sexual intercourse with incubi. Intercourse with incubi was always distinguished from the ceremonial copulation of witches with the Devil.

If demons had the power to take the forms of incubi and succubi, they had the power to take other shapes as well.[24] These shapes, it was generally agreed, were illusions. Demons had no power to transform things in their essences, but they could change their appearances. There was some disagreement about how this was accomplished. Skeptics, including William de Bechis and Martin of Arles, believed that no transformation was really accomplished at all but that the demons were merely deluding the senses of those who were beholding the supposed marvels. The more credulous—for example, Vignate—argued that demons condensed and formed air into whatever shape they wished to take: a man, sometimes black or deformed, a woman, a black cat, a stallion, a goat, a boar, a dog, or another animal. Less frequently, demons used their powers to transform other creatures: a man into a mouse or a crone into the form of a black cat. Mamoris argued that with the use of unguent men could change into werewolves. The most lurid shapeshifting story is in Nider's *Praeceptorium,* in which a knight who has been tupping a pretty girl awakes to find himself rolling in the mud with a dead beast.

In the tradition of heresy, the witches hold secret meetings at night, though some writers are skeptical of this.[25] Sometimes the night is specified as Thursday, according to the old folk custom of celebrating revels on the Day of Jupiter. The witches are bound to keep these assemblies secret in order to protect themselves from the authorities. The witches are identified with Catharists, Waldensians, or Jews, and their assemblies are called synagogues.[26] The term "sabbat," used so promiscuously by modern writers on witchcraft, appears only twice in the fifteenth-century literature; the first time it was used by Peter Mamoris in 1461–1462, and the second by Vincent.

Those who attended these meetings were heretics or even members of a formal sect, a witch cult. Even the most skeptical accepted this idea. Everything the witches believed was an illusion, Bernard Basin insisted, but that belief in itself was heretical. Indeed, their sect was worse than any other. Other heresies, Jacquier argued, are propagated by men, but witchcraft is led by the Devil himself. Since the witches' crime is so particularly loathsome, they should not be given the opportunity afforded other heretics of abjuring their errors and thereby obtaining readmission to society: they must burn at their first conviction. It cannot be alleged in their defense, Jacquier continued, that they are only led astray by the Devil, for when the immediate illusions of the secret meeting are over, they persist in their devotion to their evil master. Hence their wills are depraved as well as their senses deluded.[27]

The concept of pact still plays a somewhat modest role in the literature. The old idea that any magic *implies* a pact with demons appears frequently,[28] but the notion of explicit pact appears only in Martin le Franc, who ridicules it, and in the *Errores Gazariorum*. In both documents, the initiate to the witch cult is obliged to sign a pact with the Devil written in blood.

The orgies described by these writers are still very much in the old traditions of folklore and heresy, and Nider specifically compares them to those practiced by the antinomian heretics. At their secret meetings, the witches feast, dance, and hold sexual orgies.[29] The orgies, like those of the earlier heretics, usually take place among the sectaries themselves rather than between them and demons. The *Errores Gazariorum* states that after the feast, the lights are put out and the cry of *"Mestlet, mestlet!"* (i.e., "get in there and mix it up") is raised, at which everyone falls lustfully upon his neighbor. Tinctoris is the only writer to specify that the orgies are homosexual: homosexuality, a common charge against the Catharists, was less commonly associated with the witches, whose lechery was directed by the ancient tradition of incubi and succubi in a healthy, natural fashion toward demons of the opposite sex. The ritual union with the Devil, which would become so common in the sixteenth century, is still rare. Only Vignate brings supernatural sexuality into the revels, and it is demons in general rather than the Devil himself who participate. Vignate, who wrote about 1468, not long after the infamous trials in Artois, where the coldness of the demon's member first appears, is the first theorist to mention this characteristic of demonic intercourse, a departure from the tradition of incubi and succubi, whose virtue lay in arousing their partners to heights of venery.

Closely associated in the heretical tradition with the sex orgies was murder and cannibalism.[30] The victims are usually children. Three reasons are alleged for the murder of children. First, they are killed so that they may be sacrificed to the Devil. The *Errores Gazariorum* specifies that the initiate to the sect must promise to go out and kill as many children under the age of three as he can, usually by smothering them in their cradles.* The witches also killed and ate their own children, first affording them Christian burial in order to circumvent the suspicions of their neighbors. After the funeral, the witch repairs to the graveyard, exhumes the child, cuts off its head, hands, and feet, and wraps up the rest of the meat to be brought to the meeting and there devoured. This is the second reason for killing the children: so that they might serve as a loathsome repast. Sometimes this cannibalism is explained simply in terms of the old tradition of bloodsucking striae, but more often the child is more completely consumed, usually after having been roasted. Nider insists that the witches cook

---

* This may be a prescientific explanation of the still common phenomenon of "crib deaths."

their own children, boil them, eat their flesh, and drink the soup that is left in the pot. Or they extract from the soup a drink with which they ply one who is being initiated into the sect, for the consumption of this liquor will render him eternally loyal. From the solid matter, they make a magical salve or ointment, the procurement of which is the third reason for child murder.

This salve or ointment is one of the most important elements of witchcraft in the fifteenth century and later. It is prepared from the flesh of babies or from other no less horrible ingredients. Tinctoris' recipe is to take toads to whom consecrated hosts have been fed, and kill them. Combine their flesh with the blood of murdered children, the bones of exhumed corpses, and menstrual blood, and mix well. Even more elaborate is the confection of ointment described by the *Errores Gazariorum*. Take a red-haired man known to be a good Catholic, take off his clothes, tie him down on a bench so that he is unable to move, and then let venomous animals loose on him. When he has expired from their bites and stings, hang the body upside down and place a bowl under his head and mouth. Let the distillations falling from the body be caught in the bowl. Mix these with the fat of a hanged man, the entrails of children, and the bodies of the poisonous creatures that had been used to effect the victim's demise. The uses of the salves and powders so procured are many. By smearing them on sticks or brooms, one renders those objects capable of bearing one aloft, or else one anoints one's own body to the same end. The powder or salve is also used as a means of consecrating oneself to the Devil, of changing shapes, or of killing, causing sickness, or performing other *maleficia*. The *Errores Gazariorum* follows the tradition of attributing epidemics of disease to magical means in describing a powder made from the body of a cat stuffed with herbs, grain, and fruit, which is then hurled down from mountaintops in order to cause plague.[31]

The revolting use of the Eucharist in some preparations of the salve is a typical insult to Christianity. The *Errores Gazariorum* describes a host made out of excrement, and in other accounts the witches trample the consecrated bread or the cross.[32]

Another manifestation of contempt for Church and society was formal renunciation of the Christian religion, God, Christ, baptism, the Virgin, and the cross. This was expected of each initiate into the sect and sometimes ritually performed by all the witches at their assemblies.[33]

The most important element of witchcraft in the minds of the theorists was the direct relationship between the witches and the Devil or his demons. They followed the old tradition of attributing the success of magic to the invocation of demons and defining it as heretical. Even William de Bechis, skeptical of every other attribute of witchcraft, accepted the idea that sorcerers performed their magic by calling up evil spirits. Precisely because invocation was so generally attributed to the activity of sorcerers, it in itself was no indication of witchcraft. To be a witch rather than a sorcerer, one had not only to invoke, but also to worship, the Devil.[34]

As Thomas Ebendorfer pointed out, following William of Auvergne, all worship addressed to any creature other than God is idolatry, and superstitious reverence even of God himself is impermissible. Worse than ordinary idolatry was worship of demons, but worst of all was worship of the supreme spirit of evil. Jacquier explains that this is why the witches are the most evil of all heretics: they worship and attempt to please the Devil, *knowing that he is the Devil*. Knowing and willful subjection of oneself to the total abnegation of the Christian God and society: this is the essence of witchcraft.[35]

This worship of the Devil could be expressed in a number of ceremonies, sacrifice being the most natural in terms of either pagan or Christian tradition, so that it is difficult to be certain whether the element of sacrifice in witchcraft is meant to be a parody of Christianity or an extension of ancient pagan or magical ritual. Both traditions seem to be present. Sometimes the theorists condemn sacrifice to the Devil in the general terms similar to those used in the old injunctions against worship of pagan idols;[36] sometimes they are more explicit. Children were ritually sacrificed to the Devil, as noted above, but other gifts, such as a black rooster, food, a part of the human body, or even one's own semen, are also deemed appropriate.[37]

In an age still retaining many of the institutions of feudalism, homage was another natural form of worship. The initiate paid homage to demons or the Devil, sometimes by placing his own hands in those of his demonic lord in direct imitation of feudal practice. Sometimes whoever acted as "master" or "president" of the assembly was presumed to be the Devil, and then homage was rendered directly to him. In the oath of fidelity, the initiate had to promise to keep the meetings secret, to persuade others to join the cult, to kill children under three whenever he was able, to come to the "synagogue" whenever called, and by causing impotence or aversion to impede as many marriages as possible. Since the feudal ceremony of homage was often closed by the kiss of peace and a similar kiss of peace formed part of the mass, the obscene kiss was employed at the witches' meetings in imitation of either or both. The *Errores Gazariorum* says that the witches kiss the backside of the Devil, who has sometimes taken the form of a goat or of a wild boar.[38]

The Devil's mark, another common feature of later witchcraft, rarely appears in the writings of the theorists. Jacquier mentions it, but only in citing the record of a trial in which the accused confessed that a demon named Tonyon marked him, his brother, and his sister on the hips with the tip of his toe.[39] Jordanes de Bergamo, credulous enough in other ways, explicitly refutes the belief that witches bear a Devil's mark under their body hair because he has seen so many shaved without discovering one. He did, however, believe that the witches might conceal on their persons amulets or charms that protected them from hurt or that anesthetized certain areas of their body (a belief that became common in the next century and led to the unsavory practice of pricking).

Familiar spirits formed no great part of the theorists' beliefs, either, though even the skeptical William de Bechis believes in them. What references there are concern spirits only, not the animal forms assumed by familiars in the trials and in later literature.[40]

Though the witch phenomenon continued to develop even through the seventeenth century, the idea of witchcraft was in all major respects complete by the end of the fifteenth. In part this was due to the synthetic labors of the theorists. Yet theorists lagged behind the witch trials in the formation of the phenomenon. Some of the ideas that appear only seldom and tentatively among the theorists, like the *osculum infame,* appear frequently and are better developed in the trials. It is not possible to posit the spread of the witch trials in this century as a result of the existence of the treatises. More often, theory followed what was being done at the practical level of the courts, where popular beliefs, the legal heritage of the heresy trials, and the activity of the Inquisition were most effective. Few of the theorists (except Vineti, Jacquier, and the authors of the *Malleus*) were themselves Inquisitors or had practical experience at the trials.

Heresy and Witchcraft in the Fifteenth Century

By the fifteenth century, witchcraft had not only been firmly defined as heresy but also identified with the so-called Gazarii, the Fraticelli, and especially the Waldensians, whose name became almost a synonym for witchcraft. The reasons for the confusion between the Waldensians and the witches have already been discussed, but the fact that the real Waldensians of the period took refuge in Alpine caves to hide from their enemies may well have reinforced the idea that these heretics performed obscene rites in secrecy.[41] Even the English Lollards were connected by their enemies with sorcery if not with witchcraft. Some few Lollards held such libertine views as that adultery and fornication are not sin, or that "whoever died in faith would be saved irrespective of his way of life." There are even some closer approximations of witch beliefs, though very few. At Standon in Hertfordshire two Lollards claimed that there were no gods but the sun and moon, and a Berkshire man had taught that the Our Father should be said backwards.[42]

Witch Trials, 1427–1486

There were over a hundred significant witch trials in the period as compared with a lesser number over the preceding two full centuries. The great majority of alleged witches were accused of maleficium as well as witchcraft, but many cases of pure sorcery were tried, indicating that even at so late a date maleficium had not necessarily been pressed into the mold of witchcraft. Trials in secular courts now outnumbered those in episcopal and Inquisitorial courts, demonstrating that the Inquisition had nothing even vaguely resembling a monopoly on witch prosecutions, though the theorists drew more upon Inquisitorial than upon other trials, and the records of the Inquisitorial courts were fuller. Moreover, in some secular trials, for example, at Bressuire or in Valais, the picture of witchcraft is as complete as in the more lurid of the Inquisitorial trials. Influential as the Inquisition was in spreading the witch craze, it was representative of, and supported by, the society in which it existed.

The steady increase of the use of torture in both kinds of courts is in large part responsible for the growth of the witch phenomenon, for it elicited the implication of many more people than before. As the use of torture grows, our credence in the sources declines. The vast prosecutions in Artois in 1459–1460, for example, were so blatantly fabricated by the Inquisition through the systematic employment of terror that the condemnations were belatedly quashed by the Parlement of Paris in 1491. Though the continued activity of real heretics is a token of the continued existence of people who practiced witchcraft—indeed, the heightening of the terror probably produced a paradoxical heightening of the real practice—we cannot rely at all upon Inquisitorial testimony.

The trials are now too numerous to deal with individually; they will instead be dealt with as a group, analytically.[43]

The worship of Diana is not mentioned in any of the trials. A sinister note appears in the trials conducted by the Inquisition in Artois. The Inquisitors there obtained confessions that the witches had to promise the Devil to try to persuade people that the sabbats were sheer fantasy. In other words, the Inquisition was maneuvering those who were trying to check the witch frenzy, by appealing to the *Canon Episcopi,* into the dangerous position of appearing to be dupes of the witches or, even worse, witches themselves. The Inquisitors' success caused resistance to the witch craze to decline.[44]

The riding out, originally part of the Diana legend, had become an integral part of witchcraft, but it was now invariably associated with demonically induced flight through the air. The witches now almost always fly to their meetings, though some, if they live close enough, go on foot.[45] The Devil bears them through the air, often in the form of a beast, such as a wolf, a dog, a cat, or a goat, or else in that of a black man.[46] Sometimes the witches anoint themselves in order to prepare for this flight, but more often they anointed sticks, brooms, or even chairs. Sometimes the brooms flew without ointment, through the direct power of the Devil. The most unusual mode of diabolical travel was locomotion upon the excrement of horses or mules.[47]

Occasional references to the bonae and their practices link the witches to the bona societas, but only in one instance was the accused deliberately asked whether she was one of the boni.[48] Demons helped witches pass through doors by disassembling and reassembling their bodies more quickly than the eye could see or by rapidly opening and shutting the doors for them. Once the witches went at night through closed doors into cellars, where they took wine out of barrels and left urine in its place.[49]

The old idea of incubi was now associated with the ritual union of the witch with the Devil at the secret meetings, the Devil taking the form of a man or a woman as the circumstances required.[50]

Other varieties of shapeshifting were now more common. To help the witches or to receive their worship the Devil or one of his demons (the distinction is often blurred) took a number of forms. Usually he was an animal of some kind: a goat, a wolf, a cat, a dog, a bull, or a pig, sheep, gelding, horse, she-goat, cow, bear, monkey, hare, bird, or fox.[51] Often the animal's color was black. (Once the Devil appeared as "black water.")[52] Or he could take on the form of a person, in which event he was most often a black man or a man dressed in black. Once he was a brown man with a lowing voice, and once he was invisible. He could also be an old man in dirty clothes, a child, a pretty girl, queen of the revels, or half-man, half-goat.[53] As human, he took a name typical of the region in which he appeared. The belief that the Devil might take any kind of human form raised a question that became important for Inquisitors, who noted that some people defended accused witches on the grounds that it was not they, but rather the Devil in their forms, who had been seen at the sabbat.

In these trials, the appearance of the Devil is described in detail for the first time, and in a fashion similar to his appearance in the paintings of the period. His body is deformed, imperfectly solid, and unpleasantly cold and soft. His odor is foul, and the semen that he emits is yellow, cold, and corrupt. He is black, hairy, and horned, with large, red, shining, fiery, bulging eyes, a big, crooked nose, ears that stick out and shoot fire, a tongue that protrudes, a jutting chin that twists monstrously over towards one cheek, and a neck that is sometimes abnormally long and sometimes abnormally short. He has long, bony limbs and hooked and taloned fingers and toes. His feet may be cleft or curved like horses' hooves. His voice is harsh and dissonant, and of a terrifying timbre that causes people to fall to the ground in horror or else go mad. Here, in other words, is the modern image of the Devil. One thing only is lacking: the "pitchfork" or trident: in the fifteenth century the threefold power of Satan over air, earth, and underworld is symbolized by the tripod on which he presides over the witches' assembly.[54]

Less often, the Devil helped the witches change their own shapes into cats, wolves, foxes, goats, asses, or flies. Sometimes the Devil rendered them invisible at the witches' meeting, a procedure that made it possible for the Inquisitors to prosecute a suspect for witchcraft even when no one alleged that he had been seen at the meeting.[55]

The assembly is the aspect of witchcraft that almost universally appears in these trials, and when it is not mentioned specifically its existence is implied.[56] Where the witch cult was believed to be widespread, numerous meetings were supposed to be held concurrently. In the persecutions of Dauphiné in 1427–1447, for example, it was said that up to 10,000 witches had attended the revels. The size of each meeting varied from a few individuals to a few hundred, but there is no evidence whatever for the "coven" of thirteen. The meetings took place at night, though in one instance it was specified that they occurred in caves. Whenever the day of the meeting was mentioned specifically, it was Thursday or a Christian holiday, Thursday being in the ancient tradition of the celebrations on the day of Jupiter and Thor, and the Christian holidays either a sign of ancient pagan survival or of mockery of Christian custom.[57]

Nothing was surer evidence of witchcraft than attendance at the assembly, and courts were energetic in trying to force admissions of guilt on this score. In Artois and at Lyon, descriptions of the circumstances of the meetings were detailed. In Artois, the meetings were called conventicles or "assemblies," and they took place at night, usually between 11 P.M. and 3 A.M., often in the woods. The meetings were held frequently, and some of the more eager witches attended every night. In earlier accounts, the president was sometimes human, sometimes demonic. But in these trials he is universally supposed to be the Devil. In Artois he was called "the Great Master of the World," and the sectaries sat round him in a circle back to back and face to face, i.e., ◯ ◯ ◯. The Lyon account, which is by an Inquisitor, is the first to mention the special meetings four times a year that became a prominent characteristic of later witchcraft. The author wrote that the witches met three or four times a year in large meetings of special solemnity. The dates of these meetings were Holy Thursday, Ascension, Corpus Christi, and the Thursday nearest Christmas. Holy Thursday and Ascension Day could both be celebrations of spring.[58] On some years Corpus Christi fell close to Midsummer's Eve, and Christmas was the pagan feast of the rebirth of the sun. There is no mention here of the autumn festival of All Hallows' Eve. The Inquisitor's explanation is that the witches chose these dates in order to make mock of Christianity, but it is strange that these particular feasts were chosen: they come at times associated with pagan worship, and neither Ascension nor Corpus Christi is more important than a number of other feasts that might have been chosen if it was the witches' purpose to mock Christianity.

The frequent use of terms such as "synagoga" and "secta" in the trial records indicates how closely the Inquisitors identified the witches with other kinds of infidels and heretics. The witches were often equated explicitly with the Waldensians.[59] The term "sabbat" is still uncommon. At Dijon in 1470–1471 it appears, but only in a French summary of the trial, the Latin term that it translates being unknown. The first specific reference to a *sabat* in the original document occurs at Bressuire in 1475, which is also the first time mention is made of a new baptism given the witch at the time of her initiation and a special cult name bestowed upon her. These innovations, which became standard in later witch trials, originated in secular, rather than in Inquisitorial, courts. At Briançon in 1437 the witches' meeting is described as taking place on Saturday night, further indication of the derogation of Judaism intended.

Pact is also relatively unimportant in these fifteenth-century trials. The author of the *Recollectio* of Arras about 1460 argued that in all pact the human contractor agrees to give his soul to the Devil, the bargain sometimes being marked by some physical symbol such as the gift of a part of the body. At Annecy, for example, the witch's little finger was withered as a sign that she had given her soul to Satan. At Neuchâtel in 1481, the Devil was offered a fingernail or the whole little finger. In return for these gifts, the Devil would grant riches or magical powers. The explicit pact written and signed in blood is mentioned only once.[60]

In these witch trials as in the earlier heresy trials, the orgy, including dancing, feasting, drinking, and promiscuity, is one of the most important features. The feasting and drinking usually precede the sex orgy, as does the dancing. The loathsome nature of the feast is described in the Inquisitor's version of the heresy at Lyon: the witches consumed a coarse and horrible black bread as well as other food that had been dragged through offal; they drank a nauseating black potion out of a cup into which they then urinated. Only once is it specified that they danced widdershins (counterclockwise), a common characteristic in later trials. The most important element is the sex orgy, which in many respects follows the descriptions of the earlier heresies. This is clearest in the accusations lodged against the Fraticelli (the Reformist Franciscans): that they held their orgy after extinguishing the lights and killed the children born as a result, grinding their bones into a sacramental powder.[61]

The sex orgy is sometimes described in general terms; sometimes perversions such as homosexuality or intercourse "after the manner of beasts" are specified. The Devil or his demons take the form of incubi or succubi the better to service all the members of the sect, although the most significant sexual element, ritual copulation with the Devil, is as yet relatively uncommon. At Bressuire, the Devil caused his followers to dance and then, in the shape of a man dressed in black, copulated with the women, leaving the men alone. At Brescia in 1480, the witches had ritual intercourse with their master, Lucibello. The most specific account comes from the trials in Artois, where the accused were subsequently exonerated by the Parlement of Paris. First the witches allegedly had an orgy among themselves, in the fashion of the heretics of old. Then followed ritual intercourse with Satan, who took male or female form as the situation suggested. Sodomy, homosexuality, and other "crimes against nature" were committed, and the female witches, not content with receiving their demon lover in human form, delighted in submitting to him in the form of a bull, a fox, or even a hare.[62]

The Inquisitorial author of the *Recollectio* was even more susceptible to prurient imagination. The Devil's whole body, he says, is cold and soft, but most especially his penis. His sperm is yellow, corrupt, and fetid, for he has gathered it from the nocturnal and other emissions of humans. No one has any pleasure from sexual relations with the Devil but complies with his will only out of obedience or fear. The fact that of all fifteenth-century prosecutions those of Artois are the least credible confirms that this particular aspect of the witch phenomenon was more likely an invention of the Inquisitorial imagination rather than the result, as some have suggested, of the actual use at the revels of an artificial phallus by a human posing as the Devil who in turn is posing as a human.

Closely associated with the sex orgies in the heretical literature was child murder, which appears frequently in these trials. The witches kill their own children or those of others, sometimes specializing in the unbaptized. The murders are committed by the witches either individually for purposes of maleficium or else ritually at the meetings. Sometimes adults were killed too. There were three distinct purposes in child killing, all traditional: sacrifice to the Devil, cannibalism, and the preparation from the bodies of salves or powders to be used in maleficium. The case of Jubertus in 1437 provides an unusual example of the last: from the powder obtained from the murdered infants he manufactured facsimile children whose factitious bodies demons inhabited.[63]

The cannibalism of the witches is usually restricted to children, whose flesh they consume sometimes raw and sometimes roasted, or whose blood they suck or drink. They occasionally dig up their meals from the graveyard, being contented with corpses of any age or sex but leaving behind the heads, which have presumably been protected by the water of baptism.[64]

The magical salves and powders of the witches are made from the bodies or parts of children mixed with other unsavory objects. At Todi in 1428 they were confected of the blood of babies mixed with the fat of vultures. In Artois, the Inquisitors alleged that the accused had put consecrated bread and wine into a pot full of toads. When the toads had devoured the sacrament, they were killed and burned. Then the ashes of the toads were mixed with the powdered bones of dead Christians, the blood of children, herbs, and the recipe was completed with "other things." At Lyon in 1460 the Inquisitor distinguished between the magical powder confected from toads and the salve procured from the heart of an unbaptized child or other murdered infant. The salve made from children's guts or bones was usually employed to render one airborne and for this purpose was rubbed on one's hands and palms, or, more commonly, upon a stick, a chair, or a broom. Sometimes the salve, or the powders procured in similar fashion, were used for maleficium or in a blasphemous sacramental meal.[65]

Ceremonial desecration of the sacraments or the cross was sometimes performed by the group as a whole and sometimes enjoined upon the proselyte. This deliberate insult was a sign of the witches' faith in the Devil and should be distinguished from the use of the Eucharist or other sacraments in maleficium, an ancient custom associated with sorcery throughout the Middle Ages. The cross, the most powerful symbol of Christian orthodoxy, was most often chosen as the object of their contempt. Like the Reformist Peter of Bruys or like the Catharists who believed that the crucifix was an insult to Christ because he had never had a real material body, the witches trampled the cross and spat or even excreted on it. In 1437, Jubertus seized every opportunity to expectorate upon statues of the Virgin as well. The Inquisitor at Lyon alleged that the witches retained the host in their mouths after receiving and then took it home either to use in maleficium, to insult it at the assembly, or simply to desecrate it by mixing it with urine and feces. Another witch not only desecrated the Eucharist but showed her contempt of Christianity by defecating in the nave of the Church and urinating into the holy water font. The Inquisitor at Artois reports that the witches there poured holy water out onto the floor and stamped on it.[66]

Occasionally the alleged outrages were even more lurid. A Jewish sorcerer supposedly burned statues of Christ and the Virgin and insulted the Agnus Dei by crucifying a lamb and giving it to the dogs to eat, another indication of how the orthodox could identify witchcraft and Judaism as the two most heinous rejections of Christian society. At Porlezza people groaned and howled during mass and vomited up hairs and other objects, not because

they were witches themselves, but because they had been bewitched by heretics determined to make mock of the Eucharistic
feast.[67]

The first and only example of anything like a "black mass"
recorded in medieval witch trials occurred at Brescia in 1480,
where the witches celebrated masses in honor of their god
Lucibel. The black mass is for the most part a literary invention
of the nineteenth-century occultists, though something very like
it was performed by the degenerates of the court of Louis XIV in
the famous *Chambre Ardente* affair. The Brescia account mentions
only the parody of the Christian service and includes none of the
titillating details of the seventeenth-century masses. The absence
of black masses in the Middle Ages is a strong point against those
who argue that witchcraft originated as an explicit distortion of
Christian rite. Had this been true, the mass, the central feature
of Christian worship, would surely have been blasphemously enacted at the witches' conventicles. Here is further proof that witchcraft was drawn from heresies which, however gross, lacked this
ultimate outrage.

Directed toward the same end of repudiating Christian church
and society was the formal renunciation of the faith required of
witch postulants and sometimes jointly affirmed by the entire
assembly. The witches abjured the faith as a whole or specified
their renunciation of God, Christ, the Virgin, the saints, the
sacraments, the cross, or the Church.[68]

Witchcraft, unlike sorcery or heresy, is centered upon the
explicit worship of the Devil, either in private meetings or, more
usually, at the conventicles. It is not often specified whether the
Devil appears at the meetings simply by appointment or whether
he is called up by his worshipers. The charge of invocation, like
that of maleficium, is almost standard in the witch trials. But now
in the fifteenth century the demon summoned is likely to be the
Devil himself, and he comes, not to be the servant of the witch,

but to receive his worship. In 1438, for example, Pierre Vallin called up Beelzebub, whom he received as his master. In 1475, Sathanas appeared, and, in 1480, Lucibel. Most curious was the elaborate invocation at Provins in 1452 of three demons or Devils: Balsebur, Sathanas, and Lucifer. Faustian high magic seems to have had an influence here, as these evil ones were summoned in a ceremony that included the use of magic circles.[69]

When the Devil appeared, the witches worshiped him as their "true Lord and master," or, even more specifically, as their "God and Lord," this clearly being deliberate latria (as was specified at Barcelona in 1434) and not merely dulia. Sometimes they gave themselves to the Devil "as their Savior." Jubertus worshiped "as gods" the three demons he had summoned, kneeling before them with his face to the west and his buttocks elevated towards the east, a parody of the Christian custom of constructing altars facing in the direction of Jerusalem. The Inquisition in Artois said that the witches believed that there was no god other than their prince, Lucifer, but it also accused them of holding the belief that though Lucifer was the supreme deity they themselves were also immortal gods. Such a doctrine is consistent only in terms of Satanist pantheism. Indeed, the author of the *Recollectio* goes on to allege that the witches held other even more specifically antinomian beliefs: they defined Paradise as membership in their sect, they believed that things ordinarily considered sinful are not sins at all, that if you sin you should enjoy it, and that there is no heaven or hell, only this world, whose god and lord is the Devil.[70]

Worship of Satan was expressed in a variety of ceremonies, notably sacrifice, homage, and the obscene kiss. The witches sacrificed children or animals to their master, or offered him oblations of money, parts of their own bodies, or a lighted candle of black wax. Homage was rendered the Devil in ceremonies that sometimes directly parodied those of feudalism: the witch knelt, sometimes nude, sometimes with bared buttocks, in front of the

Devil and placed his hands between those of his master, swearing an oath of fidelity to him. At Neuchâtel one witch signified homage by putting his foot on the Devil's foot. Then there sometimes followed an infernal version of the kiss of peace. Pierre Vallin kissed the Devil's thumb, and other witches kissed his hands or feet, but usually the kiss was in the form of the *osculum obscenum* or *infame* of the buttocks, anus, or genitals, a procedure that had first achieved fame in the trial of the Templars. As in their sexual relations with Satan, the witches observed this practice, not from desire, but from obedience, for the Devil frequently appeared in the form of a goat with posteriors that were fetid, cold, and either revoltingly soft or repellently hard.[71]

In token of his favor, and to set them forever apart as his own, the Devil signed his followers with a visible mark, just as Christian baptism sets a person apart for God with an invisible mark. There is great diversity in the size and shape of the Devil's mark as well as in the manner in which it was bestowed, and it may have been wholly the invention of the witch hunters, who in the fifteenth century began the practice of shaving the accused from head to toe in their search for the sign. The Devil marked both men and women by touching them with his finger or toe, the result being a mark on the flesh that was pale, red, and about the size of a pea, or larger. It was found on the arm, shoulder, under the body hair, or elsewhere, or it might be a withered finger or other deformity. Such broad definitions, used in the secular as well as in the Inquisitorial processes, made it possible for the prosecution to define almost any physically distinguishing characteristic as a Devil's mark.[72]

The familiar, a manifestation of lesser demons, sprites, and other only mildly malevolent spirits, was not an essential part of the witch phenomenon, but it was mentioned in a number of trials. Usually the familiar is a spirit who aids and encourages the witch rather than dominates him. Sometimes he has a pet name, like Galifas, Bara, Oberycom, Krütli, or Federwisch. But the increasing importance of the *worship* of the Devil in witchcraft caused a confusion between the pet demon and the Devil, so that at Barcelona in 1434 a woman was accused (and acquitted) of rendering latria to her familiar; in 1436 a spirit named Mermet was worshiped as the Devil, and Antoine of Annecy venerated a spirit named Robinet,* who acted as president of the witches' revels. Other names used were Josaphat, Raphas, Ragot, and Robin.[73] There is no trace of the animal familiar.

Pierre Vallin and Maria "la Medica"

Of these fifteenth-century witch trials two of the most typical and most interesting were those of Pierre Vallin and Maria la Medica.

The trial of Pierre Vallin began March 15, 1438 at La Tour du Pin in Dauphiné.[74] The Inquisition had been especially active in Dauphiné since about 1425 and had systematically prosecuted both heresy and witchcraft, particularly in those areas where the Waldensians were reputed to be strong. The case of Pierre Vallin seems to be the first in this area in which accusations of witchcraft, as opposed to Waldensian Reformism, were made. The Inquisition may have been, as Hansen suggests, taking its cue from the bulls of Eugenius IV in 1434–1437. Nider's *Formicarius*, which appeared about 1430, may also have had an influence upon the trial. What is perhaps most curious is that in spite of the facts that witches were often equated with Waldensians, and that the very Inquisitor that tried Vallin had long been prosecuting those heretics, Vallin himself was never accused of any relationship with them. His only alleged crime was witchcraft.

The case was first brought before a court under the joint jurisdiction of the Franciscan Inquisition and the officials of the archbishop of Vienne, Jean de Norri, in whose diocese La Tour

* Compare Alice Kyteler's Robin Artisson.

du Pin was located.[75] The representative of the Inquisition was Antoine Andrée, the vicar of the Inquisitor Pontius Fougeyron, who had long been active in prosecuting both Waldensians and magicians. The archbishop's representative was Jean de Scalone, a canon lawyer and a sacristan of Die. The cooperation between the Inquisition and the archiepiscopal authority was quite normal here as in all areas where the Inquisitors were tactful and did not attempt to infringe upon episcopal authority.

Their procedure was also typical: the accused (of whose life and personality we are told almost nothing) was allowed no defense and was tortured into confessing. The sentence states that he made his statement voluntarily, which simply means that he was tortured, removed from the place of torture, and then given the choice of confessing voluntarily or of being returned to the torture chamber. According to his confession, he invoked his "master," Beelzebub, to whom he knelt and rendered homage by kissing the thumb of his left hand and to whom he paid a *liard* as yearly tribute. Vallin confessed that he had given himself to Beelzebub sixty-three years previously and that he had always remained faithful to him. He had denied God and trampled and spat upon the cross. He had sacrificed his daughter Françoise to the Devil when the child was only six months old. With the help of the Devil he raised storms, performed other *maleficia*, and flew through the air to the witches' assembly. At this "synagogue," he copulated with Beelzebub, who conveniently had taken the form of a twenty-year-old girl, and he joined the other witches in devouring the bodies of innocent children. The judges condemned him as a heretic, idolater, apostate, and invoker of demons. He was delivered to the secular arm with a plea for mercy, a common and wholly empty formula designed to cleanse the hands of the Inquisitors of the blood of the victim while insuring that the blood be spilled. All his worldly possessions were confiscated and, after the expenses of the trial were deducted, a third of the remaining portion was reserved for the archibishop and the Inquisition.

Pierre Vallin was delivered on the next day, March 16, to the secular authority, which was the court of the Lady of Tournon, Elinor of Grolea, whose vassal Pierre was. Representing the Lady as judge in her court was Etienne de Saint Georges; François Dupont, castellan of the Lady of Tournon's castle, was also present. The interrogation of Vallin by this court differed in no essential respect from that of the ecclesiastical tribunal, save that the Lady's court noted that he had already been convicted for magic (*sortilegiis*) in 1431, been fined, and threatened with burning if he should relapse. After interrogation, Vallin was made to stand out in the courtyard in front of the kitchen and there make a public confession of all his crimes in the presence of the judge, the castellan, a notary named G. Maréchal, and a number of other witnesses. In addition, he named four accomplices, three men and a woman, all four long since dead.[76]

Though Vallin pleaded to be exempted from further interrogation and though the judge set the date of March 21 for his formal sentencing, the higher authorities did not consider his averral sufficiently forthright. Philippe Baile, a judge of Vienne and representative of the higher secular authority of the Dauphin, intervened and ordered a further interrogation under torture. As Hansen and Lea both observed, the careful investigation of the Vallin case by both the lower and the higher secular powers shows that the secular authority did not always simply receive the condemned from the hands of the Inquisition and proceed to sentence and execution without further ado; sometimes the care they took exceeded that of the ecclesiastical tribunals. What bothered Philippe Baile was the lack of living accomplices. Under his express order, Etienne de Saint Georges went on March 23 to the castle, where Vallin was being kept prisoner, and resumed the interrogation, insisting that it was incredible that in his sixty-three years as servant of Beelzebub, Vallin could remember no more than four other witches, and those long dead. There must be living accomplices, whose names the Devil was urging him to conceal. Under repeated torture, Vallin now implicated not only the woman who had originally led him astray but also many people of both sexes and all social classes. He specifically indicated, giving their names, that eight men and four women, some of whom were now living, had been at the witches' meeting, and had ridden there upon sticks. Etienne de Saint Georges was still unsatisfied, and the next day, March 24, he again interrogated Vallin, insisting that he must remember others who had participated, not only poor men, but "priests, clerics, nobles, . . . and rich men." But Vallin steadfastly refused to implicate anyone else, even, he said, if they would promise to set him free for doing it, a resistance of extraordinary courage in a man who had now faced torture and constant threats of torture for more than a week.

Unfortunately, this is all we know of the case of Pierre Vallin. The documents relating to the civil trial were collected and notarized by Maréchal and sent on to the court of the Dauphin, which, it may be presumed, passed final sentence upon the victim.

Our suspicion of the evidence that emerges from a trial in which torture is so freely employed is bound to be great. One can only guess at what truth might lie behind the proceedings. Vallin had been tried for magic eight years previously, and it is probable that he did practice some kind of sorcery, was a heretic of sorts, and may even in some fashion have worshiped the powers of evil. But it is certain that whatever truth there was behind the accusations was systematically embroidered, first by the episcopal, and then by the secular courts. The motives of Vallin's persecutors were only too clear: to prove their own orthodoxy, to impress their superiors with their zeal in rooting out heresy, and to acquire as much property by way of confiscations as possible. Vallin's own goods were held confiscate, of course, but the efforts of Etienne de Saint Georges, evidently under pressure from Philippe Baile, the Dauphin's officer, to augment these spoils by extracting the names of nobles and other rich people, would be laughable if they were not so gross.

At Calcinato in the diocese of Brescia, a woman of low degree called Maria "la Medica" was tried alone by Brother Antonio Petoselli, a Dominican Inquisitor, on September 17, 1480. She was charged with having been a witch for fourteen years and of having attended the witches' conventicle three times a week. She worshiped the patron and lord of the assembly, knowing consciously that he was the Devil. The second time she went to the meeting, she ceremonially denied God and Christ and promised to worship the Devil as her only god. She offered him homage, her usual posture in this rite being nude and kneeling. She frequently called up the Devil, whom she called Lucibel, on each occasion renewing her renunciation of the Christian God and her faith in him. She participated in masses with lighted candles, which were celebrated in the name of the Trinity but in fact dedicated to Lucibel. At the witches' assembly, there was habitually a feast followed by an orgy including both normal sexual acts and acts against nature. The witches copulated both with one another and with Lucibel. Maria made an explicit pact with Lucibel, offering him the blood of children or a live animal, usually a hen, dove, dog, or cat. These offerings were symbols of her soul, which she delivered to him, and the words she used in these offerings were: "I offer you, o lord my god, the soul you made and that I promised I would give you, and the animal that you have created."

In return, Lucibel helped her in her magic, especially in her cures of her own diseases and those of others, and taught her how best to kill children. Her medical cures, which won her her nickname, were performed either in the name of the Trinity, like

260

the magical cures of the earlier Middle Ages, or through the direct intervention of Lucibel. Maria, however, could kill as well as cure. She was charged with having bewitched at least thirty girls and boys of the diocese, causing half to die but releasing the other half (for unspecified reasons) from her spell. She misused the sacraments, particularly holy chrism, which she employed as an aphrodisiac or smeared upon sticks in order to use them for divining the location of buried treasure. The Inquisitor, considering that this was her first conviction and that she confessed and repented, meted out the unusually light punishment of life imprisonment.[77]

Political Trials

In the fifteenth century, unlike the fourteenth, there was little inclination to introduce witch charges into trials motivated by political or economic hostility. The two most lurid political trials of the century—those of Joan of Arc in 1431 and of Gilles de Rais in 1440—did involve accusations of witchcraft, but in fact they were extremely peripheral. It is often stated that Joan of Arc was burned as a witch, and some modern writers, following Margaret Murray, have argued that she really was one. The idea is unfounded. The political nature of her trial, the need of the English and Burgundians to do away with Joan, and the mean and self-serving betrayal of the Maid of Orléans by her own king, are too well known to need any elucidation. It has long been clear that most of the charges leveled against Joan were deliberate falsifications. But the irrelevance of witchcraft in her case is even more fundamental. During the exhaustive and almost interminable interrogations, certain charges relating to witchcraft were made: namely, that Joan danced with fairies, adored them, called up demons, and made a pact with the Devil. Her voices, it was alleged, far from proceeding from the lips of saints and angels, were in fact those of Belial, Satan, and Behemoth. Now in the first place, these charges, except for invocation and pact, were quite removed from the usual witch tradition. Dancing with fairies or adoring them was an accusation drawn from old folklore, not from the thoroughly developed witch traditions of the mid-fifteenth century. Had Joan's accusers really believed she was a witch, or had they even wanted seriously to charge her with witchcraft, the accusations would have been much fuller, more detailed, and would have drawn upon the already wide experience of other witch trials as well as upon the scholastic theories of witchcraft. The court was so uninterested in this aspect of the matter that it withdrew the charges of sorcery and witchcraft altogether. Joan was condemned as a heretic, and there was nothing of witchcraft in the sentence that condemned her. The trial of Saint Joan deserves no place of importance in the history of the witch phenomenon.

The other spectacular trial of the period, that of Gilles de Rais, is only slightly more relevant. Again, the story of the fall of the wealthy and powerful Marshal of France and his destruction by his political enemies is too well known to bear detailed discussion here. Gilles was tried first in an ecclesiastical court under the joint jurisdiction of the bishop and the Inquisitor, who took the charges of witchcraft and sorcery more seriously than in Joan's case. Gilles was accused of having used alchemy and magic, of causing his magicians to invoke demons, who appeared under the names of Barron, Orion, Beelzebub, Satan, and Belial, or in the form of a serpent, and of making a pact with the Devil, to whom he sacrificed the heart, eyes, and hand of a child or a powder confected from the bones of children. Next he was tried in a secular court for the sex murders of over a hundred children.

Some writers have accepted all the charges against Gilles and made of him one of the most monstrous devotees of Satan in human history; others have exonerated him entirely and deemed him the innocent victim of his political enemies. The truth, I believe, lies between these extremes. Clearly, many of these witch charges were fabrications for the purpose of embroidering the case against a man who had many powerful political enemies and few friends left in any position of influence. But in his own confession, in which torture may not have been used, Gilles admitted to having used alchemy and to having murdered children. Neither of these two admissions has much, if anything, to do with the development of the witch phenomenon. Gilles had formed enormously expensive habits when he was in a position of power, and during the 1430's he had run up huge debts that he was unable to pay. He had alchemists and other magicians in his entourage and fell in with them very naturally in the hope that they would be able to procure him gold by the transmutation of baser metals. Alchemy was coming much into vogue at this time, and many magnates both secular and ecclesiastical employed alchemists in the hopes of augmenting their coffers. Alchemy, however, belongs to the tradition of high magic and has nothing properly to do with witchcraft.

Gilles probably did not sacrifice children to the Devil, but he all too probably murdered them. The volume and extent of the evidence that Gilles was a vicious sexual pervert is too great to be dismissed. His unspeakable habits were no doubt exploited by his political enemies, but any argument that they are too horrible to be believed can be dismissed by reference to similar (though no doubt less extensive) crimes in the police dossiers in every major city in the world. The Moor Murders of 1965 in England demonstrated the extent to which human beings are capable of deriving pleasure from the sexual abuse and murder of children. But that Gilles was a murderous pervert does not indicate that he was a witch. Witches sacrificed or ate children or made them into magical salves or powders, but they did not abuse them sexually. Gilles' pleasures were his own, not a part of the phenomenon of witchcraft.

The theories and trials of the fifteenth century were continued in the next two centuries, when during the Renaissance and Reformation the witch frenzy reached its height. This book cannot deal with witchcraft in that period, but it must now ask why and how society permitted witchcraft to arise in the Middle Ages.

Witchcraft and the Medieval Mind

T H E concept of madness is of only limited use in explaining the medieval witch phenomenon, for not all witches were psychologically disturbed or psychotic individuals. An alleged witch or Inquisitor, holding views of the supernatural that appear mad to the commonly accepted philosophical materialism of our own day, cannot in any meaningful way be assumed to have been mad, because these views were commonly accepted in his society. As the anthropologist Alan C. Elms has shown in a study of radical right-wing political sentiment in Dallas, people holding irrational ideas are not necessarily personally irrational if those ideas are held by the society in which they live, or at least by those with whom they associate.[1] It might be argued that the witch craze must at least have been initiated by madmen, but this would again be to ignore the relativity of the term madness and, more specifically, to forget that witchcraft arose within the context of a coherent and widespread magical world view and developed in the context of the system of medieval Christianity. Even if an individual witch or witch hunter was mad, the particular expression his madness took was largely determined by his social environment. Today some disturbed people imagine themselves machines: such a form of madness would have been extremely unlikely in the Middle Ages. On the other hand, in a world that was populated with spirits, many of them malignant, one might without difficulty have imagined oneself a witch. Though nourished by individual psychological difficulties, witchcraft was a social phenomenon.

Medieval witchcraft was the product of a social psychology shaped by Christian and feudal mythology. Mythical and associative mental processes had greater influence upon popular thought than the rational structures of philosophers or the carefully phrased canons of lawyers. The ubiquity of evil spirits was confirmed by the consonance of pre-Christian mythologies, the Bible, the Fathers, and even the philosophers. Hell was a reality to which a just God delivered the guilty, there to be tormented by demons. Belief in possession—involuntary seizure by demons— was seldom denied, having as it did the authority of the exorcisms performed by Christ and the apostles. Oesterreich and others have shown that charlatanry is out of the question in many or even most cases of possession, particularly in the Middle Ages: both those who felt themselves possessed and those who observed the possessed were convinced of the reality of the diabolical presence. In such a society, where the spiritual world was considered as real or even more real than the material, tension and hostility tended to be expressed in spiritual rather than material terms. This explains the wide emotional appeal of heresy. But whereas heretics claimed to have a more valid and direct understanding of Christ's teachings than the orthodox had, witches denied every aspect of Christianity and claimed to worship the Enemy of Christ. Witchcraft was therefore the strongest possible religious expression of social discontent. Even the infidels—Jews or Muslims—were far less dangerous to the faith than the witches. This tension in the spiritually oriented society of the Middle Ages produced irrational terror of witches as well as of witchcraft itself.[2]

Medieval Christianity was a dynamic religion capable of assimilation. In the early centuries, it had assimilated much paganism and sorcery into saints' cults and festivals. Later, in the fourteenth and fifteenth centuries, it at least partly absorbed mysticism and other prophetic movements. Since most popular heresy in the Middle Ages contained many elements of orthodoxy, however exaggerated, some exchange of ideas between the two was possible. But witchcraft, though it was the creation of Christianity, was also its uttermost antithesis.

The irrational terror that witches inspired in turn fed the witches' own belief in their magical powers, a psychological process of introjection brilliantly illustrated in the Danish film *Vredens Dag* ("Day of Wrath"), based upon an historical case in seventeenth-century Bergen. To some extent, the witches behaved precisely as they were expected to, *for the reason that* they were expected to. This point must, however, not be carried so far that one falls into a variety of the simplistic and erroneous belief that the Inquisition caused witchcraft. In England, for example, where the Inquisition did not exist and torture was used sparingly, confessions of witchcraft occurred. People were convinced of their guilt by suggestion as much as or more than by coercion. Parrinder shows the existence of many fantastic witch beliefs in Africa completely unelicited by force or threat.[3]

Further explication of the function of witchcraft in medieval society is limited by the scantiness of social and psychological indications in the sparse sources. Medieval writers—chroniclers, notaries, ecclesiastics—did not think or write in such categories, so that only the roughest kind of statistical suggestions are possible.

The sources yield little information about the social class of the people indicted for witchcraft. As nearly as we can tell, all sorts of people were involved. The sources most frequently mention priests and peasants, but they also refer to noblemen, knights, rich men, professional people, and others.[4] Nothing suggests that each social class had its own peculiar kind of witchcraft. Neither does there seem to be any substantial correlation between outbreaks of witchcraft and rebellions, famines, or plagues, except in the general sense that the phenomenon grew most rapidly during the troubled times of the fourteenth and fifteenth centuries.

Certain general patterns, however, can be ascertained. Some areas of Europe were much more susceptible to witchcraft than others. Spain, though it had a strong tradition of high magic, had little witchcraft, a point in favor of Trevor-Roper's view that the two are wholly unrelated. Portugal, southern Italy, Scandinavia, Ireland, and, until the fourteenth century, England, were also relatively untouched. Witchcraft was strongest in France, the Low Countries, the Rhineland, northern Italy, and the Alpine regions. With the exception of the Alps, these areas were the richest, most populous, most highly industrialized, and most intellectually advanced in Europe. Witchcraft appeared in the Alps only after the witches and heretics took refuge from persecution in those mountain fastnesses. The geographical facts thus strongly suggest that Lea, Hansen, Murray, Trevor-Roper, and even to some extent Runeberg and Ginzburg, all of whom have emphasized the agrarian or mountainous nature of witchcraft, are in error on this point. This in turn gravely weakens the hypothesis that witchcraft was fundamentally a fertility cult with roots in agriculture or in the chase. To be sure, such mythical elements had always been present, and they were somewhat reinforced when witchcraft fled the centers of population for the Alps. But in the early Middle Ages the elements of agricultural myth in witchcraft had already been subjected to the influence of Christianity, a transmutation that accelerated from the thirteenth century onward. Witchcraft thrived best, not in mountainous or agricultural areas, but wherever and whenever (often slightly after, suggesting a displacement from heresy to witchcraft) heresy flourished. Where heresy was absent, witchcraft—as distinct from simple sorcery

—was either wholly absent or appeared only in rare and peculiar cases. The geographical and chronological consonance of witchcraft and heresy, conjoined with their internal similarities, demonstrates the closeness of their relationship.

Social tension in the Middle Ages, expressed in terms of transcendental Christian myth, produced crazes of fear that were directed against outcasts from Christian society. Jews were accused of praying to the Devil, doing him homage, practicing sexual orgies, cannibalism, and murder, and using in their rites loathsome materials like blood and semen.[5] Lepers were accused (along with Jews and occasionally witches) of spreading poison from hilltops or dropping it into wells. Political outcasts were, particularly in the fourteenth century, charged with maleficium.

Yet on the whole witch charges were not loosely bandied about. In the fifteenth century, while the witch phenomenon was rapidly spreading, the practice of using charges of maleficium in political trials declined rapidly. The full bill of witchcraft was seldom leveled against the Jews, and even some superficially similar charges were at heart quite different: the Jews were absurdly believed to stab the Eucharist in order to do hurt to Christ, not a charge found in the witch trials; on the other hand, Jews, unlike witches, were not supposed to eat their sacrificial victims or render them into magical ointment. Even at the height of the medieval witch craze, simple sorcerers, heretics, Jews, lepers, political pariahs, and other outcasts, though occasionally touched with the brush of witchcraft, were for the most part dealt with quite differently. Why were witches singled out for a more total and hysterical hatred than any of the other outcasts of Christian society? Perhaps because, unlike Jews, lepers, or out-of-favor politicians, they were *not* physically identifiable, so that the number upon whom guilt and fear could be projected was almost unlimited.

Social tensions do not of course cause intellectual or mythological phenomena, but they may provide conditions favorable to their growth. Periods of rapid change tend to produce unusual anxieties and may encourage the development of mythologies of hostility like witchcraft. This may have been especially true in the Middle Ages. Most medieval people held the archaic view that cosmos and society were essentially unchanging, and through much of the Middle Ages, change was in fact slow and generally imperceptible. But in periods when perceptible change did occur, people were unable to understand it and became frightened. As society's patterns shifted, people's roles became undefined, and in that condition they developed greater anxieties. In a state of anxiety, they were open to the suggestion that the cause of their misery was a hostile and powerful group of people with access to diabolical aid.

Donald M. Lowe has created categories that help explain the deterioration of mental order in time of social crisis.[6] He postulates three zones of consciousness extending outward from the center of the ego toward the unbounded horizon: *perspective, symbolic order,* and *institutionalization. Institutionalization* is the most external, being the structure of perception established by the society in which the subject lives. But this structure is always changing, and when it changes rapidly and radically, a situation of "de-institutionalization" results, where the hitherto unquestioned values of the structure are now open to question. "In a de-institutionalizing situation, the subject will have to fall back upon a much more autonomous symbolic order." The *symbolic order* is objective truth as perceived by the subject. In situations in which institutionalization is stable and almost universally accepted, the symbolic order of most subjects will closely approximate the institutional. When the subject is forced by de-institutionalization to use his own resources to construct a symbolic order for himself, he finds the task enormously taxing to his intellect and emotions. He demands freedom from decaying institutions but is frustrated by his own limitations when he tries to utilize this freedom to construct his own symbolic order. Consequently he either seeks another system he can embrace with a commitment total enough to blot out his insecurity, or else declines into nihilism, anomic despair, violence, or espousal of whatever ideas he can think of that most directly contradict the system whose failure has betrayed him. We are familiar with the results of de-institutionalization in the twentieth century. In the Middle Ages, one result of de-institutionalization was the witch craze. Terrified by changes in a cosmos that was not supposed to change, some people were driven to embrace witchcraft; others were driven by the same terrors to irrational fear of withcraft.

Impetus was given to witchcraft by social change and dislocations. Many of the most important elements of witchcraft were being assembled and amalgamated in the heresy trials beginning in the eleventh century, a period of marked economic change. Population was growing swiftly, land holdings were divided, and the surplus population began to move into the towns, where new industry and trade developed. There were considerable spiritual reactions to these commercial changes, including movements of apostolic poverty, heresy, and reform within the monastic orders and the ecclesiastical structure. Additionally, these changes caused a break in the sense of community, a break causing anonymity and alienation.

The restlessness of the eleventh and twelfth centuries was increased by the great plagues and famines of the fourteenth century followed by the wars and social rebellions of the fifteenth century, and the rapid changes in the political, social, and religious order, of which perhaps the most important were the Babylonian Captivity of the papacy and the subsequent Great Schism. Plagues and famines caused radical changes in agricultural society and its organization. The continued population shift to the towns and the development there of an industrial proletariat had a number of unsettling effects, as did the shift from manorialism to hired labor, encouraged by the reduction of the population. The extended family structure of the agricultural population, where one lived surrounded by uncles, aunts, and cousins, tended in the cities to be gradually replaced by the nuclear family—parents, children, and perhaps grandparents. The adjustment to the nuclear family caused increased emotional strain, and new forms of anxiety were instilled in children. Another effect was the isolation of old men and women when the family emigrated to the towns or moved to take jobs as hired laborers. Abandoned, the old people were prey to anxieties and fears that might cause them to adopt witchcraft or at least drive them to eccentric behavior that could cause them to be considered witches.[7]

The results of these changes upon religious sensibilities were considerable, though it is difficult to demonstrate any direct connection. In art, visions of hell, flames, torment, of death, demons, and grotesque monsters proliferate in the fourteenth and fifteenth centuries, culminating in the grotesqueries of Bosch in the sixteenth.[8] The rise of mysticism, of the flagellants, of the dance cult, and the expansion of popular heresy occurred at the same time as the rapid growth of the witch phenomenon from the mid-fourteenth century onward. All, to one degree or another, were rejections of an institutional structure that was felt wanting. All had their origins in, and drew their greatest strength from, those areas of Europe, such as the Low Countries, France, the Rhineland, and northern Italy, where economic and social change was most pronounced.

Most people expressed social discontent in forms other than witchcraft. One must therefore inquire why some chose such an extreme form of protest. We need not impose our own ideas of mental illness upon the Middle Ages to recognize that there were individuals then as now seriously impeded from functioning in society by their idiosyncratic views of reality. Such persons, particularly during times of unusual change and stress, might have either embraced witchcraft or been seized by unreasoning terror of witchcraft.*

But it will not do to assume that the witches were on the whole mentally ill. They were responding to human needs more universal than those of individual fantasy: universal enough to be described in terms of myth. The most fundamental psychological phenomenon relating to the myth of witchcraft is the perennial fascination with evil. In the mythology of almost every society, evil is reified. The ancient dualist opposition of good and evil, light and darkness, underlay all medieval thought, and from the twelfth century it was strongly reinforced by Catharist influences. The fundamental idea of this myth is that at one time all had been good, united, harmonious, One, and that dissension, evil, and alienation had then crept in to destroy that harmony. The individual must either confront or submit to the disruption of that harmony, the disruption being defined as evil.

The social psychology of medieval witchcraft is underlain by myth, itself in part a product of the social psychology of earlier peoples now molded into a tradition. The mythological origins of witchcraft are a mixture of elements Teutonic, Celtic, and especially Greco-Roman. But here we are not considering the spe-

---

* The possible permutations of mental illness in witches are almost infinite. Freud discussed an unusual illuminating case in his *Eine Teufelsneurose im siebzehnten Jahrhundert* (Leipzig, 1924): the painter Christoph Haitzmann, ambivalent in his feelings toward his dead father, made a pact with the Devil, whom he substituted in his mind for his father, endowing him with both good and evil attributes. In witchcraft generally the Devil is imbued with good and evil qualities: the witches are ambivalent toward him. To them he is benevolent: he teaches them, guides them, helps them fulfill their needs, and promises to lead them into bliss when he regains his rightful kingdom. Yet they realize that to society in general and to individuals outside their group he is destructive and hostile, and their own fear of him is indicated by the pain that they experience in sexual intercourse with him.

cific myths or their origin, but rather their social functions in medieval witchcraft. Freud believed that both myth and religion are projections of inner conflicts, hopes, and fears onto the external world. If one feels guilty and deserving of punishment, he is likely to assume that there are forces in the world seeking to punish him: he fears air crashes, Communists, Jews, earthquakes, white men; in Greek myth he feared the Erinnyes and Nemesis; in the Middle Ages he feared pursuing demons. Freud's view is perhaps best tempered by Frankl's concept of myth as a variety of explanation of man and the world.[9] Myth may be distinguished from fantasy in this way: fantasy is wholly individual expression —it may or may not strike chords of understanding in others. Myth, by virtue of offering explanations within an accepted structure, will be universally understood (though not necessarily interpreted in the same way) by those sharing that structure. As Buber, Heschel, and Cassirer have shown, man is not merely a rational, but also a symbolizing and mythologizing animal. Myths are stories explaining things, not by deductive or inductive reason, but by association, at the level of the dream: disjointed, illogical, but symbolically meaningful.

The witch appears in the mythologies of most societies. The witch—whether considered human or supernatural—is an archetypical figure, frightening, numinous, threatening, associated with awe, wildness, and evil.[10] The psychological origins of the myth lie in the projection outside ourselves of our feelings of alienation, threat, misery, and persecution. We ourselves cannot be responsible for our lack of ability or failure; it cannot be the result of chance, for the universe is alive and not blind; nor can it be the will of God, who is good, unless it is punishment for our sins. The difficulties in our lives must therefore be caused by malevolent and superhuman beings. Medieval witchcraft is a part of this universal myth. The combination of the bonae, who bring prosperity, with the cannibalistic strigae, is comparable to the composite figure of the Indian goddess Kali, both the giver of good and the killer and cannibal wife of Siva, himself a composite of beneficence and malevolence. The wild hunt associated with early witchcraft originated in a pagan Teutonic myth in which the souls of dead warriors rode through the night in a destructive, raging procession. This myth carries with it the cathexis of the release of violence and brings together hunting, war, and menstruation: hence by the Middle Ages, the wild hunt was led by Artemis-Hecate, goddess of both fertility and of killing.[11] In similar fashion, the wild man or wild woman sometimes associated with witchcraft represents the libidinal hairy ape, Stevenson's Mr. Hyde. The animal forms that the witches or their demons are often alleged to take are also closely related to the idea of the wild man. Shapeshifting into animals (usually those considered vicious, for example, wolves or vampire bats) is a myth found in many societies. The fundamental cathexis of the myth is the release felt in believing that one is someone or something else. One is permitted things as a wild man or a wolf that are forbidden in one's ordinary shape. Some psychologists have suggested that shapeshifting originates in the common nightmare vision of transformations, nocturnal wanderings, murder, or even cannibalism, activities not lacking Freudian wish-fulfillment. There seems little doubt that there are strong sexual implications in such myths. Fur may, as Freud suggests, suggest the *crines pubis,* and the connections between cannibalism, bloodsucking, and eroticism have been clearly demonstrated by Nicolas Perella.[12]

Though witchcraft is rooted in ancient mythology, it can hardly be supposed that the witches were learned in ancient traditions. In the Middle Ages, as in any society, one might adopt witchcraft for the sense of superiority it gives one in the possession of secret knowledge, or for the pleasure of the titillating fear experienced from contact with the occult. The witch may be moved by the Promethean urge to acquire the means to bend both nature and other people to his own ends. He may expect to obtain as reward from Satan knowledge enabling him to do this. He may hope through witchcraft to obtain the object of his pecuniary or amatory desires, or he may expect thereby to exact revenge upon those whom he fears or hates. A neurotic may believe he can do harm by wishing ill upon his enemy; in the witch cult such beliefs were institutionalized and generally accepted. Witchcraft thus became a socialized channel for the expression of aggressive impulses.

In his profound and shocking study of the attractiveness of war, *The Warriors,* J. Glenn Gray hints that what distinguishes men from animals may precisely be the demonic. A man, like a brute, may rage in mindless destruction, but far more terrifying than brutalized soldiers are the sensualists of warfare, those who contemplate and luxuriate in their cruelty. Such men obtain sexual satisfaction, aesthetic pleasure, and delight in destruction, rape, and killing. "It is as if they are seized by a demon."[13] This satisfaction, Gray argues, is peculiarly human. An animal, for example, cannot degrade its sexual partner because it has not the power to regard it as a subject, as a Thou. Only a human has the power to degrade its partner, a Thou, into an object, to make him something less than he is, and by virtue of his powers of self-consciousness to take sensual pleasure in the process. It is precisely the dignity and power of man that makes this degradation possible, just as it is the existence of humane principles that makes wanton cruelty possible, and the existence of Christianity that made witchcraft possible. The witch, like the sensual warrior, takes pleasure in corrupting all that a peaceful and just society holds dear. Gray also observes a less repellent aspect of the warrior mentality that is nonetheless relevant to the witch phenomenon. This is the quasi-sacramental feeling of communion among comrades. Unlike friendship, in which the partners retain and develop their individuality, comradeship brings people together in a common cause, submerges their personalities in the common quest, and causes them to abandon themselves to the group and to one another in a kind of ecstasy of self-surrender. This abandonment to something greater than oneself is among the psychological principles that make war possible; it is at the heart of mob action; it sustains revolutions; it is a major part of the traditional Christian conception of the Eucharist; and it seems to lie at the heart of the idea of witchcraft as well. As the Dionysiacs had long before discovered, orgy, as well as warfare, can produce the ecstasy of assimilation and self-annihilation.

One might choose to embrace witchcraft in the hope of avoiding death either by obtaining a share of eternal life in the Devil's kingdom or, more basically, by displacing fear of implacable death with fear of a Devil whom one can at least hope to mollify. It cannot be wholly an accident that medieval art, even the grotesque art of the late fourteenth and fifteenth centuries, seldom portrays death and the Devil together. It was as if medieval men could not contemplate both horrors at once. In the perception of the immanent and tremendous power of the Devil can be recognized a component of the religious experience, the awesome dread, the sense of the *mysterium tremendum* that, particularly in a society where demons are felt to be omnipresent, might well be ascribed to the Devil rather than to God. Devil-worship is aimed at propitiating this infinitely powerful hostility. As Bruno Bettelheim suggests, orgiastic rituals may not be the result of the heedless unleashing of the id that Freud posited, but rather a kind of effort on the part of the ego to rationalize, control, and integrate instinctive fears and anxieties.

Similarly, medieval man was able to lessen the sense of the intolerable majesty of God by transferring at least some of the functions and powers of the severe and remote Deity to more accessible entities. Thus the emergence in the late eleventh century of the suffering and humanized Christ, of the compassionate Virgin, and of the approachable Devil. No one can face the immeasurable reality of God without fear and trembling, and medieval people by and large cared for that sensation no more than do people today. Both the deepest theism, like that of Kierkegaard or Tillich, and the deepest atheism, like that of Sartre or Camus, have dared to face the ultimate terror of the universe. But the function of most modern religion has been to escape terror by transforming God into something manageable through simple rituals of piety; and the function of most modern atheism has been to avoid the problem by pretending that it is not there. It is not surprising that some people in the Middle Ages tried to escape from the precariousness of all ontology.

Whatever their origins, these fears were reinforced by social alienation in periods of stress. Alienation generally produces not only a rejection of existing institutions and the "establishments" that are believed to operate them, but also a belief in the futility of generally accepted societal values and a conviction that the universe is inherently meaningless and chaotic, the result being either a nihilistic denial of all values or their total reversal. Another aspect of alienation may be a "systematic undermining of repression and denial, two of the most common adaptive techniques in . . . society."[14] Witchcraft shared these common characteristics of alienation. As Lynn White has observed, "Witchcraft is always a turning upsidedown of the moral standards of the world in which the witch lives. It is a drastic and spectacular way of rebelling, a repudiation of things as they are. It is an ultimate denial, a form of nihilism which is demanded by mentally and emotionally unstable people in any time of rapid change."[15] In the Christian society of the Middle Ages this meant a specific rejection of Christian values and Christian ritual. If Christianity worshiped the majesty and holy dread of God, then the witches worshiped the majesty and holy dread of God's opposite. If the Christians had their creed, their Eucharist, their kiss of peace, the witches formally forswore the faith, confected obscene parodies of the sacrament, and bestowed kisses upon the Devil's fundament. The fervor of their rejections of the faith should not surprise us. People wholly alienated from society escape ambiguity, dissonance, and despair only by throwing themselves totally into another symbolic order. In turning away from God, the witches naturally sought to discover their identity in total union with the Devil.

An important question in the social psychology of witchcraft is why more women than men participated. The sources are too sparse and uneven to yield any reliable statistical sample, but it seems that though men and women were about equally cited through the fourteenth century, in the fifteenth century women are cited significantly more often than men. In addition, when accusations are lodged against groups rather than individuals, women are much more frequently named. As early as the thirteenth century, Alexander of Hales and Thomas Aquinas argued that women were more prone to witchcraft, and it will be recalled that the *Canon Episcopi* and its long tradition specify that it is women who ride out with Diana; ordinarily, too, the *bonae* are *femine*, as the gender of the noun indicates. But in the fifteenth century, both the trials (such as those in Artois) and the writings of Nider, Visconti, Torquemada, and other theoreticians assign women an increasingly greater part in witchcraft. This trend culminated in the *Malleus Maleficarum*, in whose very title the gender of the witches is feminine, and in which the explanation was adduced that women were in every way morally and mentally inferior to men. This image, once set in the fifteenth century, was constantly confirmed in the sixteenth and the seventeenth, until it was generally assumed that witches were necessarily female.[16]

The prevalence of women in witchcraft may be discussed in two ways: in what respects and for what reasons the prevalence may have been true; and to what extent it was a delusion caused by the witch hunters. In many other cultures sorcerers are more likely to be women than men. This is true in some areas of India, for example, as well as in Africa.[17] Though deriving primarily from heresy, European witchcraft did have roots in sorcery, and the reasons why women tend to be sorcerers may relate to a similar inclination on their part to witchcraft. Women are associated with sorcery more often than men because of their traditional roles as cooks, nurses, midwives, and keepers of the home. In terms of ultimate origins, some numinous power was of course attached to the childbearing powers of women and to menstruation, which is regarded in most societies as having great *numen*. It is women who gather the herbs that can cure or poison, they who preside over the mysteries of childbirth, and they who know the charms or the potions that can cause hatred or love, fertility or impotence. Thus in the tradition of sorcery and in that of folklore there was a predisposition to consider that witches were more likely to be women. Yet that predisposition was apparently not acted upon to any large extent in the early Middle Ages. Since witchcraft's origins are more in heresy than in sorcery, we must look to the heretical movements of the eleventh century and later for an indication of female preponderance there.

The changing function of women in medieval thought is a subject that has not yet been fully explored. Everyone is aware that in the late eleventh and twelfth centuries an enormous shift took place in the attitude toward women, a shift that constitutes one of the most fundamental social changes in Western history. Women, who had previously been considered somewhat as chattels created especially to bear children and tend to the house, were suddenly given a new image. It is true that the image seldom improved the treatment of women and was applied only to ladies of high social standing, but it represented a revolutionary shift nonetheless. In the theory of courtly love, the lady became a being more spiritual, more delicate, and more refined than the man, who addressed her with a devotion bordering upon religious adoration.

At the same time as courtly love, veneration of the Virgin Mary developed, placing one woman closer to God than any other human being save Christ himself. But most women had the ill fortune to be born neither noble nor the Mother of God. The Church banned women from holy orders and considered their entrance into the sanctuary a profanation; women could not preach, nor could they attend the cathedral schools or the universities that succeeded them; they were passed over whenever possible in the succession to thrones and fiefs, for the feudal system was based upon war, and with a few exceptions women did not go to war. The Jewish tradition of the Old Testament, the tradition of Roman literature and law, the warrior tradition of the Teutons, and the tradition of Christian theology all united to confirm that woman's place was to serve man. St. Paul advised slaves to obey their masters and wives to obey their husbands. The relation of the wife to the husband, the head of the family, was compared to the relationship of mankind to Christ, the head of the Church.

It is not surprising that under such circumstances women were prominent among heretics. Medieval writers put this down to the natural gullibility of women, but modern writers, both Marxist and non-Marxist, have seen in the female support of religious dissent a form of rebellion against the male establishment.[18] Women of all classes participated, being active in orthodox, monastic, and semimonastic reform movements as well as in heresy. The lead was often taken by women of social standing, power, and wealth. To consider these religious movements as efforts to remove social inequities would be to read into the medieval mind concepts it was incapable of entertaining. The reform movements, both orthodox and heretical, were indeed motivated by the ideal of poverty and the rejection of wealth, but this was an ideal based upon the Christian theory that material concerns distract one from the contemplation of the true reality which is God's. The thrust of these apostolic movements of poverty was not to obtain for the poor a greater share in the wealth of the world, but the exact opposite: to abolish the wealth of the world as much as possible so that people might be freed to seek spiritual riches. Neither orthodox reform, nor heresy, nor witchcraft can be considered movements for material improvement.

Yet they were motivated by more subtle considerations of social alienation. The thrust of the apostolic movements was a quest for dignity and for meaning in a society that had begun to seem dislocated. To the reformers, for example, the tension between the ideals of Christianity and their tarnished practice seemed intolerable. The fact that women made their presence felt in orthodox reform, heresy, and witchcraft—all three—to a greater extent than anywhere else in medieval society suggests that they felt deprived, not of wealth, but of the dignity and worth they deserved as human beings. In turn, the activity of women disturbed, even frightened, the male establishment, as it would again when John Knox first blasted the "trumpet against the monstrous regiment of women." The trumpet had certainly been sounded five centuries earlier than that of the Scottish reformer. Male writers sympathetic to women, like Jacques de Vitry or Martin le Franc, who composed his *Champion des dames* as a reply to the slurs of the *Roman de la rose* upon the female sex, were outnumbered by those who had every intention of keeping women in their place. Faced with a lack of sympathy on the part of the orthodox establishment, many women turned to less usual expressions of piety. Hildegard of Bingen, Elizabeth of Schönau, Mechtild of Magdeburg, and later, Catherine of Siena, were among the most original mystics of the Middle Ages. An exceptional number of women joined Catharism, in which religion they could become *perfecti*. Women joined Valdes in his movement of apostolic poverty, and the fact that his bishop forbade Valdes to allow women to preach was one of the irritants that drove the Waldensians to break with orthodoxy. Women not only played a larger part than men in the movement associated with the Beguines and Beghards but also a large part in the subsequent movements of antinomian heresy associated with the Brethren and Sisters of the Free Spirit. If the stirrings of feminine discontent can be seen in all this, such discontent can be perceived in a more violent form in the feminine attachment to witchcraft.

The participation of women in witchcraft may have been exaggerated by antifeminist writers eager to attribute to the female sex the utmost weaknesses. No one who reads the ravings against women by Heinrich Institoris in the *Malleus Maleficarum* can regard that worthy Inquisitor as wholly sane, yet Institoris' hatred is only a grotesque exaggeration of a tradition that is as old, indeed far older, than Christianity. The fear of women lies deep in the mythic consciousness of men. The assorted concepts behind this fear are commonly recognized—I do not propose to discuss here the forms of the hag, the phallic mother, or the fertile killer that populate the mythologies of the world; it seems probable that the Inquisitors' idea of the female witch is an expression of them.[19] The Christian tradition from the very beginning incorporated the ancient fear of women. For the Greeks, Pandora let evil into the world from her jar. The Fathers of the Church debated whether all sin entered the world through Eve or whether the demons originally fell because they lusted after the daughters of men. *Janua diaboli*—"the gate by which the Devil enters"—was a patristic epithet for woman. The fear of women in Christianity was heightened by the suspicious attitude that most of the Fathers took toward sexual relationships: virginity was the most desirable state, and woman was the temptress luring man away from perfection. Woman was more carnal, more concerned with material things; her lust and her greed turned man's eyes from the path to heaven. There have been many Christian women in the past two thousand years, but very few have been canonized who did not die virgins. Even motherhood received qualified praise; the Fathers knew what preceded it, and St. Augustine argued that intercourse even in marriage cannot be wholly free from sin. St. Jerome admonished a widow to mourn the previous loss of her virginity more than the loss of her husband, and suggested to a matron asking his advice about child care that children of opposite sexes be isolated from one another. It would be interesting to trace the origins of the modern idea that men are more prone to carnality than women: the idea was certainly not common before the introduction of courtly love.

The rise in the status of ladies caused by courtly love and the cult of the Virgin may actually have encouraged the development of the witch image as a reaction. The basic mythological image of the female has both good and bad qualities, and when the good qualities are extracted, refined, and elevated to the status of a principle, the evil qualities that remain also attain the status of a principle. The witch is then the natural mythological counterpart of the Virgin. It should be noted that though the female sex in general was blamed for witchcraft, little girls in particular were not. If their mothers had exposed them to the evil, they were sometimes flogged and forced to witness the execution of their parents, but only seldom was a prepubertal girl herself executed. Perhaps the authorities had some pity for children, but this was not a common medieval trait. More likely, it was simply that a girl who was not yet nubile was not regarded as a threat: as yet she possessed neither the *numen* of fertility nor the carnality that lured good men to their doom.

There is more to the sexual psychology of witchcraft than its emphasis upon women. The orgiastic elements of the witches' revels are directly comparable to the rites of Tantric Buddhism, the Dionysiac cult, and other worldwide practices, in which sexual release is associated with the ecstasy of religious experience. The psychosexual element in some of the experiences of the

Christian mystics is well known. In witchcraft, the feasting, drinking, dancing, fornication, incest, even cannibalism and the ritual kiss, may represent a violent and deliberate release from the ascetic and antisexual morality of Christianity.[20] One difficulty of interpreting the orgiastic aspects of witch practices wholly as pleasurable release is the evidence that the sexual intercourse of women with the Devil was usually unpleasant, his phallus being cold and painful. The witches' dislike of what one hesitates to describe as the act of love with Satan may be a reaction of guilt or fear: we cannot suppose that, no matter how alienated, a woman submitting sexually to a being she believes to be the Devil can be wholly relaxed. The sexual possession of the woman by the Devil may be comparable to involuntary demonic possession, which was always violent and unpleasant.[21] Or, of course, the whole idea of the Devil's coldness may be an interpolation of the prosecutors, to whom cold would suggest itself as a symbol of sterility, barrenness, and death, heat generally being considered in mythology a fertile and creative principle. Again, the witches' prosecutors may have considered the unpleasantness of the act a fitting punishment for the insatiable lust of women. Curiously, in those rarer occasions when men had intercourse with the Devil in female form, the experience was usually neither painful nor unpleasant. The earlier tradition of relations with both incubi and succubi was that they were pleasurable, as were the orgies among the worshipers at the witches' meeting. Ritual copulation with the Devil was a relatively late development, and the coldness of his organ is mentioned in the medieval literature very seldom and only toward the end of the fifteenth century, though it became a common phenomenon in the following two hundred years.

Both the osculum and the feasting have direct sexual implications. The obscene kiss of the Devil's backside or foot[22] has implications that go beyond the obvious. The kiss is a symbol of eating the beloved, and the kiss had enormous importance in

Christian art, literature, and liturgy, even symbolizing the Holy Spirit's binding of the Father and the Son. The osculum infame may signify a kind of dark communion, an eating of the god, a total taking into oneself of the Devil. The osculum, connected as it is to formal renunciation of Christianity, may also have been an allusion to the Judas kiss. The kiss is the link between the sexual in witchcraft and the cannibalistic devouring of children.

Social psychology illuminates the nature of the witch hunters as well as that of the witches. "The witch and the witch-hunter were children of one bewilderment, sharing one blind vengefulness, reflecting one mentality, and stemming from one inner necessity."[23] The same elements of human psychology, magical world view, and social tensions that produced the atmosphere of fear and tension creating witchcraft also produced the craze against witchcraft. That is why throughout this book witchcraft, regardless to what degree it was embraced by the witches and to what degree it was the invention of witch hunters, has been treated as one phenomenon.

The repression of witchcraft cannot be ascribed solely to Inquisitorial, episcopal, or secular courts. The crowds that witnessed the executions, the occasional lynchings of heretics and witches by angry mobs, the total lack of any popular resistance to the repression of the witches as well as the paucity of such resistance in intellectual circles, all indicate widespread support for the persecution. Indeed, the witch hunters could not have conducted public executions over centuries and throughout wide territories without the support, or at least the tacit acquiescence, of the public.

The behavior of the authorities is understandable. Particularly in times of rapid social change like the fourteenth and fifteenth centuries, the rulers of society felt their status threatened and proceeded ruthlessly against those whom they feared. Heretics, witches, and Jews were the most visible nonconformists, and these three groups were subject to the most bitter persecution in these centuries. The persecutors justified their bloody elimination of witches, as well as of heretics and Jews, by dehumanizing them. In medieval thought, there was no concept of individual rights extending beyond the idea that each person had his proper place in Christian society. Liberty was perceived in terms of the duties pertaining to one's proper station. Those who deliberately set themselves apart from Christian society had no standing and, like outlaws, no rights. It was argued that because the dissenters had cut themselves off from the mystical body of Christ, they had become limbs of Satan and could with a clear conscience be consigned to the flames or the noose. The Inquisitors even argued, many of them with sincere conviction, that their prosecution was a kindness, for by extracting confessions and repentance from the witches, by torture if necessary, they might save their souls from the fires of hell even as their bodies were consumed by the fires of the stake. It should be remembered that if witches existed who believed in what they were doing, they had at least criminal intentions; and if their actions were indeed real, they were criminal and could legitimately be prosecuted.

The persecution of the witches, like that of the Jews and the heretics, sprang from two developments of the eleventh and following centuries. As in those years Christian society became more orderly, the Church could turn its attention from mere survival to the construction of a tightly controlled hierarchical system, the organization of a coherent body of canon law, and the establishment of instruments of repression. Second, the movements of popular enthusiasm for reform also produced widespread support for the Crusades, pogroms of the Jews, and hatred, sometimes mob violence, against heretics. The increased internal pacification of Western Europe tended to focus hostility upon those considered outside the pale of society. Sometimes, of course, the hostilities were personal and direct: one accused a man as a witch because one was his personal enemy; or an Inquisitor condemned him in order to confiscate his property for the Inquisition.

Yet the essential sanity of most of those who defended the prosecution of witches is currently argued with force by Chadwick Hansen and E. William Monter. Monter demonstrates that it is absurd to assume stupidity, madness, villainy, or even inconsistency in those who defended the reality and danger of witchcraft. There was no paradox in the fact that Jean Bodin (1530–1596) was both a brilliant philosopher and enemy of witchcraft: indeed, his belief in witchcraft was entirely reasoned and coherent with the rest of his philosophical system.[24] As we have defined superstition, it is a belief or a set of beliefs, whether spiritual or material, natural or supernatural, that do not fit into a reasoned and coherent world view. Most of the philosophical defenders of the witch belief cannot by this definition be regarded as superstitious. But the fact that the witch hunters and their supporters were neither insane nor superstitious does not make their position workable even in terms of their own goals. As the persecution of witches increased, the number of witches did not decrease. Quite the contrary, the supply rose to meet the demand. The most direct reason for this, of course, was that the accused under torture often implicated alleged accomplices. The resulting growth in the number of accused was then taken as evidence by the witch hunters that the practice of witchcraft was growing. In consequence, popular hysteria about witchcraft grew, and in consequence of that, more people convinced themselves that they were witches. In their misguided efforts to preserve the framework of Christian orthodoxy, the witch hunters launched one of the most disgraceful episodes in the history of Christianity, an episode that did not conclude until the mid-eighteenth century. It is useless to judge the hunters individually, but their policies must be judged callous and in every way destructive.

The phenomenon of witchcraft, whether we are talking about

the persecutors or the witches, was the result of fear, expressed in supernatural terms in a society that thought in supernatural terms, and repressed by a society that was intolerant of spiritual dissent. In most respects a variety, or at least an outgrowth, of heresy, witchcraft was one manifestation of alienation in medieval society. With heresy it increased in importance as the changing society of the eleventh century provoked dissent and as the ecclesiastical organization found itself strong enough to prosecute it more vigorously. Like heresy, witchcraft became more virulent as medieval society began to decline and disintegrate in the fourteenth and fifteenth centuries. That witchcraft continued with mounting fervor for nearly three centuries after the end of the Middle Ages indicates that its significance transcends time and place. European witchcraft is unthinkable in anything like the form it took without the shaping influence of Christian myth and theology. But in a deeper sense, witchcraft springs out of hostility and violence that are at the same time as old as man and as contemporary. Now once again institutions are failing and men are being thrust back upon their own formulations of symbolic order. Once again, lacking the framework of a coherent rational system, we are increasingly subject to propaganda, nihilism, and mindless violence. Dogmatic and unreasoning ideologists are preparing for us a new witch craze, couched now in secular rather than in transcendental terms.

It is in this universal context that European witchcraft is best understood. Medieval witchcraft was in one sense only the first stage of a long period of witch delusion; in another sense it was a manifestation of the innate and perennial darkness of the human soul.

Appendix

The *Canon Episcopi* and Its Variations

There are two basic versions of the *Canon Episcopi,* both appearing originally in Regino's *De synodalibus causis et disciplinis ecclesiasticis libri duo.* The first is shorter than the second.

1. The shorter version.

This appears in Regino (II, 45) and is reproduced by Burchard of Worms in two almost indistinguishable forms in his *Decretum* (I, 94, and X, 29). It appears again, this time in a somewhat different form, in Burchard's *Corrector,* which is a tenth-century penitential incorporated by Burchard as Book 19 of his *Decretum* (XIX, 70).

    a. The version of Regino (II, 45) and Burchard (I, 94, and X, 29). I give Regino's version and portions where all three agree in regular print. I note where Burchard I ends; the portion of Burchard X which differs I give in italics:

> Perquirendum si aliqua femina sit quae per quaedam maleficia et incantationes mentes hominum se immutare posse dicat, id est, ut de odio in amorem, aut de amore in odium convertat, aut bona hominum aut damnet aut subripiat. Et si aliqua est quae se dicat cum daemonum turba in similitudine mulierum transformata certis noctibus equitare super quasdam bestias et in earum consortio annumeratum esse, [Burchard I Concludes Here] (*haec talis omnimodis scopis correpta ex parochia ejiciatur*) haec talis omnimodis ex paroechia ejiciatur.

    b. The version of the *Corrector* (Burchard, XIX, 70):

> Credidisti ut aliqua femina sit, quae hoc facere possit, quod quaedam, a diabolo deceptae, se affirmant necessario et ex praecepto

facere debere, id est cum daemonum turba in similitudinem mulierum transformatam, quam vulgaris stultitia hic strigam [six out of seven MSS omit strigam] holdam vocat, certis noctibus equitare debere super quasdam bestias, et in eorum se consortio annumeratum esse? Si particeps fuisti illius incredulitatis, annum unum per legitimas ferias poenitare debes.

2. The longer version.

This is the *Canon Episcopi* proper, from which the English translation in the text is taken. It appears originally in Regino (II, 364) and is reproduced by Burchard (X, 1, and again in XIX [the *Corrector*], 90) in the form of a penitential. I give Regino II, Burchard X, and where all agree in regular type; I note where Burchard XIX pauses, and give variants in Burchard XIX in italics:

Ut episcopi episcoporumque ministri omnibus viribus elaborare studeant ut perniciosam et a diabolo inventam sortilegam et maleficam artem penitus ex parochiis suis eradant, et si aliquem virum aut feminam huiuscemodi sceleris sectatorem invenerint, turpiter dehonestatum de parochiis suis eiciant. Ait enim Apostolus: Haereticum post unam et secundam admonitionem devita, sciens, quia subversus est, qui eiusmodi est. (Titus 3.) Subversi sunt et a diabolo capti tenentur, qui derelicto creatore suo a diabolo suffragia quaerunt. Et ideo a tali peste mundari debet sancta ecclesia. Illud etiam non omittendum, quod quaedam sceleratae mulieres [Corrector, which has been silent till now, begins] *Credidisti aut particeps fuisti illius incredulitatis, quod quaedam scelerate mulieres . . .* [and then continues with Regino] retro post Satanam conversae (1 Timothy 5:15), daemonum illusionibus et phantasmatibus seductae, credunt se et profitentur nocturnis horis cum Diana paganorum dea et innumera multitudine mulierum equitare super quasdam bestias, et multa terrarum spatia intempestate noctis silentio pertransire, eiusque iussionibus velut dominae obedire, et certis noctibus ad eius servitium evocari. Sed utinam hae solae in perfidia sua perissent, et non multos secum in infidelitatis interitum pertraxissent. Nam innumera multitudo hac falsa opinione decepta haec vera esse credit, et credendo a recta fide deviat et in errorem paganorum revolvitur, cum aliquid divinitatis aut numinis extra unum esse arbitratur. [Here Corrector pauses.] Quapropter sacerdotes per ecclesias sibi commissas populo cum omni instantia praedicare debent ut noverint haec omnimodis falsa esse, et non a divino sed a maligno spiritu talia phantasmata mentibus infidelium irrogari, siquidem ipse Satanas, qui transfigurat se in angelum lucis, cum mentem cuiuscunque mulierculae ceperit et hanc sibi per infidelitatem et incredulitatem subiugaverit, illico transformat se in (*Sed diabolus transformat se in*) diversarum personarum species atque similitudines, et mentem, quam captivam tenet, in somnis deludens, modo laeta, modo tristia, modo cognitas, modo incognitas personas ostendens, per devia quaeque deducit, et cum solus eius spiritus hoc patitur, infidelis mens haec non in animo, sed in corpore evenire opinatur. Quis enim non in somnis et nocturnis visionibus extra se ipsum educitur et multa videt dormiendo, quae nunquam viderat vigilando? Quis vero tam stultus et hebes sit, qui haec omnia, quae in solo spiritu fiunt, etiam in corpore accidere arbitretur?

The rest of the canon is a web of scriptural passages and of no great relevance, except that on several occasions the derivative nature of the *Corrector* from Regino is established: it skips a passage inadvertently, rendering the sentence meaningless; and at another point it adds a pedantic little gloss. It is thus certain that the *Corrector* is not an independent source.

3. Other tenth-century beliefs relating to witchcraft and found in the *Corrector* are in XIX, v, 60, 63, 65, 68, 69, 92, 151, 152, 159, 169, 170, 171, 186, all reproduced in Hansen, *Quellen*, pp. 40–42.

Notes

Works appearing in the bibliography are cited in short form in the footnotes.

AASS: *Acta Sanctorum,* Antwerp and Brussels, 70 vols., 1643–1940.

AASSOSB: *Acta Sanctorum Ordinis Sancti Benedicti,* Paris, 9 vols., 1668–1701.

Du Cange: Charles du Fresne Du Cange, *Glossarium mediae et infimae latinitatis,* 3d ed., Paris, 10 vols., 1937–1938.

HDA: *Handwörterbuch des deutschen Aberglaubens,* Berlin-Leipzig, 10 vols., 1927–1942.

Hef-L: Karl Hefele and H. Leclercq, *Histoire des Conciles,* 2d ed., Paris, 12 vols., 1907–1952.

Jaffé: Philipp Jaffé, *Regesta Pontificum Romanorum,* ed. by G. Wattenbach, 2d ed., Leipzig, 2 vols., 1885–1888.

Mansi: Johannes Mansi, *Sacrorum Conciliorum Nova, et Amplissima Collectio,* 2d ed., Paris-Arnheim-Leipzig, 53 vols., 1901–1927.

MPG: Jacques-Paul Migne, *Patrologiae Cursus Completus: series graeca,* Paris, 167 volumes, 1857–1876.

MPL: Jacques-Paul Migne, *Patrologiae Cursus Completus: series latina,* Paris, 221 volumes, 1841–1864.

MGH: *Monumenta Germaniae Historica.*

MGH Epp: *Monumenta Germaniae Historica Epistolae.*

MGH Legg: *Monumenta Germaniae Historica Leges.*

MGH SS: *Monumenta Germaniae Historica Scriptores.*

MGH SS rer germ: *Monumenta Germaniae Historica Scriptores rerum germanicarum.*

Potthast: August Potthast, *Regesta Pontificum Romanorum.* Berlin, 2 vols., 1874–1875.

Recueil: Martin Bouquet *et al., Recueil des historiens des Gaules et de la France,* Paris, 24 vols., 1738–1904.

Chapter 1

1. Peter Berger, *The Sacred Canopy* (New York, 1967), p. 73.

2. See Francis M. Cornford, *From Religion to Philosophy* (New York, 1957; originally published, 1912); Murray and Rosalie Wax, "Notion of Magic" and "Magical World View"; E. E. Evans-Pritchard, *Theories of Primitive Religion* (Oxford, 1965), chap. 2.

3. Lynn Thorndike, *History of Magic,* II, 973–974, defines magic as "all superstitious arts and occult sciences."

4. See Malinowski, "Magic, Science, and Religion," in his collection by that name; Edmund R. Leach, "Magical Hair," in Middleton, ed., *Myth and Cosmos,* pp. 104–105.

5. There have been many studies of the sociology of magic in modern Africa, America, and Oceania. See, for example, Maxwell G. Marwick, *Sorcery in Its Social Setting* (Manchester, 1965), or Clyde Kluckhohn, *Navajo Witchcraft* (Cambridge, Mass., 1944).

6. *De hominis dignitate,* ed. E. Garin (Florence, 1942), p. 105.

7. Sir James Frazer, *The Golden Bough* (London, 1911), I, xx.

8. *The Living God* (London, 1933), p. 36; Ehnmark.

9. *Religion among the Primitives* (New York, 1951), pp. 50–54.

10. Barb; Olaf Petterson, "Magic-Religion," *Ethnos,* XXII (1957).

11. Jérôme-Antoine Rony has a good discussion of magic and science in his *History of Magic* (New York, 1962), pp. 109–120.

12. Browe gives numerous examples of the magical use of the Eucharist, including placing it in food to cause disease or to obtain love, or even to procure abortion or death, or taking it prior to a battle or a trial in order to insure victory or success. The black mass, however, is not a medieval phenomenon but is first found in the seventeenth century and fully developed by the occultists of the nineteenth century.

13. See, for example, J. D. Krige, "The Social Function of Witchcraft," *Theoria* (Natal), I (1947), 9; Monica Hunter Wilson, "Witch Beliefs and Social Structure," *American Journal of Sociology,* LVI (1951), 307–308, who argues that witchcraft involves the belief in a supernatural power innate in the witch and used by him to cause harm, while sorcery simply involves the illegal use of medicine to cause harm; and Parrinder. Wayland Hand, drawing largely upon American folklore, identifies sorcery with conjury (both of whose practitioners take money to do magic for others) and distinguishes them from witchcraft, which is used to obtain retaliation against personal enemies.

14. This list is only a selection drawn from the superb and unique collec-

tion of folklore materials made by Wayland Hand at the Center for the Study of Comparative Folklore and Mythology at UCLA. Since Professor Hand's chief interest is in a comparison of American and European motifs, there is a bias in the preponderance of materials drawn from these traditions. Yet there is much material from Africa, Oceania, and the Amerinds as well, and the size of the collection and the care with which it has been assembled and organized make it unparalleled anywhere in the world. A curious modern Amerind variation of the witches' flight is that they use little airplanes; see Helen Zunser, "A New Mexican Village," *Journal of American Folklore*, XLVIII (1935), 155. For another list of witch characteristics, see Stith Thompson.

15. J. Franck, "Geschichte des Wortes Hexe," in Joseph Hansen, *Quellen*, pp. 614–670; and the entry *Hexe* in HDA. HDA (col. 1838) claims that *haguzussa* originally meant hedge-woman or fence-woman, from *zussa* (woman) and *haga* (fence or hedge). The word *Hexe* is first used by Notker in the tenth century but did not become common until the thirteenth and fourteenth centuries (HDA, col. 1833).

16. P. 43.

17. See Karl Plenzat, *Die Theophiluslegende in den Dichtungen des Mittelalters* (Berlin, 1926).

18. *History Sacred and Profane* (London, 1964), p. 186.

Chapter 2

1. Here I discuss only the serious historical studies undertaken since the eighteenth century. I cite works on related subjects like heresy and the Inquisition only when they contain a substantial amount of material dealing with witchcraft or have had a significant effect upon the interpretation of witchcraft. I have omitted works specifically dealing with Joan of Arc, the Templars, and Gilles de Rais, because each of these subjects has a vast literature of its own only tangentially related to witchcraft.

2. *An Historical Essay Concerning Witchcraft with Observations upon Matters of Fact* (London, 1718). Another rational, if historically inaccurate, account of witchcraft was Sir Walter Scott's *Letters on Demonology*.

3. The most important of these were Johann Beaumont, *Traktat von Geistern, Erscheinungen, Hexereyen, Zauberhändeln* . . . (Halle, 1721); Eberhard David Hauber, *Bibliotheca, acta, et scripta magica* (Lemgo, 1738–1745), which was revised and extended by Georg Conrad Horst, *Zauberbibliothek*, 6 vols. (Mainz, 1821–1826); Graesse gave a bibliography of the materials in Hauber and Horst and all other works known at the time of his writing.

4. Some of the more influential, but not less worthless, of these writers include Charles Leland, whose *Aradia, or the Gospel of the Witches of Italy* (London, 1899) purports to be an ancient document establishing the antiquity and high religious purpose of witchcraft—it is of course completely spurious; Alphonse Louis Constant, who wrote under the name of Eliphas Levi; Paul Pitois, who used the pseudonym Paul Christian; Arthur Edward Waite; and, most recently, Gerald Gardner, whose books, including *Witchcraft Today* (London, 1954; reissued paperbound, 1966), are an amiable introduction to the nonsense of witchcraft as a higher religion by a man who considered himself the leader of living English witches.

5. Joseph Fehr, *Der Aberglaube und die katholische Kirche des Mittelalters* (Stuttgart, 1857) is an impassioned defense; Nikolaus Paulus, *Hexenwahn und Hexenprozess vornehmlich im 16 Jahrhundert* (Freiburg-im-Breisgau, 1910) is sensible and corrects only the exaggerations of the anti-Catholic polemicists. P. Séjourné, "Sorcellerie," in the *Dictionnaire de théologie catholique,* 15 vols. (Paris, 1924–1950); Gallus M. Manser, "Thomas von Aquin und der Hexenwahn," *Jahrbuch für Philosophie und spekulative Theologie,* 2d ser., vol. IX (1922). A balanced judgment of the part played in the development of witchcraft that avoids the apologetics of Manser while correcting the anti-Thomist excesses of Soldan and Hansen is Charles Edward Hopkin, *The Share of Thomas Aquinas in the Growth of the Witchcraft Delusion* (Philadelphia, 1940).

6. *Malleus Maleficarum* (London, 1928), p. xvi.

7. *Inquisition,* III, 539.

8. See the section "The Agency of Witches" in his enormously influential book *A History of the Warfare of Science with Theology in Christendom* (New York, 1896).

9. Burr wrote little but influenced great numbers of students. Much of his work consists of unedited notes and marginal comments in books. More readily available material appears in Bainton and Gibbons. In that volume see especially Burr's "A Witch-Hunter in the Book-Shops," originally published in 1902; "The Literature of Witchcraft," originally printed in 1890 and dripping with liberal contempt for the superstitions of another age; and his introduction to Lea's *Materials.* Burr, who had become interested in witchcraft as early as 1878 when as a sophomore at Cornell he heard President White's lectures on legal procedures, was long in correspondence with Lea and in charge of editing Lea's papers, a task he turned over to his pupil Arthur Howland because of his own advancing age. The White collection has no published catalog and is restricted to serious scholars. Some idea of its contents can be obtained from Heinrich Schneider's article. The library is noted for its almost complete collection of early editions of the great sixteenth- and seventeenth-century works on witchcraft and of early mono-

graphs on the subject, as well as a few fifteenth-century manuscripts. It has little that is not elsewhere available on the medieval period. Burr kept the collection centered upon witchcraft as classically defined in these works and avoided materials dealing with the occult, magic, and folklore.

10. "The Literature of Witchcraft," in Bainton, p. 166.

11. "Introduction" to Lea's *Materials,* I, xxix.

12. Taking a similar position were Jakob Burckhardt, *The Civilization of the (Period of the) Renaissance in Italy* (London, 1878); Hauréau; Otto Henne-am-Rhyn, *Der Teufels- und Hexenglaube, seine Entwickelung, seine Herrschaft und sein Sturz* (Leipzig, 1892); Fredericq, "L'Historiographie de l'Inquisition"; Paul Kajus, Graf von Hoensbroeck, *Inquisition, Aberglaube, Teufelsspuk, und Hexenwahn,* vol. I of *Das Papstthum in seiner sozial-kulturellen Wirksamkeit* (Leipzig, 1901); Carl Lemperns, *Das grösste Verbrechen aller Zeiten* (Halle, 1904); J. Français, *L'Eglise et la sorcellerie: Précis historique suivi des documents officiels des textes principaux et d'un procès inédit* (Paris, 1910); Herman Haupt, "Inquisition, Aberglauben, Ketzer, und Sekten des Mittelalters," *Zeitschrift für Kirchengeschichte,* XV (1895), XVI (1896), XVII 1897); Ferdinand Riegler, *Hexenprozesse, mit besonderer Berücksichtigung des Landes Steiermark* (Graz, 1926); and Davies.

13. See Emil van der Vekené, *Bibliographie der Inquisition: Ein Versuch* (Hildesheim, 1963); Coulton, *Inquisition and Liberty,* p. 262. The liberal point of view is still frequently expressed. See Samuel and Vera Leff, *From Witchcraft to World Health* (New York, 1957) and the works of Rossell Hope Robbins.

14. P. 29.

15. Georg Längin, *Religion und Hexenprozess: Zur Würdigung des 400-jährigen Jubiläums der Hexenbulle und des Hexenhammers* (Leipzig, 1888) and Ennemoser both lacked the thoroughness of Soldan–Heppe.

16. *Zauberwahn,* p. 328.

17. The latest *Britannica* article attempts to avoid controversy and succeeds only in being insufficient. Miss Murray died a centenarian in 1963.

18. The most unforgivable gap is her failure to utilize the collection of medieval sources in Joseph Hansen's *Quellen,* available for twenty years before the publication of the *Witch-Cult.* Murray also failed to use many other valuable French, German, and Latin materials, and her notes and bibliography show an unfortunate degree of reliance upon British sources and incidents at the expense of the richer continental materials.

19. For example Hugh Ross Williamson, *The Arrow and the Sword* (London, 1947); Thomas C. Lethbridge, *Witches: Investigating an Ancient Religion* (London, 1962); and Hughes. Hughes' book is a cut above Williamson's and numerous cuts above Lethbridge's.

20. Jean Palou, *La Sorcellerie* (Paris, 1957), emphasizes social elements. The best Marxist arguments regarding heresy have been made by Koch, Werner, and Erbstösser. Some sociologists who have emphasized European witchcraft are Lucien Febvre, "Sorcellerie, sottise ou révolution mentale?" in *Annales: Economies-sociétés-civilisations*, III (1948), 9–15, republished in *Au Coeur religieux du seizième siècle* (Paris, 1957); Croissant; Mandrou; and Held, who relies heavily upon Durkheim.

21. Bernard, p. 55.

22. P. 33.

23. *Ibid.*, p. xv.

24. *European Witch-Craze*, p. 115; see also pp. 100–101, 106–115.

Chapter 3

1. Cf. magical passages in Montague Rhodes James, *The Apocryphal New Testament*, 2d ed. (Oxford, 1953), pp. 45, 68, 74–75, 110–111, 459.

2. See Paul Christian, pseud. of Paul Pitois, *The History and Practice of Magic*, 2 vols. (London, 1952), I, 272 ff., and Summers, *Geography*, pp. 387–388.

3. III, 1045.

4. Bernheimer; Höfler. A late survival of the wild hunt is the scene in ⌄ *The Merry Wives of Windsor* where Mrs. Page and her allies, garbed as fairies, gather at the oak of Herne the Hunter to dupe Falstaff, who has dressed himself as the stag god. In certain isolated villages varieties of the morris dance reveal similar survivals even in the twentieth century.

5. James, *Seasonal Feasts*; Mircea Eliade, *The Myth of the Eternal Return: Cosmos and History* (New York, 1954); Runeberg. Continuing condemnations of these pagan festivals by Church synods through the early Middle Ages is testimony to this persistence.

6. Pp. 239, 225.

7. James, *Seasonal Feasts*, pp. 288–289, 298–299. Grimm, II, 502 ff.

8. Forbes, "Midwifery and Witchcraft."

9. The important passages of the Old Testament dealing with magic are Exod. xxii:18; Lev. xix:26–31, xx:6, 27; Deut. xviii:10–12; I Sam. xv:23, xxviii:7–25; II Kings ix:22, xxi:6, xxiii:24; Isa. viii:19; II Chron. xxxiii:6. See Lea, *Inquisiton*, III, 388, for a list of the varieties of Jewish divination.

10. See Acts viii and Acts xvi:16.

11. "She called upon three hundred deities in her incantations: Erebus, Chaos, and three-formed Hecate, the three faces of the maiden Diana." *Aeneid*, IV, ll. 510–511. Luck's short book on magic in Roman poetry is good.

12. See J. A. MacCulloch, *Medieval Faith and Fable* (London, 1932)

for a description of numerous relics of pagan practices. General condemnations of such practices occurred at the Synod of Elvira, c. 300 (Hef-L, I, 212–264 ff.; Mansi, II, 1 ff.); at the synod of Ancyra, 314 (Hef-L, I, 298 ff.), which has nothing to do with the ninth-century *Canon Episcopi* that used to be ascribed to it; at the synod of Laodicea between 343 and 381 (Hef-L, I, 1017; Henry R. Percival, *The Seven Ecumenical Councils of the Undivided Church* [Oxford, 1900], p. 151); at the synod of Carthage, 398 (Hef-L, II, 119; Mansi, III, 979 ff.); at the synod of Carthage, 401 (Hef-L, II, 126; Mansi, III, 763 ff.); at the second synod of Arles in 443 or 452 (Hef-L, II, 466–472; Mansi, III, 231; see Blum; Joseph Hansen, *Zauberwahn,* p. 41); and by the Theodosian Code of 438, which incorporated the laws of Constantine and other earlier emperors against magic (Joseph Hansen, *Zauberwahn,* p. 49). Martroye observes that Book xvi, Title x, of the Theodosian Code, the section dealing with magic, consists of two distinct parts, one less severe and written before 395, the other stricter and written after that date. A letter of Pope Damasus I referring to a Roman synod of 367 dealing with witchcraft is spurious (Bonomo, pp. 17–18). Maurice, p. 112, shows that before Constantius II the term *superstitio* was limited to magic and not used as a synonym for pagan religion. The confusion began in the fifth century, the first mention of paganism as superstition being found in a law of Honorius dated August 3, 415 (Martroye, p. 682). As Martroye (p. 671) indicates, Constantine the Great did not prohibit all pagan sacrifices but only those involving magic and divination. Constantius II usually distinguished between paganism and superstition, and the other, later emperors permitted the continuation of public pagan worship but forbade private sacrifice behind "closed doors" because it was assumed that magic would be performed within (Martroye, p. 679). Martroye suggests that it may well have been, for late Roman paganism was darkly colored with magic. The distinction between paganism and magic, which had begun to be clouded in the fifth century, was wholly lost by the sixth (Martroye, p. 673), so that it is often difficult to understand exactly what early medieval writers have in mind by the term "superstition."

13. Dracontius' *Romulea,* X, 305–306, written about 490–500, shows that the image of the *strix* was still alive (MGH *Auctores antiquissimi,* XIV, 188.) The early Teutonic laws, e.g., the Lex Salica, 64.2., the Pactus Alamannorum, frag. II, 31, and the Edictus Rotharii, 197–198, condemn the *striga* or *stria.* But the Irish "synod of Patrick" about 457 anathematizes Christians who believe that there are such things in the world as lamias and strigae. McNeill notes that there are two synods of the fifth century ordinarily ascribed to Patrick, and it is canon 16 of the former that is in question. See also Hef-L, II, 893; Mansi, VI, 513–538; Ludwig Bieler, "Patrick's Synod: A Revision," *Mélanges offertes à Christine Mohrmann*

(Utrecht, 1963), pp. 96–102; and *The Irish Penitentials* (Dublin, 1963), pp. 56–57.

14. *Vita Sancti Simeonis Stylitae,* MPL, LXXIII, 326 ff., chap. 6.

15. In the fifth century Severian, Peter Chrysologus, and Maximus of Turin protested against this practice. See Angelo Mai, *Spicilegium romanum,* 10 vols. (Rome, 1839–1844), X, 222 ff., for Severian; Chrysologus' *Sermo CLV* in MPL, LIII, 609; and Maximus' *Homilia XVI de Kalendis Ianuarii,* MPL, LVII, 255.

16. *On Christian Doctrine,* ii ,24; *The City of God,* xxi, 6. Augustine's ideas on demons appear most clearly in *On Christian Doctrine,* Book ii, *The City of God,* Books viii–x, xviii, xxi; and *On the Divination of Demons.* See Thorndike, I, 504 ff. for Augustine's views on magic.

17. St. Maximus of Tours' *Sermo XI* in MPL, LVII, 734, describes how the priests of Diana got their worshippers drunk to prepare them for the cult. This is still going on, he says, among the peasants. See Severian, in Mai.

18. Gratian, in *Corpus Juris Canonici,* 2 pts. (Leipzig, 1879–1881), I, 1021–1022.

19. Procopius in *De Bello Gothico,* II, 25, complained that the Christian Franks still practiced pagan rites. See Elphège Vacandard, "L'Idolatrie en Gaule au VIe et au VIIe siècle," *Revue des questions historiques,* LXV (1899), 430, 432, 433; canons 15 and 16 of the Frankish national synod at Orléans in 549; Carlo de Clercq, *La Législation religieuse franque de Clovis à Charlemagne* (Louvain-Paris, 1936), pp. 27–31. De Clercq establishes the proper date for this council, which is dated 541 in Hef-L, II, 1167; Mansi, IX, 111; MGH Legg, III, i, 90; and Blum, p. 34. Further complaints against idolatry were made in canon 3 of the synod of Eauze (near Auch) in 551 (Hef-L, III, 166; MGH Legg, III, i, 114); a letter of Pope Pelagius I to Bishop Sapaud of Arles in 558–560 (MGH Epp, III, 445); canon 1 of the synod of Braga, 572 (Hef-L, III, 194; Mansi, IX, 835 ff.); a letter of Pope Pelagius II to the Bishop of Auxerre on October 5, 580 (MGH Epp, III, 449); canons 16 and 23 of the 5th synod of Toledo in May 589 (Hef-L, III, 227; Mansi, IX, 977 ff.); and a letter of Gregory I to Bishop Januarius of Sardinia in July 599 (MGH Epp, I, 257). Similar letters of Gregory the Great on the same subject are in MGH Epp, I, 318, 322, 324; II, 237, 305, 308, 331. King Childebert I of the Franks demanded the destruction of pagan idols, and St. Radegunda tried to destroy a temple where an idol was worshipped: Vacandard, pp. 426, 431. Many of the condemnations of idolatry, magic, and other such practices that one finds in the synods of the sixth and seventh centuries and even later, are borrowed from the decrees of the synods of Ancyra (314) and Laodicea (c. 350), decrees that formed part of the large collection of canons issued by Dionysius Exiguus about 500 and that passed from his collection into the body of canon law.

20. Menendez y Pelayo, I, 235–264. For Visigothic laws and magic, see Lea, *Inquisition,* III, 399. The *Breviarium* was the basis for much of the law of the later medieval *fueros* and consequently had great influence on the Spanish law of the later Middle Ages. The most relevant passage of the *Breviarium* is IX, 13, 3 (see the edition of Gustavus Haenel, Leipzig, 1849, pp. 186 ff.), where the punishment for the worship of demons is death. In IX, 13, 1, the code condemns those who by the invocation of demons "distort the minds of men," that phrase of the Theodosian Code that is repeated again and again throughout medieval condemnations of witchcraft. Canon 3 of the synod of Tours in 567 also condemns offering food to *daemones:* Blum, p. 34; MGH Legg, III, i, 133. Sacrifice to spirits not specified as demons was condemned by the laws of Childebert (511–558) (Blum, p. 35; MGH Legg, II, i, 2–3); by canon 30 of the synod of Orléans of 511 (Blum, p. 41; Hef-L, II, 1014; MGH Legg, III, i, 9; Mansi, VIII, 347 ff.); by canon 15 of the synod of Orléans in 549 (de Clercq, pp. 27–31); and in the letter of September 597 from Gregory the Great to Queen Brunhilda (MGH Epp, II, 7). For similar condemnations at the synods of Narbonne (589), Reims (624–630), and Rouen (650), see Joseph Hansen, *Zauberwahn,* p. 42.

21. Gregory I's letter to Brunhilda condemns the persistence of pagan festivals. Gregory of Tours in his *History of the Franks,* VIII, 15, in MGH *Scriptores rerum merovingicarum,* I, 334, mentions a huge idol of Diana at Ivois near Trier, for which rituals were still being practiced, and the *Life of Caesarius of Arles* refers to a demon "whom the peasants call Diana" (MGH *Scriptores rerum merovingicarum,* III, 491). The *Vita Sancti Eugendi Abbatis* also refers to a demoniac spirit called Diana (MGH *Scriptores rerum merovingicarum,* III, 159), and in Spain the peasants offered sacrifices to Hecate, Diana, and Minerva (Menendez y Pelayo, I, 235–264). The curious thing about the mention of Minerva here is that she will appear again, very occasionally, in the later literature as a companion of, or substitute for, Diana as the leader of the wild ride of women. The masquerade of men as beasts on the Kalends of January was condemned by Caesarius of Arles (*Sermo CXXIX* in MPL, XXXIX, 2001), by canon 23 of the synod of Tours, 567 (Blum, p. 34; de Clercq, p. 43; MGH Legg, III, i, 133; Hef-L, III, 191, here called canon 22), and by canon 1 of the highly influential synod of Auxerre, which took place sometime between the synod of Tours and 605 (see de Clercq, pp. 75–78). Auxerre forbade masquerading as beasts or cattle and the offering of *strenas* (gifts or sacrifices of some kind) on the first of January. It also condemned offerings placed at rocks, trees, and springs, or anywhere except in church, a prohibition that becomes a *topos* of the laws of the following two centuries. The first specific condemnation of festivals on Thursday (*dies Iovis*) occurred at the 6th synod

of Toledo on November 1, 589, canon 15 (Mansi, IX, 1013 ff.). On Thursday, sacred to the ruler of the gods both in the Mediterranean and in the north, fell the most important of the daily observances of rites dedicated to the seven planets and their influences. The passage from Caesarius is translated by John T. McNeill and Helena M. Gamer, *Medieval Handbooks of Penance* (New York, 1938), p. 277, n. 10, from MPL, XXXIX, 2001. Caesarius, like the synod of Auxerre, condemns the offering of *strenas*.

22. King Childebert ordered property owners to refuse to permit such revels on their land. MGH Legg, II, i, 2–3. The synod of Orléans in 533 condemned those who had made vows to sing, drink, or cause other disorders in church, as well as those who ate idolothytes: canons 12 and 20, Hef-L, II, 1134–1135; de Clercq, p. 16.

23. For Spain: Menendez y Pelayo, I, 235–264. HDA, III, 1835–1836, maintains that the identification of spirits and humans was well under way at the time of these laws. See *Lex salica*, 64, 2; *Pactus alamannorum*, II, 31; *Edictus Rotharii*, 197–198. For these and related laws, see Blum, pp. 25–27; Karl August Eckhardt, ed., *Die Gesetze des Merowingerreiches, 481–714,* 2d ed., 2 vols. (Göttingen, 1955–1957); Eckhardt, ed., *Lex salica* (Weimar, 1953); Eckhardt, *Leges Alamannorum* (Göttingen, 1958). Fara: *Lex salica,* 64, 5–6; Joseph Hansen, *Zauberwahn*, p. 58.

24. This is of course an example of wergeld, the system, very common in Teutonic law, in which most crimes are punishable by fines. Prison was virtually unknown; death, or occasionally slavery, was reserved for those who could not pay the fines. The law reads "If a *stria* is proved to have eaten a man." (Eckhardt, *Gesetze*, I, 114: article 64, 2, a.) The edict of Rothari in 643 denied that such a crime was possible. The Salic Law was codified by Clovis at the beginning of the century from earlier existing material and then modified by Chilperic II (d. 584). It was subsequently revived and revised many times.

25. Penitential of Columban, no. 24, in McNeill and Gamer, p. 256. Other seventh-century condemnations of pagan customs: St. Amand of Maastricht struggled against them (Vacandard, pp. 436–437; AASSOSB, II, 714–715); they were discovered in the diocese of Thérouanne (Vacandard, p. 437; AASSOSB, II, 560); St. Géry found idols at Cambrai in 623–626 (Vacandard, pp. 437–438); idols were worshipped at Beauvais and Amiens (Vacandard, p. 438; AASSOSB, II, 84, 718); a duke named Boso near Sens still practiced paganism (Vacandard, pp. 438–439; AASS, Sept., I, 259); the synod of Nantes in 658 repeated the condemnations by previous synods of the reverence of trees and stones sacred to demons (canon 20, in Mansi, XVIII, 172) as did the 16th synod of Toledo, May 2, 693 (Hef-L, III, 582; Mansi, XII, 59 ff.). The 17th synod of Toledo in 694 prohibited the magical practice of saying a mortuary mass for a living

man for the purpose of killing him (Lea, *Inquisition,* III, 447). References to the cult of Diana or similar chthonic deities are ill defined. The *Life of St. Eli* (MPL, LXXXVII, 528) speaks of widespread reverence of Neptune, Orcus, Diana, Minerva, and Ginescus, evidently persistent chthonic paganism. Minerva is described here as a goddess of misfortune. St. Romain discovered a temple to Venus at Rouen (Vacandard, p. 441), and the *Vita Sancti Ciliani* (d. 689) speaks of the cult of "the goddess" in France (AASS, July 8, p. 616). For the synod of Toledo, see Hef-L, III, 540 ff. and Mansi, XI, 1023 ff. Erwic's laws were based in part on the *Liber Iudiciorum* or Fuero Juzgo of King Receswinth in 654, Book XII, title 2 (MGH Legg, I, i, 411 ff.).

26. Canon 14 of the synod of Reims in 624–625, followed by canon 16 of the synod of Clichy in 626, forbids the eating of idolothytes. For Reims, MGH Legg, III, i, 61; Mansi, X, 592; Hef-L, III, 262. For Clichy, Mansi, X, 592; MGH Legg, III, i, 198; de Clercq, pp. 62–65. De Clercq established the date as 626. The *Breviarium* affects the ideas of Isidore of Seville, who says that incantations to demons are the source of magic: see Thorndike, I, 629–630, the Fuero Juzgo, and the Penitential of Theodore. The Fuero Juzgo influenced the Spanish codes of the eleventh to thirteenth centuries. Book vi, 2, condemns nocturnal sacrifices to the Devil and the invocation of demons in much the same terms as the *Breviarium* (MGH Legg, I, i, 257 ff.). The *Liber Poenitentialis* of Theodore of Canterbury (668–690) is one of the most influential books of penance, and its injunctions against nocturnal sacrifice, borrowed from the *Breviarium,* had considerable influence upon later penitentials. The penitential distinguishes between sacrifice to demons in trivial matters, which calls for a penance of one year, and sacrifice in serious matters, which demands ten. The influence is intertwined, for the *Liber* in its present form, though based on Theodore's ideas, was compiled only in the course of the eighth century. See Theodore, I, xv, 1–5, in McNeill and Gamer, p. 198. The law of King Wihtraed of Kent in 690 (Felix Liebermann, ed., *Die Gesetze der Angelsachsen,* 2d ed., 3 vols. [Halle, 1903–1916], I, 13) and canon 13 of the synod of Berkhamstead or Berghamstead in 697 (Hef-L, III, 588–590; Mansi, XII, 111–113), which Wihtraed summoned, condemned sacrifice to demons and to idols.

27. Vacandard, pp. 443–445; MPL, LXXXVII, 528–529. The sermon also refers to the January 1 festival. The synod of Rouen, c. 650 (Hef-L, III, 288; Mansi, X, 1199 ff.), canons 4, 13, and 14, condemn the January 1 rites, incantations to preserve animals, and other pagan practices. The Penitential of Theodore assigns a penance of three years to those who go about as a stag or a bull, dressing in the animal's skin or donning its head. St. Aldhelm of Malmesbury and Sherbourne wrote in condemnation of people worshipping goats and stags (MPL, LXXXIX, 93). San Paciano of

Barcelona wrote a book called *Cervus* ("The Stag"), now lost, in which he attacked the custom of dressing up as animals (Menendez y Pelayo, I, 235–264).

28. MGH Legg, I, v-2, 23; Eckhardt, *Gesetze*, II, 268. MGH Legg, I, iv, 87; Blum, p. 28; Joseph Hansen, *Zauberwahn*, pp. 49–50.

Chapter 4

1. For example, chapter 18 of Charlemagne's *Admonitio Generalis* of 789, MGH Legg, II, i, 52 ff.; Blum, pp. 36–37; Carlo de Clercq, *La Législation religieuse franque de Clovis à Charlemagne* (Louvain-Paris, 1936), pp. 171–178, 311.

2. Russell, *Dissent and Reform*, pp. 172–175, 193–194. Gregory II's successor, Gregory III, issued similar exhortations to Boniface: *Dissent*, p. 173.

3. Canon 5 of the German council of 742, in Hef-L, III, 823. Other such condemnations were issued by the synod of Soissons, 744, canon 6 (Hef-L, III, 858; Mansi, XII, 388 ff.; MGH Legg, III, ii, 35), by the Frankish council of 747 (Hef-L, III, 896; Mansi, XII, 409–410; MGH Legg, III, ii, 47), by the English synod of Cloveshoh, 747 (Hef-L, III, 906; Mansi, XII, 387–408; Arthur West Haddan and William Stubbs, *Councils and Ecclesiastical Documents Relating to Great Britain and Ireland*, 3 vols. (Oxford, 1869–1878), III, 360–383), by the Bavarian synod of Neuching, 772, canons 2, 4, 6 (Hef-L, III, 965–967; MGH Legg, III, ii, 100–101, involving the swearing of oaths on phallic sticks), by the Lombard council of 786 (Hef-L, III, 995; MGH Legg, I, 50–52), and by the council of Frankfurt, 794, especially canon 43 (Hef-L, III, 1059; MGH Legg, III, ii, 170; Blum, p. 37). See also Ludwig Bieler, *The Irish Penitentials* (Dublin, 1963), pp. 204–205; Joseph Hansen, *Zauberwahn*, p. 48.

4. Mansi, XII, 278; MPL, LXXXIX, 595; Mansi, XII, 294; John T. McNeill and Helena M. Gamer, *Medieval Handbooks of Penance* (New York, 1938), p. 227; Hermann Joseph Schmitz, *Die Bussbücher und die Bussdisciplin der Kirche*, 2 vols. (Mainz, 1883–1898), II, 556. Sacrifices to demons are also reported by Bede (*Ecclesiastical History*, ed. Plummer, [Oxford, 1896], I, 116.), the penitential of Egbert, c. 750 (Schmitz, II, 667), a capitulary of 769 (MGH Legg, II, i, 45), and in a letter of May 1, 748 of Pope Zachary to St. Boniface, in Michael Tangl, *Die Briefe des heiligen Bonifatius und Lullus* (Berlin, 1916), pp. 172–180.

5. Translation by Ephraim Emerton, *The Letters of Saint Boniface* (New York, 1940), p. 142.

6. Hef-L, III, 836–844. The date of the *indiculus* is uncertain; the date

of the synod was fixed by de Clercq, pp. 120–121, at 744. See Blum, pp. 36–37. St. Boniface was very likely instrumental in devising the *indiculus*. Summers (*Geography,* p. 355) and Baroja (p. 54) both mistake the *indiculus* for a decree of Childeric III, who issued none; the quotation is from Hef-L, III, 835–836; MGH Legg, I, i, 19.

7. MGH Legg II, i, 68–70. See Blum, pp. 29, 37–38; and McNeill and Gamer, p. 389. Chapter 21 of the same capitulary forbids, in the old tradition of the penitentials, sacrifices to demons at rocks and springs. The "Pseudo-Cummean" penitential (Schmitz, II, 626–627), the Bobbio penitential (Schmitz, II, 324), and the Paris penitential (Schmitz, I, 683) of about 750 all repeat the prohibitions of the Theodosian Code against disturbing men's minds by invoking demons.

8. General condemnations of the rites on New Year's were made by the Burgundian penitential (Schmitz, II, 322), and a letter from Pope Zachary to Boniface in 741 (MGH Epp, II, 301). Stags or calves: The Pseudo-Cummean Excarpsus; the early eighth-century penitential ascribed to Bede; the Bobbio penitential; the Burgundian penitential (McNeill and Gamer, pp. 276–277); the Scarapsus of St. Permin in Alamannia, c. 724 (McNeill and Gamer, p. 277, n. 10), which also refers to the feast of the Vulcanalia; and the Merseburg penitential (Schmitz, II, 360). Chapter 31 of the Fleury penitential, 775–800 (Schmitz, II, 342 ff.). The Teutonic gods were often drawn in carts as a sign of their power; and this custom was extended to the Merovingian kings, who rode in carts to symbolize their royal dignity. *Poenitentiale Vigilianum,* in F. W. H. Wasserschleben, *Die Bussordnungen der abendländischen Kirche,* 2 vols. (Halle, 1851), I, 533. The feast mentioned by the *indiculus* may be in honor of the goddess Freyjas or Frias, whose name may yield *yrias,* which has no other known meaning.

9. The penitential ascribed to Bede; the synod of Leptinnes; the penitential of Egbert (Schmitz, II, 667); and the double penitential of Egbert and Bede (Schmitz, II, 694–695); canon 9 of the Council of Rome, 743 (Hef-L, III, 852; MGH Legg, III, ii, 16; Mansi, XII, 384); synodal statutes of Boniface, c. 745 (Hef-L, III, 931, derived from canon 9 of the synod of Auxerre in the sixth century); Boniface's *Sermo* XV in MPL, LXXXIX, 870. See Lea, *Materials,* p. 111; and Joseph Hansen, *Zauberwahn,* p. 60.

10. For Aldebert, see Russell, *Dissent and Reform,* pp. 103–104; and Jeffrey B. Russell, "Saint Boniface and the Eccentrics," *Church History,* XXXIII (1964), especially pp. 239–241 for the strange angels.

11. Karl August Eckhardt, ed., *Lex salica* (Weimar, 1953), pp. 236–237. On the cauldron, see J. J. Jones, "The Cauldron in Ritual and Myth," *Aberystwyth Studies,* 1923, especially pp. 79–81. The cauldron has a sinister tradition: it is less often a cooking pot than a ritual receptacle for the blood of, or a vessel in which to boil, victims for the purposes of sacrifice or

divination. See also C. G. Jung, "Psychological Aspects of the Mother Archetype," *The Basic Writings of C. G. Jung,* ed. V. S. de Lazlo (New York, 1959), p. 333.

12. Chapter 6 of the capitulary, translated by McNeill and Gamer, p. 389. The word for witch here is *striga.* This was followed almost word for word by canon 6 of the synod of Paderborn in 785 (Hef-L, III, 992–993; Mansi, XII, 935 ff.). Cathwulf: MGH Epp, IV, 504.

13. Canon 9, Hef-L, III, 852; MGH Legg, III, ii, 16; Mansi, XII, 382.

14. Thorndike, I, 672 ff., especially p. 673. Crawford's "Evidences for Witchcraft" is concerned primarily with low magic and takes witchcraft to mean maleficent magic. She does note that, as against Murray, she can find no evidence of witch organization in England in her period, nor any sign of what she calls "Satanism" before the thirteenth century.

15. Tours, 813: Mansi, XIV, 89–90. Lea and Summers both exaggerate the importance of the synod of Paris in the history of capital punishment for witchcraft. Nonetheless the citation of the terrible passage of Exodus had an influence upon later legislation. On this synod, see Blum, p. 46; Lea, *Inquisition,* III, 414; Hef-L, IV, 61–72; Mansi, XIV, 529–604; MGH Legg, III, ii, 605–680; Summers, *Geography,* p. 356. Worms: Joseph Hansen, *Zauberwahn,* p. 67; Mansi, XIV, 529 ff. Regino: MPL, CXXXII, 190.

16. Capitulary of 805: Mansi, XIV, app. 295–300; Lea, *Inquisition,* III, 413. The penitentials: penitential of Columban, no. 24, McNeill and Gamer, pp. 252–253; the penitential of Theodore, Book I, xv, 1, in McNeill and Gamer, p. 198, which assigns a penance of one year for sacrificing to demons in trivial matters but one of ten years for sacrificing in important matters. Since some magical practices might bring only forty days' penance, Theodore's penitential is evidence that the distinction between simple magic and magic with the demons' aid was kept in mind. Remedius of Chur: MGH Legg, V, 372, 442; Joseph Hansen, *Zauberwahn,* p. 65. Quierzy: Hansen, *Zauberwahn,* pp. 68, 106; MGH Legg, II, ii, 345; Blum, p. 86.

17. Felix Liebermann, ed., *Die Gesetze der Angelsachsen,* 2d ed., 3 vols. (Halle, 1903–1916), I, 134, 153; Lea, *Inquisition,* III, 420; MGH Legg, I, v, 2, p. 23. Note that two alleged cases of witchcraft in the tenth century are certainly spurious. No witches were burnt in Westphalia in 914, as Soldan-Heppe, relying upon the unreliable *Annales Corbeienses,* claimed (see Lea, *Inquisition,* III, 416; Summers, *Geography,* p. 359, who follows Soldan-Heppe's error; Joseph Hansen, *Zauberwahn,* p. 116). The story of the bewitching of King Duff (967–972) of Scotland is also wholly fabulous, *pace* Baroja, p. 51; Summers, *Geography,* p. 203. The story of Duff appears only in the sixteenth century with the *Buik of the Chroniclis of Scotland* by William Stewart, edited by William B. Turnbull, 3 vols. (London, 1858),

II, 512–517. This is an inordinately long epic poem about Scottish history whose earlier parts are drawn wholly from fable and totally unworthy of credence.

18. For the reaction to the reintroduction of paganism into England, see a letter of Pope Formosus to the English bishops in Mansi, XVIII, 114–115; and the laws of Alfred, Liebermann, I, 39; MPL, CXXXVIII, 458. No better evidence for the untrustworthiness of Summers and Murray can be found than their use of these laws, which are general and unsensational and aimed largely at the practices that the Danish pagans had imported. There is little in them that does not appear in one form or another in many penitentials and synodal statutes. Yet Murray, *God of the Witches,* pp. 15–16, insists that they prove not only the persistence of the "Old Religion" but that it was at that time more common than Christianity. And Summers, *Geography,* p. 72, says that they enjoin against man-worship, of which there is in fact no trace.

19. The *Poenitentiale Casinense,* McNeill and Gamer, p. 429; Schmitz, I, 412–414; *Poenitentiale Valicellanum I,* c. A.D. 800, McNeill and Gamer, p. 430; Schmitz, I, 301–330; *Poenitentiale capitula judiciorum,* c. 800, Schmitz, II, 236–238; the canons of Angilramnus of Metz (d. 804), MPL, XCVI, 1036; the capitulary of Aachen, MGH Legg, II, i, 100; Joseph Hansen, *Zauberwahn,* p. 66; the so-called penitential of Halitgar of Cambrai, c. 830, McNeill and Gamer, pp. 305–306; Jaffé, vol. I, no. 3496; Russell, *Dissent and Reform,* p. 177; See the letter of John IX to Hervé, Jaffé, vol. I, no. 3553; MPL, CXXXI, 27; Mansi, XVIII, 189–190; and the letter of Hervé to Bishop Wido of Rouen: Mansi, XVIII, 193 ff. The accusation brought against Pope John XII in 963 that he called upon Jupiter and Venus at dice, unimpressive to begin with, has been shown to be a normal way of calling out throws in a medieval dice game; see Hef-L, IV, 807. That he drank the health of Satan in wine may also be doubted; Russell, *Dissent and Reform,* p. 146.

20. "Life of San Barbato," ed. Georg Waitz, *Scriptores rerum Langobardicarum et Italicarum saec. VI–IX* (Hanover, 1878), p. 557; see Croce.

21. MGH SS, V, 455–460. See also the *Poeta saxonicus* of the year 814, in André Duchesne, *Historiae Francorum Scriptores,* 5 vols. (Paris, 1636–1649), II, 173; a sermon of Stephen V (885–891), Joseph Hansen, *Zauberwahn,* p. 69; the so-called confessional of Egbert (c. 950–1000), McNeill and Gamer, pp. 246–247; the Arundel Penitential (tenth or eleventh century), McNeill and Gamer, p. 427, and Schmitz, I, 460–461; and the laws of King Edgar the Peaceful.

22. The Tripartite St. Gall penitential, c. 800 (Schmitz, II, 181, 377); the *Poenitentiale capitula judiciorum* (Schmitz, II, 236–238); the peniten-

tial of Silos, c. .800 (McNeill and Gamer, p. 288); the *Poenitentiale Valicellianum I,* c .800 (McNeill and Gamer, p. 430; Schmitz, I, 311); the simple St. Gall penitential (Schmitz, II, 347); the *Poenitentiale Hubertense* (Schmitz, II, 344 ff.); the penitential of Halitgar of Cambrai, c. 830 (Mc-Neill and Gamer, pp. 305–306); Regino of Prüm, *Ecclesiastical Discipline* (McNeill and Gamer, p. 318; Wasserschleben, I, 533; Schmitz, II, 353). The Spanish penitential reads: "Qui in saltatione femineum habitum gestiunt et monstrose se fingunt et maiam et orcum et pelam et hic similius exercent. . . ." Bernheimer, p. 43, suggests, as part of his theory that a cult of the wild man existed (pp. 49–50), that Maia is here to be interpreted *Holz-moia,* the "Wildwoman." Pela he does not identify; Orcus he says is the leader of the dead, and thus the passage is to be interpreted as referring to a masquerade as Maia, Orcus, and Pela. This interpretation is vitiated by the reading of the Vienne penitential: "Si quis in Kalendas Januarias vadit in cervulo aut in Kalendas Maias quecunque potionem acciperit. . . ." We are dealing with a May festival, in other words, not with a wildwoman or a goddess named Maia, let alone a Holz-moia. To *"exercere"* Orcum, I suggest, is merely to practice a hellish rite; *pelam* may very likely be a corruption of *pellacem (pellax)* and to *"exercere pelam"* would then simply mean donning animal skins. Regino of Prüm condemned diabolical songs, jokes, and dancing at funerals: McNeill and Gamer, pp. 318–319. In another passage of *De Synodalibus causis et disciplinis ecclesiasticis,* Blum, p. 36, this is given a somewhat different wording, derived primarily from Hincmar; see Wasserschleben, I, 180–216. Burchard of Worms repeated this at the beginning of the eleventh century, again in somewhat different words; see Schmitz, II, 429.

23. Storms, pp. 2–4.

24. Joseph Hansen, *Zauberwahn,* p. 60; Lea, *Inquisition,* III, 417; Haddan and Stubbs, II, 329. (This synod however, may really date from 457.) Hincmar, *De Divortio Lotharii et Tetbergae,* MPL, CXXV, 716–725.

25. Hef-L, IV, 53; MGH Legg, III, ii, 581; Storms, pp. 106, 245–247. The idea that Herodias ruled *one-third* of the world may well be derived from the three-fold powers of Hecate. There is no particular reason why this one Biblical villainess should be selected as a leader of troops of evil beings other than the superficial resemblance of her name to that of the goddess. This argument is confirmed by the subsequent commonplace of linking Herodias' name with that of Diana in accounts of the witches' flight.

26. See Appendix: The *Canon Episcopi* and Its Variations.

27. The capitulary has never been found, so this explanation must remain in doubt, but the doubt is not very great. Etienne Baluze, the first modern editor of the "canon," declared in his *Capitularia regum Francorum,*

2d ed., 2 vols. (Paris, 1780), II, 361 ff. (1st ed., Paris, 1677) that it was a capitulary of the reign of Louis II issued in 867. If Baluze had any evidence for this precision, however, he does not offer it, and no such capitulary of 867 has been found. E. Vacandard in "L'Idolatrie en Gaule au VIe et au VIIe siècle," *Revue des questions historiques,* LXV (1899), 424–454, and Baroja, p. 65, as well as others have made the mistake of following Baluze on this point, though Baroja compounds his error by confusing the capitulary with that of Quierzy in 873. Although the capitulary has never been found, the supposition that that is what the "canon" must be is soundly based. In the first place, if this lurid material actually did derive from an earlier synod, it would surely have been reproduced before 906. It almost certainly does not derive from a ninth-century synod, both because most of the Carolingian synods are fairly well known to us and, more importantly, because of its form. It is an instruction to bishops and begins with the phrase: "(Ut) episcopi episcoporumque ministri omnibus viribus elaborare studeant." This opening would be unusual for a synodal canon but is very common in capitularies. Compare the following capitulary openings of the ninth century: "Ut episcopi universique sacerdotes habeant advocatos"; "Ut omnes episcopi, abbates, et comites"; "Ut nulli episcoporum et sacerdotum"; "Quidam autem episcopi et rectores monasteriorum." Joseph Hansen, *Quellen,* p. 38, n. 1, agrees that the "canon" is a capitulary of the ninth century, probably of the later ninth century, and there is no reason to dispute this judgment. It is just possible that Baluze had some evidence now lost to us and that the "canon" can be assigned to the year 867, but caution does not permit such a precision at present.

28. Translation by Lea, *Materials,* I, 178–180. The Latin of this version of the canon appears, among other places, in Joseph Hansen, *Quellen,* pp. 38–39, and MPL, CXXXII, 352–353. On the canon, see especially Lea, *Inquisition,* III, 494; Rose, pp. 106 ff.; Joseph Hansen, *Zauberwahn,* pp. 78–88; Robbins, *Encyclopedia,* pp. 74–77.

29. Including Ivo of Chartres, Gratian, Bartholomew of Exeter, Aquinas, Alexander of Hales, and Hostiensis. For others and for commentary, see Lea, *Materials,* I, 187–192.

30. It used to be believed that the *Corrector* had been taken verbatim from a tenth-century source, but Fournier proved that it was Burchard who systematized it. See McNeill and Gamer, p. 321. It is likely that the passages dealing with witchcraft are of late tenth-century or early eleventh-century origin, however. There are passages dealing with magic and paganism that derive from well-known earlier penitentials, but no earlier form is known of the passages having to do with witchcraft proper. For

texts of the *Corrector*, see MPL, CXL, 949–1014; Schmitz, II, 407–467. Parts are translated in McNeill and Gamer, pp. 323–325. The relevant passages are reproduced in Joseph Hansen, *Quellen*, pp. 40–42.

31. The shorter version of the Canon appears in *Decretum*, XIX, 70; the longer in XIX, 90.

32. *Decretum*, XIX, 60–69, deals with common sorcery, and there are many other passages dealing with pagan practices: no. 94, for example, enjoins against the eating of idolothytes, and no. 99 against the New Year's masquerade; no. 91 forbids dancing and singing of diabolical songs at funerals; no. 92 condemns making diabolical phylacteries or characters as charms (presumably amulets) or worshipping Jupiter (Thor) on Thursdays. The passages relevant to the history of witchcraft are nos. 151, 152, 170, and 171.

33. It is reminiscent of the cloud ships of Agobard. Professor Will-Erich Peuckert has kindly informed me that his seminar has shown that the Frisians and Low Saxons were already speaking of the flight of witches over the sea before the great migrations to the East began in the twelfth century.

34. McNeill and Gamer, p. 335.

35. Capitulary of Aachen, MGH Legg, II, i, 99; capitulary of Ansegis, MGH Legg, II, i, 281, 276. See Russell, *Dissent and Reform*, p. 177. Cf. Aldebert in the eighth century with his letter from heaven and his uncanonical angels.

36. Agobard, *Liber contra insulsam vulgi opinionem de grandine et tonitruis*, MPL, CIV, 147–158, especially 148. See Lea, *Inquisition*, III, 414–415.

37. Russell, *Dissent and Reform*, pp. 107–109.

38. The treatise dealt with the divorce of the Emperor Lothar II and Queen Theutberga: MPL, CXXV, 716–725. Hincmar also condemns feasts with wild eating and drinking.

39. *Gesta Karoli*, MGH SS, II, 742.

40. I argue this, in agreement with Raoul Manselli and Raffaello Morghen, in my *Dissent and Reform*. See Manselli, and Raffaello Morghen, *Medioevo cristiano* (Bari, 1951; 2d ed., 1958). Also of this opinion are Henri Puech, "Catharisme médiéval et Bogomilisme," *Convegno "Volta" di scienze morali, storiche, e filologiche, Atti*, 8th ser., XII (1957), 56–84; Emile G. Leonard, "Remarques sur les 'Sectes,'" *Annuaire de l'Ecole pratique des hautes études, section des sciences religieuses* (1955–1956); and, with some reservations, Wakefield and Evans, p. 19. Other writers, including the eminent Father Dondaine, have disputed this position, claiming that at least some dualist influence stemming from Bogomilism appeared in the West in the eleventh century. I am unconvinced. The evidence does

not permit us to exclude the possibility of Bogomil influence in that century, but there is absolutely no external evidence for Bogomil penetration, and there is nothing in the doctrines of eleventh-century heretics that cannot be explained—usually quite obviously—in terms of the indigenous, ascetic Reformist tradition.

41. Russell, *Dissent and Reform,* pp. 110–113, 197, 207–215, 237–240; Wakefield and Evans, pp. 71–75.

42. Russell, *Dissent and Reform,* pp. 27–35, 197, 276–277; Wakefield and Evans, pp. 74–81. Historians of heresy have always been plagued by the conflicts among the sources for the Orléans heresy. The best source is Paul of Saint-Père de Chartres. Though he wrote almost fifty years after the trial, he was personally acquainted with some of the principals. He mentions secret conventicles at night, the carrying of lamps, the litany of demons, the appearance of Satan in the form of a beast, the extinction of the lights in order to have a carnal orgy, a viaticum made from the ashes of murdered children, and demonic transportation. Adhémar of Chabannes, a good source who wrote soon after the events (1028), mentions sex orgies; spitting on the image of Christ; adoration of the Devil, who appeared as a black man or as an angel of light; the Devil's giving money to the heretics; sacred food made out of the ashes of dead children. Baldwin of Thérouanne, a much less reliable source, mentions the secret worship of pagan gods. Radulf Glaber, almost wholly unreliable, says that the heretics believed that lust was not a sin and consequently was not punishable. Andreas of Fleury, the *Historiae Francicae Fragmentum,* and Jean of Fleury, all sources inferior to Paul and Adhémar, do not mention the witch charges. See *Dissent and Reform,* pp. 276–277; and Malcolm Lambert's forthcoming book.

43. James, *Sacrifice and Sacrament;* C. G. Jung, *Symbols of Transformation,* 2d ed. (Princeton, 1967), especially pp. 224, 341; Samuel Angus, *The Mystery Religions and Christianity* (New York, 1925); Briffault, III, 196–209; W. K. C. Guthrie, *Orpheus and Greek Religion* (New York, 1966), pp. 264 ff. In the Far East, the practices of Tantric Buddhism form the closest analogy.

44. George E. Mylonas, *Eleusis and the Eleusinian Mysteries* (Princeton, 1961), pp. 224–285.

45. See Lev., 20:2; Deut., 18:10–11; Judg., 11:30–40; II Kings, 3:27; 16:3–4; 23:10 (sacrifice to Moloch); Ps., 106:35–38.

46. Strack.

47. Indeed, sexual irregularities were not unknown among the Christians, witness I Cor. 5–6. See Schulze, pp. 304–306; Waltzing; W. H. C. Frend, *Martyrdom and Persecution in the Early Church* (New York, 1967), p. 188; Dölger, "Sacramentum infanticidii"; Theodor Keim, *Rom und das Christentum* (Berlin, 1881), pp. 362–510; Max Conrat, *Die Christenver-*

fölgung im römischen Reiche vom Standpunkte des Juristen (Leipzig, 1897), pp. 29–42.

48. Augustine, *De Moribus Manichaeorum*, MPL, XXXII, 1374–1375. The passage is translated by Richard Stothert in *The Nicene and Post-Nicene Fathers*, 14 vols. (New York, 1886–1890) Ser. I, vol. IV, 88. The term *lucerna exstincta* is used here twice. See also MPL, XXXII, 1373; *De Haeresibus*, ed. and trans. Liguori G. Müller (Washington, D.C., 1956), pp. 84–97.

49. The Euchites were accused of eating feces in honor of the Devil, they went at night to rites presided over by a black man, and they were attended by hordes of demons. Svoboda, pp. 47–48; Garsoian, pp. 27–29; Karapet ter-Mkrttschian, *Die Paulikianer im byzantinischen Kaiserreiche und verwandte ketzerische Erscheinungen in Armenien* (Leipzig, 1893); Dmitri Obolensky, *The Bogomils* (Cambridge, Eng., 1948), pp. 186–187, 251–252. That these traditions persisted in the East well into the fourteenth century is clear from the *Responsio fratris Danielis ad impositos Hermensis,* a mid-century treatise of Daniel of Thaurizio appearing in G. Shefer and L. de Mas Latrie, *Recueil des historiens des croisades, documents arméniens,* II, 559–650. Garsoian, p. 107, n. 95, cites Daniel's account. In a village called Tondray near Manzikert are heretics speaking Armenian who are neither Christians, Saracens, nor Jews. They worship the sun, and twice a year they assemble in a humble home at night. No lights are kindled, and they engage in indiscriminate intercourse. The children begotten during these revels are slain and burnt, their ashes then being added to food as a sacred ingredient. The Christian Armenians abhorred these heretics "like demons."

50. Psellos, *On the Operation of Demons* was written about 1050; Paul wrote about 1070. It is extremely unlikely that Paul borrowed from Psellos in any event, and the similar charges reported by Adhémar in 1028, two decades before Psellos, makes borrowing from the East even less likely. It seems most probable that both the Eastern and Western literary traditions derived independently from the Fathers.

51. Herbert Grundmann argued against accepting these reports: "Der Typus des Ketzers im mittelalterliche Anschauung," *Kultur- und Universalgeschichte: Festschrift W. Goetz* (Leipzig-Berlin, 1927). Grundmann associated these sexual accusations with similar allegations against the early Christians and believed them to be the product of a psychological release mechanism, too vague an explanation.

52. Russell, *Dissent and Reform,* pp. 35–38, 198; Wakefield and Evans, pp. 86–93.

53. Russell, *Dissent and Reform,* pp. 54–68, 201–202, 207–215; Wakefield and Evans, pp. 96–101.

54. Russell, *Dissent and Reform*, pp. 68–80; Wakefield and Evans, pp. 101–104, 107–117, 122–126.

55. Russell, *Dissent and Reform*, pp. 77–78, 114–124; Wakefield and Evans, pp. 120, 138–139, 141–146.

56. Adam of Bremen, *History of the Archbishops of Hamburg and Bremen*, II, 61 (59); Lea, *Inquisition*, III, 421–422; H. Schwarzwälder, "Geschichte des Zauber- und Hexenglaubens in Bremen"; MGH SS rer germ, II, 160–162; Joseph Hansen, *Zauberwahn*, p. 77; Radulf Glaber, *Historia*, IV, 11, in MPL, CXLII, 672.

57. Joseph Hansen, *Zauberwahn*, pp. 82–88. Minerva is added by pseudo-Augustine in the twelfth century: "cum Diana paganorum dea vel cum Herodiade et Minerva." See MPL, XL, 799. The other most important derivations from Burchard are the *Summa de judiciis omnium peccatorum*, eleventh century (see Schmitz, II, 484–496); Book 8 of Ivo of Chartres' *Panormia* and Book II of his *Decretum*, which deal with the old traditions of paganism and sorcery and repeat much of Burchard (see MPL, CLXI, 752–753, and Joseph Hansen, *Zauberwahn*, p. 88); Gratian's *Decretum*, the most influential compilation of canon law for most of the Middle Ages (see MPL, CLXXXVII, 1349–1351, and Joseph Hansen, *Zauberwahn*, pp. 93–95). That these old traditions were handed down by the canonists and not by theologians is clear. Peter Lombard, the author of the *Sentences*, which occupies in the history of theology a place similar to that occupied by Gratian's *Decretum* in canon law, is absolutely silent in regard to the canon or the pagan practices linked with it by Burchard and his successors.

58. Orderic, *Historia Ecclesiastica*, in MPL, CLXXXVIII, 607–612.

59. Stephen's laws, caput 31, *De strigibus*. See A. Szendrey, "Hexe-Hexendruck," *Acta Ethnographica*, IV (1955), 129–169; Mansi, XX, 777; Joseph Hansen, *Zauberwahn*, pp. 76–78. Szendrey and Andor Komáromy, *Magyarországi boszorkányperek oklevéltára* (Budapest, 1910) are unconvincing in their argument that King Stephen could not have believed in vampires or succubi because he was too holy and intelligent.

60. Map is not concerned that we take this story seriously. See *De Nugis Curialium*, ad ann. 1127; Kittredge, p. 43. Ethelred II: Mansi, XIX, 300; Joseph Hansen, *Zauberwahn*, p. 77; Liebermann, I, 248–249, 254–255. Cnut: MPL, CLI, 1178; Mansi, XIX, 561; Liebermann, I, 312.

61. Baroja, p. 45.

62. The story was later used by Vincent of Beauvais, Olaus Magnus, and others, possibly including Caesarius of Heisterbach, though it does not appear in the *Dialogus Miraculorum*, and eventually was made famous in a poem by Southey. The Malmesbury version appears in the *De Gestis Regum Anglorum*, ed. William Stubbs (Rolls Ser.), 2 vols. (London, 1887–1889), I, 253–255.

63. *Historia rerum anglicarum,* ed. Thomas Sebright (Oxford, 1719), I, 28. William of Newburgh also records instances of vampirism (V, 22–23).

Chapter 5

1. Langton, *Essentials of Demonology,* pp. 68–71.

2. Lea, *Materials,* I, 78–79. The evil spirit (Germanic mara) who is supposed to sit on one's chest at night, causing feelings of suffocation, has left its name in the English "nightmare" and the French *cauchemar.* For the popular tales about demons told by Caesarius of Heisterbach, see Philipp Schmidt, pp. 78–97.

3. Because of their association in the Christian mind with evil, Jews were often portrayed with horns and a tail. See Trachtenberg, pp. 44–52. Michelangelo's Moses is horned. This is partly a consequence of the artist's having followed the Vulgate's mistranslation of the Hebrew of Exod. 34:29, 35: the Hebrew says that Moses' face shone; the Vulgate says that it bore horns. The confusion goes back beyond the Vulgate. The Hebrew *keren* can mean both "horn" and "power," so that in Jewish imagery horns could be identified with strength, as in II Sam. 22:3. The conception of supernatural entities with horns is common in the Ancient Near East. For example, an Ugaritic inscription has: "He (*El*) meets Chaby, the lord of horns and tail," this Chaby being associated with the evil god Resheph. See Mission de Ras Shamra, vol. XVI (*Ugaritica V*) (Paris, 1968), 545–548.

4. See Naselli. The red devil, very uncommon in the Middle Ages, has become a common figure in current irreverent portraiture of Satan. This is partly because of the association of the Devil with the flames of hell. It is possible that in the early New World fear of the American Indian reinforced this image.

5. "*Tali primum parente generati nigri sumus.*" And yet, Jerome was obliged to note that the Bridegroom in the Song of Songs found his beloved "black but comely."

6. Lea, *Inquisition,* I, 214; Wakefield and Evans, pp. 93 and 670, n. 14.

7. The pitchfork may appear as two- or three-pronged. When three-pronged, it is really a trident, possibly associated—through Neptune—with the watery substance ascribed to demons by some authors or with the three-fold power over earth, sea, and air (or underworld, earth, and air: cf. Hecate) ascribed to Satan. The Devil's trident is not primarily a phallic symbol, as Masters, p. 17, asserts.

8. Thorndike, *A History of Magic,* II, 155 ff.

9. Jacob Grimm, *Deutsche Rechts-Alterthümer* (Göttingen, 1828), p.

646; Joseph Hansen, *Zauberwahn*, p. 138; John T. McNeill and Helena M. Gamer, *Medieval Handbooks of Penance* (New York, 1938), pp. 349–350.

10. Witch stories in this period are a subcategory of devil and demon stories. Their quantity is enormous, and we mention here only those relating to witchcraft. That the Devil's presence was taken for granted is seen in this bald statement from the *Annales Floreffienses*, MGH SS, XVI, 625: "1185. . . . In this year the Devil visited a citizen of Brussels in a ship."

11. *De nugis curialium*, ed. Montague Rhodes James (Oxford, 1914). The stories related here are found on pp. 72–82, 159–171.

12. Gervaise, *Otia Imperialia*, ed. G. W. von Leibnitz in *Scriptores rerum Brunsvicensium*, 3 vols. (1707–1711), I, 881 ff.; or in MGH SS, XXVII, 359–394. The most relevant passages are Books I, 17; and III, 85, 86, 93, and 120.

13. H. von E. Scott and C. C. Swinton Bland, trans., *Dialogus Miraculorum*, 2 vols. (London, 1929). For the tales related here, see I, 86 ff., 138 ff., 315 ff., 338–341, 354–355, 360–368, 373–374, 385–386, 467 ff.; and II, 61–63, 172 ff., and 310–313.

14. Joseph Hansen, *Zauberwahn*, pp. 191–211.

15. Lea, *Inquisition*, III, 424.

16. *Ibid.*, 422.

17. Russell, *Dissent and Reform*, pp. 188–192.

18. *Ibid.*, pp. 192–229; Wakefield and Evans, pp. 26–50. Wakefield's is the best brief account of the spread of Catharist ideas.

19. The close connection between witchcraft and Catharism is demonstrated by the derivative term *gazarus*, which in the fourteenth and fifteenth centuries was commonly used to denote a witch. Borst, pp. 241–242, gives nearly a dozen examples of the use of *gazarus* or similar forms in the thirteenth and fourteenth centuries.

20. Translation by Walter Wakefield, in Wakefield and Evans, pp. 230–235. The original text is in Antoine Dondaine, "Durand de Huesca et la polémique anti-cathare," *Archivum fratrum praedicatorum*, XXIX (1959), pp. 268–271.

21. Gerhart Ladner, "*Homo Viator*: Medieval Ideas on Alienation and Order," *Speculum*, XLII (1967), 233–259.

22. Rigord, *Gesta Philippi Augusti: Recueil*, XVII, 38.

23. Scott and Bland, I, 352.

24. Alan of Lille, *De fide catholica contra haereticos sui temporis*, MPL, CCX, 377–380; translation by Wakefield in Wakefield and Evans, pp. 219–220.

25. *Tractatus de haeresi pauperum de Lugduno auctore anonymo* in Edmond Martène and Ursin Durand, *Thesaurus novus anecdotorum*, 5

vols. (Paris, 1717), V, 1781–1782. See Wakefield and Evans, p. 637; *Dictionnaire de théologie catholique*, 15 vols. (Paris, 1924–1950), IX, 1047; Joseph Hansen, *Zauberwahn*, pp. 232–233; Wilhelm Preger, "Der Traktat des David von Augsburg über die Waldesier," *Abhandlungen der historischen Classe der königlich bayerischen Akademie der Wissenschaften*, XIV (1878), 181–235, (p. 211 has the section *De Adoratione Luciferi*); Dondaine, pp. 93–94, 104–105, 180–183.

26. Translation by Walter Wakefield, in Wakefield and Evans, pp. 305–306.

27. For a full discussion of the problem of libertinism, see Koch, pp. 113–121. See also W. Schmithals, *Die Gnosis in Korinth: Eine Untersuchung zu den Korintherbriefen* (Göttingen, 1965); Hans Jonas, *The Gnostic Religion* (Boston, 1958); Anders Nygren, *Agape and Eros*, trans. Philip S. Watson (Philadelphia, 1953); Büttner and Werner, pp. 73–134; Antoine Dondaine, "Nouvelles sources de l'histoire doctrinale du néomanichéisme au moyen âge," *Revue des sciences philosophiques et theologiques*, XXVIII (1939), 465–488. Koch suggests (p. 116) that the indiscriminate sexual intercourse practiced at orgies at which members of different classes were present produced a sense of comradeship that helped to break down undemocratic social barriers.

28. Büttner and Werner, pp. 98, 110–111, 131.

29. Kurze, p. 53.

30. Geoffrey of Auxerre, *Super Apocalypsim*, ed. Jean Leclercq, in *Analecta monastica*, 2d ser. (*Studia Anselmiana*, no. 131; Rome, 1953), 196–197; Leclercq, "Les écrits de Geoffroy d'Auxerre," *Revue Bénédictine*, LXII (1952), 274–291; Russell, *Dissent and Reform*, p. 208; Joachim, *Espositio in Apocalypsim* (Venice, 1527); *Dictionnaire de théologie catholique*, IX, 1046–1047. That the Patarines, or Publicans, as they were sometimes called, were identified with the Catharists and witches is seen in a phrase in the edict of Otto IV in 1210 published in L. A. Muratori, *Rerum Italicarum Scriptores*, 25 vols. (Milan, 1723–1751), V, 89: "*Pathurenos sive Gazaros.*" The origin of this use of the word Patarine is uncertain: it may derive from the eleventh-century Patarines of Florence, reformers who were charged by their enemies with heresy, or from the Patarenoi, as the Bogomils of the Illyrian coast were called. Walter Map, *De nugis*, pp. 57–59. See the translation in Wakefield and Evans, pp. 254–256. See also Joseph Hansen, *Zauberwahn*, pp. 228–229.

31. *De fide catholica contra haereticos sui temporis*, chaps. 62–63, MPL, CCX, 365. Joseph Hansen, *Zauberwahn*, p. 229. Further references to the sexual immorality of the Catharists in this period appear in the testimony of heretics converted by the legate Henry of Albano (see his letter of 1181 in MPL, CCIV, 235 ff.); in the chronicle of Geoffrey of Vigeois in *Recueil*,

XII, 448; and an anonymous fragment of c. 1200 published by Jacob Gretzer, *Opera Omnia,* 17 vols. (Regensburg, 1734–1741), XIIb, 96.

32. Gerhoh of Reichersberg; Heisig, pp. 271–274. The idea of sperm communion derives from St. Augustine. See St. Augustine, *De Haeresibus,* ed. Liguori G. Müller (Washington, D.C., 1956), p. 89. The Manichean elect "consume a sort of eucharist sprinkled with human seed in order that the divine substance may be freed even from that, just as it is from other foods of which they partake." (St. Augustine had described their belief that in eating foods, they liberated their spirit from the enclosing matter). Later, Augustine describes the unappetizing custom of sprinkling flour beneath a couple in intercourse so that a batter can be made of their seed (p. 91).

33. In his sermon for the eighth Sunday after Trinity, written sometime in the latter half of the twelfth century, MPL, CLV, 2011.

34. Ralph of Coggeshall, *Chronicon Anglicanum,* Rolls Ser., LXVI (London, 1875), 121–125; Wakefield and Evans, pp. 251–254.

35. Translation by Walter Wakefield, in Wakefield and Evans, p. 254.

36. A similar story was told earlier of a nobleman of Maastricht about 1160 by Alberic of Trois-Fontaines, in his *Chronica,* MGH SS, XXIII, 845. There demons in the shape of fair folk lured the gentleman to a table where a magnificent repast had been laid. Having been forewarned by his bishop, the noble made the sign of the cross over the food, whereupon he saw it for what it really was: "the diverse excrements of men, hogs, asses, and other filthy things; the delicious wine turned into urine."

37. He suggests two other, equally false derivations—from *catha,* meaning flux, and from *castus,* because they feign chastity.

38. Thus the Catharists of Cologne in 1163. Russell, *Dissent and Reform,* p. 222; Wakefield and Evans, pp. 243–244.

39. See Wakefield, p. 728, n. 10, for a different view.

Chapter 6

1. For Rutebeuf, see W. T. H. Jackson, *The Literature of the Middle Ages* (New York, 1960), pp. 312–313. Another such Faustian story, describing how a young man was seized by the Devil after calling him up in order to obtain the affections of a young lady, was told about 1260 by Siegfrid the Priest in his *Epitome,* in Charles du Plessis d'Argentré, *Collectio judiciorum de novis erroribus,* 3 vols. (Paris, 1724–1736), I, 172. The influence of Berthold of Regensburg's immensely popular sermons on the development of popular demonology and, indirectly, upon witchcraft was great, but Burchard tells no stories other than those about pact that

are typical of classical witchcraft. On Berthold, see Lea, *Inquisition*, I, 268; Joseph Hansen, *Zauberwahn*, p. 170.

2. De Gaiffier and De Tervarent.

3. Thomas of Cantimpré, *Bonum universale de apibus* (Douai, 1627), II, chap. 56, pp. 536–537. In the same chapter, Thomas tells how a monk tried to prevent his sister from being carried away unwillingly at night by demons, but no matter how hard he clung to her she would disappear from his arms.

4. Jacques de Vitry, *La Légende dorée*, ed. and trans. J.-B. M. Roze, 3 vols. (Paris, 1902), II, 314–321. See Joseph Hansen, *Zauberwahn*, p. 136.

5. Lea, *Materials*, I, 175.

6. Brooke, pp. 115–131, points out that *zwîvel* is at the center of Wolfram von Eschenbach's *Parzival* and of many other monuments of medieval thought.

7. Fredericq, *De Secten der Geeselaars*. This movement was reflected in the more grotesque dances of death that passed into art and literature. See Hecker, p. 153, for the Erfurt incident. The great outbreak of the dancers occurred in 1374. Some dance stories seem to be moral *exempla* rather than actual fact. At Utrecht in 1278 (Hecker, p. 153), two hundred dancers are said to have danced on a bridge over the Moselle until it collapsed and they drowned; but this is similar to the famous account of the dancers of Kolbig (Hecker, pp. 153–154), who in 1021, unheeding the pleas of the priest to stop their revels, were forced supernaturally to continue their dance for a full year without ceasing.

8. "The Dance is a kind of sermon," says Clark, p. 94. On the dance, see Clark, Rosenfeld, and Stegemeier.

9. On the flagellants, see Leff, *Heresy in the Later Middle Ages*, II, 485–493; Fredericq, *Geschiedenis der Inquisitie*, II, 61–78; Norman Cohn, *The Pursuit of the Millennium* (London, 1957), pp. 124–148. J. M. Fearns is currently at work on a book on the subject.

10. Borst, pp. 128–142; Wakefield and Evans, pp. 265–446; Joseph Hansen, *Zauberwahn*, p. 233.

11. Grundmann, *Religiöse Bewegungen*, pp. 319–438; Grundmann, *Ketzergeschichte*, pp. 41–58; Wakefield and Evans, pp. 259–263, 406, 411; Leff, *Heresy in the Later Middle Ages*, I, 167–258, 308–410; Cohn, pp. 149–194; Friess, pp. 209–272; Antonino de Stefano, "Intorno alle origini e alla natura della 'secta spiritus libertatis,'" *Archivum Romanicum*, vol. XI (1927); Decima L. Douie, *The Nature and the Effect of the Heresy of the Fraticelli* (Manchester, 1932); McDonnell; Russell, *Medieval Religious Dissent*, pp. 86–91; Erbstösser and Werner. Norman Cohn points out (pp. 186–187) that mysticism was itself associated with antinomianism in

its insistence upon internal justification. The great Rhenish mystic Heinrich Suso himself became attached to the heresy of the Free Spirit.

12. Similar confessions by Johann Hartmann and Konrad Kannler are discussed by Ernst Werner, in Büttner and Werner, pp. 109–110.

13. Cohn, p. 190. Norman Cohn no longer trusts the source from which this was derived.

14. Pyarali Rattansi, "Alchemy and Natural Magic in Raleigh's *History of the World*," *Ambix*, XIII (1966), 127–128. Rattansi's excellent article, to which Hugh Trevor-Roper directed me, makes the valuable distinction between Neoplatonic and Aristotelian views of magic that I follow here. Trevor-Roper's own interpretation of witchcraft has been influenced by Rattansi.

15. Joseph Hansen, *Zauberwahn*, pp. 121, 179–189.

16. William of Auvergne, *De Universo*, Book III, chap. 24, in *Guilielmi Alverni, Opera Omnia*, 2 vols. (Orléans, 1674), I, 1066.

17. Lea, *Materials*, I, 187–188.

18. Especially in *De Legibus*, chaps. 26–27; and in *De Universo*, II, 94, and III, 12, 24, in *Opera Omnia*, 2 vols. (Paris, 1674), I, 948–1066. Joseph Hansen, *Zauberwahn*, pp. 134–136, 229–239; Lea, *Materials*, I, 202.

19. Joseph Hansen, *Zauberwahn*, pp. 229–239, suggests that William and other writers probably derived these ideas from Konrad of Marburg's inquisition in Germany in the 1230's, but, as we have seen, all the elements existed earlier in the century.

20. At Cologne in 1074, a witch was hurled off the town walls: Lambert of Hersfeld, *Annales*, MGH SS, V, 213–214; Joseph Hansen, *Zauberwahn*, pp. 117–118; Lea, *Inquisition*, III, 419. At Vötting in 1090, a witch was burned by the "diabolical zeal" of the people: *Annales Sancti Stephani Frisingensis*, MGH SS, XIII, 52. In 1128, a sorceress at Ghent was lynched by disemboweling, and later in the same year another was burned by the people: *The Murder of Charles the Good*, MGH SS, XII, 614; Joseph Hansen, *Zauberwahn*, p. 119. R. C. Van Caenegem, *Geschiedenis van het Strafrecht in Vlaanderen van de XIe tot de XIVe eeuw* (Brussels, 1954), suggests that rather than lynching, the disemboweling was a revival of ancient Germanic custom.

21. Jaffé, I (1885), no. 5164. However, the first formal execution of heretics in the Middle Ages occurred at Orléans in 1022, and in 1115 thirty sorcerers were burned at Graz: Byloff, p. 19.

22. Delhaye, "L'Ignorantia juris," *Etudes . . . Le Bras*, II, 1131–1141.

23. Maisonneuve, "Le Droit romain," *Etudes . . . Le Bras*, II, 931–942.

24. Lea, *Inquisition*, III, 432; Joseph Hansen, *Zauberwahn*, pp. 366–367; MGH Legg, IV, ii, 401. This code was issued in 1230 by Henry (VII),

the son of Frederick II, not by Henry VI, as Summers states in his *Geography of Witchcraft,* p. 361. For the influence of Roman law on Inquisitorial procedures, see Eberhard Schmidt.

25. A. Lübben, *Der Sachsenspiegel* (Oldenburg, 1879), p. 44; Joseph Hansen, *Zauberwahn,* pp. 367–368; Friedrich L. A. Freiherr von Lassberg, *Der Schwabenspiegel* (Tübingen, 1840), p. 368. On the city laws: Joseph Hansen, *Zauberwahn,* p. 372; Schwarzwälder; C. Trummer, *Vorträge über Tortur, Hexenverfolgung, und Vehmgerichte,* 3 vols. (Hamburg, 1844–1850), I, 102.

26. Gaston Bachelard, *La Psychoanalyse du feu* (Paris, 1949). From the Old Testament, see especially the rescue of Abraham from the fire of the Chaldeans (Gen., 11:31), the burning bush (Exod., 3:2), the fiery furnace (Dan., 3), the rescue of Lot from Sodom and Gomorrah (Gen., 19), the pillar of fire (Exod., 14); from the New Testament, see the descent of the Holy Spirit in tongues of fire (Acts, 2), and the consumption by fire of the fruitless vine (John, 15:6).

27. For the best account of the implications of the ordeal, see Benz.

28. For torture, see Parry; G. R. Scott; Esmein; Mellor; Lea, *Superstition;* Joseph Hansen, *Zauberwahn,* pp. 99–110. I am indebted to the assistance provided by my student Leon McCrillis in the preparation of the section on torture.

29. William Holdsworth, *A History of English Law,* 2d ed., 13 vols. (London, 1922–1938), V, 170 ff.

30. For a list of later papal bulls dealing with witchcraft and sorcery, see Lea, *Materials,* I, 220–229.

31. Edmond Martène and Ursin Durand, *Thesaurus novus anecdotorum,* 5 vols. (Paris, 1717), IV, 1485–1486. See, for example, the trial on July 3, 1245, at Le Mas Saintes-Puelles near Castelnaudary. There a woman was accused of bewitching her neighbors' clothing and curing illnesses by magical means. Nothing could be more clearly a case of simple sorcery, but the Inquisition insisted on asking her whether she had been associated with heretics. Joseph Hansen, *Quellen,* pp. 445–446; *Zauberwahn,* pp. 308–309.

32. Joseph Hansen, *Quellen,* pp. 42–44; William Durand, Bishop of Mende, *Speculum iudiciale,* 4 vols. (Frankfurt, 1668), III, 491. See also the formulary in the Collection Doat de la Bibliothèque Nationale, Vol. XXXVII, fol. 258.

33. *Quod super nonnullis,* confirmed by bulls of December 13, 1258, and January 10, 1260, excerpted in Joseph Hansen, *Quellen,* p. 1.

34. Stephen of Bourbon, *Anecdotes historiques,* ed. A. Lecoy de la Marche (Paris, 1877), esp. pp. 319–325; see Lea, *Materials,* I, 174; Joseph Hansen, *Zauberwahn,* pp. 137, 230.

35. Fehr, "Gottesurteil und Folter"; "Zur Lehre vom Folterprozess."

36. See Evans; Darwin; and Brown. Boniface VIII gave some support to the accused when he ordered the Inquisitors to draw up lists of the personal enemies of the accused and to refuse to admit their testimony. One legitimate—in the context of the idea system—reason for the secrecy regarding the witnesses' names was their frequently honest terror of magical revenge. Albert Shannon argues that the secrecy granted witnesses, unjustifiable though it may seem, was in fact necessary to forestall physical harm to them, especially in the Midi, where feelings against the Inquisition ran very high. Similar precautions were taken in the secular courts at that time. In any event a full transcript of testimony that suppressed only the witnesses' names was given the accused. Or, if defense counsel was allowed at all, it was very late in the proceedings, often after the interrogations. Defense counsel was sometimes denied all the information pertinent to the case. The Emperor Frederick II in 1231 and Pope Innocent IV in 1243 both specifically denied the right of appeal to notorious criminals such as murderers, poisoners, robbers, and heretics.

37. Baroja, pp. 75–76; Joseph Hansen, *Zauberwahn*, pp. 229–231, 240–241; Emile Amann in the *Dictionnaire de théologie catholique*, XIV, 2583–2586; Schwarzwälder, pp. 178–181; Balthasar Kaltner, *Konrad von Marburg und die Inquisition in Deutschland* (Prague, 1882), pp. 58–62, 130–149; Lea, *Inquisition*, II, 334–336.

38. Potthast, no. 7260; Kaltner, pp. 90–95; Joseph Hartzheim, *Concilia Germaniae*, 11 vols. (Cologne, 1759–1790), III, 515–516. *Gesta Treverorum*, MGH SS, XXIV, 401; Fredericq, *Corpus*, I, 81–82; Mansi, XXIII, 241.

39. Alberic des Trois-Fontaines, *Chronica*, MGH SS, XXIII, 930–932.

40. MGH Epp, saec. xiii, I, 413. Potthast, no. 9229. Konrad's reports themselves have been lost. It is necessary to state here that *Vox in Rama* has nothing to do with the north German rebellion of the Stedingers and that the Stedingers had nothing to do with witchcraft. The connection, based on a misreading by Raynaldus in his *Annales ecclesiastici*, 37 vols. (Bar-le-Duc, 1864–1887), XXI, ad ann. 1233, has long been rejected by scholars, but it nonetheless continues to be repeated. It is one of the more unforgivable mistakes in Baroja (pp. 75–77), because Joseph Hansen clearly denied the connection in *Zauberwahn*, p. 229, n. 3. The Stedingers were peasants in revolt against the archbishop of Hamburg-Bremen because of the taxes that that prelate imposed upon them in his capacity of temporal lord. The see was in dispute between two candidates from 1207 to 1216, and that one of the candidates (Gerhard I, who eventually was recognized as archbishop in 1216) supported the Stedingers is an indication that they could hardly have been Luciferans. Gerhard I's friendliness to the Stedingers also explains why after his death his unsympathetic successor, Gerhard II, held a

synod in 1230 in which he accused the Stedingers of heresy, divination, and magic. But even Gerhard II alleged no witch practices against them. Gregory IX's bulls of July 26, 1231, October 29, 1232, January 19, 1233, and June 17, 1233, deal with the Stedingers, but *Vox in Rama,* June 13, 1233, deals exclusively with the Rhenish heretics prosecuted by Konrad of Marburg. See Lea, *Inquisition,* III, 426.

41. Because of the presence of the endura in this case, it probably dates from the latter part of the thirteenth century, though it might be earlier. The document appears in Ignaz Döllinger, *Beiträge zur Sektengeschichte des Mittelalters,* 2 vols. (Munich, 1890), II, 369–373, under the title *Confessio Manichaei,* from St. Gall MS. 974, fols. 616–619. It consists not of one, but of two depositions, one by a Burchard, which is of little relevance, the other by a Lepzet. Lepzet's confession, much abridged, appears also in Döllinger, II, 295–296, where Lepzet appears as "Lebzer." This is from Munich CLM MS., 7714, fol. 64a. I am indebted to Walter Wakefield for his help in identifying the manuscript sources.

42. Baltrušaitis, *Le moyen âge fantastique,* pp. 212–213.

43. Toledo: Alberic, MGH, XXIII, 932; Joseph Hansen, *Zauberwahn,* p. 239. Mont-Aimé: Alberic, MGH, XXIII, 945; Hansen, *Zauberwahn,* pp. 236–237. Pistoia: Roberto Davidsohn, *Firenze ai tempi di Dante* (Florence, 1929), p. 195, from *Bollettino pistoiese,* XXVI (1924), 109. Toulouse: Hansen, *Zauberwahn,* pp. 234, 309–310; Joseph Hansen, *Quellen,* p. 446; Lamothe-Langon, II, 614; Lea, *Inquisition,* III, 384.

44. E. Battisti, *L'Antirinascimento* (Milan, 1962), plate 28, opp. p. 241.

45. Bonomo, pp. 22–23; Du Cange, under *Bensozia,* I, 635. Du Cange says that Bensoria may be a variant of Bezezia, the name of a fictitious daughter of Herodias.

46. Murray, *The Witch-Cult,* p. 23; Rose, pp. 63–64; Sir Herbert Maxwell, trans., *The Chronicle of Lanercost 1272–1346* (Glasgow, 1913), pp. 29–30. Maxwell's translation should be corrected on some points with reference to J. Stephenson, *Chronicon de Lanercost* (Edinburgh, 1839).

Chapter 7

1. Joannes Vitoduranus (Johann of Winterthur), *Chronicon,* MGH SS rer germ NS, III, 108.

2. In 1321 in Aquitaine, for example, lepers were charged with using a compound of urine and powdered Eucharist to poison wells: Cauzons, II, 313–316.

3. Betts.

4. Philip Ziegler, *The Black Death* (New York, 1969), pp. 259–279.

5. Robert of Brunne, *Handling Synne*, vss. 339–498, quoted by Kittredge, p. 51. In this, Robert follows the thirteenth-century William of Waddington. Dan Michel of Kent expressed a similar opinion in the *Ayenbite of Inwit*, ed. Richard Morris (London, 1866), p. 19. Michel terms an apostate anyone who "deth manhod to the dyeule and becomth his threl." On Oresme, see Thorndike, *History of Magic*, III, 398–471. See G. R. Owst, "*Sortilegium* in English Homiletic Literature of the XIVth Century," *Studies Presented to Sir Hilary Jenkinson* (London, 1957), pp. 272–303, on John Bromyard's sermons.

6. Lea, *Inquisition*, III, 449. Throughout the century secular courts in most of Europe maintained their interest in the trials: a Prussian law of 1310 ordered branding and fines, though not capital punishment, as punishment for sorcery (Lea, *Inquisition*, III, 432); many German cities issued codes based on the Sachsenspiegel ordering burning for heretics and magicians: Schleswig, Goslar, Groningen, Berlin, and others (Joseph Hansen, *Zauberwahn*, pp. 370–374); in 1355 the Emperor Charles IV issued a codification of the law of Bohemia, the *majestas carolina*, which was not used until the next century but specified burning for heretics and magicians (Hansen, *Zauberwahn*, pp. 369–370). Hansen notes (*Zauberwahn*, p. 370) that many German cities had laws against heresy but not sorcery, indicating which was considered the greater threat.

7. Thorndike, *A History of Magic*, III, 18 ff.; Cauzons, II, 327–341; Bock, XXVII, 109–134; Lea, *Inquisition*, III, 452–454, 458–459; Hugues Géraud was burned in 1316 for using magic to cause the pope's death (Joseph Hansen, *Zauberwahn*, p. 252; Lehugeur, pp. 415–416; Cauzons, II, 318–327). In 1317 a number of people in Reggio were arrested for plotting against John's life. (Lea, *Inquisition*, III, 452–454). In 1320 Galeazzo Visconti was accused of trying to kill the pope with a wax doll: Robert Michel, "Le Procès de Matteo et de Galeazzo Visconti," *Mélanges d'archéologie et d'histoire publiés par l'école française de Rome* (1909), pp. 277–327. On the bishop of Béziers: Joseph Hansen, *Zauberwahn*, pp. 259–260; Joseph Hansen, *Quellen*, pp. 11–13; Thorndike, *A History of Magic*, III, 31.

8. Enguerrand: Joseph Hansen, *Zauberwahn*, p. 356; Cauzons, III, 308–309; Lea, *Inquisition*, III, 451. Pierre de Latilly: Langlois, pp. 56–57. Jeanne de Latilly: Hansen, *Zauberwahn*, p. 357. Gaetani: Langlois, pp. 56–71; Hansen, *Zauberwahn*, pp. 356–357; Lehugeur, pp. 416–417. Accusations among nobles: Hansen, *Zauberwahn*, p. 355, n. 1; Lehugeur, pp. 416–417. Matilda of Artois: Lehugeur, pp. 115, 168 ff. Toulouse, 1323–1326: Hansen, *Zauberwahn*, pp. 257, 357; Lea, *Inquisition*, I, 230; III, 458. Philip VI: Hansen, *Zauberwahn*, p. 257; Joseph Hansen, *Quellen*, pp. 7–8; Thorndike, *A History of Magic*, III, 31.

9. Lea, *Inquisition*, III, 458; Frederick Pollock and Frederick W. Maitland, *The History of English Law before the Time of Edward I*, 2 vols., 2d ed. (rpt. Cambridge, Eng., 1952), II, 534.

10. For the bull of 1320: Lea, *Materials*, I, 231–232; Hansen, *Quellen*, pp. 4–5; Hansen, *Zauberwahn*, pp. 254–255; J. M. Vidal, *Bullaire de l'inquisition française au xive siècle et jusqu'à la fin du Grand Schisme* (Paris, 1913), pp. 61–62. For the bull of 1330: Hansen, *Zauberwahn*, pp. 256–257; *Quellen*, pp. 6–7; Lea, *Inquisition*, III, 459; Thorndike, III, 31.

11. Hansen, *Zauberwahn*, pp. 255–258; Hansen, *Quellen*, pp. 5–16; Lea, *Inquisition*, III, 454, 460; HDA, III, col. 1855; Thorndike, *A History of Magic*, III, 30–31. There is some question as to the authenticity of this document, but it fits John's policies. It was used by Eymeric in his *Directorium Inquisitorum*, Rome, 1503, pt. II, qu. 43. See also the bulls of 1327 and 1331 against the invocation of demons, in Hansen, *Quellen*, pp. 671–672.

12. Oldrado was a doctor of both laws. See Hansen, *Quellen*, pp. 55–59, and *Zauberwahn*, pp. 263–266. "Si enim adorares, hereticum esset vel heresim sapiat manifeste," is the phrase relating to the worship of demons. On Ugolini: Hansen, *Zauberwahn*, pp. 268–270; *Quellen*, pp. 59–63. Anonymous treatise: Hansen, *Zauberwahn*, p. 267; *Quellen*, p. 63. Johannes Andreae: Hansen, *Zauberwahn*, p. 240.

13. Hansen, *Quellen*, pp. 47–55; Wakefield and Evans, pp. 444–445; Hansen, *Zauberwahn*, pp. 299–300; see the edition of the *Practica* by Célestin Douais (Paris, 1886), pp. 150–159, 292–301.

14. The use of the term *res* here seems to be "measure," so that the *bonae res* are in effect those who give good measure. In Italy, the "good people" were sometimes called *buone robbe*, probably from *roba* meaning "property." See Cesare Cantù, *Gli Eretici d'Italia*, 3 vols. (Turin, 1865–1867), II, 377.

15. Owst, pp. 275–278. The treatise appears in part in Andrew G. Little, *Studies in English Franciscan History* (New York, 1917), app. 3, pp. 228–231. The expanded version of the manuscript, Owst observes, substitutes "King Arthur with his knights" for Onewone and Wade, who were mythical giants. On Onewone and Wade, see Raymond Wilson Chambers, *Widsith: A Study in Old English Heroic Legend* (Cambridge, Eng., 1912), pp. 95–100 and 219–254. The translation quoted is by Owst, p. 278.

16. John of Freiburg, Astesanus, and the synod of Trier of 1310, for example: Lea, *Materials*, I, 141, 188–189; Edmond Martène and Ursin Durand, *Thesaurus novus anecdotorum*, 5 vols. (Paris, 1717), IV, 257. In 1318, John XXII wrote to the bishop of Fréjus accusing three clergymen of

magic and witchcraft, including the use of succubi, which the pope, under the influence of the *Canon Episcopi*, calls *dianae*. (Hansen, *Quellen*, pp. 2–4).

17. The first story is from the *Speculum morale* once mistakenly attributed to Vincent of Beauvais, III, p. iii, dist. 27; Hansen, *Zauberwahn*, p. 136; Bonomo, pp. 25–36; *Dictionnaire de théologie catholique*, 15 vols. (Paris, 1924–1950) XV, 3028. For Passavanti, see Lea, *Materials*, I, 175–176.

18. To say that the cause of the flagellant sect was the plague would be to oversimplify: not every outbreak of plague produced flagellants. But the plague was clearly the most important of the terrors the flagellants and their followers wished to repel. On the flagellants, see Fredericq, *De secten der geeselaars*; Fredericq, *Corpus*, I, 202–203; Ziegler, pp. 86–97; Norman Cohn, *The Pursuit of the Millennium* (London, 1957), pp. 129–148. See also Erbstösser, p. 384; and Delaruelle, pp. 109–145.

19. The medieval Luciferans had nothing to do with the ancient Luciferan heresy that, related to the old Arian controversy, took its name from Bishop Lucifer of Sirmia. Kurze argues unconvincingly in his otherwise excellent article "Zur Ketzergeschichte" (pp. 58 ff.) that the Luciferans of Brandenburg were nothing but misunderstood Waldensians. That was the name given them, but their practices are Luciferan. The obvious confusion of witches and *Vaudenses* in the fifteenth century should make us skeptical of Kurze's argument, and since the doctrines ascribed to the Brandenburg heretics are similar to those of the Austrian and Bohemian Luciferans, there is no good reason to suppose that the sources are not reasonably accurate. In any event, the essential point again is that, whatever the reality, witch beliefs were current in Brandenburg as well as in Austria and Bohemia.

20. Friess, pp. 254 ff.

21. The *Annales Novesienses* (Annals of Neuss) ad ann. 1315, in Edmond Martène and Ursin Durand, *Veterum Scriptorum*, 9 vols. (Paris, 1724–1733), IV, 581–582. See also the *Anonymi auctoris brevis narratio de nefanda haeresi adamitica in variis Austriae locis saeculo XIV grassente*, in Hieronymus Pez, *Scriptores rerum austriacarum*, 2 vols. (Leipzig, 1721–1725), II, 533–536. The name "Adamite" is given these heretics, not by the chronicler, but by Pez, who was confusing them with the fifteenth-century Bohemian sect of that name. The Adamites were probably affiliated to, but not identical with, the Luciferans. See also Friess, pp. 254 ff.; Bernard; and the *Dictionnaire de théologie catholique*, IX, 1052–1053.

22. Palacky, pp. 11–12.

23. Joannes Vitoduranus (Johann of Winterthur), *Chronicon*, in Johan-

nes Georg von Eckhart (Eccard), *Corpus historicum,* 2 vols. (Leipzig, 1723), I, 1834–1840; see also Lea, Materials, I, 202; Joseph Hansen, *Zauberwahn,* p. 233; *Dictionnaire de théologie catholique,* IX, 1054. In 1327–1328 Abbot Johannes Victoriensis (Johann of Victring) in his *Liber certarum historiarum,* MGH SS in usus scholarum, XXXVI, 130, reports heretics who summoned a demon masquerading as the Holy Spirit in the form of a dove. See Kurze, pp. 56–58; Bernard, pp. 50 ff. It is possible, but far from clear, that this incident has some connection with the Luciferans. The statement by Byloff, p. 19, that there were no trials for magic or witchcraft in Austria before 1500 demonstrates the fundamental limitations of looking for the origins of witchcraft in sorcery rather than in heresy.

24. *Anonymi Leobensis Chronicon,* in Pez, I, 957; Friess, pp. 232–238; Bernard, pp. 56–57; *Dictionnaire de théologie catholique,* IX, 1054; Lea, *Inquisition,* II, 376.

25. Magdeburg: *Gesta archiepiscoporum Magdeburgensium,* MGH SS, XIV, 434; Kurze, p. 55; Christopher U. Hahn, *Geschichte der Ketzer im Mittelalter,* 2 vols. (Stuttgart, 1845–1850), II, 524, n. 4. Kurze suggests that the events of 1336 may be closely related to the events of 1338 reported in Brandenburg: in the latter year, Brandenburg heretics were found who held nightly gatherings under the presidency of a *"rector puerorum,"* who invoked demons, one of whom took the shape of God the Father, one of God the Son, and one of the Holy Spirit. See note 19 above. On Brandenburg, 1338, see Kurze, pp. 56–58; Lea, *Materials,* I, 175; Joannes Vitoduranus, *Chronicon,* MGH SS rer germ NS, III, 151. The *rector puerorum* and his followers were detected by a Minorite friar and burned as heretics. Prenzlau: Kurze, pp. 55–56 (especially p. 55, n. 18), 67–68, 91–93.

26. Our knowledge of the trials comes exclusively from Lamothe-Langon, who published a French summary of original Latin documents in the archives of southern France, documents which have since been lost or destroyed. Consequently we must rely upon a summary translation, and though Lamothe-Langon was a careful scholar, we have no way of knowing what was the word he translated as "sabbat." The use of the term at this early date is isolated, and I suggest that Lamothe may, under the influence of his knowledge of the later trials, have translated *synagoga* by "sabbat." Lamothe-Langon, III, 226–238.

27. For the first trial: Lamothe-Langon; Joseph Hansen, *Zauberwahn,* pp. 314–315; Joseph Hansen, *Quellen,* pp. 449–450; Lea, *Materials,* I, 230–233. For the second trial: Lamothe-Langon, III, 233–238; Hansen, *Zauberwahn,* pp. 315–317; *Quellen,* pp. 450–453.

28. As Hansen observes (*Quellen,* p. 452), this demon also appears at Paris in 1323. With Robin Artisson in the Alice Kyteler case, these are the first mentions of demons not associated with Judaeo-Christian demonology.

29. Hansen, *Zauberwahn*, pp. 331–332; Lamothe-Langon, III, 256–260; Hansen, *Quellen*, p. 454; Lea, *Materials*, I, 232; Lea, *Inquisition*, III, 534. A vague reference in the *Tractatus de strigis* of Bernard of Como, written in 1508 or earlier, seems to indicate that Bernard placed the origins of witchcraft at Como around 1360. See Hansen, *Quellen*, pp. 282, 454.

30. Hansen, *Zauberwahn*, pp. 334–337; Hansen, *Quellen*, pp. 64–66, 453; Lea, *Materials*, I, 232–233; Bonomo, p. 133.

31. The following reports of magical activity involving invocation occur from the period 1300–1360. (1) The Devil was invoked and the sacraments were commonly abused c. 1300 at Rijsel and throughout the diocese of Tournai: Fredericq, *Corpus*, I, 149. (2) Secret conventicles and invocations were held in England in 1311: *Registrum Radulphi Baldock*, Robert C. Fowler, ed., Canterbury and York series (London, 1911), VII, 144–145; Kittredge, pp. 51–52. (3) Invocation and magic were condemned at the Chapter General of the Franciscan Order at Barcelona in 1313: Hauréau. (4) Raising of the dead and invocation were practiced at Pamiers, 1318–1325: Riezler, p. 46; Charles Molinier, "Rapport," *Archives scientifiques et littéraires*, 3d ser., XIV (1888), 231; Thorndike, *A History of Magic*, III, 23; Vidal, pp. 53–54; Joseph Hansen, *Zauberwahn*, pp. 312–313; Joseph Hansen, *Quellen*, pp. 446–447. (5) Numerous trials were held at Carcassonne and Toulouse, 1320–1350, mostly for maleficium, a few with invocation, but none except the trial of 1335 involved real witchcraft: Lamothe-Langon, III, 211–212, 226, 246–247; Collection Doat, XXVII, fols. 42–50. In Doat, three cases of 1327–1328, related to that published in Hansen, *Quellen*, pp. 447–449, are recorded. Involved were three clerics who had practiced invocations and two of whom had made an explicit pact with the Devil, signing their names, one of them in blood, on a contract promising service to the Devil in return for learning magic arts. (6) A monk of Morigny near Etampes in 1323 had a book containing the names of demons who would do service to anyone who signed his name in the book: *Continuatio Chronici Guillelmi de Nangiaco* (Guillaume de Nangis), *Recueil*, XX, 634. (7) A canon at Agen in 1326 invoked evil spirits to produce hail and thunder: Thorndike, *A History of Magic*, III, 29. (8) A canon of Mirepoix, Guillaume Lombardi, was investigated in 1337 by order of Pope Benedict XII for having invoked demons: Hansen, *Quellen*, pp. 10–11. (9) A priest named Pepin was tried for sorcery and invocation of demons in Gévaudan in 1347: Falgairolle. (10) Further trials were held for sorcery at Toulouse and Carcassonne, 1350–1357: Hansen, *Quellen*, p. 454; Lamothe-Langon, III, 246–267.

32. Peter Recordi: Hansen, *Zauberwahn*, pp. 312–313; Hansen, *Quellen*, p. 449; Collection Doat, XVII, fols. 150v–156v; Riezler, pp. 45–46; Lea, *Inquisition*, III, 455–456, and 657–659 (where the Doat document is

edited); Lea, *Materials*, I, 230. Ehingen: Hansen, *Zauberwahn*, p. 388, from Johann of Winterthur, *Chronica*, MGH SS rer germ NS, III, 108. Fréjus: Hansen, *Zauberwahn*, p. 260; Hansen, *Quellen*, pp. 13–14. Grenade: Hansen, *Zauberwahn*, p. 331; Lamothe-Langon, III, 242. Torrenbüren: Johann of Winterthur, *Chronica*, MGH SS rer germ, NS, III, 270.

33. Hansen, *Zauberwahn*, p. 251; Lea, *Inquisition*, III, 451.

34. *Continuatio Chronici Guillelmi de Nangiaco* (Guillaume de Nangis), *Recueil*, XX, 633–634; Hansen, *Zauberwahn*, p. 332; Lea, *Inquisition*, III, 454–455.

35. Mathias von Neuenburg, *Chronica*, MGH SS rerum germanicarum, IV, pt. i, 125–126.

36. For fuller accounts of the case, see Thomas Wright, ed., *A Contemporary Narrative of the Proceedings against Dame Alice Kyteler, Prosecuted for Sorcery in 1324, by Richard Ledrede, Bishop of Ossory* (London, 1843), an edition of the anonymous account that is the fullest primary source for the trial. Other sources, such as Raphael Holinshed, *The Chronicles of England, Scotland, and Ireland*, 3 vols. (London, 1587) and James Grace, *Annales Hiberniae*, ed. Richard Butler (Dublin, 1842), are derivative from the *Narratio*; Lea, *Inquisition*, III, 456–458; Hansen, *Zauberwahn*, pp. 341–343; Summers, *Geography*, pp. 85–91; Rose, pp. 65 66; Patrick F. Byrne, *Witchcraft in Ireland* (Cork, 1967), pp. 18–27; St. John Seymour, *Irish Witchcraft and Demonology* (London and Dublin, 1913), pp. 47 ff.; Murray, *The Witch-Cult*, pp. 23, 40, 104, 148, 154, 228.

37. Seymour, p. 47.

38. E. K. Heller, "The Story of the Sorcerer's Serpent: A Puzzling Medieval Folk Tale," *Speculum*, XV (1940), 338. The article, which reports the Wisse-Colin version, extends to p. 347.

39. Citations are from the translation by Edward Hutton, originally made in 1620 and published again in London in 1909.

40. (1) Thomas Rymer, *Foedera*, 17 vols. (London, 1704–1717), II, 932–934; Hansen, *Zauberwahn*, p. 251; Hansen, *Quellen*, p. 2; Kittredge, pp. 241–242, 546–547; Pollock and Maitland, II, 554. (2) Hansen, *Zauberwahn*, pp. 355–356; Cauzons, II, 303–304; Rigault. (3) Kittredge, p. 242. (4) Hansen, *Zauberwahn*, p. 253; Hansen, *Quellen*, pp. 2–4. This is reported in a letter of John XXII dated February 27, 1318. (5) Hansen, *Zauberwahn*, pp. 253–254; Lea, *Inquisition*, III, 451–452; Thorndike, *A History of Magic*, III, 23; Hauréau; Dmitrewski. (6) Hansen, *Zauberwahn*, p. 334. (7) Hansen, *Zauberwahn*, p. 333. (8) Lea, *Inquisition*, III, 197–203; Cauzons, II, 344–347. (9) Kittredge, p. 53. (10) The literature on the Templars is enormous, and I cite here only some of the most useful works: Lamothe-Langon, III, 39 ff.; Hansen, *Zauberwahn*, pp. 188, 233–234, 356; George Campbell, *The Knights Templars*; Carrière; Claude Bertin et al.,

Les Templiers: L'Affaire Calas, vol. VII of *Les Grands procès de l'histoire de France: Les procès d'intolérance* (Paris, 1967); Gmelin; Lizerand; Le Comte de Loisne, "Bulles de papes pour l'ordre du Temple conservées aux archives nationales (1155–1312)," *Comité des travaux historiques et scientifiques: Bulletin historique et philologique* (1917); Jules Michelet, ed., *Le Procès des Templiers,* 2 vols. *Collection de documents inédits sur l'histoire de France* (Paris, 1841–1851). Gmelin gives a very complete tabular summary of all the trials.

Chapter 8

1. Germain Bazin, "The Devil in Art," in Charles Moeller et al., *Satan* (New York, 1951).

2. Rosen, "Dance Frenzies," p. 13.

3. On the dancers and the flagellants in this period, see Rosen, "Dance Frenzies"; Hecker, pp. 143–192; Fredericq, *De Secten der Geeselaars;* Fredericq, *Geschiedenis der Inquisitie,* II, 103–113; Fredericq, *Corpus,* I, 190–203, 231–236; J. S. Van Veen, "Maatregen tegen de Flagellanten," *Archief voor de Geschiedenis van het Aartsbisdom Utrecht,* XLVI (1920), 176–178.

4. Josiah Cox Russell, *British Medieval Population* (Albuquerque, 1948), pp. 368–369.

5. Lea, *Inquisition,* III, 464.

6. Lucerne: Hansen, *Zauberwahn,* p. 385; Hansen, *Quellen,* p. 528; Lea, *Materials,* I, 247; Bader, p. 101. Interlaken: Hansen, *Zauberwahn,* p. 385; Hansen, *Quellen,* p. 530.

7. Lea, *Inquisition,* III, 460–463, 511; Hansen, *Zauberwahn,* p. 261; Hansen, *Quellen,* pp. 15–16.

8. Summers, *Geography,* p. 101.

9. Hansen, *Zauberwahn,* p. 373; Szendrey, p. 132; Trachtenberg, p. 67.

10. Hansen, *Zauberwahn,* p. 301; Mansi, XXVI, 619 ff.; Hef-L, VI, 1393–1398; Lea, *Inquisition,* III, 466; Hansen, *Zauberwahn,* p. 301.

11. Hansen, *Zauberwahn,* pp. 262–263; Hansen, *Quellen,* pp. 16–17.

12. The original is therefore lost, and the work is known only through the writings of Eymeric, who attacked it in his *Directorium,* pt. II, *question* 10; see the Venice edition, 1607, pp. 262–264; Hansen, *Quellen,* p. 67.

13. Lea, *Materials,* I, 209–210; Hansen, *Zauberwahn,* pp. 270–275; Hansen, *Quellen,* pp. 66–67. There are many editions of the *Directorium:* I use the Venetian edition of 1607. Pt. II, questions 42–43, is most relevant.

14. Jauer: Hansen, *Quellen,* pp. 67–71; Herolt: "Sermo xi in die Nativitatis," in Herolt's *Sermones discipuli de tempore et de sanctis,* cited

in Grimm, III, 933. Guaineri, *De egritudinibus capitis:* Thorndike, *History of Magic,* IV, 229–230, 670–674. Johann von Frankfurt: Hansen, *Quellen,* pp. 71–82. Cologne treatise: Hansen, *Quellen,* pp. 82–86. Gerson: edited in the Lyon, 1669 edition of the *Malleus Maleficarum,* Book II, 45–51; and in Hansen, *Quellen,* pp. 86–87. Sozzini: Thorndike, IV, 296–297.

15. A fifteenth-century regulation for the administration of penance in the Archdiocese of Cologne follows the Canon Episcopi in forbidding women (and men) to believe that they ride out at night with Diana. (See Emil Pauls, "Zauberwesen und Hexenwahn am Niederrhein," *Beiträge zur Geschichte des Niederrheins,* XIII [1898], 233). The battles may have been similar to those occurring at the time of Ginzburg's sixteenth-century *benandanti.*

16. The term *zobianae* is unique here. Du Cange gives *Zobellina,* "a fur," a variant of *sabelum,* "sable."

17. Charles Emmanuel Dumont, *Justice criminelle des duchés de Lorraine et de Bar,* 2 vols. (Nancy, 1848), II, 69.

18. Thomas Favent, *Historia sive Narratio de modo et forma mirabilis Parliamenti,* ed. May Mc Kisack, *Camden Miscellany,* XIV (1926), 18. See Kittredge, pp. 54–55.

19. Portagruaro: Bonomo, p. 478, n. 1; Filippo da Siena, *Assempri,* cited by Bonomo, p. 139.

20. Hansen, *Zauberwahn,* p. 384; Hansen, *Quellen,* pp. 524–526; Lea, *Materials,* I, 247.

21. Foucault, p. 293.

22. Hansen, *Quellen,* pp. 454–455; Kittredge, p. 59.

23. James Tait, ed., *Chronica Johannis de Reading et Anonymi Cantuariensis, 1346–1367* (Manchester, 1914). See Kittredge, p. 242.

24. The term used to describe her was *fattuchiera,* a cognate of the French *faiturière.* The word derives from the Latin *facere,* Italian *facere,* or French *faire* meaning "to make" and is related to the *-ficium* suffix of *maleficium,* so that a *fattuchiera* is one who does (makes) ill. "*Facturas facere*" was a Latin phrase used during the Middle Ages to mean "work magic," and a *fatuus* was one who was bewitched or enchanted. See Du Cange under *factura,* meaning no. 7, and *fatuarii.* See also Zdekauer, pp. 107–109; Bonomo, pp. 136–138; and Aldo Cerlini, "Una Dama e una strega dell'Ariosto," *Lares,* XX (1954), fasc. iii–iv, pp. 75–76. Ariosto assigns the name Gabrina to a sorceress in *Orlando Furioso,* canto xiii.

25. Cerlini, p. 85.

26. Brucker, pp. 19–20. This is one of the few mentions of Beelzebub in a medieval witch trial. Presumably the name was introduced by a scholarly observer.

27. Hans Vintler, *Pluemen der Tugent,* a free translation, done in 1410,

of Tommaso Leoni's *Fiori di Virtù* (c. 1320), in which the parts dealing with witchcraft, however, are Vintler's own additions. Vintler's translation was edited by Ignaz von Zingerle (Innsbruck, 1874). See vss. 7737 ff., 7952 ff., 7993 ff., 8023 ff., and 8168 ff. See also Hansen, *Zauberwahn*, p. 406.

28. Hansen, *Zauberwahn*, p. 338, n. 1; Lea, *Inquisition*, III, 547.

29. Milan 1370: Ginzburg, p. 50; Valpute: Marx, p. 31, from the archives of Isère. Wild men were reported near Bedford in 1402: John Capgrave, *Chronicle of England*, ed. Francis C. Hingeston (London, 1858), p. 251; See Kittredge, p. 58. Nieder-Hauenstein: Hansen, *Zauberwahn*, p. 385; *Quellen*, p. 529; Lea, *Materials*, I, 247. In 1407, werewolves made one of their rare appearances in the Middle Ages at Basel: Hansen, *Zauberwahn*, p. 382, n. 5; *Quellen*, p. 527; Lea, *Materials*, I, 247.

30. Bonomo, pp. 15–17; Verga; Luigi Fumi, "L'Inquisizione romana e lo stato di Milano," *Archivio storico lombardo*, ser. 4, XIII (1910), p. 97. Verga (p. 181) derives the name "Oriente" from a declaration against demonolatry issued by the University of Paris in 1381, in which one demon was described as *"rex Orientis,"* or "king of the East." I believe the derivation is from the "Her-" deities of the north who led the wild chase. *"Her-"* is transformed into *"Or-"*; the rest of the word is then transmuted to resemble a known word, *oriente*, possibly with reference to the demon mentioned by Verga. There is no reason to assume with Verga (p. 179) that this was specifically a cult of Diana.

31. For the trial of 1390, see Hansen, *Zauberwahn*, pp. 358–360; Hansen, *Quellen*, pp. 518–520; H. Duplès-Agier, *Régistre criminel du châtelet de Paris*, 2 vols. (Paris, 1861–1864), I, 327–362. For the trial of 1391, see Hansen, *Zauberwahn*, pp. 362–364; Hansen, *Quellen*, pp. 520–523; Duplès-Agier, II, 280–343. For both, see Battifol, LXIII (1897), 266–283; Foucault, pp. 283–292); Lea, *Materials*, I, 246; Lea, *Inquisition*, III, 461–463.

32. Hansen, *Zauberwahn*, pp. 437–438; *Quellen*, pp. 91–92, 523.

33. The date is sometimes given as 1420 or 1421. Riezler (p. 68) makes the best case for 1424. Lea, *Inquisition*, III, 535; Hansen, *Zauberwahn*, pp. 349–350; Hansen, *Quellen*, pp. 110, 131, 529–530; Jakob Burckhardt, *The Civilization of the Renaissance in Italy*, trans. S. G. C. Middlemore (London, 1960), p. 289. The original sources are Stephen Infessura, *Diarium Urbis Romae*: in Johann Georg von Eckhart, *Corpus historicum*, 2 vols. (Leipzig, 1723), II, 1874; or edited by Oreste Tommassini (Rome, 1890), p. 25. Felix Hemmerlin, *Dialogus de nobilitate et rusticitate* (Strasbourg, 1490), chap. 32; Johann Hartlieb, *Buch aller verbotenen Kunst, Unglaubens und der Zauberei*, ed. Dora Ulm (Halle, 1914), chap. 33. Hansen, *Quellen*, p. 131.

34. Marx, pp. 33 ff.

35. Carcassonne: Hansen, *Zauberwahn*, p. 331; Hansen, *Quellen*, p. 454; Lamothe-Langon, III, 285–286; Boffito, pp. 392–396. Toulouse: Hansen, *Zauberwahn*, p. 331; Hansen, *Quellen*, p. 455; Lamothe-Langon, III, 299–300. Catharists in Piedmont in 1412 were accused of holding "Synagogues" and conventicles: Boffito, p. 422. Toulouse-Carcassonne: Hansen, *Zauberwahn*, p. 331; Hansen, *Quellen*, p. 456; Lamothe-Langon, III, 307–308.

36. On the Waldensian connection, see Hansen, *Zauberwahn*, pp. 414–416; Hansen, *Quellen*, pp. 408–415; Fredericq, *Corpus*, I, 347; Bourquelot, pp. 81–109. Note that the term "voodoo," however, does not derive from *Vaudois* but from the West African Ewe *vodu*. The *Errores Valdensium* is edited by Thomas Wright and James Orchard Halliwell, *Reliquiae Antiquae* (London, 1845), p. 246; see Hansen, *Quellen*, p. 413. Hansen corrects the date assigned the manuscript (which is in the British Museum) by Wright.

37. Bader, p. 132. The Swiss origins of the usage caused some writers of the last century to suppose that the term *Vaudenses* may have derived from the canton of Vaud, or Waadt, on the northern shore of the Lake of Geneva. The term *Vaudensis* or—in French—*Vaudois*, could signify either a "Waldensian" or an "inhabitant of Vaud." Hansen denies the connection in his *Quellen*, p. 408, with the argument that the terminology was too widespread. Yet the curious fact remains that in most of the early trials the term used for the witches was *Waudenses* or *Vaudenses* rather than *Valdenses*, which was usually reserved in the earlier fifteenth century for true Waldensians. It is possible that the presence of witches in the canton of Vaud reinforced in the public mind the application of the term *Vaudois* to them, but the derivation directly from the heresy rather than from the canton is sufficient in itself.

38. Hansen, *Zauberwahn*, p. 414; Hansen, *Quellen*, pp. 18–19. Eugenius uses the terms *stregule, stregones,* and *Waudenses* as equivalents.

39. Hansen, *Zauberwahn*, pp. 416–420; Hansen, *Quellen*, p. 455; Runeberg, pp. 22–27.

40. For the trials at Pinarolo and nearby, see Boffito; Lea, *Materials,* I, 203–204; Hansen, *Zauberwahn*, p. 411; Riezler, p. 46; Amati, I, 16–52, and II, 3–61; published in abbreviated form by Ignaz von Döllinger, *Beiträge zur Sektengeschichte des Mittelalters,* 2 vols. (Munich, 1890), II, 251–273.

41. The chief source is a notarial act of June 12, 1411, reproduced in Fredericq, *Corpus*, I, 267–280. See Leff, *Heresy in the Later Middle Ages,* I, 395–399.

42. On the Bohemian Adamites, see "Adamites," *Dictionnaire de théologie catholique,* I, 391–392; Palacky; Lea, *Inquisition,* II, 517–518;

F. G. Heymann, *John Žižka and the Hussite Revolution* (Princeton, 1955), p. 263; Büttner and Werner, pp. 73–141; Werner, "Adamitische Praktiken"; Leff, *Heresy in the Later Middle Ages*, I, 399–400; the original source is Aeneas Silvius, *Historica Bohemica*, chap. 41, in Charles du Plessis D'Argentré, *Collectio judiciorum de novis erroribus*, 3 vols. (Paris, 1728–1736), I, 216–217.

Chapter 9

1. Trevor-Roper, *The European Witch Craze*, pp. 102–108.

2. Since a much greater amount of material is available for the fifteenth century than for the earlier centuries, this chapter shifts from analysis of individual incidents to a correlation of data, though a certain degree of distortion is inherent in all procedures that bring together materials from different times and places. As usual, cases of pure *maleficium* are omitted; this chapter also omits those incidents for which no details are available beyond the mere mention of witchcraft, on the grounds that these provide no elucidation of the phenomenon.

3. The quantum leap in the size of the persecution will be obvious from any perusal of Lea's *Materials* or Hansen's *Quellen*. As an example, Guido Bader gives an approximate number of 1150 persons tried and 350 executed for witchcraft between 1400 and 1500 in Switzerland alone. Even these numbers pale in comparison with the bloodbaths of the following two centuries.

4. See, for example, the synod of Rouen, 1445 (Lea, *Materials*, I, 141), and the execution of heretics and magicians by the bishop of Regensburg about 1446 (Hansen, *Zauberwahn*, pp. 424, 433–436; Riezler, p. 63).

5. For prosecution without reference to heresy: Hansen, *Zauberwahn*, p. 427; J. A. Lilienthal, *Die Hexenprozesse der beiden Städte Braunsberg* (Königsberg, 1861). For the equation of the two: Hansen, *Zauberwahn*, p. 353.

6. Pugh, *Imprisonment*; William Holdsworth, *A History of English Law*, 2d ed., 12 vols. (London, 1903–1938), IV, 273. As an example of torture and burning employed by the secular courts on the continent, see the case at Marmande near Bordeaux in 1453: Hansen, *Quellen*, pp. 559–561; Lea, *Materials*, I, 252. At Marmande, the mob seized and tortured some of the victims to death, one of the rare instances of witch lynching in the Middle Ages. By mid-century, the Inquisition was using extensive torture as a matter of course, as in the trials in Artois in 1459–1461.

7. An example of the resistance of the secular power is the case at Brescia in 1486: Lea, *Materials*, I, 241. The episcopal courts were often

even more vigorous, as for example the strong resistance to Heinrich Institoris offered by the bishop of Brixen: Lea, *Inquisition*, III, 541; Riezler, pp. 90–93. That the Inquisition was never the sole instigator of witchcraft can be seen in the case at Torcy in 1455, where the secular court entirely on its own tried and severely punished witchcraft: Hansen, *Quellen*, p. 565; Lea, *Inquisition*, III, 537–538.

8. Bulls of Eugenius IV: (1) February 24, 1434; (2) 1437; (3) March 23, 1440; (4) July 17, 1445. See Hansen, *Zauberwahn*, pp. 412–415; Hansen, *Quellen*, pp. 17–19; Lea, *Inquisition*, III, 512; Lea, *Materials*, I, 204.

9. *"Etiam si haeresim non sapiant manifeste."* The relevant bull was published August 1, 1451: Hansen, *Zauberwahn*, p. 415; Hansen, *Quellen*, p. 19; Lea, *Inquisition*, III, 512. Calixtus III (1455–1458) and Sixtus IV (1471–1484) supported the Inquisition against sorcery but made no reference to the specific crimes of witchcraft: Hansen, *Quellen*, pp. 19–24.

10. For this and Innocent's other witchcraft bulls, see Hansen, *Zauberwahn*, pp. 467–475; Hansen, *Quellen*, pp. 24–30; Lea, *Inquisition*, III, 540; Lea, *Materials*, I, 304–305; Trevor-Roper, pp. 101–102.

11. See, for example, his three bulls of June 18, 1485 to the archbishop of Mainz, the archduke of Austria, and Abbot John of Weingarten, and his letter of September 30, 1486, to the bishop of Brescia. He uses the phrase *Hereticorum et maleficorum secta.*

12. The best account of their lives, with pertinent documentation, is in Hansen, *Quellen*, pp. 360–407. See also Hansen, *Zauberwahn*, pp. 425–426, 474–500; Lea, *Inquisition*, III, 540–545; Lea, *Materials*, I, 306–353. The *Malleus* has been usably but not always accurately translated by Montague Summers, *Malleus Maleficarum* (London, 1928). The *Malleus* was first translated into English in 1584; there were numerous subsequent editions in that language, as well as in German, French, and Italian. It was first published in Latin in 1486, and had by 1520 appeared in no fewer than fourteen Latin editions. Summers' translation must be checked with especial care against the Latin. Institoris is sometimes known as Krämer, a translation of *Institor* ("peddler") into the vernacular. Institoris is the best form of the name and was not uncommon in Germany in that period (Hansen, *Quellen*, p. 380, n. 1). Hansen proved Sprenger's role minor in *Quellen*, pp. 404–407.

13. Hansen, *Zauberwahn*, pp. 431–432; Riezler, pp. 78–79, 90–93; Lea, *Inquisition*, III, 541; Lea, *Materials*, I, 241; Müller.

14. There is an excellent discussion of the theorists in Hansen, *Zauberwahn*, pp. 445–467, and there are additional particulars about their lives and works in his *Quellen*. I summarize Hansen's information in Appendix II with the addition of references and information that have become availa-

ble since his time, but I have seen no point in reproducing his information in detail. In the notes that follow, the theorists are for the sake of brevity referred to in abbreviated fashion.

15. The most striking account of the triumph of magic in the late fifteenth and sixteenth centuries and its integral relationship to the scientific thought of the period is Yates' *Giordano Bruno*.

16. Martin le Franc, Barrientos, *Errores,* Jacquier, Alfonso, Visconti, Martin of Arles, Vignate, Kemnat, Basin, Bernard of Como. Jordanes has a whole catalog of names for witches: *strigae, strigones, maliarde, herbarie, fascinatrices, fastineres* or *festurieres, pixidarie, bacularie.*

17. See Monter, "Witchcraft in Geneva."

18. Accepting it are Nider, Torquemada, Martin of Arles, Socinus; rephrasing it are Barrientos, Alfonso, Basin; accepting it in part is Raphael of Pornasio, who rationalizes that witches walk, though they do not fly, to the meeting.

19. Vineti, Jacquier, Bernard of Como.

20. Tostado, *Errores,* Vineti, Hartlieb, Jacquier, Alfonso, Visconti, Mamoris, Vignate, Jordanes de Bergamo, Kemnat, and Bernard of Como all accept it—*Errores,* Visconti, and Kemnat specifying the stick, and Tostado, Hartlieb, and Kemnat the beasts. Martin le Franc, Torquemada, Bechis, Martin of Arles, Vincent, and Galateo dismissed flight as illusion.

21. Ebendorfer, *Errores,* Vineti, Mamoris, Bernard of Como.

22. Martin le Franc, Raphael, Bechis, Vineti, Mamoris, Jordanes, Galateo, Basin.

23. Nider, Raphael, Vineti, Jacquier, Alfonso, Visconti, Mamoris, Martin of Arles, Vignate, Jordanes, Bernard of Como. Bechis dissents.

24. Nider, Martin le Franc, Tostado, *Errores,* Hartlieb, Jacquier, Alfonso, Visconti, Mamoris, Vignate, Kemnat, Vincent, Galateo, Basin, Bernard of Como, Jordanes.

25. The believers are Tostado, *Errores,* Vineti, Jacquier, Alfonso, Visconti, Mamoris, Vignate, Kemnat, Bernard of Como. The skeptics are Martin le Franc, Bechis, Martin of Arles, Galateo, and Basin.

26. Martin le Franc, *Errores,* Vineti, Jacquier, Kemnat.

27. Vineti, Visconti, Tinctoris, Behaim, Martin of Arles; Cult: Nider, *Errores,* Jacquier, Vignate, Basin, Bernard of Como.

28. Nider, Ebendorfer, Wunschilburg, Vineti, Tinctoris, Mamoris, Martin of Arles, Vincent, Garcia. Garcia's argument tends to bear out Trevor-Roper's theory of an opposition between the Aristotelian and Neoplatonic traditions. As an Aristotelian, Garcia violently attacks the Neoplatonic idea that there is such a thing as natural magic. All magic, he insists, is diabolical.

29. Tostado, *Errores,* Jacquier, Visconti, Tinctoris, Mamoris, Kemnat, and Bernard of Como. Martin le Franc, Bechis, and Galateo are skeptical.

30. Nider, *Errores,* Vineti, Jacquier, Mamoris, Vignate, Kemnat. Only Vignate specifically indicates that adults are killed, though other writers imply it. Martin le Franc, Bechis, Vincent, Galateo, and Basin are skeptical of cannibalism.

31. Nider, Tostado, *Errores,* Hartlieb, Alfonso, Tinctoris, Mamoris, Jordanes, Vincent. Tostado, Jordanes, and Vincent accept the salve but reject the idea of flight. Jordanes calls the witches *pixidarie* from the jars in which they keep their ointment.

32. Nider, *Errores,* Jacquier, Visconti, Vignate, Bernard of Como. Bechis is skeptical.

33. Nider, Hartlieb, Jacquier, Visconti, Mamoris, Vignate, Bernard of Como. Martin le Franc is skeptical.

34. Nider, Ebendorfer, Bechis, Vineti, Vignate, Francis, Basin, Bernard of Como.

35. Ebendorfer, Martin le Franc, Wunschilburg, Raphael, *Errores,* Vineti, Jacquier, Alfonso, Visconti, Mamoris, Bernard of Como. Only Visconti explicitly denies that the witches worshiped Satan.

36. Ebendorfer, Jacquier, Visconti.

37. Nider, *Errores,* Jacquier.

38. Nider, *Errores,* Vineti, Alfonso, Mamoris, Kemnat, Bernard of Como. There is an excellent depiction of the obscene kiss in a Parisian manuscript of Martin le Franc (who was skeptical), reproduced in Hansen, *Quellen,* p. 184.

39. Hansen, *Quellen,* p. 137.

40. Jacquier and Alfonso also believe; Martin le Franc dissents.

41. See Boffito.

42. See the cases of John Boreham, c. 1430–1450, John Crayer, c. 1500–1510, and John Pasmer, 1507, in John Thomson, *The Later Lollards,* pp. 83, 179–180, 185, 241. See also pp. 67, 106, 177, 241.

43. The notes that follow are abbreviated references to the incidents listed here; a brief reference is given for each incident. Basel, 1423: Joseph Hansen, *Quellen,* p. 529. Interlaken, 1424: *Quellen,* p. 530. Benevento, 1427: Bonomo, p. 120. Dauphiné, 1427–1447: *Quellen,* pp. 459–466. Todi, 1428: Bonomo, p. 119. Valais, 1428–1480: *Quellen,* pp. 531–539, 551–552. Briançon, 1428–1447: *Quellen,* pp. 539–544. Neuchâtel, 1430–1439: *Quellen,* p. 455. Savoy, 1430–1440: *Quellen,* pp. 118–122, 455. Rome, 1431: Riezler, p. 68. Barcelona, 1434: *Quellen,* p. 457. Carcassonne, 1435: *Quellen,* pp. 457–458. Mâcon, 1437: *Quellen,* p. 546. La Tour du Pin: *Quellen,* pp. 459–466. Fribourg, 1438: *Quellen,* p. 546. France, 1438–1458: *Quellen,* pp. 466–467. Nivernais, 1438: *Quellen,* p. 141. Draguignan, 1439: Aubenas. Savoy, 1439: Bourquelot, p. 83. Dauphiné. 1440 ff: *Quellen,* pp. 466–467, Marx, pp. 42 ff.

Fribourg, 1440: *Quellen*, p. 546. Rouen, 1445: Lea, *Materials*, I, 141. Perugia, 1446: *Quellen*, pp. 547–548. Solothurn, 1447: *Quellen*, pp. 548–551. Rouen, 1447: *Quellen*, p. 552. Béarn, 1448–1452: *Quellen*, p. 552. Lucerne, c. 1450: *Quellen*, p. 556. Provins, 1452: *Quellen*, pp. 556–559. Châlons-sur-Saône, 1452: Fredericq, *Corpus*, I, 333–334. Bordeaux, 1453: *Quellen*, pp. 559–561. Evreux, 1453: *Quellen*, pp. 467–472. Lucerne, 1454: *Quellen*, pp. 561–565. Fribourg, 1454: Quellen, p. 561. Locarno, 1455: *Quellen*, p. 565. Edolo, 1455: *Quellen*, p. 472. Metz, 1456: *Quellen*, pp. 567–569. Como, 1456: Bonomo, pp. 260–261. Falaise, 1456: *Quellen*, p. 565. Lorraine, 1456–1457: Lea, *Materials*, I, 253. Fribourg, 1457: *Quellen*, p. 569. Faido, 1457: *Quellen*, p. 570. Metz, 1457: *Quellen*, pp. 569–570. Faido, 1458–1459: *Quellen*, p. 570. Dauphiné and Gascony 1458–1460: *Quellen*, p. 148. Andermatt, 1459: *Quellen*, pp. 571–575. Artois, 1459–1460: *Quellen*, pp. 149–183, 413–415, 476. Lyon, c. 1460: *Quellen*, pp. 188–195. Italian Alps c. 1460: *Quellen*, pp. 202, 216, 281, 476. Ascanio, 1462: Bonomo, pp. 263–265. Bologna, 1462: Bonomo, pp. 263–265. Chamonix, 1462: *Quellen*, pp. 477–484. Alpnach, 1462: *Quellen*, p. 576. Milan, 1463–1464: Bonomo, p. 143. Porlezza, c. 1465: Bonomo, pp. 276–277. Solothurn, 1466: *Quellen*, p. 577. Paris, 1466: Charles du Plessis d'Argentré, *Collectio judiciorum de novis erroribus*, 3 vols. (Paris, 1728–1736), I, 256. Valais, 1466: *Quellen*, pp. 576–577. Holland, 1467: *Quellen*, p. 577. Valais, 1467: *Quellen*, pp. 531–539. Rome, 1467: Lea, *Materials*, I, 203–204. Italy, 1467–1480: Bonomo, p. 97. Ferrara, 1471–1505: Cerlini. Holland, 1472: Sinnighe. Canavese, 1474: Bonomo, p. 101, *Quellen*, pp. 485–487. Bressuire, 1475: Filhol. Lucerne, 1477: Bader, p. 102, Hoffman-Krayer, "Luzerner Akten," p. 24. Annecy, 1477: *Quellen*, pp. 487–499. Bern, 1478: *Quellen*, p. 580. Valais, 1478: *Quellen*, p. 580. Pavia, 1479: Fumi, pp. 109–110. Fribourg, 1479: *Quellen*, p. 581. Brescia, 1480: Bonomo, p. 121. Lucerne, c. 1480: Hoffman-Krayer, pp. 81–86. Sardinia, 1480–1489: Thorndike, *History of Magic*, IV, 499. Neuchâtel, 1481: *Quellen*, pp. 499–500. Murten, 1482: *Quellen*, p. 583. Fribourg, 1482: *Quellen*, p. 582. Hamburg, 1482: *Quellen*, p. 582. Innsbruck, 1485: Byloff, pp. 31–32, Riezler, pp. 90 ff. Bresica, 1486: Bonomo, p. 97.

44. Artois, 1459–1460.

45. Savoy, 1430–1440; Lorraine, 1456–1457; Artois, 1459–1460; Lyon, c. 1460; Holland, 1472.

46. Dauphiné, 1427–1447; Todi, 1428; Neuchâtel, 1430–1439; Basel, 1423; La Tour du Pin, 1438; Lucerne, c. 1450; Falaise (Normandy), 1456; Andermatt, 1459; Ascanio, 1462; Italy, 1467–1480; Bressuire, 1475; Lucerne, c. 1480; Neuchâtel, 1481.

47. Dauphiné, 1427–1447; Briançon, 1428–1447; Faido, 1458–1459;

Artois, 1459–1460; Lyon, c. 1460; Bressuire, 1475; Annecy, 1477; Neuchâtel, 1481.

48. Como, 1456; Artois, 1459–1460; Lyon, c. 1460; Annecy, 1477.

49. Artois, 1459–1460; Lyon, c. 1460.

50. Todi, 1428; Briançon, 1428–1447; Artois, 1459–1460; Lyon, c. 1460; Valais, 1467; Constance, 1482–1486; Como, 1485.

51. Dauphiné, 1427–1447; Todi, 1428; Briançon, 1428–1447; Faido, 1432; Basel, 1423; Isère, 1436; Dauphiné, 1440 ff.; Rouen, 1447; Lucerne, c. 1450; Evreux, 1453; Faido, 1457; Faido, 1458–1459; Andermatt, 1459; Artois, 1459–1460; Chamonix, 1462; Valais, 1467; Bressuire, 1475; Annecy, 1477; Lucerne, c. 1480; Neuchâtel, 1481. The she-goat appears at Briançon if one reads *capra* for the meaningless *tapia*.

52. Isère, 1436; Faido, 1458–1459; Valais, 1467; Bressuire, 1475; Annecy, 1477; Neuchâtel, 1481.

53. Briançon, 1428–1447; Isère, 1436; Dauphiné, 1440 ff.; Faido, 1457; Faido, 1458–1459; Artois, 1459–1460; Lyon, c. 1460; Valais, 1467; Italy, 1467–1480; Bressuire, 1475; Annecy, 1477; Neuchâtel, 1481.

54. Isère, 1436; Artois, 1459–1460; Lyon, c. 1460.

55. Todi, 1428; Valais, 1428–1480; Rome, 1431; Provins, 1452; Andermatt, 1459; Lyon, c. 1460; Ascanio, 1462.

56. Benevento, 1427; Briançon, 1428–1447; Valais, 1428–1480; Neuchâtel, 1430–1439; Genoa, 1430–1450; Draguignan, 1439; Solothurn, 1447; Lucerne, c. 1450; Provins, 1452; Como, 1456; Metz, 1456; Faido, 1457; Faido, 1458–1459; Dauphiné and Gascony, 1458–1460; Italian Alps, c. 1460; Canavese, 1474; Neuchâtel, 1481.

57. Briançon, 1428–1427; Lucerne, c. 1450; Artois, 1459–1460; Lyon, c. 1460; Annecy, 1477. In Germany the meeting was called a *Rat* (Andermatt, 1459); in Italy, a *barlotto* (Faido, 1458–1459), *noce di Benevento* (Benevento, 1427; Todi, 1428), or *ludus* ("game": Italy, 1467–1480; Brescia, 1480). In France the terms *synagogue, factum, factium, le fait* (i.e., "the deed"), or *le Martinet* (after the feast of St. Martin on November 11) were favored: La Tour du Pin, 1438; Artois, 1459–1460; Lyon, c. 1460; Chamonix, 1462.

58. James, *Seasonal Feasts,* pp. 217–220.

59. The term *synagogue* is frequent: La Tour du Pin, 1438; Evreux, 1453; Artois, 1459–1460; Lyon, c. 1460; Chamonix, 1462; Annecy, 1477; Neuchâtel, 1481. Witchcraft is explicitly labelled a heretical sect at Briançon, 1428–1447; Savoy, 1430–1440; Fribourg, 1438; Provins, 1452; Artois, 1459–1460; Chamonix, 1462; Annecy, 1477; Pavia, 1479; Neuchâtel, 1481. The witches are described as Waldensians in Savoy, 1430–1440; Fribourg, 1438; Savoy, 1439; Dauphiné, 1440 ff.; Fribourg, 1440; Provins, 1452; Evreux, 1453; Fribourg, 1454; Fribourg, 1457; Artois, 1459–1460;

Lyon, c. 1460; Fribourg, 1479; Neuchâtel, 1481; Fribourg, 1482. Another common appelation is one or another form of *faicturiers,* those who attend the *factium:* Briançon, 1428–1447; Perugia, 1446; Béarn, 1448–1452; Lyon, c. 1460. Yet another is one variation or another of *striga:* Savoy, 1430–1440; Savoy, 1439; Locarno, 1455; Como, 1456; Faido, 1457; Canavese, 1474; Pavia, 1479. *Hexe* appears at Lucerne, c. 1450: Lucerne, 1454; Alpnach, 1462; Solothurn, 1466; Bern, 1478; Valais, 1478. Other terms are *wichelarij* (Holland, 1467); *frangules* (Savoy, 1439); *mascae* (Canavese, 1474), and *Gazarii* (Savoy, 1430–1440).

60. Todi, 1428; Savoy, 1430–1440; Andermatt, 1459; Artois, 1459–1460; Bressuire, 1475; Annecy, 1477; Brescia, 1480; Neuchâtel, 1481; Innsbruck, 1485.

61. Benevento, 1427; Evreux, 1453; Faido, 1458–1459; Artois, 1459–1460; Lyon, c. 1460; Rome, 1467; Canavese, 1474; Bressuire, 1475; Annecy, 1477; Brescia, 1480; Neuchâtel, 1481.

62. Interlaken, 1424; Benevento, 1427; Fribourg, 1438; La Tour du Pin, 1438; Dauphiné, 1440 ff.; Provins, 1452; Evreux, 1453; Artois, 1459–1460; Lyon, c. 1460; Chamonix, 1462; Bressuire, 1475; Annecy, 1477; Brescia, 1480; Neuchâtel, 1481.

63. Todi, 1428; Briançon, 1428–1447; Valais, 1428–1480; Savoy, 1430–1440; Provins, 1452; Bordeaux, 1453; Edolo, 1455; Metz, 1456; Faido, 1457; Artois, 1459–1460; Lyon, c. 1460; Chamonix, 1462; Milan, 1463–1464; Rome, 1467; Annecy, 1477; Lucerne, 1477; Brescia, 1480; Sardinia, 1480–1489; Neuchâtel, 1481; Brescia, 1485–1487.

64. Todi, 1428; Valais, 1428–1480; Savoy, 1430–1440; Rome, 1431; La Tour du Pin, 1438; Châlons-sur-Saône, 1452; Artois, 1459–1460; Chamonix, 1462; Annecy, 1477; Neuchâtel, 1481.

65. Todi, 1428; Valais, 1428–1480; Lucerne, c. 1450; Metz, 1456; Faido, 1458–1459; Andermatt, 1459; Artois, 1459–1460; Lyon, c. 1460; Bologna, 1462; Bressuire, 1475; Annecy, 1477; Brescia, 1480; Neuchâtel, 1481.

66. Briançon, 1428–1447; La Tour du Pin, 1438; Nivernais, 1438; Solothurn, 1447; Lucerne, c. 1450; Artois, 1459–1460; Lyon, c. 1460; Chamonix, 1462; Bressuire, 1475; Annecy, 1477; Neuchâtel, 1481; Hamburg, 1482; Murten, 1482; Brescia, 1485–1487.

67. Dauphiné, 1440 ff.; Porlezza, c. 1465.

68. Valais, 1428–1480; Cologne, c. 1430; Savoy, 1430–1440; La Tour du Pin, 1438; Heidelberg, 1446–1447; Provins, 1452; Evreux, 1453; Metz, 1457; Andermatt, 1459; Artois, 1459–1460; Lyon, c. 1460; Chamonix, 1462; Valais, 1466; Italy, 1467–1480; Canavese, 1474; Bressuire, 1475; Annecy, 1477; Brescia, 1480; Neuchâtel, 1481; Innsbruck, 1485; Brescia, 1485–1487.

69. Todi, 1428; Briançon, 1428–1447; Savoy, 1430–1440; Faido, 1432; Carcassonne, 1435; Isère, 1436; Mâcon, 1437; La Tour du Pin, 1438; France, 1438–1458; Draguignan, 1439; Dauphiné, 1440 ff.; Rouen, 1447; Provins, 1452; Como, 1456; Faido, 1457; Artois, 1459–1460; Paris, 1466; Italy, 1467–1480; Bressuire, 1475; Brescia, 1480; Neuchâtel, 1481.

70. Briançon, 1428–1447; Valais, 1428–1480; Savoy, 1430–1440; Barcelona, 1434; La Tour du Pin, 1438; Nivernais, 1438; Rouen, 1445; Evreux, 1453; Edolo, 1455; Metz, 1457; Dauphiné and Gascony, 1458–1460; Artois, 1459–1460; Lyon, c. 1460; Chamonix, 1462; Valais, 1466; Italy, 1467–1480; Ferrara, 1471–1505; Annecy, 1477; Lucerne, 1477; Brescia, 1480; Brescia, 1485–1487.

71. Briançon, 1428–1447; Valais, 1428–1480; Savoy, 1430–1440; La Tour du Pin, 1438; Rouen, 1447; Evreux, 1453; Fribourg, 1454; Edolo, 1455; Artois, 1459–1460; Lyon, c. 1460; Chamonix, 1462; Valais, 1466; Canavese, 1474; Annecy, 1477; Brescia, 1480; Neuchâtel, 1481; Brescia, 1485–1487.

72. Fribourg, 1438; Provins, 1452; Artois, 1459–1460; Ferrara, 1471–1505; Bressuire, 1475; Annecy, 1477.

73. Barcelona, 1434; Isère, 1436; Dauphiné, 1440 ff.; London, 1444; Solothurn, 1447; Lucerne, c. 1450; Munich, 1456; Artois, 1459–1460; Neuchâtel, 1481.

74. Hansen, *Zauberwahn,* pp. 440–441; Hansen, *Quellen,* pp. 459–466 (Martin le Franc, in *Quellen,* pp. 99–104 also is relevant); Lea, *Materials,* I, 233–235.

75. The document that relates to this portion of the trial is a sentence of heresy dated March 15, 1438, reproduced in Hansen, *Quellen,* pp. 459–461.

76. The document describing the procedure of the secular court is published, from a manuscript in the archives of Grenoble, by Hansen, *Quellen,* pp. 461–466.

77. Bonomo, p. 121; Paolo Guerrini, *Le Cronache bresciane inedite dei secoli XV–XIX* (Brescia, 1922), p. 183.

Chapter 10

1. *Newsweek,* March 2, 1970, p. 54.

2. Oesterreich. See comparable observations in M. G. Marwick, "The Sociology of Sorcery in a Central African Tribe," Middleton, ed., *Magic, Witchcraft, and Curing,* p. 114; and Epstein, in Middleton, p. 149.

3. Lévi-Strauss, *Anthropologie structurale,* chap. 9; Parrinder, pp. 160–165.

4. In sources before 1486, priests are mentioned 18 times, peasants, 17, and noblemen and knights, 9.

5. Trachtenberg, pp. 26, 31, 44, 48, 60, 140–141, 150–151, 207–216.

6. Donald Lowe, "Intentionality and the Method of History," M. Natanson, ed., *Phenomenology and the Social Sciences* (Evanston, Ill., 1972). For similar insights, see Kenneth Keniston, *The Uncommitted: Alienated Youth in American Society* (New York, 1965); Hadley Cantril, *Psychology of Social Movements* (New York, 1951).

7. On the importance of a sense of community, see Robert A. Nisbet, *The Quest for Community* (New York, 1953). On alienation in medieval society, see Ladner; see also Philippe Aries, *Centuries of Childhood,* trans. Robert Baldick (London, 1962), esp. pp. 33–49.

8. Baltrušaitis, *Réveils et prodiges.*

9. Viktor Frankl, *Man's Search for Meaning,* rev. ed. (New York, 1963); original title: *From Death-Camp to Existentialism* (New York, 1959).

10. Both Vordemfelde and Runeberg make the point that whether the witch is considered human or supernatural the symbol has the same strength.

11. Erich Neumann, *The Origins and History of Consciousness,* 2 vols. (New York, 1962), I, 33, 35.

12. Sigmund Freud, *Three Contributions to the Theory of Sex,* in A. A. Brill, ed., *The Basic Writings of Sigmund Freud* (New York, 1938), p. 567; Perella, pp. 1–11.

13. J. Glenn Gray, *The Warriors: Reflections on Men in Battle* (New York, 1959), p. 51.

14. Keniston, p. 197.

15. Lynn White, p. 23.

16. In the fifteenth century, excluding instances where both sexes were involved or sex not mentioned, there were 25 instances in which individual women were accused as against 20 for men, and there were 17 instances in which groups of women were cited as against 3 for men. In instances where men and women were mixed, the women usually outnumbered the men.

A short discussion of the emphasis upon women in witchcraft appears in Hansen, *Quellen,* pp. 416–423, with illustrative passages pp. 423–444. See also Parrinder, pp. 60–63. The ascription of the origins of evil to women, typified by the myths of Eve and Pandora, is worldwide. In *The Mothers,* Briffault says that "the power of witchcraft (he means sorcery) is . . . universally regarded as appertaining specifically to women" (II, 556). In II, 555–562, Briffault discusses the preponderance of women in sorcery all over the world.

17. See Epstein, p. 149; Edwin M. Loeb, "Kuanyama Ambo Magic," *Journal of American Folklore,* LXVIII (1955).

18. See Werner, "Die Stellung der Katharer zur Frau"; Koch. Both of these writers are Marxists. The anti-Marxist Herbert Grundmann in his *Religiöse Bewegungen,* esp. pp. 170–198, 452–475, diverges from Werner, insisting that women of all classes participated in the movement and that consequently no class motivations were involved.

19. See Joseph Campbell, esp. I, 73; Anton Mayer, *Erdmutter und Hexe;* Neumann, I; W. H. Trethowan, "The Demonopathology of Impotence," *British Journal of Psychiatry,* CIX (1963), 344; Lederer.

20. This is a common suggestion made by those who study witchcraft from a psychological point of view. See Masters; Barnett; Lauritz Gentz, "Vad förorsakade de stora häxprocesserna?" *Tidskrift för Nordisk Folkminnesforskning,* X (1954); and many others in a long tradition back to the eighteenth century that suggest the witches obtained erotic sensations, or even the illusion of growing hair (shapeshifting), or of flight, by the use of hallucinatory drugs taken orally or rubbed upon the skin.

21. See Oesterreich, esp. pp. 8, 131, 161–163, 177–185.

22. Which Freud, p. 567, indicates may be a phallic symbol. It should be pointed out, however, that kissing the foot is an ancient mark of subjugation found as far back as Egypt and Mesopotamia and employed at the Byzantine court and even, rarely, in the West.

23. White, p. 33. White shows how, after World War II, Navajo society was dislocated by the return of alienated former soldiers, the result being a concomitant growth of the witch cult and of murders of supposed witches.

24. Monter, "Inflation," p. 389.

Bibliography

THIS bibliography is selective, referring only to books and articles likely to be of direct value to the reader. With the exception of certain works that I have been unable to obtain (and that are indicated), I believe that I have looked at all the relevant published material relating to medieval witchcraft; the reader can be assured that all works of value published before 1972 are cited. Brief notes of caution or explanation are attached to some entries.

In principle, and with a few exceptions, the following categories are excluded: (1) works relating to magic and heresy unless also directly related to witchcraft; (2) works dealing with witchcraft outside the chronological borders 300–1486 unless directly relevant to an understanding of medieval witchcraft; (3) works written chiefly for occult or sensational purposes, or works oversimplified for popular consumption; (4) all but the most important works written before the publication of Hansen's books in 1900–1901; (5) works of a general nature or on subjects other than witchcraft but containing occasional references to witchcraft, unless those references are unusually illuminating; (6) works peripheral to witchcraft, mentioned only once or twice in this book and for specific or unique purposes (full references to such items will be found in the footnotes); (7) original sources, references to which appear in the footnotes.

The first section of the bibliography is a list of the major witch theorists of the classical period, 1430–1484, and their works. For earlier similar lists, see Hansen, *Zauberwahn*, pp. 445–447 and Rossell Hope Robbins, *The Encyclopedia of Witchcraft and Demonology* (New York, 1959), pp. 145–146. The effort here is to bring the information up to date and provide references to discussions of these authors in recent books and articles.

Theorists of Witchcraft, 1430–1486

Johann Nider was born between 1380 and 1390 in Swabia. He studied theology at Vienna and Cologne. He was a Dominican but served only occasionally, if at all, as an Inquisitor, and his knowledge of witchcraft was based in part upon the experiences of Peter of Berne, a secular judge. He died in 1438. His chief works are (a) *De morali lepra,* written about 1430. The earliest edition of this work is about 1470 and the latest 1490. See Joseph Hansen, *Quellen,* pp. 423–437. Like (b) his sermon in marriage, partially edited in *Quellen,* pp. 437–444, it connects women with witchcraft. (c) The *Formicarius* was written between 1435 and 1437. The first edition is Basel, 1470(?) and the latest 1692. The fifth book, which deals most explicitly with witchcraft, was frequently published separately, in part or as a whole. See *Quellen,* pp. 88–89; Lea, *Materials,* I, 177, 260–272; Lea, *Inquisition,* III, 534–535. (d) The *Praeceptorium divinae legis,* first edited about 1470. See Lea, *Materials,* I, 265–272.

Thomas Ebendorfer (Ebendorffer) of Haselbach wrote his *De decem praeceptis* in 1439. It has never been edited. See Thorndike, *History of Magic,* IV, 294–295; Ginzburg, p. 51; A. E. Schönbach, "Zeugnisse zur deutschen Volkskunde des Mittelalters," *Zeitschrift des Vereins für Volkskunde,* XII (1902), 1–12.

Martin le Franc (Martin Franc), a secretary of the Antipope Felix V, wrote a poem entitled *Le Champion des dames* in 1440 and dedicated it to Duke Philip of Burgundy in defense of the female sex. Martin exonerates women from the crime of witchcraft and takes a generally skeptical attitude toward witch beliefs. The first edition of the poem is Lyon, 1485; the last is Paris, 1530. See *Quellen,* pp. 99–104; Lea, *Materials,* I, 177; Félix Bourquelot, "Les Vaudois du XVe siècle," *Bibliothèque de l'école des chartes,* II (2d series), 82–84.

The theologian Johann Wunschilburg (Wünschelburg) wrote a

Tractatus de superstitionibus about 1440; it has never been edited. See *Quellen*, p. 104; Thorndike, *History of Magic*, IV, 274.

Alfonso Tostado (Tostatus), who studied theology in Salamanca and became bishop of Avila in Spain, wrote a *Commentary on Genesis* about 1435; it has not been edited. See *Materials*, I, 190–191. He also wrote a *Commentary on Matthew* about 1440, which was first edited in Venice in 1507 and last printed in 1728. See *Quellen*, pp. 105–109; *Materials*, I, 189–191.

John of Torquemada (Turrecremata), uncle of the infamous Inquisitor Thomas Torquemada, was a Dominican who spent most of his life in Rome after studying in Paris. His *Super toto Decreto commentaria* was written about 1445, first edited at Lyon in 1519 and last edited at Venice in 1578. See *Quellen*, pp. 112–118; *Materials*, I, 191; Stephen Lederer, *Der spanische Cardinal Johann von Torquemada, sein Leben und seine Schriften* (Freiburg im Breisgau, 1879).

Raphael of Pornasio (Pornassio), an Inquisitor at Genoa about 1430 to 1450, wrote *De arte magica*, which has not been printed, about 1450. See Thorndike, *History of Magic*, IV, 308–313.

William de Bechis wrote *De potestate spirituum*, which has not been edited, about 1450. See Thorndike, *History of Magic*, IV, 298–299.

Lope Barrientos, a Dominican theologian who was also bishop of Segovia, Avila, and Cuenca, was the author of an unedited *Tratado de la Divinanza*, which he wrote about 1450. See *Quellen*, pp. 123–124.

The *Errores Gazariorum* were the work of an anonymous Savoyard Inquisitor about 1450. There is no edition, but see *Quellen*, pp. 118–122 for a portion of the work; see also *Materials*, I, 273–275.

Jean Vineti, Dominican, professor of theology at Paris, and Inquisitor at Carcassonne, wrote *Tractatus contra demonum invocatores* about 1450. There is no edition. See *Quellen*, pp. 124–130 and *Materials*, I, 272–273. Trevor-Roper (*Encounter*, I, 9–10) mistakenly says that Vineti was the first to call witchcraft heresy. The tradition was much older.

Johann Hartlieb, the author of *Buch aller verbotenen Kunst, Unglaubens, und der Zauberei*, produced his work in 1456, but the first edition was not prepared until 1914: Dora Ulm, ed., *Johann Hartliebs*

Buch aller verbotenen Kunst (Halle an der Saale, 1914). See *Quellen*, pp. 130–133; *Materials*, I, 275; Sigmund Riezler, *Geschichte der Hexenprozesse in Bayern* (Stuttgart, 1896), pp. 64–65.

Nicholas Jacquier was a Dominican who was first Inquisitor at Tournai (1465) and then in Bohemia and finally at Lille. His *Flagellum haereticorum fascinariorum*, written in 1458, was first edited at Frankfurt in 1581. See *Quellen*, pp. 133–145; *Materials*, I, 276–285; Lea, *Inquisition*, III, 497–498, 538.

Alfonso de Spina, a Minorite theologian at Salamanca and bishop of Orense, wrote his *Tabula fortalicii fidei*, more commonly known as the *Fortalicium fidei*, in 1458–1460. The first edition was 1464 or 1467 and the last, 1525. This was the first book on witchcraft to be printed. See *Quellen*, pp. 145–148; *Materials*, I, 285–292; Lea, *Inquisition*, III, 445, 496.

Girolamo (Jerome, Hieronymus) Visconti, the author of *Lamiarum sive striarum opusculum* and *An striae sint velud heretice judicande*, was a member of the princely family of Milan who became a Dominican and a professor of logic at Milan. The two tracts were both written about 1460 and were first edited at Milan in 1490. See *Quellen*, pp. 200–207; *Materials*, I, 295–296; Lea, *Inquisition*, III, 540, 546.

Johannes Tinctoris, born at Tournai, became a professor of theology and eventually rector of the University of Cologne. His *Tractatus (Sermo) de secta Vaudensium*, never edited, was written about 1460. A few pages are published in Fredericq, *Corpus*, I, 357–360. See also *Quellen*, pp. 183–184 and, for a French version, pp. 184–188.

Michael Behaim's *Meistergesang* was written about 1460, first edited in 1835, and last edited in 1839. See *Quellen*, pp. 207–208; *Materials*, I, 297.

Peter Mamoris, a professor of theology at Poitiers and regent of that university, wrote a treatise for Louis de Rochechouart, bishop of Saintes, in 1461–1462. This treatise, *Flagellum maleficorum*, was first edited in 1490 and was last printed in 1669 in an edition of the *Malleus*. See *Quellen*, pp. 208–212; Thorndike, *History of Magic*, IV, 299–305; *Materials*, I, 298.

Martin of Arles, a professor of theology and canon of Pampelona in

Spain, wrote at an unknown date a *Tractatus de superstitionibus contra maleficia seu sortilegia, quae hodie vigent in orbe terrarum*. Hansen places the date of this treatise in 1515, but Lea put it in the "middle third of the fifteenth century." The first edition was 1581. See *Quellen*, pp. 308–310; *Materials*, I, 297–298.

Marianus Socinus (Soccini, Sozzini) was a professor of canon law at Padua and Siena. A humanist, he wrote a skeptical *Tractatus de sortilegis*, which deals with magic more than with witchcraft proper. Written about 1465, it has never been edited. See *Quellen*, pp. 212–215; *Materials*, I, 299; Thorndike, *History of Magic*, IV, 295–298.

Ambrose de' Vignate, a professor of law at Padua, Bologna, and Turin, produced an *Elegans tractatus de haeresi; Quaestio de lamiis seu strigibus et earum delictis* about 1468; it was first edited at Rome in 1581 and last appeared in an edition of the *Malleus* in 1669. See *Quellen*, pp. 215–227; *Materials*, I, 299, 301.

The Dominican theologian Jordanes de Bergamo wrote a *Quaestio de strigis* about 1470–1471. It was never edited. See *Quellen*, pp. 195–200; *Materials*, I, 301–303.

Francis of Florence, a Minorite who became dean of theology at Florence, wrote *De quorundam astrologorum parvipendendis iudiciis pariter et de incantatoribus ac divinatoribus nullo modo ferendis* in 1472–1473. There is no edition. See Thorndike, *History of Magic*, IV, 313–330.

A court chaplain to Elector Frederick of the Palatinate, Mathias Widman von Kemnat, wrote a *Chronik* about 1475. It was first edited in *Quellen zur bayerischen und deutschen Geschichte*, II (1862), 102 ff. See *Quellen*, pp. 231–235; *Materials*, I, 304.

Jean Vincent (Vincenti), prior of the church of Les Moustiers at Lay in the Vendée, wrote *Liber adversus magicas artes* about 1475. There is no edition. See *Quellen*, pp. 227–231; *Materials*, I, 303–304.

Antonio Galateo (de' Ferrari), a humanist professor at the University of Naples, wrote a *De Situ Japigiae* in 1480, which was first edited at Basel in 1558(?). See Joseph Hansen, *Zauberwahn*, p. 517; *Quellen*, pp. 239–240, note.

Pedro Garcia (Garsia, Garsias), bishop of Usellus in Sardinia, wrote

In determinationes magistrales contra conclusiones apologiales Ioannis Pici Miranduli . . . proemium in 1480–1489, the first edition appearing in 1489. See Thorndike, *History of Magic,* IV, 497–509.

Bernard Basin, a theologian of Saragossa, wrote his *Tractatus exquisitissimus de artibus magicis et magorum maleficiis* in 1482. The first edition appeared in Paris in 1483 and the last in a 1669 edition of the *Malleus.* See *Quellen,* pp. 236–238; Materials, I, 304; Thorndike, *History of Magic,* IV, 488–493, 578, 615.

Angelus Politiani (Angelo Poliziano) wrote a treatise called *Lamia* in 1483. Its first edition is 1492; its last is Rome, 1542. Though sometimes cited by later writers on witchcraft, the treatise contains nothing about witchcraft as such and only a little related to it. See *Quellen,* p. 239; Joseph Hansen, *Zauberwahn,* p. 517; Thorndike, *History of Magic,* IV passim.

Bernard of Como (Bernardo Rategno), a Dominican Inquisitor at Como, wrote a *Tractatus de strigiis,* which was published first in Rome in 1584 along with another of Bernard's works, the *Lucerna inquisitorum haereticae pravitatis.* The last edition seems to have been Venice, 1596. The date of composition is unknown: Lea argues for c. 1500; Hansen for c. 1508; but the most recent writer on Bernard, Bonomo, places the tracts in 1484–1487. See Bonomo, pp. 141, 260; *Quellen,* pp. 279–284; Lea, *Inquisition,* III, 498.

I have omitted consideration of the following: Felix Hemmerlin (because he deals only with magic, not with heresy or witchcraft proper); the *Recollectio* of the Arras heretics (which I treat in connection with the Arras case of 1459–1460); *La Vauderye de Lyonois en brief* (which I treat in connection with the prosecution of witches at Lyon).

Books and Articles

Abel, Armand. "Aspects sociologiques des religions 'manichéens,'" *Mélanges offerts à René Crozet.* Poitiers, 1966. Pp. 33–46.

Albe, Edmond. *Autour de Jean XXII, Hugues Géraud, évêque de Cahors: L'affaire des poisons et des envoûtements en 1317.* Cahors-Toulouse, 1904.

Albers, Johann H. *Das Jahr und seine Feste.* Stuttgart, 1917.

Allier, Raoul. *Magie et religion.* Paris, 1935.

Amati, N. "Processus contra valdenses in Lombardia superiori anno 1387," *Archivio storico italiano,* 3d ser., vols. I and II (1864).

Ammann, Hartmann. "Der Innsbrucker Hexenprozess von 1485," *Neue Zeitschrift des Ferdinandeums für Tirol und Vorarlberg.* Innsbruck, 1890.

Anagnine, Eugenio. *Dolcino e il movimento ereticale all'inizio del trecento.* Florence, 1964.

Aubenas, Roger. *La Sorcière et l'inquisiteur: Episode de l'Inquisition en Provence, 1439.* Aix en Provence, 1956.

Aureggi, O. "Stregoneria eretica e tortura giudiziaria," *Bolletino della società storica valtellinese,* XVII (1963–1964). I have not seen this work.

Bader, Guido. *Die Hexenprozesse in der Schweiz.* Affoltern, 1945.

Bächtold-Stäubli, Hanns, ed. *Handwörterbuch des deutschen Aberglaubens.* 11 vols. Berlin-Leipzig, 1927–1942. Especially vol. III: entry *Hexe.*

Bainton, Roland H., and Lois O. Gibbons, eds. *George Lincoln Burr, His Life: Selections from His Writings.* Ithaca, 1943.

Baissac, Jules. *Histoire de la diablerie chrétienne: Le Diable, la personne du Diable, le personnel du Diable.* Paris, 1882.

Baltrušaitis, Jurgis, *Le moyen âge fantastique: Antiquités et exotismes dans l'art gothique.* Paris, 1955.

———. *Réveils et prodiges: Le gothique fantastique.* Paris, 1960.

Bamberger, Bernard. *Fallen Angels.* Philadelphia, 1952.

Barb, A. A. "The Survival of Magic Arts," in Arnaldo Momigliano, ed., *The Conflict between Paganism and Christianity in the Fourth Century.* Oxford, 1963. Pp. 100–125.

Barnett, Bernard. "Witchcraft, Psychopathology, and Hallucinations," *British Journal of Psychiatry,* CXI (1965), 439–445.

Baroja, Julio Caro. *The World of the Witches.* Chicago, 1964. A translation of *Las brujas y su mundo* (Madrid, 1961).

Barton, George A. "The Origin of the Names of Angels and Demons in the Extra-Canonical Apocalyptic Literature to 100 A.D.," *Journal of Biblical Literature,* XXX (1911), XXXI (1912).

Baschwitz, Kurt. *Hexen und Hexenprozesse: Die Geschichte eines Massenwahns.* 2d ed. Munich, 1966.

Bataille, Georges, ed. *Le Procès de Gilles de Rais: Les documents.* Montreuil, 1965.

Battifol, Louis. "Le Chatelêt de Paris vers 1400," *Revue historique,* LXI (1864), 225–264; LXII (1865), 225–235; LXIII (1866), 42–55; 266–283.

Bavoux, Francis. "Les Caractères originaux de la sorcellerie dans le Pays de Montbéliard," *Mémoires de la Société pour l'histoire du droit et des institutions des anciens pays bourguignons, comtois, et romands,* fasc. 20 (1958–1959), pp. 89–96.

———. *La Sorcellerie au Pays de Quingey.* Besançon, 1947.

Béliard, Octave. *Sorciers, rêveurs, et démoniaques.* Paris, 1920.

Belknap, G. N. "The Social Value of Dionysiac Ritual," *Revue de l'histoire des religions,* CVI (1932).

Benz, Ernst. "Ordeal by Fire," in Joseph M. Kitagawa and Charles H. Long, eds., *Myths and Symbols: Studies in Honor of Mircea Eliade.* Chicago, 1969.

Berge, François, James Frazer, and Marcel Renault. *Folklore et religion, Magie et religion,* vol. V of *Histoire générale des religions.* Paris, 1951.

Berger, Peter L., and Thomas Luckman. *The Social Construction of Reality: A Treatise in the Sociology of Knowledge.* Garden City, 1966.

Bernard, Paul P. "Heresy in Fourteenth Century Austria," *Medievalia et Humanistica,* X (1956), 50–63.

Bernheimer, Richard. *Wild Men in the Middle Ages.* Cambridge, Mass., 1952.

Bettelheim, Bruno. *Symbolic Wounds: Puberty Rites and the Envious Male.* Rev. ed. New York, 1962.

Betts, Reginald R. "Correnti religiose nazionali ed ereticali dalla fine del secolo XIV alla metà del XV," *Relazioni del X Congresso internazionale di scienze storiche,* III (1955), 485–513. In English.

Beurmann, Arno. *Der Aberglaube der Jäger: Von den beseelten Magie, von Mystik und Mythen und allerlei Zauberwahn der Jäger.* Hamburg and Berlin, 1961.

Beyschlag, F. "Ein Speyerer Ketzerprozess vom Jahre 1392," *Blätter für Pfälzische Kirchengeschichte*, III (1927), 61–65. I have not been able to obtain this work.

Bickermann, E. "Ritualmord und Eselskult," *Monatschrift für Geschichte und Wissenschaft des Judentums*, LXXI (1927), 171–187.

Biscaro, Girolamo. "Guglielmina la Boema e i Guglielmiti," *Archivio storico lómbardo*, LVII (1930), 1–67.

Bitter, Wilhelm, ed. *Massenwahn in Geschichte und Gegenwart: Ein Tagungsbericht*. Stuttgart, 1965. Includes Arno Borst, "Mittelalterliche Sekten und Massenwahn"; Wanda von Baeyer-Katte, "Die historischen Hexenprozesse—der verbürokratisierte Massenwahn"; Erich O. Haisch, "Psychiatrische Aspekte der Hexenprozesse"; Herbert Auhofer, "Der Hexenwahn in der Gegenwart."

Bloomfield, Morton. *The Seven Deadly Sins*, 2d ed. East Lansing, 1967.

Blum, Elisabeth. *Das staatliche und kirchliche Recht des Frankenreichs in seiner Stellung zum Dämonen-, Zauber-, und Hexenwesen*. Paderborn, 1936.

Bock, Friedrich. "Studien zum politischen Inquisitionsprozess Johanns XXII," *Quellen und Forschungen aus italienischen Archiven und Bibliotheken herausgegeben vom preussischen historischen Institut in Rome*, XXVI (1935–1936); XXVII (1937).

Boffito, Giuseppe. "Eretici in Piemonte al tempo del gran schisma 1378–1417," *Studi e documenti di storia e diritto*, XVIII (1897).

Bonomo, Giuseppe. *Caccia alle streghe: La credenza nelle streghe dal secolo xiii al xix con particolare riferimento all'Italia*. Palermo, 1959.

Bonser, Wilfrid. *A Bibliography of Folklore*. London, 1961.

Borst, Arno. *Die Katharer*. Stuttgart, 1953.

Bouisson, Maurice. *Magic: Its History and Principal Rites*. New York, 1961. Translation of *La Magie: Ses grandes rites, son histoire* (Paris, 1958).

Bourquelot, Félix. "Les Vaudois du XVe siècle," *Bibliothèque de l'École des chartes*, 2d ser., vol. III (1846).

Brandt, William J. "Church and Society in the Late Fourteenth Century: A Contemporary View," *Medievalia et Humanistica*, XIII (1960), 56–67.

Briffault, Robert. *The Mothers: a Study of the Origins of Sentimental Institutions*. 3 vols. New York, 1927.

Briggs, Katherine Mary. *Pale Hecate's Team: An Examination of the Beliefs on Witchcraft and Magic among Shakespeare's Contemporaries and His Immediate Successors*. New York, 1962.

Brooke, Christopher. "Heresy and Religious Sentiment, 1000–1250," *Bulletin of the Institute of Historical Research*, XLI (1968).

Browe, Peter. "Die Eucharistie als Zaubermittel im Mittelalter," *Archiv für Kulturgeschichte*, XX (1930).

Brown, Ralph. "Examination of an Interesting Roman Document: *Instructio pro formandis processibus in causis strigum*," *Jurist*, XXV (1964), 169–191.

Brucker, Gene. "Sorcery in Early Renaissance Florence," *Studies in the Renaissance*, X (1963), 7–24.

Brunner, Gottfried. *Ketzer und Inquisition in der Mark Brandenburg im ausgehenden Mittelalter*. Berlin, 1904.

Bruno de Jésus Marie, O. C. D. *Satan*. New York, 1951.

Büttner, Theodora, and Ernst Werner. *Circumcellionen und Adamiten: Zwei Formen mittelalterlichen Haeresie*. Berlin, 1959.

Burr, George Lincoln. "The Literature of Witchcraft," *American Historical Association Papers*, IV (1889–1890), pt. 3, pp. 235–266.

——. "A Witch-Hunter in the Book-Shops," *The Bibliographer*, I (1902), 431–446.

——. "The Witch-Persecutions," *Translations and Reprints from the Original Sources of European History*. Philadelphia, 1902.

Burris, Eli. "The Terminology of Witchcraft," *Classical Philology*, XXXI (1936). Greek and Roman.

Burstein, Sona Rosa. "Aspects of the Psychopathology of Old Age," *British Medical Bulletin*, VI (1949).

——. "Folklore, Rumor, and Prejudice," *Folklore*, LXX (1959), 361–381.

——. "Social and Situational Hazards of the Ageing Individual," *Acts of the Fourth Congress of the International Association of Gerontology* (1957).

——. "Some Modern Books on Witchcraft," *Folklore*, LXXII (1961), 520–534.

Buxtorf-Falkeisen, Karl. *Basler Zauberprozesse aus dem 14 und 15 Jahrhundert*. Basel, 1868.

Byloff, Fritz. *Hexenglaube und Hexenverfolgung in den österreichischen Alpenländern*. Berlin and Leipzig, 1934.

Cabanès, Augustin. *Moeurs intimes du passé: Le Sabbat a-t-il existé?* Paris, 1935.

Campbell, George Archibald. *The Knights Templars: Their Rise and Fall*. London, 1937.

Campbell, Joseph. *The Masks of God*. 4 vols. New York, 1959–1968.

Capelle, G. C. *Autour du décret de 1210, III, Amaury de Bène: Etude sur son panthéisme formal*. Paris, 1932.

Carcopino, Jérome. "Survivances par substitution des sacrifices d'enfants dans l'Afrique romaine," *Revue de l'histoire des religions*, CVI (1932), 592–599.

Carnoy, E. Henri. "Les Acousmates et les chasses fantastiques," *Revue de l'histoire des religions*, IX (1884).

Carrière, Victor. *Histoire et cartulaire des Templiers de Provence avec une introduction sur les débuts du Temple en France*. Paris, 1919.

Castelli, Enrico. *Il Demoniaco nell'arte*. Milan, 1952.

——, ed. *L'Umanesimo e il demoniaco nell'arte*. Rome, 1952.

Cauzons, Thomas de (pseud.). *La Magie et la sorcellerie en France*. 4 vols. Paris, 1910–1911.

Cavendish, Richard. *The Black Arts*. New York, 1967.

Cerlini, Aldo, "Una dama e una striga dell'Ariosto," *Lares*, XX (1954), 64–86.

Chabloz, Fritz. *Les Sorcières neuchâteloises*. Neuchâtel, 1868.

Champion, Pierre. *Procès de condamnation de Jeanne d'Arc*. 2 vols. Paris, 1920–1921.

Charpentier, John. *L'Ordre des Templiers*. Paris, 1944.

Chochod, Louis. *Histoire de la magie et de ses dogmes*. Paris, 1949. Magic tied uncritically to witchcraft.

Cirlot, Juan. *A Dictionary of Symbols*. New York, 1962.

Clark, James M. *The Dance of Death in the Middle Ages and the Renaissance*. Glasgow, 1950.

Cohn, Norman. *The Pursuit of the Millennium.* Rev. ed. New York, 1970. References in the text and notes are to the first edition of 1957.

Comba, Emilio. *La Storia dei Valdesi.* 4th ed. Torre Pellice, 1950.

Cordier, Jacques. *Jeanne d'Arc: sa personnalité, son rôle.* Paris, 1948.

Corsi, Domenico. "Le *Constitutiones Maleficorum* della provincia di Garfagnana del 1287," *Archivio storico italiano,* CXV (1957).

Coulton, George G. *The Death Penalty for Heresy from 1184 to 1921* A.D. London, 1924.

———. *Inquisition and Liberty.* London, 1938.

Crawford, Jane. "Evidences for Witchcraft in Anglo-Saxon England," *Medium Aevum,* XXXII (1963), 99–116.

Crecelius, W. "Frau Holde und der Venusberg (aus hessischen Hexenprozessen)," *Zeitschrift für deutsche Mythologie und Sittenkunde,* I (1853).

Croce, Benedetto, "Un dramma sulla noce di Benevento," chap. 21 of *Saggi sulla letteratura italiana del seicento.* Bari, 1911.

Croissant, Werner. *Die Berücksichtigung geburts- und berufsständischer und soziologischer Unterschiede im deutschen Hexenprozess.* Mainz, 1953. I have not seen this work.

Cumont, Franz. "Les Anges du paganisme," *Revue de l'histoire des religions,* LXXII (1915).

D'Alatri, Mario. *L'Inquisizione francescana nell'Italia centrale nel secolo XIII.* Rome, 1954.

Darwin, Francis. "The Holy Inquisition," *Church Quarterly Review,* CXXV (1937) 226–246; CXXVI (1938) 19–43; CXLI (1945) 38–71; CXLII (1946) 176–195.

Davidson, Gustav. *A Dictionary of Angels.* Glencoe, 1967.

Davidson, Thomas. "The Needfire Ritual," *Antiquity,* XXIX (1955), 132–136.

Davies, Reginald Trevor. *Four Centuries of Witch Beliefs, with Special Reference to the Great Rebellion.* London, 1947.

De Gaiffier, Baudouin, and Guy de Tervarent. "Le Diable voleur d'enfants," *Analecta sacra tarraconensia,* XII (1936).

Delaruelle, E. "Les Grandes processions de pénitents de 1349 et 1399," in *Il Movimento dei disciplinati nel settimo centenario dal suo inizio.* Perugia, 1960.

Delhaye, Philippe, *"L'Ignorantia juris* et la situation morale de l'hérétique dans l'Eglise ancienne et médiévale," in *Etudes d'histoire de droit canonique dédiées à Gabriel Le Bras.* 2 vols. Paris, 1965.

De Rougemont, Denis. *The Devil's Share.* New York, 1944. Discursive rather than historical.

Diehl, Katherine Smith. *Religions, Mythologies, Folklores: An Annotated Bibliography.* New York, 1956.

Di Maria, Costantino. *Enciclopedia della magia e della stregoneria.* Milan, 1967.

Dmitrewski, Michel de. "Fr. Bernard Délicieux, O.F.M. Sa lutte contre l'inquisition de Carcassonne et d'Albi, son procès 1297–1319," *Archivum Franciscanum Historicum,* XVII (1924); XVIII (1925).

Dölger, Franz Joseph. *Antike und Christentum.* 7 vols. Münster, 1929–1950. Vol. IV, pp. 188–228: "Sacramentum infanticidii."

Doncoeur, Paul, and Yves Lanhers. *Documents et recherches relatifs à Jeanne la Pucelle.* 5 vols. Paris, 1952–1961.

Dondaine, Antoine. "Le Manuel de l'inquisiteur," *Archivum Fratrum Praedicatorum,* XVII (1947), 85–194.

Dossat, Yves. "L'Evolution des rituels cathares," *Revue de synthèse,* LXIV (1948), 27–30.

Douglas, Mary, ed. *Witchcraft Confessions and Accusations.* New York, 1970.

Driesen, Otto. *Der Ursprung des Harlekin: Ein kulturgeschichtliches Problem.* Berlin, 1904.

DuCange, Charles du Fresne. *Glossarium mediae et infimae latinitatis,* 3d ed., Paris, 10 vols, 1937–1938.

Dujčev, Ivan. *Medioevo Bizantino-Slavo.* Rome, 1965.

Durban, Pierre. *Actualité du catharisme.* Toulouse and Bordeaux, 1968.

Duverger, Arthur. *La Vauderie dans les états de Philippe le Bon: Le premier grand procès de sorcellerie aux Pays-Bas.* Arras, 1885.

Eckstein, F. "Zum Diersburger Hexenprozess vom Jahre 1486," *Zeitschrift für die Geschichte des Oberrheins,* XL (1927), 635–636.

Ehnmark, Erland. "Religion and Magic—Frazer, Söderblom, and Hägerström," *Ethnos,* XXI (1956), 1–10.

Eitrem, Samson. *Some Notes on the Demonology of the New Testament.* Oslo: Symbolac Osloenses, fasc. supplet. 12, 1950.

Endter, A. *Die Sage vom wilden Jäger und von der wilden Jagd. Studien über der deutschen Dämonenglauben.* Gelnhausen, 1933. I have not seen this work.

Enklaar, Diederik, and R. R. Post. *La Fille au grand coeur: Études sur Jeanne d'Arc.* Groningen, 1955.

———. "Was Jeanne d'Arc een Duivelvereerster?" *Medelingen der koninklijke Nederlandse Akademie van Wetenschappen, afd. Letterkunde*, N.S., vol. XVI (1953).

Ennemoser, Joseph. *Geschichte der Magie.* Leipzig, 1844.

Epstein, Scarlett. "A Sociological Analysis of Witch Beliefs in a Mysore Village," in John Middleton, ed., *Magic, Witchcraft, and Curing.* Garden City, 1967. Pp. 135–154.

Erbstösser, Martin. "Ein neues Inquisitionsprotokoll zu den sozial-religiösen Bewegungen in Thüringen Mitte des XIV Jahrhunderts," *Wissenschaftliche Zeitschrift der Karl-Marx-Universität Leipzig,* XIV (1965), 379–388.

———, and Ernst Werner. *Ideologische Probleme des mittelalterlichen Plebjertums: Die freigeistige Häresie und ihre sozialen Würzeln.* Berlin, 1960.

Le Eresie popolari dei secoli XI–XIII: Relazioni degli studenti che hanno partecipato al Seminario di storia medievale nella primavera del 1968, raccolte in onore di Ernesto Sestan per il suo 70. Florence, 1968.

Esmein, Adhémar. *A History of Continental Criminal Procedure with Special Reference to France.* Boston, 1913.

Evans, Austin P. "Hunting Subversion in the Middle Ages," *Speculum,* XXXIII (1958), 1–22.

Falgairolle, Edmond. *Un envoûtement en Gévaudan en l'année 1347.* Nîmes, 1892.

Fastin, Léon, *La Légende de Théophile.* Brussels, 1966.

Fearns, James. "Peter von Bruis und die religiöse Bewegung des 12 Jahrhunderts," *Archiv für Kulturgeschichte,* XLVIII (1966), 311–355.

Febvre, Lucien. "Sorcellerie, sotise ou révolution mentale?" *Annales: économies—sociétés—civilisations,* III (1948), 9–15.

Fehr, Hans. "Gottesurteil und Folter: eine Studie zur Dämonologie des

Mittelalters und der neuren Zeit," *Festgabe für Rudolf Stammler.* Berlin and Leipzig, 1926.

——. "Zur Erklärung von Folter und Hexenprozess," *Zeitschrift für schweizerische Geschichte,* XXIV (1944), 581–585.

——. "Zur Lehre vom Folterprozess," *Zeitschrift der Savigny-Stiftung für Rechtsgeschichte: Germanistische Abteilung,* LIII (1933).

Ferguson, Ian. *The Philosophy of Witchcraft.* London, 1924.

Ferraironi, Francesco. *Le Streghe e l'inquisizione: Superstizioni e realtà.* Rome, 1955.

Fiertz, Gertrude. "An Unusual Trial under the Inquisition at Fribourg, Switzerland, in 1399," *Speculum,* XVIII (1943), 340–357.

Filhol, R. "Procès de sorcellerie à Bressuire, août-septembre 1475," *Revue historique de droit français et étranger,* 4th series, XLII (1964), 77–83.

Finke, Heinrich. *Papsttum und Untergang des Templerordens.* Münster, 1907.

Flade, Paul. *Das römische Inquisitionsverfahren in Deutschland bis zu den Hexenprozessen.* Leipzig, 1902.

Flasdieck, Hermann. "Harlekin: Germanischer Mythos in romanischer Wandlung," *Anglia,* LXI (1937), 225–340.

Förg, Ludwig. *Die Ketzerverfolgung in Deutschland unter Gregor IX: Ihre Herkunft, ihre Bedeutung, und ihre rechtliche Grundlagen.* Berlin, 1932.

Forbes, Thomas Rogers. *The Midwife and the Witch.* New Haven, 1966.

——. "Midwifery and Witchcraft," *Journal of the History of Medicine and Allied Sciences,* XVII (1962), 417–439.

——. "Witch's Milk and Witches' Marks," *Yale Journal of Biology and Medicine,* XXII (1950).

Foucault, Maurice. *Les Procès de sorcellerie dans l'ancienne France devant les jurisdictions seculières.* Paris, 1907.

Fredericq, Paul. *Corpus documentorum inquisitionis haereticae pravitatis neerlandicae.* 5 vols. Ghent and The Hague, 1889–1906.

——. *Geschiedenis der Inquisitie in der Nederlanden.* 2 vols. Ghent and The Hague, 1892–1897.

BIBLIOGRAPHY
Books and Articles

———. "L'Historiographie de l'inquisition," preface to the French translation of Lea's *History of the Inquisition* (Paris, 1900).

———. "Les Récents historiens catholiques de l'inquisition en France," *Revue historique*, CIX (1912), 307–334.

———. *De Secten der Geeselaars en der Dansers in de Nederlanden tijdens de XIVe eeuw.* Brussels, 1896.

Friedrich, J. "La Vauderye (Valdesia): ein Beitrag zur Geschichte der Waldesier," in *Akademie der Wissenschaften; Sitzungsberichte: philosophisch-philologische Klasse* (Munich, 1899).

Friess, Godfrid Edmund. "Patarener, Begharden, und Waldenser in Oesterreich während des Mittelalters," *Oesterreichische Vierteljahrschrift für katholische Theologie*, XI (1872), 209–272.

Fumi, Luigi, "L'inquisizione romana e lo stato di Milano," *Archivio storico lombardo*, XIII (1910).

Gabory, Emile. *Alias Bluebeard. The Life and Death of Gilles de Raiz.* New York, 1930.

Gallinek, Alfred. "Psychogenic Disorders and the Civilization of the Middle Ages," *American Journal of Psychiatry*, XCIX (1942–1943), 42–54.

Garinet, Jules. *Histoire de la magie en France, depuis le commencement de la monarchie jusqu'à nos jours.* Paris, 1818.

Garsoian, Nina G. *The Paulician Heresy: A Study of the Origin and Development of Paulicianism in Armenia and the Eastern Provinces of the Byzantine Empire.* New York, 1967.

Ginzburg, Carlo. *I Benandanti: Ricerche sulle stregoneria e sui culti agrari tra Cinquecento e Seicento.* Turin, 1966.

Girand, Albert. *Etude sur les procès de sorcellerie en Normandie.* Rouen, 1897.

———. *Fragments d'histoire de la folie: La sorcellerie au moyen âge; Une épidémie de délire de nos jours.* Bar-le-Duc, 1883. One of the earliest efforts to explain witchcraft as a phenomenon of mass social deviation.

Gmelin, Julius. *Schuld oder Unschuld des Templerordens: Kritischer Versuch zur Lösung der Frage.* 2 vols. Stuttgart, 1893.

Gokey, Francis X. *The Terminology for the Devil and Evil Spirits in the Apostolic Fathers.* Washington, D.C., 1961.

Gonnet, Giovanni. "Casi di sincretismo ereticale in Piemonte nei secoli XIV e XV," *Bolletino della società di studi valdesi*, CVIII (1960).

——. "I Valdesi d'Austria nella seconda metà del secolo XIV," *Bolletino della società di studi valdesi*, CXI (1962).

——. "Il movimento valdese in Europa secondo le più recenti ricerche (sec. 12–16)," *Bolletino della società di studi valdesi*, C (1956), 21–30.

——, ed. *Enchiridion fontium valdensium: Recueil critique des sources concernant les vaudois au moyen âge du IIIe concile du Latran au synode de Chanforan (1179–1532)*. Torre Pellice, 1958.

Gosler, Sieglinde. *Hexenwahn und Hexenprozesse in Kärnten von der Mitte des 15 bis zum ersten Drittel des 18 Jahrhunderts*. Graz, 1955. I have not been able to obtain this work.

Graesse, Johann Georg. *Bibliotheca magica et pneumatica*. Leipzig, 1843. An important early bibliography used by Burr to build the Cornell collection.

Grattan, John H. G., and Charles Singer. *Anglo-Saxon Magic and Medicine*. London, 1952.

Grimm, Jakob. *Teutonic Mythology*. 4 vols. New York, 1883–1888. Reprinted by Dover Publications in 1966.

Grundmann, Herbert. *Bibliographie zur Ketzergeschichte des Mittelalters (1900–1966)*. Sussidi eruditi no. 20. Rome, 1967.

——. *Ketzergeschichte des Mittelalters*. Göttingen, 1963.

——. "Ketzerverhöre des Spätmittelalters als quellenkritisches Problem," *Deutsches Archiv für die Erforschung des Mittelalters*, XXI (1965), 519–575.

——. *Religiöse Bewegungen im Mittelalter*. 2d ed. Hildesheim, 1961.

Guarnieri, Romana. *Il movimento del Libero Spirito: Testi e documenti*, Rome, 1965.

Hadfield, James A. *Dreams and Nightmares*. Harmondsworth, 1954.

Haisch, Erich. "Der Hexenwahn," *CIBA Zeitschrift*, IX, no. 101 (1963).

Hansen, Chadwick. *Witchcraft at Salem*. New York, 1969.

Hansen, Joseph. "Heinrich Institoris, der Verfasser des Hexenhammers, und seine Tätigkeit an der Mosel im Jahre 1488," *Westdeutsche Zeitschrift für Geschichte und Kunst*, XVII (1898).

————. "Der Hexenhammer, seine Bedeutung, und die gefälschte Kölner Approbation vom Jahre 1487," *Westdeutsche Zeitschrift für Geschichte und Kunst,* XVII (1898).

————. "Inquisition und Hexenverfolgung im Mittelalter," *Historische Zeitschrift,* LXXXI (1898).

————. *Quellen und Untersuchungen zur Geschichte des Hexenwahns und der Hexenverfolgung im Mittelalter.* Bonn, 1901. Reprinted, Hildesheim, 1963.

————. *Zauberwahn, Inquisition, und Hexenprozess im Mittelalter und die Entstehung der grossen Hexenverfolgung.* Munich, 1900. Reprinted, Munich, 1964.

Hartmann, Wilhelm. *Die Hexenprozesse in der Stadt Hildesheim: Quellen und Darstellungen zur Geschichte Niedersachsens,* vol. XXXV. Hildesheim and Leipzig, 1927. Little on the Middle Ages.

Hauréau, Jean. *Bernard Délicieux et l'inquisition albigeoise 1300– 1320.* Paris, 1877.

Hecker, Justus F. C. *Die grossen Volkskrankheiten des Mittelalters.* Berlin, 1865.

Heisig, Karl. "Eine gnostische Sekte im abendländischen Mittelalter," *Zeitschrift für Religions- und Geistesgeschichte,* XVI (1964), 271– 274.

Held, Gerrit. *Magie, Hekserij, en Toverij.* Groningen, 1950.

Hemphill, R. E. "Historical Witchcraft and Psychiatric Illness in Western Europe," *Proceedings of the Royal Society of Medicine,* LIX (1966), 891–902.

Hernandez, Ludovico. *Le Procès inquisitorial de Gilles de Rais, maréchal de France, avec un essai de réhabilitation.* Paris, 1921.

Höfler, Otto. *Kultische Geheimbünde der Germanen.* Frankfurt a/M, 1934.

Hoffman-Krayer, E. "Die Frau Faste," *Schweizerisches Archiv für Volkskunde,* XIV (1910).

————. "Die Hexe von Binzen," *Schweizerisches Archiv für Volkskunde,* XIV (1910).

————. "Luzerner Akten zum Hexen- und Zauberwesen," *Schweizerisches Archiv für Volkskunde,* III (1899).

Hole, Christina. *A Mirror of Witchcraft*. London, 1957. A book of readings.

——. "Winter Bonfires," *Folklore*, LXXI (1960), 217–227.

——. *Witchcraft in England*. London, 1945.

Hughes, Pennethorne. *Witchcraft*. London, 1952.

Hugon, Augusto, and Giovanni Gonnet. *Bibliografia valdese*. Torre Pellice, 1953.

Jaffé, Philipp, *Regesta pontificum romanorum*, 2d ed., 2 vols. Leipzig, 1885–1888.

Jaide, Walter. *Wesen und Herkunft des mittelalterlichen Hexenwahns im Lichte der Sagaforschung*. Leipzig, 1936.

James, Edwin O. *Prehistoric Religion*. New York, 1957.

——. *Sacrifice and Sacrament*. London, 1962.

——. *Seasonal Feasts and Festivals*. New York, 1962.

Jeanneret, Frédéric-Alexandre. *Les Sorciers dans le pays de Neuchâtel aux 15e, 16e, et 17e siècle*. Locle, 1862.

Jones, Alfred Ernest. *Nightmare, Witches, and Devils*. New York, 1931.

——. *On the Nightmare*. London, 1931.

Jones, J. J. *The Cauldron in Ritual and Myth*. Aberystwyth, 1923.

Kämpfen, Peter Joseph. *Hexen und Hexenprozessen im Wallis, nach bewährten Quellen bearbeitet und kritisch beleuchtet*. Stans, 1867.

Keenan, Mary E. "The Terminology of Witchcraft in the Works of Augustine," *Classical Philology*, XXXV (1940), 294–297.

Kelly, Henry A. *The Devil, Demonology, and Witchcraft: the Development of Christian Beliefs in Evil Spirits*. Garden City, 1968. Published in London (1968) as *Towards the Death of Satan: The Growth and Decline of Christian Demonology*.

Kerdaniel, Edouard-L. de. *Sorciers de Savoie*. Annecy, 1901.

Kiessling, Edith. *Zauberei in den germanischen Volksrechten*. Jena, 1941.

Kittredge, George Lyman. *Witchcraft in Old and New England*. Cambridge, Mass., 1929.

Klélé, J. *Hexenwahn und Hexenprozesse in der ehemaligen Reichsstadt und Landvogtei Hagenau*. Hagenau im Elsass, 1893.

Koch, Gottfried. *Frauenfrage und Ketzertum im Mittelalter: Die*

Frauenbewegung im Rahmen des Katharismus und des Walden-sertums und ihre sozialen Wurzeln (12.–14. Jahrhundert). Berlin, 1962.

Kocher, Ambros. "Regesten zu den solothurnischen Hexenprozessen (1466–1715)," *Jahrbuch für solothurnische Geschichte*, XVI (1943), 121–140.

König, Bruno Emil. *Hexenprozesse: Ausgeburten des Menschenwahns im Spiegel der Hexenprozesse und der Autodafés*. 2d ed. Schwerte/Ruhr, 1966.

Kretzenbacher, Leopold. " 'Berchten' in der Hochdichtung," *Zeitschrift für Volkskunde*, LIV (1958), 185–204.

——. "Totentänze im Südosten," *Jahrbuch des ostdeutschen Kulturrates*, VI (1959), 125–152.

Kulcśar, Zsuzsánna. *Eretnekmozgalmak a XI–XIV században*. Budapest, 1964.

Kurze, Dietrich. "Zur Ketzergeschichte der Mark Brandenburg und Pommerns vornehmlich im 14. Jahrhundert: Luziferianer, Putzkeller, und Waldenser," *Jahrbuch für Geschichte Mittel- und Ostdeutschlands*, XVI–XVII (1968), 50–94.

Kyll, Nikolaus. "Hexenprozesse im Bitburger Land," *Heimatkalendar für den Kreis Bitburg*, 1963. I have not seen this article.

Ladner, Gerhart B. "Homo Viator: Medieval Views on Alienation and Order," *Speculum*, XLII (1967), 233–259.

Lamothe-Langon, Etienne de. *Histoire de l'inquisition en France, depuis son établissement au XIIIe siècle . . . jusqu'en 1772, époque définitive de sa suppression*. 3 vols. Paris, 1829.

Langlois, Charles-V., "L'Affaire du cardinal Francesco Caetani," *Revue historique*, LXIII (1897).

Langton, Edward. *Essentials of Demonology: A Study of Jewish and Christian Doctrine, Its Origin and Development*. London, 1949.

——. *Good and Evil Spirits: A Study of the Jewish and Christian Doctrine, Its Origin and Development*. London, 1942.

——. *Satan, a Portrait: A Study of the Character of Satan through All the Ages*. London, 1946.

Lavanchy, Joseph-Marie. *Sabbats ou synagogues sur le bord du lac d'Annecy: Procès inquisitorial à St. Jorioz en 1477*. Annecy, 1896.

Lavaud, René, and René Nelli. "Débat de la sorcière et de son confesseur," *Folklore,* XIV (1951).

Lea, Henry Charles. *The History of the Inquisition of the Middle Ages.* 3 vols. New York, 1883. Reprinted, New York, 1955.

———. *Materials toward a History of Witchcraft.* 3 vols. Edited by Arthur Howland. Philadelphia, 1939. Reprinted, New York, 1957.

———. *Superstition and Force: Essays on the Wager of Law, the Wager of Battle, the Ordeal, and Torture.* 4th ed. Philadelphia, 1892.

Lederer, Wolfgang. *The Fear of Women.* New York, 1968.

Leff, Gordon. "Heresy and the Decline of the Medieval Church," *Past and Present,* XX (1961), 36–51.

———. *Heresy in the Later Middle Ages.* 2 vols. Manchester, 1967.

Legman, Gershom. *The Guilt of the Templars.* New York, 1966.

Lehrman, Nathaniel S. "Anti-Therapeutic and Anti-Democratic Aspects of Freudian Dynamic Psychiatry," *Journal of Individual Psychology,* XIX (1963), 167–181.

Lehugeur, Paul. *Histoire de Philippe le Long, Roi de France (1316–1322).* Paris, 1917.

Leigh, Dennis. "Recurrent Themes in the History of Psychiatry," *Medical History,* I (1957).

Lerner, Robert E. "The Uses of Heterodoxy: The French Monarchy and Unbelief in the Thirteenth Century," *French Historical Studies,* IV (1965), 189–202.

Lévi-Strauss, Claude. *Anthropologie structurale.* Paris, 1958. Translated by Claire Jacobson and Brooke Grundfest as *Structural Anthropology* (New York, 1963). Chap. 9: "The Sorcerer and His Magic."

Levron, Jacques. *Le Diable dans l'art.* Paris, 1935.

Lightbody, Charles W. *The Judgments of Joan: Joan of Arc, a Study in Cultural History.* Cambridge, Mass., 1961.

Linderholm, Emanuel. *De stora häxenprocesserna i Sverige.* Uppsala, 1918.

Lizerand, Georges, ed. *Le Dossier de l'affaire des Templiers.* Paris, 1923.

Luck, Georg. *Hexen und Zauberei in der römischen Dichtung.* Zürich, 1962.

McCasland, S. Vernon. *By the Finger of God: Demon Possession and*

Exorcism in Early Christianity in the Light of Modern Views of Mental Illness. New York, 1951.

McDonnell, Ernest W. *The Beguines and Beghards in Medieval Culture.* New Brunswick, N.J., 1954.

Macfarlane, Alan. *Witchcraft in Tudor and Stuart England.* New York, 1970.

McNeill, John T. "Folk-Paganism in the Penitentials," *Journal of Religion,* XIII (1933), 450–466.

Mager, Hans Wolfgang. *Inquisition und Hexenwahn.* Dresden, 1938. I have not seen this work.

Maillet, Henri. *L'Eglise et la répression sanglante de l'hérésie.* Liège, 1909.

Mair, Lucy. *Witchcraft.* New York, 1969.

Maisonneuve, Henri. "Le Droit romain et la doctrine inquisitoriale," in *Etudes d'histoire du droit canonique dédiées à Gabriel le Bras.* 2 vols. Paris, 1965. Pp. 931–942.

——. *Etudes sur les origines de l'Inquisition.* 2d ed. Paris, 1965.

Malinowski, Bronislaw. *Magic, Science, and Religion, and Other Essays.* Boston, 1948.

Mandrou, Robert. *Introduction à la France moderne, 1500–1640: Essai de psychologie historique.* Paris, 1961.

Manselli, Raoul. "L'Eresia del male," in *Coll. di storia diretta da Arsenio Frugoni,* vol. I. Naples, 1963.

Mansi, Johannes. *Sacrorum conciliorum nova, et amplissima collectio,* 2d ed. Paris–Arnheim–Leipzig, 53 vols. 1901–1927.

Martin, Edward J. *The Trial of the Templars.* London, 1928.

Martroye, F. "La Répression de la magie et le culte des gentils au IVe siècle," *Revue d'histoire de l'église de France,* IX (1930), 669–701.

Marwick, Maxwell G. *Witchcraft and Sorcery.* Baltimore, 1970.

Marx, Jean. *L'Inquisition en Dauphiné: Etude sur le développement et la répression de l'hérésie et de la sorcellerie du XIVe siècle au début du règne de François Ier.* Paris, 1914.

Masters, Robert E. L. *Eros and Evil: the Sexual Psychopathology of Witchcraft.* New York, 1962.

Matrod, H. "Les Bégards: Essai de synthèse historique," *Etudes franciscaines,* XXXVII (1925) 5–20; 146–168.

Maurice, Jules. "La Terreur de la magie au IVe siècle," *Revue historique de droit français et étranger,* VI (1927), 108–120.

Mayer, Anton. *Erdmutter und Hexe: Eine Untersuchung zur Geschichte des Hexenglaubens und zur Vorgeschichte der Hexenprozesse.* Munich and Freising, 1936.

Mayer, Ernst. *Geschworenengericht und Inquisitionsprozess: Ihr Ursprung dargelegt.* Munich and Leipzig, 1916.

Mellor, Alec. *La Torture: son histoire—son abolition—sa réapparition au XXe siècle.* Paris, 1949.

Menendez y Pelayo, Marcelino. *Historia de los heterodoxes españoles.* 3 vols. Madrid, 1880–1882. Vol. I, chap. 7: "Artes mágicas, hechicherías, y supersticiones en España desde el siglo VIII al XV." The *Historia* has since been reprinted many times and in variant forms.

Meunier, Georges. *Gilles de Rais et son temps.* Paris, 1949.

Michelet, Jules. *Satanism and Witchcraft.* New York, 1965. Translated from the French *La Sorcière* (Paris, 1862).

Michl, Johann. "Katalog der Engelnamen," in *Reallexikon für Antike und Christentum,* vol. V. Stuttgart, 1962. Pp. 200–239.

Middleton, John, ed. *Magic, Witchcraft, and Curing.* Garden City, 1967.

——. *Myth and Cosmos: Readings in Mythology and Symbolism.* Garden City, 1967.

Midelfort, H. C. Erik. "Recent Witch Hunting Research, or Where Do We Go from Here?" *The Papers of the Bibliographical Society of America,* LXII (1968), 373–420.

——. "Witchcraft and Religion in Sixteenth-Century Germany: The Formation and Consequences of Orthodoxy," *Archiv für Reformationsgeschichte,* LXII (1971), 266–278.

Monter, E. William. "Inflation and Witchcraft; the Case of Jean Bodin," in Theodore K. Rabb and Jerrold E. Siegel, eds., *Action and Conviction in Early Modern Europe.* Princeton, 1969.

——. "Trois historiens actuels de la sorcellerie," *Bibliothèque d'humanisme et Renaissance. Travaux et documents,* XXXI (1969), 205–213.

——. ed. *European Witchcraft.* New York, 1969. Readings with critical introductions. Essentially post-medieval.

———. "Witchcraft in Geneva, 1537–1662," *Journal of Modern History,* XLIII (1971), 179–204.

Moore, R. I. "The Origins of Medieval Heresy," *History,* LV (1970), 21–36.

Müller, Karl Otto. "Heinrich Institoris, der Verfasser des Hexenhammers, und seine Tätigkeit als Hexeninquisitor in Ravensburg im Herbst 1484," *Württemberg Vierteljahrshefte für Landesgeschichte,* XIX (1910).

Murray, Margaret. "Child-sacrifice among European Witches," *Man,* XVIII (1918).

———. *The Divine King in England.* London, 1954.

———. *The God of the Witches.* 2d ed. London, 1952.

———. *The Witch-Cult in Western Europe.* London, 1921.

Naselli, Carmelina. "Diavoli bianchi e diavoli neri nei leggendari medievali," *Volkstum und Kultur der Romanen,* XV (1941–1943).

Neumann, Eva G. *Rheinisches Beginen–und Begardenwesen.* Meisenheim, 1960.

Nickerson, Hoffman. *The Inquisition.* 2d ed. London, 1968.

Notestein, Wallace. *A History of Witchcraft in England from 1558 to 1718.* Washington, D.C., 1911.

Nugent, Donald. "The Renaissance and/of Witchcraft," *Church History,* XL (1971), 69–78.

Odorici, Federico. *Le Streghe di Valtellina e la santa inquisizione.* Milan, 1861. Only medieval case is Brescia, 1485.

Oesterreich, Traugott. *Possession, Demoniacal and Other: Among Primitive Races, in Antiquity, the Middle Ages, and Modern Times.* London and New York, 1930.

Palacky, Franz. *Ueber die Beziehungen und das Verhaeltnis der Waldenser zu den ehemaligen Sekten in Böhmen.* Prague, 1869.

Parkes, James. *The Conflict of the Church and the Synagogue: A Study in the Origins of Antisemitism.* London, 1934.

Parrinder, Geoffrey. *Witchcraft: European and African.* London, 1963.

Parry, Leonard A. *The History of Torture in England.* London, 1934.

Parsons, Anne. "Expressive Symbolism in Witchcraft and Delusion: A Comparative Study," *Revue internationale d'ethnopsychologie normale et pathologique,* I (1956), 99–119.

Patrides, C. A. "The Salvation of Satan," *Journal of the History of Ideas,* XXVIII (1967), 467–478.

Pellegrini, Lodovico. "L'inquisizione francescana sotto Alessandro IV (1254–1261)," *Studi francescani,* LXIV (1967), 73–100.

Perella, Nicholas James. *The Kiss Sacred and Profane: An Interpretive History of Kiss Symbolism and Related Religio-Erotic Themes.* Berkeley and Los Angeles, 1969.

Pernoud, Régine. *Joan of Arc by Herself and Her Witnesses.* New York, 1966.

——. *The Retrial of Joan of Arc: The Evidence at the Trial for Her Rehabilitation, 1450–1456.* New York, 1955.

Peuckert, Will-Erich. *Deutscher Volksglaube des Spätmittelalters.* Stuttgart, 1942.

——. *Geheimkulte.* Heidelberg, 1951.

——. "Hexen- und Weiberbünde," *Kairos,* II (1960), 101–105.

——. *Pansophie: Ein Versuch zur Geschichte der weissen und schwarzen Magie.* Stuttgart, 1936.

Pitangue, François. "Variations dramatiques du diable dans le théâtre français du moyen âge," in *Etudes médiévales offertes à Augustin Fliche.* Paris, 1954. Pp. 143–160.

Potthast, August. *Regesta pontificum romanorum.* 2 vols. Berlin, 1874–1875.

Pra, Mario dal. *Amalrico di Bena.* Milan, 1951.

Pratt, Antoinette Marie. *The Attitude of the Catholic Church towards Witchcraft and the Allied Practices of Sorcery and Magic.* Washington, D.C., 1915.

Pugh, Ralph B. *Imprisonment in Medieval England.* Cambridge, Eng., 1968.

Quicherat, Jules. *Procès de condamnation et de réhabilitation de Jeanne d'Arc dite la Pucelle.* 5 vols. Paris, 1841. Reprinted 1965.

Rau, Eric. *Le Juge et le sorcier, les sacrifices humaines.* Paris, 1957. I have not seen this work.

Régné, Jean. "La Sorcellerie en Vivarais et la répression inquisitoriale ou séculière du XVe au XVIIe siècle," in *Mélanges d'histoire offerts à M. Charles Bémont.* Paris, 1913.

Rehder, Johannes. "Hexenverbrennung," *Jahrbuch für Heimatkunde im Kreis Oldenburg, Holstein,* vol. V (1961), I have not seen this work.

Reinhard, J. R. "Burning at the Stake in Medieval Law and Literature," *Speculum,* XVI (1941), 186–209. Nothing specifically relating to witchcraft.

Reyes, Antonio. "La Confesión y la tortura en la historia de la Iglesia," *Rivista española de derecho canonico,* XXIV (1968).

Reymond, Maxime. "La Sorcellerie au Pays de Vaud au XVe siècle," *Schweizerisches Archiv für Volkskunde,* XII (1908).

Rhodes, Henry T. F. *The Satanic Mass.* London, 1954.

Ricoeur, Paul. *The Symbolism of Evil.* Boston, 1969.

Riegler, Ferdinand, *Hexenprozesse mit besonderer Berücksichtigung des Landes Steiermark.* Graz, 1926.

Riezler, Sigmund. *Geschichte der Hexenprozesse in Bayern: Im Lichte der allgemeinen Entwicklung dargestellt.* Stuttgart, 1896.

Rigault, Abel. *Le Procès de Guichard évêque de Troyes, 1308–1313.* Paris, 1896.

Riol, Jean-Laurent. *Dernières connaissances sur des questions cathares: Essai de critique historique.* Albi, 1964.

Ritter, Gerhard. "Zur Geschichte des häretischen Pantheismus in Deutschland im 15 Jahrhundert: Mitteilungen aus einer vatikanischen Handschrift," *Zeitschrift für Kirchengeschichte,* XLIII (1924), 150–159.

Rivière, Jean. "Le Marché avec le démon chez les Pères antérieurs à Saint Augustin," *Revue des sciences religieuses de l'Université de Strasbourg,* VIII (1928), 257–269.

——. "Mort et démon chez les Pères," *Revue des sciences religieuses,* X (1930).

Robbins, Rossell Hope. *The Encyclopedia of Witchcraft and Demonology.* New York, 1959.

——. "The Heresy of Witchcraft," *South Atlantic Quarterly,* LXV (1966), 532–543.

——. "The Imposture of Witchcraft," *Folklore,* LXXIV (1963), 545–564.

——. "Yellow Cross and Green Faggot," *Cornell Library Journal,* Winter, 1970.

Róheim, Géza. *Magic and Schizophrenia*. Bloomington, 1955.

Rose, Elliot. *A Razor for a Goat*. Toronto, 1962.

Rosen, Barbara. *Witchcraft*. London, 1970.

Rosen, George. "Dance Frenzies, Demoniac Possession, Revival Movements, and Similar So-Called Psychic Epidemics: An Interpretation," *Bulletin of the History of Medicine*, XXXVI (1962), 13–44.

———. "The Mentally Ill and the Community in Western and Central Europe during the Late Middle Ages and Renaissance," *Journal of the History of Medicine and Allied Sciences*, XIX (1964), 377–388.

———. "A Study of the Persecution of Witches in Europe as a Contribution to the Understanding of Mass Delusions and Psychic Epidemics," *Journal of Health and Human Behavior*, I (1960), 200–211.

Rosenberg, Alfons. *Engel und Dämonen: Gestaltwandel eines Urbildes*. Munich, 1967.

Rosenfeld, Hellmut. *Der mittelalterliche Totentanz*. Münster, 1954.

Rosenthal, Theodore, and Bernard Siegel. "Magic and Witchcraft: an Interpretation from Dissonance Theory," *Southwestern Journal of Anthropology*, XV (1959), 143–167.

Rudwin, Maximilian. *The Devil in Legend and Literature*. Chicago, 1931.

Runeberg, Arne. *Witches, Demons, and Fertility Magic: Analysis of Their Significance and Mutual Relations in West-European Folk Religion*. Helsinki: Societas Scientiarum Fennica Commentationes humanarum litterarum, vol. XIV, 1947.

Russell, Jeffrey Burton. *Dissent and Reform in the Early Middle Ages*. Berkeley and Los Angeles, 1965.

———. *Religious Dissent in the Middle Ages*. New York, 1970.

Schacher von Inwil, Joseph. *Das Hexenwesen in Kanton Luzern, nach den Prozessen von Luzern und Sursee, 1400–1675*. Lucerne, 1947.

Schade, Herbert. *Dämonen und Monstren: Gestaltungen des Bösen in der Kunst des Frühen Mittelalters*. Regensburg, 1962.

Schiess, Emil. *Die Hexenprozesse und das Gerichtwesen im Lande Appenzell im 15 bis zum 17 Jahrhundert*. Trogen, 1925.

Schirmer-Imhoff, Ruth. *Jeanne d'Arc: Verurteilung und Rechtfertigung, 1431–1456*. Cologne, 1956.

Schmidt, Eberhard. *Inquisitionsprozesse und Rezepten: Studien zur*

Geschichte des Strafverfahrens in Deutschland vom 13. bis 16. Jahrhundert. Leipzig, 1940.

Schmidt, Philipp. *Der Teufels- und Daemonenglaube in den Erzählungen des Caesarius von Heisterbach.* Basel, 1926.

Schneider, Heinrich. "Die Hexenliteratur-Sammlung der Cornell Universität in Ithaca, New York," *Hessische Blätter für Volkskunde,* XLI (1950), 196–208. An explanatory essay, not a catalog. There is no printed catalog to the Cornell collection, the card catalog to which is housed in the Rare Book Room of the Olin Library.

Schneweis, Emil, O.F.M. Cap. *Angels and Demons According to Lactantius.* Washington, D.C., 1944.

Schönach, L. "Zur Geschichte des ältesten Hexenprocesse in Tirol," *Forschungen und Mitteilungen zur Geschichte Tirols und Vorarlbergs,* I (1904).

Schottmueller, Conrad. *Der Untergang des Templerordens: Mit urkundlichen und kritischen Beträgen.* 2 vols. Berlin, 1887.

Schulze, W. A. "Der Vorwurf des Ritualmords gegen die Christen im Altertum und in der Neuzeit," *Zeitschrift für Kirchengeschichte,* LXV (1953–1954).

Schwab, Moïse. "Vocabulaire de l'angélologie d'après les manuscrits hébreux de la Bibliothèque Nationale," *Mémoires présentés à l'académie des inscriptions et belles-lettres,* vol. X (1897).

Schwager, Johann Moritz. *Versuch einer Geschichte der Hexenprozesse.* Berlin, 1784. Never completed, but one of the first efforts to write an historical account of the witch phenomenon.

Schwarzwälder, Herbert. "Die Geschichte des Zauber- und Hexenglaubens in Bremen," *Bremisches Jahrbuch,* XLVI (1959), 156–233; XLVII (1961), 99–142.

Scott, George Ryley. *The History of Torture throughout the Ages.* 2d ed. London, 1949.

Scott, Sir Walter. *Letters on Demonology and Witchcraft.* London, 1830.

Shannon, Albert C. "The Secrecy of Witnesses in Inquisitorial Tribunals and in Contemporary Secular Trials," in *Essays in Medieval Life and Thought Presented in Honor of Austin P. Evans.* New York, 1955.

Shriver, George H., "A Summary of 'Images of Catharism and the Historian's Task,'" *Church History*, XL (1971), 48–54.

Sinnighe, J. R. W. "De eerste heksenprocessen en heksenvervolgingen in Nederland, XVe eeuw," *Historia*, XV (1950), 170–173.

Smith, Timothy d'Arch. *A Bibliography of the Works of Montague Summers*. London, 1964.

Snell, Otto. *Hexenprozesse und Geistesstörung: Psychiatrische Untersuchungen*. Munich, 1891. An early effort at a psychological understanding of witchcraft.

Soldan, Wilhelm Gottlieb. *Geschichte der Hexenprozesse: Aus den Quellen dargestellt*. Stuttgart, 1843. 2d ed. by Heinrich Heppe, *Geschichte der Hexenprozesse*. Stuttgart, 1880. 3d ed. by Max Bauer, *Geschichte der Hexenprozesse*. 2 vols. Munich, 1912.

Spinetti, Vittorio. *Le Streghe in Valtellina: studio su vari documenti editi e inediti del secolo XV, XVI, XVII e XVIII*. Sondrio, 1903.

Stauffer, Marianne. *Der Wald: zur Darstellung und Deutung der Natur im Mittelalter*. Berne, 1959.

Stegemeier, Henri. *The Dance of Death in Folksong, with an Introduction on the History of the Dance of Death*. Chicago, 1939.

Storms, Godfrid. *Anglo-Saxon Magic*. The Hague, 1948.

Strack, Herman. *The Jew and Human Sacrifice*. New York, 1909.

Summers, Montague. *The Geography of Witchcraft*. London, 1927.

——. *The History of Witchcraft and Demonology*. London, 1926.

——. *A Popular History of Witchcraft*. London, 1937.

——. *The Vampire: His Kith and Kin*. London, 1928.

——. *The Vampire in Europe*. London, 1929.

——. *The Werewolf*. London, 1933.

——. *Witchcraft and Black Magic*. London, 1946.

Svoboda, Karel. *La Démonologie de Michel Psellos*. Brno, 1927.

Szendrey, A. "Hexe-Hexendruck," *Acta ethnographica hungarica*, IV (1955), 129–168.

Tantsch, Werner. "Meister Hämmerlein," *Beiträge zur Namenforschung*, VII (1956), 281–293.

Thomas, Keith. *Religion and the Decline of Magic*. London, 1971.

Thompson, Richard Lowe. *The History of the Devil, the Horned God of the West*. London, 1929.

Thompson, Stith. *Motif-Index of Folk Literature.* 2d ed. 6 vols. Bloomington, 1955–1958.

Thomson, John A. F. *The Later Lollards, 1414–1520.* London, 1965.

Thomson, Samuel H. "Pre-Hussite Heresy in Bohemia," *English Historical Review,* XLVIII (1933), 23–42.

Thorndike, Lynn. *A History of Magic and Experimental Science.* 8 vols. New York, 1923–1958.

——. "Magic, Witchcraft, Astrology, and Alchemy," chap. 22 of the *Cambridge Medieval History,* vol. VIII, pp. 660–686.

——. *The Place of Magic in the Intellectual History of Europe.* New York, 1905.

——. "Relations of the Inquisition to Peter of Abano and Cecco d'Ascoli," *Speculum,* I (1926).

——. "Some Medieval Conceptions of Magic," *The Monist,* XXV (1915), 107–139.

Thouzellier, Christine. *Catharisme et valdéisme en Languedoc à la fin du XIIe siècle et au début du XIIIe siècle.* 2d ed. Louvain, 1969.

——. *Hérésies et hérétiques.* Rome, 1969.

——. *Une Somme anti-cathare: Le Liber contra manichaeos de Durand de Huesca.* Louvain, 1964.

Tisset, Pierre, and Yves Lanhers. *Procès de condamnation de Jeanne d'Arc.* Paris, 1960.

Tobler, G. "Zum Hexenwesen in Bern," *Schweizerisches Archiv für Volkskunde,* II (1898), 59–60; IV (1900), 236–238.

Trachtenberg, Joshua. *The Devil and the Jews: The Medieval Conception of the Jew and Its Relation to Modern Antisemitism.* New Haven, 1943.

Tramer, M. "Kinder im Hexenglauben und Hexenprozess des Mittelalters. Kind und Aberglaube," *Acta Paedopsychiatrica: Zeitschrift für Kinderpsychiatrie,* XI (1945), 140–149, 180–187.

Trevor-Roper, Hugh. "Witches and Witchcraft: An Historical Essay," *Encounter,* XXXVIII (May, 1967), 3–25; (June, 1967), 13–34. Reprinted as "The European Witch-Craze of the Sixteenth and Seventeenth Centuries" in Trevor-Roper, *Religion, Reformation, and Social Change* (London, 1967), pp. 90–192. Reprinted again under the second title in Trevor-Roper, *The European Witch-Craze of the Sixteenth and Seventeenth Centuries and Other Essays* (New York, 1969), pp. 90–192.

Turmel, Joseph. *Histoire du Diable*. Paris, 1931.

Ullmann, Walter. "The Defence of the Accused in the Medieval Inquisition," *Irish Ecclesiastical Record*, LXXIII (1950), 481–489.

Van Baal, J. "Magic as a Religious Phenomenon," *Higher Education and Research in the Netherlands*, vol. VII (1963).

Van der Vekené, Emil. *Bibliographie der Inquisition*. Hildesheim, 1963.

Van Nuffel, Herman. "Le Pacte avec le diable dans la littérature médiévale," *Anciens pays et assemblées d'états*, XXXIX (1966), 27–43.

Verga, Ettore. "Intorno a due inediti documenti di stregoneria milanese del secolo XIV," *Rendiconti del Reale Istituto Lombardo di scienze e lettere*, series 2, vol. XXXII (1899).

Villeneuve, Roland. *Le Diable dans l'art*. Paris, 1957. Short and popular.

Villette, P. "La Sorcellerie à Douai," *Mélanges de science religieuse*, XVIII (1961), 123–173.

——. "La Sorcellerie dans le nord de la France, du milieu du XVe siècle à la fin du XVIIe siècle," *Mélanges de science religieuse*, XIII (1956), 39–62, 129–156.

Von Blankenburg, Wera. *Heilige und dämonische Tiere: Die Symbolsprache der deutschen Ornamentik im frühen Mittelalter*. Leipzig, 1943.

Vordemfelde, Hans. "Die Hexe im deutschen Volksmärchen," in *Festschrift Eugen Mogk zum 70. Geburtstag*. Halle a/S, 1924.

Wagner, Werner-Harald. *Teufel und Gott in der deutschen Volkssage*. Greifswald, 1930.

Wakefield, Walter, and Austin P. Evans. *Heresies of the High Middle Ages*. New York, 1969.

Walker, Daniel P. *Spiritual and Demonic Magic from Ficino to Campanella*. London, 1958.

Walther, Daniel. "A Survey of Recent Research on the Albigensian Cathari," *Church History*, XXXIV (1965), 146–177.

Waltzing, J.-P. "Le Crime rituel reproché aux chrétiens du IIe siècle,"

Bulletin de l'Académie royale des sciences, des lettres, et des beaux-arts de Belgique: Classe des lettres et des sciences morales. Brussels, 1925.

Waschnitius, Viktor. "Perht, Holda, und verwandte Gestalten. Ein Beitrag zur deutschen Religionsgeschichte," *Sitzungsberichte der kaiserlichen Akademie der Wissenschaft in Wien, philosophische-historisch Klasse,* vol. CLXXIV (1913).

Wax, Murray and Rosalie, "The Magical World View," *Journal for the Scientific Study of Religion,* I (1962), 179–188.

——. "The Notion of Magic," *Current Anthropology,* IV (1964), 495–518.

Webster, Hutton. *Magic: a Sociological Study.* Stanford, 1948.

Weigel, Oswald. *Geschichte der Hexenprozesse.* Leipzig, 1912. I have not seen this work.

Werner, Ernst. "Adamitische Praktiken im spätmittelalterlichen Bulgarien," *Byzantinoslavica,* XX (1959), 20–27.

——. "Die Bogomilen in Bulgarien: Forschungen und Fortschritte," *Studi medievali,* series 3, III (1962), 249–278.

——. "Die Entstehung der Kabbala und die südfranzösischen Katharer," *Forschungen und Fortschritte,* XXXVII (1963), 86–89.

——. "Ideologische Aspekte des deutsch-österreichischen Waldensertums im 14. Jahrhundert," *Studi medievali,* ser. 3, IV (1963), 217–237.

——. *Nachrichten über spätmittelalterliche Ketzer aus tschechoslovakischen Archiven und Bibliotheken.* Leipzig, 1963.

——. "Die Stellung der Katharer zur Frau," *Studi medievali,* ser. 3, II (1961), 295–301.

Wey, Heinrich. *Die Funktionen der bösen Geister bei den griechischen Apologeten des zweiten Jahrhunderts nach Christus.* Winterthur, 1957.

White, Lynn, Jr. "The Spared Wolves," *Saturday Review of Literature,* XXXVII (Nov. 13, 1954).

Williams, Charles. *Witchcraft.* London, 1941.

Wilson, Monica, "Witch Beliefs and Social Structure," *American Journal of Sociology,* LVI (1951) 307–313.

Winwar, Frances. *The Saint and the Devil: Joan of Arc and Gilles de Rais, a Biographical Study of Good and Evil.* New York, 1948.

"Witches and the Community: an Anthropological Approach to the History of Witchcraft," *Times Literary Supplement,* no. 3583, October 30, 1970. A critical review of some recent works.

Woeller, Waltraud. "Zur Geschichte des Hexenwahns und der Hexenprozesse in Deutschland," *Wissenschaftliche Zeitschrift der Humboldt-Universität zu Berlin: Gesellschafts- und sprachwissenschaftliche Reihe,* XII (1963), 881–894.

Woods, Barbara Allen. *The Devil in Dog Form: a Partial Type-Index of Devil Legends.* Berkeley and Los Angeles, 1959.

Wunderer, Richard (pseud. of F. Bernheim). *Erotik und Hexenwahn, eine Studie der Entstehung des Hexenwahns in der vorchristlichen Zeit bis zu den Pogromen unserer Vergangenheit.* Stuttgart, 1963.

Wyndham-Lewis, Dominic. *The Soul of Marshal Gilles de Rais.* London, 1952.

Yates, Frances A. *Giordano Bruno and the Hermetic Tradition.* London, 1964.

Zdekauer, Lodovico. "La Condanna di una strega (1250)," *Bulletino storico pistoiese,* XXVI (1924), 107–109.

Inдex

Adamites (14th and 15th centuries), 127, 141-142, 181, 224-225, 327 n. 21
Agen (1326), 329 n. 31
Agobard of Lyon (814-849), 82, 312 n. 33
Ahriman, 106-107
Air, as abode of demons, 54, 56, 112
Alan of Lille, treatise of (1190-1202), 126-127, 129, 131
Alberic of Brittany (1076-1096), 94
Albertus Magnus (1206-1280), 142, 144
Alchemy, 7, 9, 142, 262-263
Aldebert (8th century), 68-69, 87
Alexander IV (1254-1261), 153, 155-156, 171
Alexander V (1409-1410), 205
Alexander of Hales (1185-1245), 6-7, 146, 279
Alfonso de Spina, treatise of (1458-1460), 236, 348
Alpnach (1462), 339 nn. 43ff.
Amalric of Bena (d. 1206), 138
Amalricians, 138-140
Amiens, idolatry at (7th century), 304 n. 25
Ancyra, synod of (314), 76-77, 301 n. 12, 302 n. 19
Andermatt (1459), 339 nn. 43ff.
Angèle de la Barthe, trial of (1275), 164
Angels, names of, 66, 69, 223
Angermünde, Luciferans at (1336), 180

Angilramnus of Metz (d. 804), 309 n. 19
Animal masquerade, see January
Animals: as demons, 105, 111; as Devil, see Devil, as animal; eating of, 211, 213; as gods, 54-55, 105; as witches' helpers, 14
Annecy (1477), 249, 256, 339 nn. 43ff.
Anthropology, see Folklore
Antichrist, 109, 162
Antinomian heresy, see Heresy, antinomian
Apostolici (13th and 14th centuries), 141
Aquinas, Thomas (1225-1274), 143-144, 146, 148-149, 279
Aquitaine, heretics in (1018-1028), 86
Aristotelianism, 111, 115-116, 133, 142-144, 147, 171, 205, 227, 233, 321 n. 14, 337 n. 28
Arles: synod of (443-452), 301 n. 12; synod of (558-560), see Pelagius I
Artois (1459-1460), 239, 245, 248-251, 254, 279, 339 nn. 43ff.
Ascanio (1462), 339 nn. 43ff.
Astrology, 7, 9, 115, 142, 144
Augustine (354-430), 19, 56-57, 71, 92-93, 109-110, 114, 118, 125, 142, 148, 208, 284; and torture, 153
Austria, 328 n. 23; Luciferans in (14th century), 177-180, 198, 327 n. 19; see also Frederick III of Austria, Graz, Hinnisperg, Innsbruck, Krems,

379

INDEX

Austria (cont.)
St. Pölten, Salzburg, Styria, and Vintler, Hans
Auvergne, see Stephen of Bourbon
Auxerre: synod of (580), see Pelagius II; synod of (c. 600), 303 n. 21

Barcelona, witchcraft at: (1313), 329 n. 31; (1434), 256, 338 nn. 43ff.
Barrientos, Lope, treatise of (c. 1450), 347
Bartolo of Sassoferrato (1314-1357), 186
Basel: council of (1431), 234; werewolves at (1407), 333 n. 29; witchcraft at (1423), 211, 338 nn. 43ff.
Basil, St. (c. 380), 19
Basin, Bernard, treatise of (1482), 238, 350
Béarn (1448-1452), 339 nn. 43ff.
Beauvais, idolatry at (7th century), 304 n. 25
Bechis, see William de Bechis
Bede (8th century), reports sacrifices to demons, 306 n. 4
Bedford, wild men at (1402), 333 n. 29
Beghards and Beguines (13th and 14th centuries), 139, 177, 219, 224-225, 283
Behaim, Michael, treatise of (c. 1460), 348
Benandanti (16th century), 41-42, 82, 211, 213, 236, 332 n. 15
Benedict XII (1334-1342), 172-173, 186-187, 329 n. 31
Benevento, 74; synod of (1378), 204; witchcraft at (1427), 338 nn. 43ff.
Berghamstead or Berkhamstead, synod of (697), 305 n. 26
Berit, demon, 181, 187-188
Berkeley, witch of (1065), 98
Bern: trials at Simmenthal, near (1395-1405), 215-216; witchcraft at (1478), 339 nn. 43ff.
Bernard of Como, treatise of (1484-1487), 236, 350
Birds, 98, 216, 242, 260
Black mass, 24, 253, 296 n. 12

Blackness: animals, 99, 131, 147, 157, 160, 182, 188, 193, 196, 216-218, 237, 242, 246; clothing, 97, 119, 208-209, 216-218, 246; darkness of the underworld, 52, 84; eyes, 160; man, 87, 88, 97, 119, 191, 216-217, 245, 314 n. 49, 316 n. 5; origins of Devil as black man, 113-114, 217; skin, 14, 183
Bloodsucking, 15, 50, 53, 56, 59, 62, 70, 79, 97, 118, 132, 156, 207, 239, 251, 275, 316 n. 63
Boars, 242
Boats, 14, 95, 317 n. 10
Boccaccio (c. 1350), 193
Bogomils, 92, 108, 121-122, 312 n. 40, 318 n. 30
Bohemia, 231; Adamites in, 181, 224-225; Luciferans in, 177, 179, 327 n. 19; see also Žižka, John
Bologna (1462), 339 nn. 43ff.
Bonae mulieres (bonae res, "Good Society"), 23, 53, 70, 82, 117-118, 134-135, 156-157, 175-176, 213, 236, 246, 274, 279, 326 n. 14
Boniface, St. (680-755), 64-66, 68, 70, 306 n. 4, 307 n. 6, n. 8, n. 9
Boniface VIII (1294-1303), 187, 323 n. 36
Bordeaux (1453), 339 nn. 43ff.
Braga, synod of (572), 302 n. 19
Brandenburg: Luciferans in (14th century), 177, 180, 327 n. 19; witchcraft in (1338), 328 n. 25; see also Angermünde and Prenzlau
Brescia, trial of Maria la Medica at, see Maria la Medica
Bressuire (1475), 244-245, 250, 339 nn. 43ff.
Breviarium of Alaric II (506), 58, 61, 72, 303 n. 20, 305 n. 26
Briançon (1428-1447), 249, 338 nn. 43ff.
Bromyard, John (14th century), 176
Brooms, 14-15, 53, 164, 236, 240, 245, 252
Brownies, 52
Brunne, Robert (14th century), 171
Bucy-le-long, see Soissons
Bulls (animals), 163, 246, 250, 305 n. 27

Burchard of Worms, *Corrector* and *Decretum* of (1008-1012), 77-78, 80-82, 96, 311 n. 30, 312 nn. 31-32; text of, 291-293
Burgand (860-876), 83
Burning: of heretics, 88, 130, 149-151, 189, 204, 325 n. 6, 328 n. 25; of witches, 61, 69, 149-151, 159, 164, 184-186, 188-189, 204, 216, 321 nn. 20-21, 325 nn. 6-7; of witches in England, 204
Burr, George Lincoln, 28, 31-32, 298 n. 9

Cabala, 8, 12-13, 142
Caesarius of Arles (d. 542), 58, 303 n. 21
Caesarius of Heisterbach (c. 1200), 118-120, 126, 216
Cambrai: idolatry in (623-626), 304 n. 25; trial at (1411), *see* "Men of Intelligence"
Canavese (1474), 339 n. 43
Candlemas, 51
Cannibalism, 23, 50, 79, 90, 100, 275, 285; and Catharism, 125; in *Corrector* of Burchard, 81; Jews and, 132; origins of, 88-93, 199; at Orléans (1022), 88, 95; in other cultures, 14; in Salic Law, 59; 7th century, 61-62; 8th century, 67, 69-70; 15th century, 239, 251; *see also* Children, eating of
Canon Episcopi (c. 960), 75-80, 87, 219, 301 n. 12; as capitulary, 310 n. 26, 311 n. 27; cited by later writers, 96, 115, 117, 146-147, 156, 175-176, 205, 232, 234-235, 245, 279, 322 n. 15; text of, 291-293; *see also* Regino of Prüm
Capitulary: of 775-790, 69; of 802, 66, 82; of 805, 73; of Ansegis (827), 82; of Quierzy (873), 73, 311 n. 27
Carcassonne: trial at (1435), 338 nn. 43 ff.; trials at, in 14th century, 173, 177, 185-186, 219, 329 n. 31; witchcraft at (1335), 181-182, 198; *see also* Cassendi, Géraud; *and* Géraud, Hugues

Carpocratians, 91-92
Carthage, synods of (398 and 401), 301 n. 12
Cassendi, Géraud, tried at Carcassonne (1410), 209
Catharism, see *Gazarius; and* Heresy, Catharist
Catholic Church, modern position on witchcraft, 29
Cats, 91, 105, 126, 131, 147, 157, 159-161, 163, 188, 191, 196, 207, 216-219, 236-237, 240, 245-247, 260
Cauldrons, 69, 307 n. 11
Cavalcade of death, 96-97, 156; *see also* Wild chase
Châlons-sur-Marne, heretics at (1043-1048), 94
Châlons-sur-Saône (1452), 339 nn. 43ff.
Chamonix (1462), 339 nn. 43ff.
Charlemagne (768-814), 63-64, 66-67, 69
Charles IV (1322-1328), 172
Childebert I (511-558), 302 n. 19, 303 n. 20, 304 n. 22
Children: burning of, 88, 95; burning of, in Old Testament, 89; conceived at orgies, burning of, 87, 93, 250, 314 n. 49; eating of, by Greeks, 89; eating of, by Manichaeans, 125; eating of, by witches, 14, 86, 92-93, 95, 146, 164, 184-185, 216, 233, 239-240, 257, 286; made into magic salve or powder, 216-218, 233, 240, 250-252, 262; murder of, by Devil, 117, 156; murder of, by Gilles de Rais, 262-263; sacrifice of, by Christians, 90-92; sacrifice of, by heretics or witches, 23, 88, 92-93, 100, 116, 146, 167, 186, 216-217, 232, 239-240, 242, 251, 254, 257, 260, 262; sacrifice of, by Jews, 92, 132, 167; seldom accused as witches, 284; stealing of, 61, 92, 118, 132, 134, 216, 236
Chilperic II (d. 584), 304 n. 24
Clement IV (1265-1268), 155
Clement V (1305-1314), 195
Clermont, *see* Stephen of Bourbon
Clichy, synod of (626), 305 n. 26

Cloveshoh, synod of (747), 306 n. 3
Cohn, Norman, 320 n. 11
Coldness, *see* Devil, coldness of
Cologne: treatise written near (1415), 207; witch at (1074), 321 n. 20; witchcraft at (1325), 141
Como (1456), 339 nn. 43ff.
Conserans, riding with Diana at (1280), 164
Consolamentum, 222
Constantius II (337-361), 301 n. 12
Corpus hermeticum, 8
Corrector, see Burchard of Worms
Courts: episcopal, 228-229; Inquisitorial, *see* Inquisition; secular, 3, 150, 152-153, 174, 199, 204, 210-211, 214-215, 229, 244, 258-260, 286, 325 n. 6, 336
Coven, 24, 36, 192, 247
Cross, desecration of, *see* Desecration, of cross
Crossroads, 14, 156, 184

D'Ailly, Pierre (at Cambrai, 1411), 224
Damasus I (366-384), 301 n. 12
Dance: cult and mania of, 136-137, 186, 200-202, 272, 320 n. 7; of Joan of Arc, 261; widdershins, 249; of witches, 14, 23, 36, 48, 52, 58, 61, 68, 70, 74-75, 96, 175, 185, 218, 238, 249-250, 285
Dauphiné: and Gascony, witchcraft in (1458-1460), 339 nn. 43ff.; trial of Pierre Vallin at (1428), *see* Vallin, Pierre; trials at (1421-1447), 216-218, 247, 338 nn. 43ff.
Death penalty: for heresy, 71, 120, 149, 303 n. 20; for malefici, 72-73, 97; for witches, 54, 73, 186, 211, 219, 304 n. 24, 308 n. 15, 335 nn. 3-4; *see also* Burning
Decretum of Burchard, *see* Burchard of Worms
Definition of witchcraft, 3-4, 16-17, 23-24, 27, 230
Délicieux, Bernard, trial of (1319), 194
Delort, Catherine, trial of (1335), 182-185

Demons: and angels, 68-69, 77, 82, 105-109, 111-112; as animals, 53, 116, 188; and animistic spirits of nature (little men), 52-53, 101, 103-105, 111, 217; distinction of, from Devil, *see* Devil; as God, 328 n. 23, n. 25; as gods, *see* Gods; names of, 111, 184; origin of, 13, 18, 103-104; physical appearance of, 86, 99, 109, 119, 188, 214, 216-217; power of, 112-113; sacrifice to, *see* Sacrifice to demons; Teutonic and Celtic ideas of, 110-111; as women, *see* Women; worship of, 16-17, 60-61, 65, 100, 147, 155, 173, 206-208; worship of, distinguishing between dulia and latria, 206, 208; *see also* Familiars
Desecration: of cross, 23, 86-88, 94-95, 100, 125, 186, 195, 218, 229, 241, 252-253, 257; of Eucharist, 87, 92, 129, 161-162, 167-168, 251-252, 296 n. 12, 319 n. 32, 324 n. 2; of sacraments in general, 23, 94, 100, 125, 180, 185, 187, 192, 233, 240-241, 252-253, 261, 278, 329 n. 31
Devil: as angel of light, 56, 77, 175; as animal, 105, 113, 188, 250; as black man, *see* Blackness; Catharist view of, 124-125; coldness of, 20, 239, 246, 250, 255, 285; distinction of, from demons, 18, 103-104, 107; growth of power of, in 12th and 13th centuries, 101-102, 111; hairiness of, 161, 163, 246, 275; horns of, 111, 113, 214, 246; in human form, 113, 117, 175, 183, 213, 216, 246; instruments used by, 114-115, 191; Devil's mark, 23, 218, 232, 242-243, 255; as monster, 110, 112-113, 246-247; origin of, 104-110; origin of name, 103; paleness of, *see* Pallidity; sacrifice to, *see* Sacrifice; shining body or clothing of, 161, 179, 218; worship of, 18, 24, 41, 72, 74, 80, 87, 125, 130, 132, 144, 147, 175, 178, 184, 194, 209-210, 216, 222-223, 235, 241, 253-255, 260, 277

Diana, 23, 55, 96, 115-116, 157, 213; attributes of, 47-49, 275; as Devil, 80, 235; ride with, *see* Ride; worship of, 41, 52, 57-58, 60-62, 245, 302 n. 17, 303 n. 21, 305

Digest of Justinian, 152-153

Dijon, trial at (1470-1471), 249

Dionysos, 47, 88-89

Divination, 7, 9, 15-16, 54, 115, 208, 215

Dogs, 90-91, 105, 191, 216, 237, 245-246, 260

Dolcino (14th century), 200

Dolls, waxen, 215

Dominicans as Inquisitors, 155, 221, 230-231, 260

Dondaine, Antoine, 127

Donkey (ass), 73, 98, 105, 163, 211-212, 247; sacred to witches, 89; as sexual athlete, 89; *see also* Mules

Doors, passing through, 81-82, 157, 237, 246

Draguignan (1439), 338 nn. 43ff.

Drugs, 38, 54, 344 n. 20

Ducks, 160

Dwarves, 52

Eauze, synod of (551), 302 n. 19

Ebendorfer, Thomas, treatise of (1439), 241, 346

Edmund, Earl of Kent, accused of witchcraft (1330), 194

Edolo, near Brescia (1455), 339 nn. 43ff.

Edric the Wild, 116

Edward II (1307-1327), 173, 194-195

Ehingen, witch at (1322), 167, 186

Elves, 13, 18, 52, 101, 111, 118, 175

Elvira, synod of (c. 300), 301 n. 12

Elyaphres, story of, in *Parzival* (1331-1336), 193

England, 40, 267-268; burning of witches in, *see* Burning; growth of witchcraft in, 40; laws of Anglo-Saxons against magic, 73, 97, 305 n. 26, 308 n. 17; letter of Formosus to the English bishops, 309 n. 18; paganism in, 309 n. 18; witchcraft in (1311), 329 n. 31; *see also* Bede; Bedford; Berghamstead; Berkeley; Bromyard, John; Brunne, Robert; Cloveshoh; Edmund, Earl of Kent; Edward II; Gervaise of Tilbury; Hereford; Lollards; Michel of Kent; Penitential Books; Perrers, Alice; Tannere, John; Tresilian, Robert; Walter, Bishop of Lichfield and Coventry; *and* William of Newburgh

Enoch, books of, 108, 178

Errores Gazariorum (c. 1450), 238-242, 347

Erwic, laws of (7th century), 305 n. 25

Etampes: Marigny, near (1323), 329 n. 31

Eucharist, *see* Desecration

Euchites, 92-93, 314 n. 49

Eudo of Brittany (1148), 95

Eugenius IV (1431-1447), 220, 229-230, 256, 336 n. 8

Evil, concept: of Christians, 108-110; of Jews, 105-108

Evil eye, 14, 185

Evreux (1453), 339 nn. 43ff.

Eymeric, Inquisitor in Aragon (1320-1393), 206, 231, 326

Factura, 16, 332 n. 24, 340 n. 57, 341 n. 59

Faido (1457-1459), 339 nn. 43ff.

Fairies, 13-14, 18, 52, 101, 103, 111, 118, 187, 191, 261

Falaise (1456), 339 nn. 43ff.

Familiars, 14, 23, 37, 52-53, 98, 197, 217-218, 232; definition of, 187; names of, 53, 111, 187, 191, 215, 217, 255-256; relationship of Devil to, 255-256; shapes of, 188, 191, 223, 243

Fasciculus morum (1320), 175

Fathers, views of: on demons, 109-110; on orgies, 90-93

Faust, 19

Feast of Fools, 47, 51-52, 210

Feasting, 23, 52, 60, 62, 68, 70, 99-100, 157, 193, 223, 232, 238, 249, 285, 312 n. 38; psychology of, 285-286

Fences, 53, 79

Ferrara (1471-1505), 339 nn. 43ff.

Fertility cults, 36, 48, 51-52, 61, 80, 105, 113, 158, 164, 213, 268-269; in Friuli (16th century), 41-42, 58-59, 81

Festivals: Christian, 50-52; pagan, 58-59, 67-68, 74-75, 300 n. 5; see also Fire, festivals

Filippo da Siena (1339-1442), 209

Finicella, tried at Rome (1424), 216

Fire, 89, 184; festivals, 50-52; ordeal by, 150; symbolism of, 150, 322 n. 26; see also Burning and Needfire

Flagellants, 126, 137-138, 164, 176-177, 200-201, 272, 327 n. 18

Flight, 20, 23, 53-54, 56, 70, 75, 79, 119-120, 132, 199; in Burchard, 82; of cloud ships, 82-83; in Dauphiné, 218; in the Eddas, 75; first picture of witch flying on a broom (1280), 164; in Gervaise of Tilbury, 117-118; and heresy, 130; in Malleus, 233; at Mont-Aimé (1239), 163; in other cultures, 14; in Passavanti, 176; of Pierina, 213; in Salic Law, 59; salve used for, 216, 218, 236, 240, 245, 252; scholastic view of, 115, 146-147; in Stephen of Bourbon, 156; alleged of Waldensians, 219; in 13th century, 134; in 15th century, 234, 236, 245; see also Ride

Florence, see Marta

Folklore, 2, 21, 25, 32-37, 40-42, 101, 175, 199, 217, 238, 262, 297 n. 14

Formosus (891-896), see England

Fortalicium Fidei (1464), 234

France: witchcraft in (1438-1458), 338 nn. 43ff.; see also Agen; Agobard of Lyon; Alan of Lille; Alberic of Brittany; Aldebert; Amalric of Bena; Amiens; Angèle de la Barthe; Angilramnus of Metz; Aquitaine; Arles; Artois; Auxerre; Béarn; Beauvais; Bordeaux; Bressuire; Briançon; Burgand; Cambrai; Carcassonne; Cassendi, Géraud; Châlons-sur-Marne; Châlons-sur-Saône; Chamonix; Charlemagne; Charles IV; Childebert I; Chilperic II; Clichy; Conserans; Dauphiné; Délicieux, Bernard; Delort, Catherine; Dijon; Draguignan; Eauze; Etampes; Eudo of Brittany; Evreux, Falaise; Fréjus; Gaetani, Francesco; Georgel, Anne-Marie de; Géraud, Hugues; Gerson, Jean; Gévaudan; Gilles de Rais; Gregory of Tours; Gui, Bernard; Gui, Pierre; Guichard of Troyes; Halfedanges; Henricians; Isère; Jacquier, Nicholas; Joan of Arc; Jubertus; Langres; Latilly, Jeanne and Pierre de; Leptinnes; Leutard; Louis X; Lyon; Mâcon; Mamoris, Peter; Marigny, Enguerrand de; Martin le Franc; Matilda of Artois; Maximus of Tours; Mirepoix; Mont-Aimé; Nantes; Narbonne; Nivernais; Orléans; Pamiers; Paris; Pastoureaux; Penitential Books; Peter of Bruys; Philip IV; Pons; Provins; Radegunda; Recordi, Peter; Reims; Robert of Artois; Robert le Bougre; Rouen; Sens; Severian; Soissons; Stephen of Bourbon; Templars; Thérouanne; Tinctoris, Johannes; Torcy; Toulouse; Tournai; Tours; Vallin, Pierre; Valois kings; Vincent, Jean; and Vineti, Jean

Francis of Florence, treatise of (1472-1473), 349

Franciscans as Inquisitors, 155

Frankfurt, council of (794), 306 n. 3

Frankish council (747), 306 n. 3

Fraticelli, 139, 213, 243, 250

Frederick II (1212-1250), 151, 323 n. 36

Frederick III of Austria (1325-1326), 188-189

Free Spirit, 140-141, 224, 283

Fréjus: alleged witchcraft in (1318), 326 n. 16; witches in (1338), 187

Fribourg, witches at: (1399), 220; (1438-1482), 338 n. 43

Friuli: Portagruaro, in (1339), 209

Frogs, see Toads

Gabrina Albetti, tried at Reggio (1375), 209-210

Gaetani, Francesco, tried under Louis X (1314-1316), 172

Galateo, Antonio, treatise of (1480), 349

Garcia, Pedro, treatise of (1480-1489), 349-350

Gazarius, 15, 235, 243, 317 n. 19; see also Errores Gazariorum

Geese, 160

Geneva: Jeannette, at (1401), 209

Geographical spread, 268-269

Georgel, Anne-Marie de, trial of (1335), 182-185

Géraud, Hugues, burned (1316), 325 n. 7

Gerbert of Aurillac (Sylvester II, 999-1003), 19, 70-71, 86

Germany: heretics in (1150-1160), 129; synod of 742, 306 n. 3; see also Angermünde; Austria; Behaim, Michael; Bohemia; Brandenburg; Burchard of Worms; Cologne; Ebendorfer, Thomas; Ehingen; Frankfurt; Frankish council; Free Spirit; Hamburg; Hartlieb, Johann; Herolt, Johann; Hildesheim; Hinnisperg; Holland; Indiculus superstitionum; Institoris, Heinrich; Jauer, Nicholas von; Johann von Frankfurt; Kemnat, Mathias Uridman von; Konrad of Marburg; Lepzet; Lorraine; Luckard; Magdeburg; Malleus Maleficarum; Metz; Neuching; Nider, Johann; Pactus Alamannorum; Paderborn; Parzival; Penitential Books; Prenzlau; Regensburg; Regino of Prüm; Salic Law; Sint-Truiden; Sprenger, Jakob; Stedingers; Tanchelm; Theuda; Torrenbüren; Trier; Vötting; Westphalia; and Wunschilburg, Johann

Gerson, Jean, treatise on spirits (1415), 207-208

Gervaise of Tilbury, writer (1214), 117-118

Gévaudan (1347), 329 n. 31

Ghent (1128), 321 n. 20

Ghosts, 50, 52, 79, 184, 212

Giants, 96-97, 108, 119

Gifts, left for spirits or bonae, 70, 82-83, 116, 118, 157, 207, 303-304 n. 21

Gilles de Rais, trial of (1440), 262-263

Ginzburg, Carlo, 41-42, 211, 236, 268

Gnosticism, 8, 45, 69, 91-92, 108, 121-122, 129

Goats, 105, 183-185, 211, 236-237, 242, 245-247, 255, 340 n. 51

Gods: and angels, 66; as demons, 13, 46-48, 58, 60, 103, 109-110; worship of, 57-58, 61, 73-74, 95-96, 99, 156, 302 n. 19

"Good Society," see Bonae mulieres

Gratian, Decretum of (c. 1140), 57, 96, 153-154

Graz (1115), 321 n. 21

Green: as color of witchcraft, 14; men, 51-52

Gregory I, the Great (590-604): letters of, 302 n. 19, 303 nn. 20, 21; and torture, 153

Gregory IX (1227-1241), 151; bulls of 1231-1233, 160-162, 323 n. 40; and the origin of the Inquisition, 155

Gregory XI (1370-1378), 173, 204

Gregory of Tours (6th century), 57

Grimoires, 142

Guaineri, Antonio (1410-1440), treatise of, 206-207

Guglielma, 13th century heretic, 141

Gui, Bernard, author of Practica (c. 1320), 174-175, 206

Gui, Pierre, Inquisitor (1335), 182

Guichard of Troyes, trial of (1308-1313), 194

Halfedanges (1372), 209

Hallowe'en, 1, 14, 50-51, 248

Hamburg (1482), 339 nn. 43ff.

Hand, Wayland, 52, 86, 296 nn. 13, 14

Hansen, Joseph, 24, 27, 33-34, 39, 53, 119–120, 133, 144, 150, 194, 199-200, 220, 268, 298 n. 5

Hartlieb, Johann, treatise of (1456), 347

Hecate, see Diana

Hell, 104, 109-110, 150

Henricians (c. 1116), 95

Herbs, 16, 59, 116, 240, 280

Hereford, idolatry in (1410), 209

Heresy, 19, 21, 23, 25, 39, 65, 79, 100, 120, 132, 155-156, 173-176, 200, 219-223, 266-269, 272; antinomian, 26, 94, 128, 138-142, 159-163, 167, 177, 223-225, 238, 254, 283, 320 n. 11; Catharist, 25, 101, 108, 111, 120-132, 138, 140, 151, 154-155, 159, 162-163, 177-178, 183, 196, 208, 219-223, 237, 252, 273, 282, 318 nn. 30, 31; Reformist, 25, 55, 63-65, 71, 82, 85-88, 94-95, 121, 139-140, 159; witchcraft defined as, 228-233, 235, 238, 241, 248, 340 n. 59; see also Fraticelli *and* Waldensians

Heretics, blamed for slandering Christians, 90

Herne the Hunter, leader of the wild chase (Harlequin, Hellequin, Herla, Herlechin, Hillikin, Berchtold, Berhtolt, Berndietrich), 49, 97, 117, 300 n. 4, 333 n. 30

Herodias: as ruler of one-third of world, 310 n. 25; see also Ride, of Diana

Herolt, Johann, sermon of (1400), 206

Hildesheim, synod of (1224), 159

Hinnisperg (c. 1315), 179

Historiography, 27-43

Holland (1467, 1472), 339 nn. 43ff.

Homage: to chief of wild chase, 211-212; to Devil or demons, 18-19, 24, 87, 119, 174, 194, 216-218, 229, 233, 242, 254-255, 257, 260, 325 n. 5

Homosexuality, 95, 141, 161-162, 180, 219, 239, 250; of Templars, 195-197

Honorius, emperor, law of (415), 301 n. 12

Honorius III (1216-1227), 151

Horns, see Devil *and* Jews

Hulda, fertility goddess (Abundia, Befana, Befania, Berhta, Berta, Epiphania, Faste, Hilde, Holda, Holle, Holt, Perchta, Pharaildis, Satia, Selda, Venus), 49, 81, 135, 146, 211

Hungary, 97; law code of Kulm (1390), 204

Idolatry, 58, 60-61, 65-66, 73, 78, 94, 96, 175, 209-210, 241-242, 257, 302 n. 19, 304 n. 25, 305 n. 26; of Templars, 196-197

Incantation, 9, 16, 18, 70, 72-73, 78, 95, 185, 207, 233

Incest: alleged of Christians, 89-92; of Luciferans, 162; at orgies, 129, 141, 285

Incubi, 23, 59, 61, 70, 75, 115-119, 145, 164, 183, 192, 207, 230, 232, 237, 239, 246, 250, 285

Indiculus superstitionum (744), 66-67, 306 n. 6, 307 n. 8

Initiation, 161-162, 239-242, 249; of Templars, 195, 197

Innocent III (1198-1216), 122, 151, 154

Innocent IV (1243-1254), 323 n. 36; and bull *Ad Extirpanda* (1252), 153, 155

Innocent VIII (1484-1492), 229-230

Innsbruck (1485), 339 nn. 43ff.

Inquisition: definition of witchcraft by, 19-20, 23, 26, 212; evaluation of, 3, 124, 167; foundation of, 25, 133, 153-155; invention of witchcraft by, 20, 22, 30, 32-33, 35, 39-40, 42, 133, 216, 223-224; jurisdiction of, 204-205, 228-232; manuals of, 155-156, 174; papal support of, 229-230; procedure of, 42-43, 155-156, 158-159, 168, 170, 174-175, 231, 257, 322 n. 24, 323 n. 36; social psychology of, 286-288; and torture, see Torture; used for political purposes, 172

Institoris, Heinrich (15th century), 205, 230-231, 283, 336 n. 12; see also *Malleus Maleficarum*

Interlaken (1424), 202, 338 nn. 43ff.

Inverkeithing, priest of (1282), 164

Invisibility, 216

Invocation of demons, 23, 62, 66, 92, 96, 118-119, 126, 149, 155-156, 173-174, 181, 186, 194, 196, 204, 206-209, 214-216, 241, 253, 257, 260-262, 305 n. 26, 307 n. 7, 326 n. 11, 328 n. 25, 329 n. 31

Ireland: penitentials of, 60; synod (800), 75; synods (5th century), 56, 301 n. 13; *see also* Kyteler, Alice

Isère: witches at Valpute, near (1395), 210

Isidore of Seville (7th century), 61, 305 n. 26

Islam, 196

Italy: witchcraft in (1460), 339 nn. 43ff.; witchcraft in (1467-1480), 399 nn. 43ff.; *see also* Ascanio; Benandanti; Benevento; Bernard of Como; Boccaccio; Bologna; Brescia; Canavese; Como; Dolcino; Edolo; *Errores Gazariorum;* Faido; Ferrara; Filippo da Siena; Finicella; Francis of Florence; Friuli; Gabrina Albetti; Galateo, Antonio; Garcia, Pedro; Ginzburg, Carlo; Guaineri, Antonio; Guglielma; Joachim of Flora; Jordanes de Bergamo; Lombardy; Maria la Medica; Marta; Milan; Monforte; Novara; Oldrado da Ponte; Passavanti; Pavia; Perugia; Pierina de' Bugatis; Pistoia; Politiani, Angelus; Porlezza; Raphael of Pornasio; Rome; Sardinia; Savoy; Segarelli, Gerard; Sibillia; Siena; Socinus, Marianus; Todi; Ugolini, Zanchino; Venice; Verona; Vignate, Ambrose de'; Vilgard of Ravenna; Visconti, Galeazzo, Girolamo, *and* Matteo; *and* William de Bechis

Ivo of Chartres, 96, 154

Ivois, *see* Trier

Jacquier, Nicholas, treatise of (1458), 235, 238, 241-243, 348

January, festival and animal masquerade on first of, 51-52, 58, 61, 67, 74-75, 303 n. 21, 305 n. 27, 307 n. 8, 310 n. 22, 312 n. 32

Jauer, Nicholas von, *Treatise on Superstitions* (1405), 206, 208

Jehanne de Brigue, *see* Paris, witchcraft at (1390-1391)

Jews: accused of slandering Christians, 90; ancient, and witchcraft, 54; angels of, 69; attacked by Agobard of Lyon (814-849), 82; as heretics, 174; and horns, 316 n. 3; and human sacrifice, 89; linked with witchcraft, 17, 167-168, 199, 237, 249, 269; and magic, 61; persecution of, 137, 171, 198, 286-287; poisoning alleged against, 181; sacrifice of children by, *see* Children

Joachim of Flora (12th century), 128, 131, 137-138, 140-141, 185, 222

Joan of Arc, trial of (1431), 261-262

Johann von Frankfurt, treatise of (1412), 206-207

Johannes Andreae (canonist), 174

John XII, accused of sorcery (963), 309 n. 19

John XXII (1316-1334), 172-174, 181, 194, 325 nn. 7ff., 326 n. 12

Jordanes de Bergamo, treatise of (1470-1471), 237, 242, 349

Jubertus, trial of (1437), 251-252, 254

Justin Martyr, 90, 93

Kelly, Henry A., 16

Kemnat, Mathias Widman von, treatise of (c. 1475), 349

Kiss: of bread, 222; of foot, 344 n. 22; obscene, 24, 126-127, 129-132, 147, 159-161, 194, 217, 219, 232, 242-243, 254-255; obscene, of Templars, 195-196; psychology of obscene, 279, 285-286

Kobolds, 18, 52, 101, 103, 111, 187

Konrad of Marburg (13th century), 138, 155, 159-160, 321 n. 19

Krems, Luciferans at (1315), 177, 179

Kyteler, Alice, trial of (1324), 189-193

La Tour du Pin, *see* Vallin, Pierre

Ladner, Gerhart, 125-126

Lamia, lama, 15, 53, 59, 61, 75, 117-118, 207, 235, 301

Langres, synod of (1404), 204

Laodicea, synod of (343-381), 301 n. 12, 302 n. 19

Lateran (Fourth Lateran Council, 1215), 154

Latilly, Jeanne and Pierre de, tried under Louis X (1314-1316), 172
Law: and magic, 56, 60-61, 64, 66, 71-73, 204, 301 nn. 12ff., 303 n. 20, 304 n. 23; Roman, 55; and witchcraft, 59, 61-62, 72, 148-151; see also England
Lea, Henry Charles, 24, 27, 30-32, 133, 150, 181, 268, 308 n. 15
Lepers, 168, 181, 269, 324 n. 2
Leptinnes, synod of (744), 66, 307 n. 9
Lepzet, heretic at Cologne (c. 1240), 161-163, 324 n. 41
Leutard, heretic at Châlons-sur-Marne (c. 1000), 86
Lights, extinction of, at orgies, 87, 90, 92-94, 126-127, 129-131, 161-162, 179, 191, 223, 250, 314 n. 48
Lilith, 105
Locarno (1455), 339 nn. 43ff.
Lollards (15th century), 244
Lombard council (786), 306 n. 3
Lombardy: trials of 1387-1388 in, 220-224; witchcraft in (1412), 334 n. 35
Lorraine (1456-1457), 339 nn. 43ff.
Louis X (1314-1316), 172
Lucerne: trial at (1419), 202; witchcraft at (1450, 1454, 1477, 1480), 339 nn. 43ff.
Lucifer (Lucibel, Lucifel, Luzabel), 108, 130, 147, 158, 178-180, 210, 213, 215, 217, 254; as true God, 159, 162-163; see also Devil
Luciferans, 94, 141-142, 177-181, 327 nn. 19ff., 328 n. 23
Lucius III (1181-1185), 151, 154
Luckard, witch at Trier (1231), 159
Lynching, see Mob violence
Lyon (1460), 248, 251, 339 nn. 43ff., 350

Maastricht, necromancer at (1234), 163
Maastricht, St. Amand of (7th century), 304 n. 25
Macète de Ruilly, see Paris, witchcraft at (1390-1391)
Mâcon (1437), 338 nn. 43ff.
Magdeburg (1336), 328 n. 25

Magic: definition of, 4, 10, 296 n. 3, by University of Paris (1398), 202; and Devil, 71-72; and heresy, 208, 215; high, 5-13, 70-71, 86, 115, 142-144, 228, 254; low, 6-7, 13-17, 23, 59-60, 62, 65, 78, 83, 191, 308 n. 14; Oresme's distinction between natural and demonic, 171; and religion, 10-11; and science, 11-12; sociology of, 296 n. 5; white and black, 6, 144
Magical world view, 4-13, 25
Maleficium, 54, 183-184, 209, 228, 235, 240, 251, 257; definition of, 7, 13, 15, 65, 71; as secular crime, 71
Malleus Maleficarum (1485-1486), 7, 25, 29, 145, 205, 228, 230-233, 243, 279, 283, 336 n. 12
Mamoris, Peter, treatise of (1461-1462), 236-238, 348
Manichaeans, 92, 106, 122, 125, 208
Map, Walter (12th century), 116-117, 129-131
Marcionites, 90
Margot de la Barre, see Paris, witchcraft at (1390-1391)
Maria la Medica, trial of (1480), 250, 253, 260-261, 339 nn. 43ff.
Marigny, Enguerrand de, tried under Louis X (1314-1316), 172
Marion la Droiturière, see Paris, witchcraft at (1390-1391)
Marta, witch at Florence (1375), 210
Martin V, bull of (1418), 205
Martin of Arles, treatise of (1460-1515), 237, 348-349
Martin le Franc, author of Champion des dames (1440), 238, 282, 346
Masca, or talamasca, 15, 116-117, 235, 341 n. 59
Matilda of Artois, tried for magic and poison (1317), 172
Maximus of Tours (5th century), 57
May Day, 51, 74
"Men of Intelligence," at Cambrai (1411), 224
Messalians, 92-93, 108
Metz (1456-1457), 339 nn. 43ff.
Michel of Kent, 325 n. 5
Midsummer Eve, 51, 248

Milan, witchcraft at: (1370), 210; (1384-1390), 211; (1463-1464), 339 nn. 43ff.
Millenarianism, 138-139, 185
Minneke, Heinrich (1224), 159
Mirepoix (1337), 329 n. 31
Mithraism, 51, 106
Mob violence, 61, 64, 73, 83, 148, 164, 286, 321 n. 20, 335 n. 6
Monforte, heretics at (1028), 94, 151, 221
Mont-Aimé, trial of Catharists at (1239), 163
Montanists, 91-92
Monter, E. William, 288
Motifs in other societies, 13-15
Mountains, alleged origin of witchcraft in, 199-200, 220, 228, 268-269
Mules, 75, 84, 85
Murder, by witches, 162, 210; see also Children, sacrifice of
Murray, Margaret, 21-22, 30, 32, 36-37, 39-41, 61, 164, 190, 192, 261, 268, 299 nn. 17-18, 308 n. 14, 309 n. 18
Murten (Morat, 1482), 339 nn. 43ff.
Mythological origins, 273-275

Names given witches, 15-16, 65, 297 n. 15, 337 n. 16, 340 n. 59
Nantes, synod of (658), 304 n. 25
Narbonne, synod of (589), 303 n. 20
Necromancy, 9, 16, 85, 120, 163, 187-188
Needfire, 51
Neoplatonism, 8, 111-112, 129, 143, 205, 227, 233-234, 321 n. 14, 337 n. 28
Neuchâtel, witchcraft at: (1430-1439), 255, 338 nn. 43ff.; (1481), 249, 339 nn. 43ff.
Neuching, synod of (772), 306 n. 3
Nicholas I (858-867), 153
Nicholas V (1447-1455), 229
Nider, Johann (c. 1380-1438), 235-239, 256, 279, 346
Night, as time for witch activities, 14, 23, 56, 59, 62, 70, 75-79, 87, 92, 99-100, 115, 125, 129, 135, 147, 192, 208, 237, 247-248, 328 n. 25
Nivernais (1438), 338 nn. 43ff.

Noon, 119
Notker Balbulus, story of pact by (883), 84
Novara, Lombardy (c. 1335), 186
Nudity, 14, 157, 181, 210, 224-225, 254, 260

Obscene kiss, see Kiss
Odin, 48-49, 67
Oldrado da Ponte (14th-century jurist), 174
Orgies, 23, 100, 145, 147, 196, 208, 232, 277; in Aquitaine, 86; Bettelheim on, 277; in Boccaccio, 193; in Bohemia (15th century), 225; of Brethren of the Free Spirit, 141; at Cambrai (1411), 224; Catharist, 125, 128-129, 132; in Dauphiné, 218; of Catherine Delort, 184-185; in Germany (1150s), 129; of Henricians, 95; idea introduced into West, 93; of Alice Kyteler, 192; of Luciferans, 141, 178-180; in Walter Map, 117, 130; of Maria la Medica, 260; origins of, 88-93, 199, 318 n. 27; at Orléans (1022), 87-88, 90, 93; in other cultures, 15; and pagan festivals, 68; psychology of, 285; reality of, 127-128; in Rhineland (1233), 161-162; at Sint-Truiden, 95; at Soissons, 94-95; in Stephen of Bourbon, 157-158; of Tanchelm, 94; at Verona (c. 1175), 126; attributed to Waldensians, 127, 138; 5th century, 57-58; 7th century, 62-62; 9th century, 70; 15th century, 238-239, 249-251; see also Underground
Orléans: synod of (511), 303 n. 20; synod of (533), 304 n. 21; synod of (549), 302 n. 19, 303 n. 20; trial at (1022), 71, 86-95, 151, 180, 185, 200, 223, 313 n. 42, 321 n. 21
Orphism, 108

Pact, 18, 23, 208; in Caesarius of Heisterbach, 118-120; of carpenter (1366), 209; in Dauphiné, 217; of Catherine Delort, 184; at Etampes (1323), 329 n. 31; described by Eugenius IV, 229; at Fréjus (1338),

Pact (cont.)
187; Freud on, 273; of Gilles de Rais, 262; of Joan of Arc, 261; in John XXII, 173; of Alice Kyteler, 191; maleficium as, 16, 73; in Malleus, 232; in Walter Map, 116; of Maria la Medica, 260; origins of, 18-19, 57; in other cultures, 14; of Pierina, 213; scholastic definition of, 18, 144, 147; of Theophilus, 59-60, 65, 134; used to link witchcraft with heresy, 62, 71, 156, 174, 200, 208-209; 9th and 10th centuries, 70, 75, 83-85; 13th century, 134; 14th century, 185, 194, 197; 15th century, 238
Pactus Alamannorum (613-623), 61, 73
Paderborn, synod of (785), 308 n. 12
Pallidity: of demons or Devil, 56, 114, 159-161, 163, 168, 216; of heretics, 114, 168
Pamiers (1318-1325), 329 n. 31
Pantheism, 138, 140
Paris: synod of (829), 7, 308 n. 15; witchcraft at (1390-1391), 214-215; witchcraft at (1404), 209; witchcraft at (1466), 339 nn. 43ff.
Parzival, version of Wisse and Colin (1331-1336), 193
Passavanti, Giacopo (d. 1357), 176
Pastoureaux, 136
Patarenes, 122, 128-129, 318 n. 30
Paul, St., 109, 119
Paulicians, 92, 122
Pavia (1479), 339 nn. 43ff.
Pedro II of Aragon, and burning of heretics (1197), 151
Pelagius I (558-560), 302 n. 19
Pelagius II, letter to bishop of Auxerre (580), 302 n. 19
Penitential Books, 60-61, 66, 305 n. 26, 306 nn. 3ff., 307 n. 9, 308 n. 16, 309 nn. 19ff., 310 n. 22
Pentacles, 9, 119, 188, 207, 215, 254
Perrers, Alice, mistress of Edward III, tried (1376), 204
Perugia (1446), 339 nn. 43ff.
Peter of Bruys (d. c. 1132), 95
Philip IV (1285-1314), 171-172, 187, 194-195, 198-199

Pierina de' Bugatis, tried at Milan (1390), 212-214
Pigs, 68, 105, 211, 246
Pinarolo, see Lombardy
Pistoia (1250), 164
Pitchfork, see Trident
Plagues, 136-138, 165, 176, 327 n. 18; causing of, by witches, 240
Platonism, 108, 111-112
Poisoning of wells, 168, 181, 324 n. 2
Poisons, 15, 172, 183, 240, 280
Politiani, Angelus, treatise of (1483), 350
Political trials: for magic, 172-173, 190; for witchcraft, 193-198, 261-263, 269
Pons, heretic (1140-1147), 95
Porlezza (c. 1465), 252, 339 nn. 43ff.
Possession, 18, 115, 201, 266, 285, 320 n. 3
Prenzlau, Luciferans at (1384), 180
Provins (1452), 254, 339 nn. 43ff.
Psellos, Michael, 90, 93
Psychological interpretations of witchcraft, 6, 37-38, 265-266, 273, 275-278, 284-286; see also Social psychology
Pythonissa, 16

Radegunda (6th century), 302 n. 19
Raphael of Pornasio (fl. 1430-1450), 347
Raymond of Tarrega, Invocation of Demons (1370), 206
Reality of witchcraft, 1, 19-22, 28-29, 42-43, 205-206, 231-232
Receswinth, fuero juzgo of (654), 305 n. 25
Recordi, Peter, trial of (1329), 186
Red, associated with Devil, 216-218, 223, 246, 316 n. 4
Regensburg, sorcerers at (1446), 335 n. 4
Reggio, see Gabrina Albetti
Regino of Prüm (c. 960), 75-76, 78-81, 96, 310 n. 22; text of, 291-293
Reims: synod of (624-630), 303 n. 20, 305 n. 26; synod of (1157), 128
Remedius of Chur (800-820), 73

Renunciation of the faith, 17, 23, 83-84, 87, 100, 119, 125, 161, 174, 179, 186, 191, 195, 223, 232, 241, 253, 260

Ride, 23, 53-54, 65, 97, 156, 197, 210-211, 218; around tree backwards, 74; in Boccaccio, 193; of Diana, 75-81, 97, 115-116, 146, 156, 164, 175-176, 183, 210-211, 232, 235-236, 279, 303 n. 31, 310 n. 25, 322 n. 15; in Gervaise of Tilbury, 117; of Alice Kyteler, 192; see also Flight and Wild chase

Robbins, Rossell Hope, 39-40, 53, 194, 234

Robert of Artois, trial of (1327), 194

Robert le Bougre (13th century), 155

Robin Hood, animistic spirit or familiar (Robin Goodfellow, Robinet), 52-53, 187, 191-192, 256, 328 n. 28

Roman law, revival of, 149, 152

Rome: spurious synod of (367), 301 n. 12; synod of (743), 70; synod of (826), 75; trial at (1424), see Finicella; witchcraft at (1431), 338 nn. 43ff.; witchcraft at (1467), 339 nn. 43ff.

Rothari, edict of (643), 61, 304 n. 24

Rouen: idolatry at (7th century), 305 n. 25; synod of (c. 650), 303 n. 20, 305 n. 27; witchcraft at (1445), 335 n. 4, 339 nn. 43ff.; witchcraft at (1447), 339 nn. 43ff.

Sabbat, 86, 167, 182, 218, 220, 230, 249; derivation of term, 17, 61; first use of term, 22, 24, 37, 131, 181, 249, 328 n. 26; origins of, 51, 59, 68; use of term in 15th century, 80, 237

Sacraments, desecration of, see Desecration, of sacraments

Sacrifice: to demons, 58, 61, 66-67, 96, 173, 175, 184, 191, 206, 210, 229, 303 n. 20, 306 n. 4, 307 n. 7, 308 n. 16; to the Devil, 18, 24, 129-130, 171, 181-182, 186, 218, 239, 242, 305 n. 26; to gods, 55, 58; human, 67, 88; origins of human sacrifice, 88-93; see also Children, sacrifice of

St. Pölten, heretics at (14th century), 179

Salic Law, 69, 304 n. 24

Salt, 131, 180, 184

Salve, 14, 23, 54, 183, 197, 216, 233, 237, 240-241, 251-252; of Alice Kyteler, 191-192

Salzburg, Luciferans at (1340), 180

Sardinia (1480-1489), 339 nn. 43ff.; see also Gregory I

Satanael, 93

Saturday, time of witches' meeting, 182-184, 218, 249

Savoy, 177; witchcraft at (1420-1430), 220; witchcraft at (1430-1440), 338 nn. 43ff.

Scandinavia, 124, 268

Scholastic definitions of witchcraft, 19-20, 22, 26, 35

Scholasticism, 115-116, 133-134, 142-147, 199

Scotland, 36, 164, 308 n. 17

Sect, witchcraft as, 24, 219, 221, 223-224, 235, 238, 248

Segarelli, Gerard (heretic, c. 1260), 141

Sens: idolatry at (7th century), 304 n. 25; witchcraft in diocese of (1323), 188

Serpent, see Snakes

Severian (5th century), 57

Sexual intercourse: between angels and women, 108, 115, 283; between demons and witches, 15, 59, 62, 196, 237; between demons and witches as distinguished from Devils and witches, 237, 239; between the Devil and men, 257, 285; between the Devil and women, 75, 115, 144-146, 157, 164, 183-184, 218, 232, 237, 239, 246, 250, 260, 273, psychological interpretation of, 285

Sexual perversion, 92; see also Gilles de Rais

Shapeshifting, 11, 23, 54, 57, 216, 275, 344 n. 20; at Bern (c. 1400), 216; in Canon Episcopi, 77, 79, 87; in Corrector of Burchard, 81; as demonic illusion, 156, 207; in Eng-

Shapeshifting (cont.)
land, 12th century, 116; in Gervaise of Tilbury, 117-118; in Malleus, 233; origins of, 56, 58, 89; in Parzival, 193; in penitentials, 68; scholastic view of, 115, 146; in Teutonic religion, 48; 7th century, 62; 9th century, 70, 84; 10th and 11th centuries, 74-75, 98, 99; 13th century, 135; 14th century, 175; 15th century, 234, 237, 240, 246-247; see also January
Sibillia, tried at Milan (1384), 211-212
Siena: Rugomago, near (1383), 210
"Signora Oriente," 211-213, 333 n. 30
Sint-Truiden (1133-1136), 95
Skepticism, 20-22; of Jean de Meun, 135; of liberal school, 30-32; 12th century, 116; 14th century, 193, 207; 15th century, 205-206, 208, 234-243; see also Canon Episcopi
Snakes, 74, 105, 107, 164, 262
Social change, 270-272, 278-279, 286-289, 344 n. 23; in 11th and 12th centuries, 100-102, 125-126; 13th century, 133-134, 136; 14th century, 165-171, 199-200; 15th century, 227-228
Social class of witches, 259, 267-268
Social protest, 2-3, 26, 38, 42, 95, 126, 139-140, 200-202, 213, 281
Social psychology, 6, 38, 203-204, 266-267, 269-275, 278-284, 289, 296 n. 13, 300 n. 20
Socinus, Marianus, treatise on spirits of (1465), 207, 349
Sodomy, 162, 196, 219, 250
Soissons: heretics at Bucy-le-long, near (1114), 94; synod of (744), 306 n. 3
Soldan-Heppe-Bauer, 33, 35, 298 n. 5, 299 n. 15
Solothurn (1447, 1466), 339 nn. 43ff.
Sortilegus or sortiarius, 15
Spain, 59, 67, 206, 303 n. 21, 304 n. 23, 306 n. 27; relatively little witchcraft in, 40, 124, 268; see also Alfonso de Spina; Barcelona; Barrientos, Lope; Basin, Bernard; Braga; Elvira; Eymeric; Gui, Bernard; Isidore of Seville; Martin of Arles;
Pedro II of Aragon; Raymond of Tarrega; Receswinth; Rothari; Toledo; Torquemada, John of; and Tostado, Alfonso
Sprenger, Jakob (15th century), 230-231
Stags, 67, 74, 98-99, 305-306 n. 27, 307 n. 8, 310 n. 22; see also January
Stedingers (13th century), 323 n. 40
Stephen of Bourbon (c. 1250), 156-158
Sticks, 53, 79, 218-219, 236, 240, 245, 252, 306 n. 3
Striga, stria, strigimaga, strix, 15, 53, 56, 61, 68-70, 75, 79, 81, 83, 97, 116-118, 132, 146, 207, 239, 274, 301, 308 n. 12, 341 n. 59; secta strigarum, 219, 235; see also Bloodsucking
Styria, Luciferans in (1310), 177, 179
Succubi, 81, 97, 110, 115, 116, 145, 183, 196, 237, 239, 250, 285, 327 n. 16; see also Incubi
Suicide, 218, 222
Summers, Montague, 29-30, 32, 308 n. 15, 309 n. 18
Summis desiderantes affectibus (1484), see Innocent VIII
Superstition,· definition of, 5
Switzerland, 177, 220; see also Alpnach, Andermatt, Annecy, Basel, Bern, Fribourg, Geneva; Interlaken, Locarno, Lucerne, Murten, Neuchâtel, Remedius of Chur, Solothurn, and Valais
Synagogue: witch meeting as, 23, 61, 131-132, 141, 167, 223, 237, 242, 248, 257, 328 n. 26, 334 n. 35, 340 n. 57, n. 59; first mention of witch meeting as, 131

Tanchelm, heretic (1110-1120), 94
Tannere, John, trial of (1314-1315), 194
Templars, prosecution of (1306-1314), 194-198, 219
Theodosian Code (438), 72, 149, 301 n. 12, 303 n. 20, 307 n. 7
Theophilus (d. c. 540), 19; see also Pact

Theorists, 14th and early 15th centuries, 205-208, 346-350
Thérouanne, idolatry in (7th century), 304 n. 25
Theuda, heretic (847-848), 83
Thorndike, Lynn, 7, 11-12
Thursday, as time of witches' meeting, 48, 52, 58, 68, 218, 237, 247-248, 303-304 n. 21, 312 n. 32
Tinctoris, Johannes, treatise of (1460), 236, 239-240, 348
Toads, 126, 147, 160-161, 163, 186, 215, 223, 240, 251
Todi, trial at (1428), 251, 338 nn. 43ff.
Toledo: necromancer from (1234), 163; synod of (589), 302 n. 19, 303 n. 21; synod of (681), 61; synods of (693, 694), 304 n. 24
Torcy (1455), 336 n. 7
Torquemada, John of, treatise of (c. 1445), 279, 347
Torrenbüren (1347), 187
Torture: by Inquisition, 153, 158-159, 257, 335 n. 6; of magicians, 73; origins of, 152-153; by secular courts, 229, 258-259, 335 n. 6; of Templars, 197; of witches, 149, 152-153, 171, 182, 185, 189, 210, 215, 221, 223, 244-245
Tostado, Alfonso, treatise of (c. 1440), 347
Toulouse: council of (1229), 151; trial at (1275), see Angèle de la Barthe; trial at (1319), 194, see also Délicieux, Bernard; trial at (1412), 219; trials at (14th century), 173, 177, 181, 185-187, 329 n. 31; witchcraft at (1335), 181-186, 198
Tournai (c. 1300), 329 n. 31
Tours, synod of: (567), 303 nn. 20-21; (813), 71
Transportation by demons, 87; see also Flight and Ride
Treatises on witchcraft (15th century), 233-243
Tresilian, Robert (1388), 209
Trevor-Roper, Hugh, 7, 35, 42, 227, 268, 321 n. 14, 337 n. 28
Trident, 191, 247, 316 n. 7
Trier: heretics at (1231), 159; heretics at Ivois, near (1102-1124), 94;

synod of (1310), 326 n. 16
Trolls, 52
Turin, see Lombardy
Turrecremata, see Torquemada, John of

Ugolini, Zanchino, Super materia haereticorum of (1330), 174
Underground, as place for orgies, 87, 94, 99-100, 115, 117, 126, 130-131, 141, 147, 157-158, 161, 180, 247
Unguent, see Salve

Valais, witchcraft in: (1428-1480), 244, 338 nn. 43ff.; (1466, 1467, 1478), 339 nn. 43ff.
Vallin, Pierre, trial at La Tour du Pin (1438), 254-260, 338 nn. 43ff.
Valois kings, 172
Vampire, see Bloodsucking
Venice, trial of Franciscans at (1422), 210
Verona: council of (1184), 154; heretics at (1175), 126
Vienna (c. 1315), 179
Vienne, council of (1311-1312), 198
Vignate, Ambrose de', treatise of (c. 1468), 236-237, 239, 349
Vilgard of Ravenna (c. 1000), 86, 151
Vincent, Jean, treatise of (c. 1475), 238, 349
Vineti, Jean, treatise of (c. 1450), 235, 243, 347
Vintler, Hans, poet (c. 1410), 210-211
Visconti, Galeazzo, accused of witchcraft by John XXII (1320), 325 n. 7
Visconti, Girolamo, treatises of (c. 1460), 279, 348
Visconti, Matteo (d. 1322), tried at Milan, 194
Voodoo, 334 n. 36
Vötting, witch at (1090), 321 n. 20

Waldensians, 126-127, 138-139, 154, 177, 200, 219-221, 235, 243-244, 248, 256-257, 283, 327 n. 19; word applied to witches, 15-16, 237, 334 nn. 36-38, 340 n. 59

Walpurga, St., 50-51
Walter, Bishop of Lichfield and Coventry, trial of (1303), 194
Weather-witching, 13, 16, 54, 83, 329 n. 31
Werewolves, 53, 55, 68, 81, 333 n. 29
Werner, Ernst, 127-128
Westphalia, spurious witch trial in (914), 308 n. 17
White, Andrew Dickson, 28, 31-32, 298-299 n. 9
White, Lynn, Jr., 22, 278
Wild chase, wild hunt, wild ride, wild rout, *wilde Jagd,* 23, 48-50, 79-80, 116, 118, 135, 156, 176, 211-213, 275, 300 n. 4, 333 n. 30; *see also* Cavalcade of death *and* Ride
Wild men and women, 23, 49-50, 81, 97, 117, 310 n. 22, 333 n. 29
William of Auvergne, scholastic (1180-1249), 142, 144-147, 241
William de Bechis, treatise of (c. 1450), 237, 241, 243, 347

William of Newburgh (12th century), 99
Witches' mark, 218, 232
Wolves, 105, 116, 156, 164, 211-212, 237, 245-247, 275; *see also* Werewolves
Women: as demons, 59, 79-81, 207; and European witchcraft, 62, 67, 74-75, 78, 81, 109, 116, 145-146, 156-158, 176, 183, 199; in other societies, 15; proportion of, in witchcraft, 343 n. 16; psychological and social interpretations of the preponderance of, 201-202, 279-284; *see also* Ride, of Diana
Wunschilburg, Johann, treatise of (c. 1440), 346-347

Yates, Frances, 11

Žižka, John (15th-century heretic), 224-225
Zoroastrianism, 106-107, 122